"When any person is known to be considering the new Religion, all his relations and acquaintances rise en masse; so that to get a new convert is like pulling out the eyetooth of a live tiger."

— Adoniram Judson

Pulling the Eye Tooth from a Live Tiger

A Memoir Of the Life and Labors of Adoniram Judson
Volume 2
by Francis Wayland

Audubon Press
& Christian Book Service

AUDUBON PRESS
2601 Audubon Drive / P.O. Box 8055
Laurel, MS 39441-8000   USA

Orders: 800-405-3788
Inquiries: 601-649-8572
Voice: 601-649-8570 / Fax: 601-649-8571
E-mail: buybooks@audubonpress.com
Web Page: www.audubonpress.com

© 2006 Audubon Press edition

All rights reserved.

Printed in the United States

Cover design by Crisp Graphics

ISBN #0-9742365-8-6

Original Publication:

To preach the Gospel in regions beyond... – 2 Cor. 10:16

In Two Volumes

Volume 2

Boston: Phillips, Sampson, and Company
London: Nisbet and Company
1853

Stereotyped at the Boston Stereotype Foundary

All Scripture quotations are from the KJV

CONTENTS

OF THE SECOND VOLUME.

CHAPTER I.

VIEWS OF MISSIONARY WORK ILLUSTRATED. — PREACHING TOURS IN THE KAREN JUNGLES. — PLAN FOR A MISSION TO PALESTINE, ...

CHAPTER II.

ADVICE TO CANDIDATES FOR MISSIONARY LABOR. — THIRD TOUR AMONG THE KARENS. — APPEALS FOR HELP. — TRANSLATION OF THE BIBLE COMPLETED. — MARRIAGE TO MRS. BOARDMAN, ... 38

CHAPTER III.

TREVELYANISM. — VIEWS RESPECTING THE METHOD OF CONDUCTING MISSIONS. — REVISION OF THE OLD AND NEW TESTAMENTS. — GROWTH AND RESULTS OF THE MISSION. — FIRST TWENTY-FIVE YEARS OF MISSIONARY LABOR, . 84

CHAPTER IV.

DECLINING HEALTH. — VISIT TO CALCUTTA. — PRINCIPLES OF TRANSLATION. — MISSIONARY WORK. — REVISION OF BURMESE SCRIPTURES COMPLETED. — CHARACTER OF THE VERSION, ... 131

CHAPTER V.

ILLNESS OF HIS FAMILY. — PASSAGE TO CALCUTTA. — BEREAVEMENT AT SERAMPORE. — VOYAGE TO THE ISLE OF FRANCE AND MAULMAIN. — INCIDENTS OF THE VOYAGE. — BURMESE DICTIONARY, ... 169

CHAPTER VI.

ILLNESS OF MRS. JUDSON. — VOYAGE TO THE UNITED STATES. — DEATH OF MRS. JUDSON. — BURIAL AT ST. HELENA. — OBITUARY NOTICE. — RECEPTION AND ADDRESSES IN THE UNITED STATES, ... 196

CHAPTER VII.

MARRIAGE. — FAREWELL SERVICES AT BOSTON. — VOYAGE TO MAULMAIN. — RECOMMENCES LABORS AT RANGOON. — RETURN TO MAULMAIN. — REMINISCENCES OF HIS LAST VISIT TO RANGOON, ... 249

CHAPTER VIII.

NUMBER OF MISSIONARIES IN MAULMAIN — MODES OF MISSIONARY LABOR. — BURMESE DICTIONARY. — STATE OF THE MISSION, ... 304

CHAPTER IX.

HIS LAST ILLNESS. — INTENDED VOYAGE TO THE ISLE OF FRANCE. — THE CLOSING SCENES OF HIS LIFE. — HIS DEATH AND BURIAL. — NOTICES OF THE PRESS. — ANECDOTES AND SKETCHES, ... 331

CHAPTER X.

GENERAL VIEW OF HIS CHARACTER AND LABORS, . 373

APPENDIX

DR. JUDSON'S OPINION ON SOME OF THE TENETS OF BUDDHISM, ... 407
PREVALENCE OF BUDDHISM, ... 409
BUDDH, ... 410
KYOUNGS AND PRIESTS, ... 417
LETTER FROM RANGOON IN 1826, ... 420
DEPOSITION OF DR. JUDSON BEFORE COMMISSIONER CRAWFURD, ... 422
THE GOLDEN BALANCE, TRANSLATED FROM THE BURMAN, 448
THE GOLDEN BALANCE IN PEGUAN, ... 457
THE THREEFOLD CORD, ... 459
A BURMAN LITURGY, TRANSLATED INTO ENGLISH, . 467
LETTER ON ORNAMENTAL AND COSTLY ATTIRE, . . . 476
SERMON AT THE ORDINATION OF REV. S. M. OSGOOD, . 486
SKETCH OF ELEANOR MACOMBER, ... 495

CONTENTS.

SKETCHES OF SERMONS, ... 498
TO A LADY, AN INTIMATE FRIEND OF MRS. JUDSON, . . 500
WAYSIDE PREACHING. 502
OBEDIENCE TO CHRIST'S LAST COMMAND A TEST OF PIETY, 519
THE MISSIONS OF THE AMERICAN BAPTIST MISSIONARY
    UNION, ... 522

MEMOIR OF DR. JUDSON.

CHAPTER I.

VIEWS OF MISSIONARY WORK ILLUSTRATED. — PREACHING TOURS IN THE KAREN JUNGLES. — PLAN FOR A MISSION TO PALESTINE.

1831–1832.

The events of the ensuing chapters illustrate still more clearly Dr. Judson's views of missionary labor. He had made himself perfectly familiar with the Burman language, so that, as a medium of communication, he seemed to prefer it to his native tongue. He was aware that this knowledge imposed upon him the duty of devoting a considerable portion of his time to the work of translation; yet he considered his appropriate business as a missionary to be the preaching of the gospel. He believed that Christianity was to be promulgated by the contact of individual mind with individual mind, and hence he diligently sought every possible occasion for personally offering to men salvation by Christ. And in this there was something distinctive and almost peculiar. He did not devise any set of measures to operate, as it is said, on the public mind, and change the views of the masses, and by a general and gradual process of illumination prepare the way for the diffusion of the gospel. He had little confidence in schools as a means for the conversion of men. For a while he gave them a modified approval; but the more he saw of them and their effects, the smaller was his confidence in them as missionary work. It was sufficient for him to know that Christ and his apostles had made it their great work to proclaim to men every where the news of salvation, and without conferring with ease, or taste, or love of civilized society, he resolutely followed their example.

There is, it seems to me, something deeply interesting in the following narrative. Here was one of the most learned and able men in India, that nursery of great men, a man of refined manners and cultivated tastes, surrounded by a company of native Christians who had yet only begun to put off their habits of barbarism, penetrating the recesses of the forest and threading every accessible rivulet for the sake of preaching to almost naked savages the gospel of our salvation. Wherever he could find listeners, were they many or few, there he stopped to discourse on the message of redeeming love. Whether from his boat or on the shore, whether by day or by night, he was always ready to reveal to these wandering barbarians the love of God in sending his Son for our redemption. In this work he was remarkably successful. Rarely did he go into the jungle without, on his return, "bringing his sheaves with him." It was, moreover, the work in which, above all others, he delighted. He had a passion for saving souls, and he had reason to believe that, by this labor, many souls were saved, who would be his joy and his crown in that heaven for which his whole life was a constant preparation. When, at length, he felt constrained to listen to the repeated solicitations of the board, and devote himself to the work of translation, it cost him many a pang; and the paper which recorded his resolution to forsake the jungle, and devote himself to a life of greater self-indulgence, was bedewed with his tears.

In another respect, his labors in this direction were peculiar. He seems to have possessed a remarkable facility for calling into active service all the gifts of the native Christians. He saw that a nation can never be evangelized except by means of its own population. Foreigners can never supply it with ministers of the gospel. Strangers may carry to it the truths of revelation, may transfer them into its language, and, by the blessing of God, may establish churches. But it is from these churches themselves that the preachers must be taken who are to carry the gospel to their brethren. Impressed with these views, he cultivated to the utmost the native talent. He was ever surrounding himself with men whom he was training up to this service. In Maulmain and Rangoon, he always employed several assistants, whom he sent daily to the different parts of the city and vicinity to preach and converse with their countrymen, and read and distribute tracts. When he went into the jungle, a company of the same kind followed him. These he would send away, two by two, into those parts of the forest to which he could not himself penetrate, appointing to them their work, and receiving their reports as they returned. He was thus greatly multiplying his own efficiency, and training up the most promising natives as preachers of the gospel.

The same method has been pursued with most remarkable success by Rev. Mr. Abbott, in Sandoway and the adjacent districts. Mr. Abbott has carried this plan farther than Dr. Judson. He has been enabled to increase very greatly the number of native preachers; some of them he has ordained; their labors have been abundantly owned of God, and many of the churches have already chosen their own pastors, and are supporting them, in a great measure, by their own contributions. When so much as this has been accomplished, Christianity has taken root among a people. They may need, and for a considerable time they will need, the encouragement and direction of a superior mind, more perfectly acquainted than themselves with the Scriptures; but after this, the main labor of evangelization may be done by themselves. Missionary efforts have been successful very much in proportion to the prevalence of these ideas. In the first instance, however, missionaries must show how the work is to be done, by their own example. Without this, it is not reasonable to expect that any thing will be accomplished.

There is one feature of the following narrative which may possibly require a brief explanation. It will be seen that, on many occasions, Dr. Judson, in his tours through the jungle, met with men and women who requested Christian baptism; and that, after conversation with them, and what is termed "a relation of their experience," with the approbation of such native Christians as were present, he admitted them by this ordinance, to the fellowship of the church. It may be asked, How, from such a brief acquaintance could he know that they were suitable candidates for the reception of this rite?

The answer to this question is briefly as follows: Dr. Judson believed that when any man becomes a Christian, or a real disciple of Christ, a specific moral change takes place in his spiritual nature. The essential elements of this change are, a deep and universal sorrow for the sins of his past life, an entire renunciation of all hope of salvation by any merits of his own, an unreserved surrender of himself to Christ, relying on him alone for pardon and acceptance with God, and an earnest desire to live henceforth in obedience to all the requirements of the gospel; and that these spiritual exercises terminate in a radical change of moral character, leading to a pure and holy life. A man's fitness for membership of a church is, therefore, to be learned, first, from the nature of these exercises, of which he himself alone can be conscious, and which, therefore, we must learn from his own lips; and, secondly, from the testimony of those who know him, that his life has corresponded with these professions. It was on this ground that Dr. Judson acted in admitting men to baptism; and he seems to have acted with good reason. "If any man," saith St. Paul, "be in Christ, he is a new creature." This new creation must comprehend not only a change in practice, but a change in motives, and in all the moral affections. What is external may be known, in part, from others; what is internal, the source of all, being apparent to his own consciousness alone, must be known from himself. The personal narrative of this change in moral character is frequently called the relation of a man's "religious experience." It was after hearing this, and learning the character which the candidate maintained among his neighbors, that he was received to membership in the church.

To the Corresponding Secretary.

Maulmain, August 7, 1831

Rev. and dear Sir: I have received very kind letters from yourself, Deacon Lincoln, Mr. E. Lincoln, and Mr. Malcom, of last November, on the subject of my visiting America; but as brother and sister Wade have just left us, which circumstance you could not foresee, and I remain almost alone in the native department of the mission, and as my health is now very good, I presume there will be no doubt in the minds of any of the board about the propriety of my remaining where I am.

There is one point which I wish respectfully to suggest — whether, in sending out future missionaries to these parts, it may not be best to assign them no definite station, or limited field of labor, but leave them to follow the path of duty as it may be opened by Providence, and recommended by their brethren of the mission. The great question whether Burmah proper is open to missionary efforts or not, must essentially affect all our movements. If it be open, we shall want to direct every thing to the centre; otherwise we must make the most of the outskirts. Such events may transpire, in the interval of your sending a missionary and his arrival, as may embarrass him and us, in case of his having received very definite instructions in regard to the particular field of labor. And the effect on his own mind may also be very bad, if he has fixed his regards on one object *exclusively*, and, on arriving, finds that object unattainable. Would it not be safe to send out missionaries to *Burmah*, to labor in any section, and among any class of people, — Burmans, Talings, or Karens, — as shall appear most advisable at the time?

A. Judson.

Journal.

Maulmain, August 14, 1831.

Since I left this, a year ago last April, nine persons have been received into the native church by baptism, besides fourteen Karens, most of them relatives of persons previously baptized; but Moung Ouk-moo, a Taling, and Moung Shway-moung, a Burman, are not of that description, and are both very promising characters. To-day were added Mah Ike and Mah Kau-mee, widows, in the neighborhood; the latter, mother of Sarah Wayland, formerly a most abusive, wicked woman, but now entirely changed; the former outrageously opposed by a large circle of connections, and, on that account, enabled to give bright evidence of sincerity.

August 24. We have just opened a school for teaching adults to read. Five scholars are engaged, two of them members of the church.

WADESVILLE, September 11.

At this place, destitute of a name, where brother Wade baptized the first Karens, I arrived on the fifth, four days' journey from Maulmain, up the Dah-gyne River. Moung Doot has been stationed here three months, and endeavored to do a little among the natives, though in the Taling language only, which some of them understand. I have seen most of the converts. They appear pretty well. Tau-nah is my interpreter, the first baptized, an intelligent Christian, and competent to the work. Eight more have this day been added to the church.

September 12. I removed a few miles, to accommodate some who could not visit me at the other place, and have here baptized five more. There are many inquirers, and some decided opposition.

September 17. Having left the Dah-gyne, I ascended another branch, called the Laing-bwai, hearing that there were several disposed to embrace the Christian religion through the preaching of Ko Myat-kyau and Moung Zuthee, who have visited these parts; but soon after my arrival, I was taken with the jungle fever, and rendered unable to do much. Nine, however, from two different villages, have been examined and baptized. To-day, finding myself hourly getting worse, I was obliged, most reluctantly, to leave the field.

Maulmain, September 27. Am just recovering from the

fever, and able to record my gratitude to God for his sparing mercy, and to brother and sister Bennett, and my attending physician, Dr. Richardson, for their kind attentions and care, by means of which another span is added to my forfeited life. Renewedly would I devote it, whether longer or shorter, to the service of my God and Saviour,—

> "If so poor a worm as I
> May to thy great glory live."

September 28. Three of the Karens whom I had selected from all the baptized, namely, Tau-nah, Pan-lah, and Chetthing, have arrived, with their wives and children, and one girl from another family — fifteen souls in all. It is our intention to place the men in the adult school, and qualify them to read and interpret the Scriptures to their countrymen. In the mean time, their families will be acquiring a little civilization and Christian knowledge, which will render them useful when they return to their native wilds. The plan will involve some expense, as they must, of course, be supported while at school. Each family will require six or seven rupees per month. But I know of no way in which a little money can be laid out to greater advantage, for the promotion of the cause of truth among this people.

October 2. A Karen lad, lately baptized, applied for admission into the school. He appears to be affectionate and sincere, but uncommonly stupid. We are willing to give him a trial.

October 8. The ship in which brother and sister Wade took passage for Bengal, on their way to America, having left this place three months, without being heard of, was generally supposed to be lost, and we were beginning to feel exceedingly distressed, when we were astonished by the news that they were on board a steam vessel at Amherst; and yesterday morning we had the happiness of seeing them walk into the house. It appears that they had a most severe time in the Bay of Bengal, and at length reached Kyouk Phyoo, on the Arracan coast, in a sinking condition. They remained there two months, during which time, and the preceding voyage, Mrs. Wade's health was so essentially amended, that they relinquished the design of prosecuting their voyage homewards, and took passage in a steam vessel which touched at Kyouk Phyoo, on her way from Bengal to the southern ports. At first they thought of proceeding to Tavoy; but, having ascertained that the vessel would touch at Mergui only, we all concluded that it was advisable for them to visit that place, in hope that a residence there of a few months will completely restore sister Wade's health, and, through the divine blessing, issue in the establishment of a church in that region. With a view to the latter object, we are writing to Tavoy, requesting that Ko Ing, who was originally destined to Mergui, his native place, may immediately proceed thither. Brother and sister Wade leave early to-morrow morning, in order to rejoin the vessel at Amherst.

October 23. We baptized Moung Zah, a pure Burman, from that favored district below Ava which is blessed with a genuine impression in stone of the foot of Gaudama! He has been considering the Christian religion about two years, being married to a Taling woman in this neighborhood, who is a Christian. The opposition in this place was never more steady and strong. The priests have all taken a most decided stand; and the people seem to have resolved to stand or fall with their priests. When any person is known to be considering the new religion, all his relations and acquaintance rise *en masse;* so that to get a new convert is like pulling out the eye tooth of a live tiger.

November 6. The school mentioned above does well. It contains about twenty persons — men, women, and children. Most of them are professors of religion, and six are Karens; the rest, inhabitants of Maulmain. Some of them are boarded in whole, some in part, and some board themselves.

To-day the hundredth member was added to the European church under the care of brother Kincaid, all baptized by him except the first fifteen.

In the printing office, brother Bennett has just completed a new edition of the Septenary or Seven Manuals, and of the Epistles of John, and of Paul to the Ephesians; also, first editions of brother Boardman's Ship of Grace, and brother Wade's Awakener — a work which he wrote during his late sojourn at Kyouk Phyoo, and which bids fair to be deserving of its title. We intended to have printed an edition of ten thousand; but having concluded that brother Bennett must go to Bengal to rectify the Burmese types, we must content ourselves with three thousand, as the ship on which he takes passage is about leaving. I close this article to be forwarded by him.

To the Corresponding Secretary.

MAULMAIN, October 11, 1831.

REV. AND DEAR SIR: We are quite convinced that the female boarding school in this place cannot be sustained without more efficient aid in that department. The case stands thus: Mrs. Mason has removed to Tavoy, and Mrs. Jones to Rangoon. Mrs. Kincaid is afflicted with one of the most dreadful scourges that human nature is subject to — the chronic thrush, which incapacitates her for any business, and will, in all probability, sooner or later, come to a fatal termination. Add to which, that brother Kincaid, whose labors were wonderfully blessed among the soldiers, has removed into town, in order to be near them and the European population. He is baptizing every Lord's day, and his church numbers nearly a hundred; so that we have no present missionary aid from that quarter. Mrs. Wade, who, having no family, has, with occasional assistance from Mrs. Bennett, done nearly all that has ever been done in the school, though now returned in comparative good health, has gone with brother Wade to spend a few months at Mergui; and if I should remain here, with a view to superintending the printing of the New Testament, &c., according to the latest instructions of the board, there is no prospect that Mrs. Wade will be able to resume her labors in the school; for brother Wade and I, being the only persons yet competent to preach in the native language, cannot conscientiously remain long together at the same station. Mrs. Bennett is therefore the only female remaining on the mission premises, and she has a young and increasing family, which requires vastly more attention than a family at home. Being, also, in a good degree, acquainted with the language, she has the native female disciples and inquirers all on her hands. It is therefore evidently impossible that she can do justice to a female school. When I first arrived from Rangoon, I found a school of fifteen, which she was endeavoring to keep alive, beyond her strength. I advised her to give it up at once; and we divided the girls between two of our best assistants, Mee A and Mee Nenyay, who were educated under Mrs. Wade, and both well competent to the business of instructing. Such, however, is the native prejudice in favor of white blood, that the arrangement gave universal dissatisfaction. And one day, when I was lying very ill, there was a general insurrection of the mothers, Christian and heathen; and they withdrew nearly all their daughters from the schools, so that now there are three girls only; and one of them is a wild Karen, that I picked up lately in my travels.

There can be no doubt that a lady appointed to this department, especially one disengaged from family cares, would be able, in the course of a few months' attention to the language, to collect an interesting school, and that she would find herself in a situation of usefulness to the cause of Christ beyond almost any in her native land.

Yours faithfully,

A. JUDSON.

To Mr. Bennett, in Bengal.

MAULMAIN, December 19, 1831.

DEAR BROTHER BENNETT: This has been a very solemn day. Mrs. ——— died about four o'clock in the morning, and at sunset we consigned her remains to the silent grave. She died clinging to life with an eagerness which it was frightful to witness; and yet we have, upon the whole, a comfortable hope that she is now at rest. Mrs. Bennett and I have just been conversing about the importance of cutting off our ties to this world before death cuts them off per force. The scene we have witnessed reads us a most solemn lesson. O, may we learn it well, and may it be sanctified to our hearts! . . . The children are all in perfect health. Mrs. Bennett walks with me every morning between gunfire and sunrise. I need not add that she is quite well. She says that she has nothing to add to the accompanying letters which she wrote a few days ago. I sent the maps and a parcel from Mah A to her husband, by Captain Landale, who went from this to Rangoon, to take passage for Calcutta, in the Indian Oak.

I expect to leave this for the Karen villages in the course of a few days, but shall not probably be long from home. We have heard nothing from you since your departure.

Yours very affectionately,

A. JUDSON.

To the Corresponding Secretary.

MAULMAIN, December 29, 1831.

REV. AND DEAR SIR: One native only has been baptized since my last — Moung Hlau, the husband of Mah Kyan, mentioned January 28, and May 29, 1829. Though his violent opposition had long ceased, he did not, till lately, become fully convinced of the truth of the Christian religion, so as to receive it into his heart. He is a very ignorant man, not even knowing how to read; but he is now in the school of Christ, and must grow in knowledge and grace.

On looking over the results of the past year, I find that seventy-six persons have been baptized at Tavoy, one hundred and thirty-six at Maulmain, and five at Rangoon; two hundred and seventeen in all; of whom eighty-nine are foreigners, nineteen Talings or Burmans, and one hundred and nine Karens; one has been excluded from the native and one from the European church in Maulmain.

The following table exhibits the number baptized in Burmah from the beginning.

The mission commenced July 13, 1813.

Year.	Place.	Native.	Foreign.	Total.
1819	Rangoon,	3	....	3
1820		7	....	7
1821		3	....	3
1822		5	....	5
1823	....	None.	....	....
1824	....	War.	....	....
1825			....	....
1826	Amherst,	3	....	3
1827	Amherst,	1	....	1
1828	Maulmain and Tavoy,	29	4	33
1829	Rangoon, Maulmain, and Tavoy,	39	12	51
1830		42	8	50
1831		128	89	217

Total, 373, of whom 260 are natives and 113 foreigners. Of the whole number 11 have been excluded, and 11 have died in the faith.

The adult school, which has prospered well, will be suspended at the close of the year, most of the scholars having learned to read and committed to memory several important portions of the tracts and Scripture.

In view of my leaving Maulmain, on a second tour among the Karens, I have appointed the two deacons, Ko Dwah and Ko Shway-ba to conduct the daily evening worship, and the public worship on Lord's days. The former acts also as teacher to Mrs. Bennett, and the latter is employed in copying translations. Ko Man-boke, the other deacon, and his wife, I send to the aid of brother and sister Wade at Mergui, where Pastor Ing also is stationed. Moung San-lone and Moung Shway-moung, I send to itinerate in the direction of Yay, and Moung Poo, from the school, and Moung Zah, to itinerate between this and Amherst, chiefly in the vicinity of Pah-ouk. Ko Shan and family I send to reside at Tara-nah, a populous Taling village, on the Gyne, a few miles above Maulmain, where he has a son settled. Moung En expects soon to revisit Rangoon. Moung Dway has gone to Bengal with brother Bennett. The three Karen families who have been in the adult school, and Moung Doot, who is now here on a visit from his station at Wadesville, I shall take with me, together with Ko Myat-kyau, who speaks the Karen well, Moung Zuthee, Moung Tau-ma-gnay, Moung Tsan-lone, the schoolmaster, and Moung Ouk-moo, just from school, "all good men and true."

Brother Kincaid lives in town, and is chiefly occupied with the Europeans; so that sister Bennett only remains in charge of the homestead, and the female disciples, who mostly stay behind, while their husbands are out on service. Scanty are our resources, and we are obliged to put every thing in requisition. May the Lord soon send us more help from our native land; or, if that be not his will, may he cause his strength to be made perfect in our weakness.

Journal. — Life in the Jungle.

WADESVILLE, January 1, 1832.

We set out from Maulmain, as purposed in my last, and leaving the Salwen on the west, and the Ataran on the east, we followed the Gyne and the Dah-gyne, as it is termed above its confluence with the Houng-ta-rau, which falls in from the east, and in three days reached this place, the distance being, by conjecture, above eighty miles. Accounts, on first arriving, are rather unfavorable.

January 8. My people have been out for several days, in different directions. One party has ascended the river to Kau-nau's village, beyond which boats do not pass. Others have been to Lausan's village, south-east of this, on the Pan-ka-rong rivulet; others have proceeded farther in the same direction, to the head of the Patah River, which also falls into the Dah-gyne. There are twenty-seven baptized disciples in these parts, who were nearly all present to-day at worship, and I am happy to find that they have all behaved well since my last visit, though they have been obliged to encounter a great deal of reproach and opposition from their unbelieving countrymen. But a number of circumstances, too tedious to detail, have conspired to damp the spirit of religious inquiry, which appeared a few months ago; and though, at one time, there were reported to be a considerable number who were ready to embrace the Christian religion, and though it is to be hoped that many of them will prove to be sincere, there seems to be a simultaneous understanding among them to consider longer, before finally committing themselves. I have not, therefore, had the happiness of adding a single individual to the branch of the church in this quarter.

January 9. The disciples at this place being desirous of changing their residence, and uniting with other disciples from different parts in forming a new settlement, we went down the river a short distance, and on the western bank, just below the mouth of the Pan-ka-rong rivulet, found a spot which, uniting the suffrages of all parties, we commended to God, praying him to come and make it his abode, and bless the inhabitants with all temporal and spiritual blessings, and cause it to be a spring whence living waters should flow into all the adjacent parts. Having performed this service, and taken leave of the disciples, we proceeded down the river.

January 10. We arrived early at the mouth of the Leing-bwai, which falls into the Dah-gyne from the north-west, and bent our course thitherward. At night, reached Ken-doot, where they have repeatedly rejected the gospel.

January 11. Continued to work our way up the river, frequently impeded by the trees which had fallen across the water, and through which we were obliged to cut a passage for the boat. At night, came to a small cluster of houses, where we found an elderly woman, who, with her daughter, formerly applied for baptism, but was advised to wait. She now received us joyfully, and united with her daughter and son-in-law in begging earnestly that their baptism might be no longer delayed. I directed them to meet me at Kwan-bee, about a mile distant, where I formerly baptized nine disciples, most of them from Tee-pah's village, a few miles to the west.

January 12. Proceeded to Kwan-bee. A few people came

together on the beach to stare at us, and we had a little meeting for worship before breakfast. We then proceeded to investigate the case of Loo-boo, who was reported to have joined, when his child was extremely ill, in making an offering to a nat (demon) for its recovery. We at first thought of suspending him from the fellowship of the church; but he made such acknowledgments and promises that we finally forgave him, and united in praying that God would forgive him. We do not hear of any other case of transgression; but on the contrary, in two instances of extreme illness, the disciples resisted all the importunities of their friends to join in the usual offerings to propitiate the demons, who are supposed to rule over diseases. In one instance, the illness terminated in death; and I have to lament the loss of Pan-mlai-mlo, who was the leader of the little church in this quarter, and the first of these northern Karens, who, we hope, has arrived safe in heaven. I ought, perhaps, to except the case of a man and wife near the head of the Patah River, who, though not baptized, and *never seen by any foreign missionary*, both died in the faith; the man enjoining it on his surviving friends to have the View of the Christian Religion laid on his breast and buried with him.

Some of the disciples have gone to Tee-pah's village to announce my arrival; and while others are putting up a small shed on the bank, I sit in the boat and pen these notices.

In the evening, held a meeting in the shed, at which several of the villagers were present.

January 13. My people returned from Tee-pah's village, bringing with them several disciples, and one woman, the wife of Loo-boo, who presented herself for baptism, with twelve strings of all manner of beads around her neck, and a due proportion of ear, arm, and leg ornaments! and, strange to say, she was examined and approved, without one remark on the subject of her dress. The truth is, we quite forgot it, being occupied and delighted with her uncommonly prompt and intelligent replies. In the afternoon, sent the boat back to Maulmain, with directions to proceed up the Salwen, having concluded to cross thither by land. In the evening, had a pretty full shed; but the inhabitants of the place do not appear very favorably inclined.

January 14. The three persons mentioned on the 11th presented themselves, with the decorated lady of yesterday. Being formerly prevented by illness from animadverting on female dress in this district, as I did in the Dah-gyne, I took an opportunity of "holding forth" on that subject before breakfast; and it was truly amusing and gratifying to see the said lady, and another applicant for baptism, and a Christian woman who accompanied them, divest themselves, on the spot, of every article that could be deemed merely ornamental; and this they did with evident pleasure, and good resolution to persevere in adherence to the plain dress system. We then held a church meeting, and having baptized the four applicants, crossed the Leing-bwai on a bridge of logs, and set out for Tee-pah's village, accompanied by a long train of men, women, children, and dogs. Towards night we arrived at that place, and effected a lodgment in Tee-pah's house. In the evening, had a pretty full assembly.

January 15, Lord's day. In the forenoon I held a meeting for the disciples only, and, as I seldom see them, endeavored to tell them all I knew. Had more or less company through the day. In the evening a crowded house. Tee-pah's father, a venerable old man, came forward, and witnessed a good confession. Some others, also, begin to give evidence that they have received the truth into good and honest hearts.

January 16. In the morning Tee-pah's mother joined the party of applicants for baptism, and her younger daughter-in-law, whose husband was formerly baptized. But Tee-pah himself, though convinced of the truth, and giving some evidence of grace, cannot resolve at once on entire abstinence from rum, though he has never been in the habit of intoxication. In the course of the forenoon, we held a church meeting, and unanimously received and baptized eight individuals from this and a small village two miles distant.

Took an affectionate leave of the people, and prosecuted our journey towards the Salwen. Came to Zat-kyee's small village, where one man and his wife embraced the truth at first hearing; and the man said, that as there was no suitable place for baptizing at that village, he would follow on, until he could say, "See, here is water," &c. I gave him leave to follow, not with that view, but to listen further to the blessed gospel. At night, reached Shway-bau's village, where they afforded us a shelter rather reluctantly. In the evening, however, had an interesting, though small assembly.

January 17. Pursued our way, and soon came in sight of the Salwen, the boundary between the British and Burmese territories. Arrived at Poo-ah's small village, consisting of three houses, not one of which had a leaf of covering. No one welcomed our arrival; so we sat down on the ground. Presently the preaching of one of the Karen disciples so wrought upon one of the householders, a Burman with a Karen wife, that he invited me to sit on his floor; and my people spread a mat overhead, which, with my umbrella, made me quite at home. The householder, in the interval of his work, and one of the neighbors, began to listen, and were present at evening worship.

January 18. Shway-hlah, the man who followed us from the village day before yesterday, appearing to be sincere in his desire to profess the Christian religion, we held a meeting, though four disciples only could be present; and on balloting for his reception, there was one dissentient vote, so that I advised him to wait longer. He appeared to be much disappointed and grieved; said that he should perhaps not live to see me again, and have an opportunity of being initiated into the religion of Jesus Christ; and after a while the two Karen disciples insisting that he should be reëxamined, we gave him a second trial, when, on cross questioning him in the Burman language, which he understood pretty well, (for we began to suspect the Karen interpreters of being a little partial to their countryman,) some circumstances leaked out which turned the scale in his favor, and he gained a clear vote. After his baptism, he went on his way rejoicing, resolving to tell all his neighbors what "great things the Lord had done for him." At morning worship, our host and the neighbor mentioned above, appeared to be very near the kingdom of heaven, but the other people of this village decidedly reject the gospel.

January 19. The boat having last night arrived from Maulmain, we prepared to proced up the river. The two hopeful inquirers requested us to make them another visit on our return. Resolve to do so; and hope to find that the seed now sown in this and the neighboring villages will have sprung up and be ripe for harvest.

Passed Panchoos' village, where we spent an hour, and Nga-koung's, too far inland to visit.

January 20. Passed the head of Kanlong Island, and breakfasted near Yetdau's village, where we found two or three inquirers. One woman followed to the boat, and listened attentively. Passed Kan-karet Island, beyond which the Yoon-zalen empties into the Salwen from the west, and about noon reached Tat-sau's small village. One man, who had heard the gospel before, appeared very favorably impressed. Crossed the river to Lee-hai's village on the Burman side. In the evening, had a considerable assembly at his house. He and his son-in-law, their wives and one or two others, appeared open to conviction.

January 21. Recrossed the river to take in Ko Myat-kyau and Chet-thing, whom I had sent away from Kwan-bee, with directions to make a circuit to the north, and meet me at this place. They have proclaimed the gospel in many places where it was never heard before, and met with some instances of hopeful inquiry. We then proceeded up the Salwen, and in passing the mouth of the Yen-being, which falls in from the east, I sent Moung Zu-thee and Tau-nah to make another circuit, and meet me at Poo-ah's village ten days hence. At night, sent the two remaining Karen disciples to a small village a few miles inland.

January 22. On their return we again set out, and at three o'clock reached the landing-place called Toung Pyouk, where trading boats from Maulmain are obliged to stop, on account of the rapids in the river. No village near, and only two boats. A most dreary place. Nothing but rocks and sand hills. Sent two of my people forward by land, intending to follow them to-morrow.

January 23. Followed the track of my people, and after travelling five hours, came to Chanbau's village, in the midst of the mountains. In the evening, had a pretty large, but not very attentive assembly. Two or three received the word with apparent joy, and none manifested decided opposition.

January 24. Set out for Bau-nah's village, two days' journey; but after travelling an hour over dreadful mountains and in the bed of a rivulet, where the water was sometimes knee deep, and full of sharp, slippery rocks, when my bare feet, unaccustomed to such usage, soon became so sore that I could hardly step; and having ascertained that such was the only road for many miles, I felt that I had done all that lay in my power towards carrying the gospel farther in this direction, and therefore relinquished the attempt, and reluctantly returned to Chanbau's village. Not so many present at evening worship as yesterday. The seed sown here appears, in some instances, to have fallen on good ground; but our short stay deprives us of the pleasure of seeing fruit brought to perfection.

January 25. Returned to the boat, which we reached in two and a half hours, by a more direct route, and proceeded down the river. Soon came to a landing-place, where, observing a few boats, we stopped, with a view to communicate the gospel to the boat people. The two Karen disciples went to a village about a mile inland. In the evening, had a considerable assembly on the sand bank.

January 26. Some of the villagers came to the boat, and after listening a while, invited me to return with them. I found three houses only, but the inhabitants listened with the best attention.

January 27. This little village may be said to have embraced the gospel. At one time we had eight applicants for baptism; but two only were finally received, Ko Shway and his wife Nah Nyah-ban. They both understand the Burmese language pretty well; and the woman possesses the best intellect, as well as the strongest faith, that I have found among this people. I invited them, though rather advanced in life, to come to Maulmain, and learn to read, promising to support them a few months; and they concluded to accept the invitation next rainy season. They followed us all the way to the boat, and the woman stood looking after us until we were out of sight.

In the afternoon, arrived again at the Yen-being River, and sent some of my people to a neighboring village two miles distant. The villagers listened a while, and then sent a respectful message, saying that they believed the religion of Jesus Christ, that it was most excellent, &c., but begged that the teacher would go about his business, and not come to disturb them.

January 28. Proceeded down the Salwen, touching at several villages, and on reaching Yet-dau's, found sufficient encouragement to spend the night.

January 29. Four persons, two men and their wives, having heard the gospel before, and being now quite settled in their minds, and giving good evidence of having the grace of God, were received into the Christian church by baptism. Enjoyed a very pleasant Lord's day, having several seasons of worship, in a little shed pertaining to the village. Two other persons request baptism, and their case will be considered to-morrow.

January 30. In the morning, held a church meeting by the river side, and received the two last applicants. The chief of the village, Yet-dau's father, and several other persons, are very favorably impressed. Not a word of opposition to be heard. Took an affectionate leave of this little church, now consisting of six members, and went down the river on the west side of Kanlong Island, having come up on the east side from Poo-ah's village. Entered the Mai-zeen rivulet, in Burmese territory, and landed at Thah-pe-nike's village, where we spent the day. In the evening, had a noisy assembly. Some professed to believe, but pleaded the fear of government as an excuse for not prosecuting their inquiries. One young man, Kah-lah by name, drank in the truth, and promised to come to Maulmain as soon as he could get free from some present engagements.

January 31. Continued our course down the river, and landed on the west side, at Ti-yah-ban's village. The chief is said to be very much in favor of the Christian religion, but, unfortunately, had gone up the river, and his people did not dare to think in his absence. In the afternoon, came to the "upper village," the first we found on Kanlong. They listened well, but, about sunset, took a sudden turn, and would give us no further hearing. We removed, therefore, to Yai-thah-kau's village. Some of my people went ashore. The chief was absent, and the principal remaining personage, a Boodhist Karen, said that when the English government enforced their religion at the point of the sword, and he had seen two or three suffer death for not embracing it, he would begin to consider, and not before; that, however, if the teacher desired to come to the village, he could not be inhospitable, but would let him come. I sent back word that I would not come, but, as he loved falsehood and darkness, I would leave him to live therein all his days, and finally go the dark way; and all my people drew off to the boat. While we were deliberating what to do, something touched the old man's heart; we heard the sound of footsteps advancing in the dark, and presently a voice. "My lord, please to come to the village." "Don't call me lord. I am no lord, nor ruler of this world." "What must I call you? Teacher, I suppose." "Yes, but not your teacher, for you love to be taught falsehood, not truth." "Teacher, I have heard a great deal against this religion, and how can I know at once what is right and what is wrong? Please to come and let me listen attentively to your words." I replied not, but rose and followed the old man. He took me to his house, spread a cloth for me to sit on, manifested great respect, and listened with uncommon attention. When I prepared to go, he said, "But you will not go before we have performed an act of worship and prayer?" We accordingly knelt down, and, during prayer, the old man could not help, now and then, repeating the close of a sentence with emphasis, seeming to imply that, in his mind, I had not quite done it justice. After I was gone, he said that it was a great thing to change one's religion; that he stood quite alone in these parts; but that, if some of his acquaintance would join him, he would not be behind.

February 1. Went on to Pa-dah's village, near the southern extremity of the island, where there is a Boodhist priest, and the people generally are worshippers of Gaudama. Met with a frigid reception. But one man, who had heard and received the truth before, came forward boldly, and requested baptism. He bore an excellent examination, and we received him gladly. The opposition here is strong. None of the villagers present at evening worship, except a brother of the chief, and one other man; but these spoke decidedly in favor of the Christian religion, as did the old man of yesterday, who followed hither by land. The priest, I hear, is very angry, and, unfortunately for his cause, uses abusive language.

February 2. Went round the northern extremity of Kanlong, and up the eastern channel, to Poo-ah's village, where we found the two disciples whom we sent away on the 21st ultimo. They have met with a few hopeful inquirers. Some who live near are expected here to-morrow. In the mean time, went down the river a few miles, to Poo-door's village. My people preceded me, as usual, and about noon I followed them. But I found that the village was inhabited chiefly by Boodhist Karens, and, of course, met with a poor reception. After showing myself, and trying to conciliate the children and dogs, who cried and barked in concert, I left word that, if any wished to hear me preach, I would come again in the evening, and then relieved the people of my presence, and retreated to the boat. At night the disciples returned, without any encouragement. One of them, however, accidentally met the chief, who said that if I came he would not refuse to hear what I had to say. On this half invitation, I set out, about sunset, and never met with worse treatment at a

Karen village. The chief would not even invite us into his house, but sent us off to an old deserted place, where the floor was too frail to support us; so we sat down on the ground. He then invited us nearer, and sat down before us, with a few confidential friends. He had evidently forbidden all his people to approach us, otherwise some would have come, out of curiosity. And what a hard, suspicious face did he exhibit! And how we had to coax him to join us in a little regular worship! It was at least an hour before he would consent at all. But in the course of worship his features softened, and his mind " crossed over," as he expressed it, to our religion; and I returned to the boat inclined to believe that all things are possible with God.

February 3. Some of my people who slept at the village returned with the report that the place is divided against itself. Some are for and some against us. The opposition is rather violent. One man threatens to turn his aged father out of doors if he embraces the Christian religion. Perhaps this is not to be regretted. Satan never frets without cause. Turned the boat's head again to the north, and retraced our way to Poo-ah's village, where we spent the rest of the day. But the two hopeful inquirers that I left here on the 29th have made no advance.

February 4. Shway-hlah's wife, mentioned the 16th ultimo, having been here three times to meet me, was this time examined and received. She came accompanied by Tat-kyee, the principal man in her village, who himself is half a Christian. He had heard that I wished to have a zayat in these parts, and invited me to go up to the mouth of the Chummerah rivulet, now dry, where some of his people intend settling, and he would assist in building the zayat. I regarded this as an intimation of the path of duty, and set out for the place, about three miles distant. It was an additional inducement, that Tee-pah's village has been lately removed towards the Salwen, and is now situated two miles inland from the spot recommended. On our way we met a deputation from Tee-pah, inviting me to fix on the same spot, and his people also would assist in building the zayat. On arriving at the place we were joined by Tee-pah's father, and several other disciples, bringing with them a lad who has for some time listened to the truth, and now earnestly requested to be baptized. We held a church meeting on the bank, twelve disciples present from different parts, and unanimously received him. I then marked out a place for the zayat, despatched Tau-nah to bring his family from the Dah-gyne district, and build a house near the zayat, as he is to be stationed here, by mutual consent of all parties; and having named the new place Chummerah, from the adjoining rivulet, we took leave of the disciples, and again went down the river to Poo-door's village, where we arrived late at night.

February 5. Went to the village and had worship. The chief was absent on some government business. Six persons appeared to be near the kingdom of heaven, among whom is the old man whose son threatens to turn him out of doors. In the afternoon, proceeded down the river, and came to a village of Toung-thoos, a race of people from whom we have never yet obtained a disciple. They are strict Boodhists. Their language is entirely different from the Karen, but the men generally understand a little Burmese. We did all in our power to gain their confidence, but in vain. They rejected our overtures, and would not even allow us to sleep in their houses.

February 6. Went on our way; entered the Maizeen rivulet, which falls into the Salwen from the east, and landed at Kai-ngai's village, where we spent a few hours, but, not meeting with much encouragement, in the evening dropped down to the mouth of the rivulet, where, finding some relations of Pan-lah, who listened well, we spent the night.

February 7. Proceeded down the river to Kappay's village, where some listened with delight; thence to a small village on the Burman side; thence to Pah-an, on the British side; and thence to Rajah's village, on the same side, where we spent the night. The chief, who had heard the gospel before, now listened with the utmost eagerness till after midnight.

February 8. Rajah made a formal request to be admitted into the Christian church, and we had no hesitation in complying. He is the first Karen chief baptized in these parts. His people show a strange aversion. Not one of them would accompany us to the water, though he gave them an invitation. They seem to take side with his eldest son, a grown man, who has been a Boodhist priest, and is still strongly attached to that religion. After the baptism, we went to a small village below Rajah's; thence to Taroke-lah, inhabited by Talings; thence to a village of Toung-thoos, where we found one man that listened; thence to a Karen village below Kan-blike. In the evening, had a considerable assembly. Three persons professed to believe.

February 9. Visited Wen-gyan, Pah-len, and Zong-ing, Taling villages, where we found a few Karens. At the latter place, collected a small assembly for evening worship. A few professed to believe; others were violent in opposing.

February 10. Visited several Taling villages in succession. In the afternoon, reached the confluence of the Salwen and the Gyne, upon which we turned into the latter, and went up to Taranah, where Ko Shan resides, as mentioned December 29. The inhabitants of this place, like the Talings in general, are inveterately opposed to the gospel, and Ko Shan has had very little success. Two or three individuals, however, appear to be favorably impressed; but the opposition is so strong that no one dares to come forward.

February 11. Left Ko Shan, with the promise of sending him aid as soon as possible, and in the afternoon reached Maulmain, after an absence of six weeks, during which I have baptized twenty-five, and registered about the same number of hopeful inquirers. I find that brother and sister Jones have arrived from Rangoon, brother Kincaid having concluded to take their place.

The two disciples who were sent to itinerate in the direction of Yay went no farther than Amherst, on account of the illness of one of them. They effected but little. The other two spent a month in the vicinity of Pah-ouk, encountering a great deal of bitter opposition, but occasionally cheered by some encouraging appearances.

February 21. Some of the Karen disciples have just returned from a visit to their countrymen on the south part of Baloo Island, where the gospel has never been preached. They found many a listening ear, but none who were disposed, on first hearing, to embrace the new religion.

February 23. Brother Kincaid leaves this for **Rangoon**, with twelve thousand tracts, preparatory to the great **annual** festival of Shway-dagong, which is near at hand.

February 26. Baptized a Burmese residing at **Pah-ouk**, but now about removing to Maulmain, on account of the persecution he receives from his old neighbors.

February 27. Have concluded to make another visit to the Karens on the Salwen, and expect to set out day after tomorrow.

I have already alluded to the profound interest with which Dr. Judson contemplated the progress of the gospel in every direction. Many years ago, he had urged upon the board at Boston the importance of directing their attention to several parts of the heathen world. He believed that a bold and aggressive policy was demanded of the conductors of missionary efforts, and that no other course will either arouse or keep alive the benevolent spirit of the churches. On a following page will be found two addresses to Christians in this country in behalf of missions to the East, which, in true eloquence and touching pathos, have been exceeded by nothing with which I am acquainted that has been written on this subject.

It was not, however, for the heathen alone that his sympathies were excited. He looked upon all men as by nature the enemies of God, who could be reconciled to him only by the preaching of the cross; and he therefore labored and prayed for the universal dissemination of the truths of the New Testament. In a special manner were his desires awakened in favor of the Jews. He once said that, though he believed one soul purchased by the blood of Christ as valuable as another, he should esteem it a peculiar favor — a favor directly from the hand of Him who understands and sympathizes with his people through his own self-imposed humanity — to be permitted to restore one of the lost sheep of the house of Israel.

Influenced by these sentiments, and having observed that his suggestions in respect to the occupation of new fields had been unheeded, he made an attempt to provide the means for establishing a mission to Palestine, in a great measure from the circle of his own friends. He interested in this plan Mr. Nisbet, a pious and intelligent officer of high rank in the East India Company's service, while he and several of his missionary brethren themselves contributed largely to the object. The sum to be raised was ten thousand dollars, which he hoped would form a permanent basis for an independent mission. Having secured so large an amount in India, he forwarded the proposals to Boston, in the hope that the necessary amount remaining would readily be provided. The plan, however, did not meet with favor. For some reason, he never received any reply from either of the ministers addressed.

The letters which follow will present in detail the steps which he took to accomplish this purpose. Whether the design was or was not wisely conceived, it is not necessary here to consider. It is enough that it illustrates the earnest longing of Dr. Judson's soul to carry the blessings of the gospel to every brother of the human race.

To the Corresponding Secretary.

MAULMAIN, May 8, 1832.

REV. AND DEAR SIR: Whereas there has been lately remitted from Madras, to the agent of the American Baptist Board of Foreign Missions in Calcutta, between three and four thousand Sicca rupees, and it is desirable that the board should understand the specific purposes for which the money has been given, I enclose a letter from Mr. Nisbet, the principal donor, which will somewhat explain those purposes, and would add more definitely, that so much of the whole sum as is sufficient to cover nine shares in the Palestine mission concern, at two hundred dollars each, belongs to that concern, and is to be refunded in case the sum of ten thousand dollars is not made up in the United States. I would here add that the remaining three shares, which have been taken by members of this mission, will be paid, as soon as we are officially informed that all the shares are taken.

In regard to the one thousand rupees given to Mrs. Wade, as she has requested my advice about the manner of disposing of it, I do hereby advise her to let it remain for the present in the funds of the board, subject to her order or her husband's, in the same way that the few hundred rupees, the remnant of my property, is allowed to remain, (with this difference only, that the latter sum appears every year in my annual account;) and that in case of death, without any particular disposal, it ultimately become the property of the board. I request, also, that this letter be preserved, in the archives of the board, superseding the necessity of any further explanation.

Yours faithfully,

A. JUDSON.

We accede to the above arrangement, in regard to the one thousand rupees.

J. WADE,
D. B. L. WADE.

RANGOON, May 13, 1832.

To the Rev. Messrs. Mercer, Manly, Taylor, Brantly, Cone, Galusha, Pattison, and Knowles.

DEAR BRETHREN: I present you the accompanying subscription paper, in good hope that, as twelve shares of the fifty are already taken, you will not hesitate to second the effort, and procure five subscribers each.

Your faithful friend,
A. JUDSON.

MAULMAIN, February 20, 1832.

P. S. Much to write on this subject, from a full heart, but no time. Excuse abruptness.

We, the undersigned, desirous of contributing to the revival of true religion in those regions where our adorable Saviour and his apostles labored and suffered, agree to raise the sum of ten thousand dollars, in fifty shares of two hundred dollars each, for the permanent support of a missionary to be sent by the American Baptist Board of Foreign Missions, in the direction of Palestine, the particular field of labor to be determined by the board; the money to be paid to the treasurer of the board as soon as the sum is completed.

A. JUDSON,	1 share.
C. BENNETT,	1 share.
J. WADE,	1 share.
J. NISBET,	3 shares.
A. FRIEND,	1 share.
R. CATHCART,	1 share.
W. K. HAY,	1 share.
E. B. MILLS,	3 shares.

From J. Nisbet, Esq.

DARWAR, November 3, 1831.

MY DEAR MR. JUDSON: I am grieved to find that I have allowed so long a space of time to elapse since the receipt of your letter, regarding the sending of a missionary to Palestine. You will, however, I hope, ere this have received intimation from Mr. Van Someren that I was doing something for the accomplishment of the object you have in view. Indeed he has informed me of his having remitted the amount subscribed by myself and others to Calcutta. In addition to the sum subscribed by me on the paper, I have sent one thousand rupees, which Mrs. Nisbet intended as an offering to Mrs. Wade, in humble imitation of her devoted zeal in giving up the things of this world. She said she felt, after reading the delightful letter from Mrs. Wade to her sister which you sent to me, as if she could have sent every trinket in her possession, (not that she possessed many,) upon which we proposed to substitute one thousand rupees. A late letter from you to Mr. Van Someren has just informed us of Mr. and Mrs. Wade having gone home, sick. I therefore beg you will dispose of the money, one thousand rupees, how you please, or as you think Mrs. Wade would have done.

I make no apology for sending the subscription paper as it is. Some very good men, but mistaken I think, objected to a Baptist missionary going where there was no minister of the same denomination, as he could not communicate with others. Mr. Mills's answer suited me better. I therefore kept it, and returned the conditional subscriptions, begging them to send one of another denomination, which perhaps may be done. I am sure you will rejoice if they should succeed in sending a servant devoted to his heavenly Master, or such a one as I feel confident the Baptist board will. Both Mrs. Nisbet and myself have been unwell lately, and are going to the Cape of Good Hope for a year. Thank God, we are not at present seriously ill; but it is thought that we might become so next hot season. May the grace of our Lord Jesus Christ, the love of God, and the fellowship of the Holy Ghost, be with you, and prosper exceedingly your labors. Pray that *we* may be kept close to our dear Saviour, "in our going out and in our coming in;" and if an opportunity should occur of writing to me at the Cape, you will confer a great favor on me by doing so, for, believe me, my dear Mr. Judson, I feel the warmest affection for you and the glorious cause in which you are so diligently laboring.

I am, and trust I ever shall be, your brother in Christ Jesus to whom be glory forever and ever.

J. NISBET.

Thus apparently ended Dr. Judson's effort on behalf of the Jews. It, however, pleased an all-wise Providence to render his servant useful to the children of Abraham in a manner which he little expected. Two or three days before he embarked on his last voyage, not a fortnight before his death, Mrs. Judson read to him the following paragraph from Rev. Dr. Hague's journal in the Watchman and Reflector:—

There * we first learned the interesting fact, which was mentioned by Mr. Schauffler, that a tract had been published in Germany, giving some account of Dr. Judson's labors at Ava; that it had fallen into the hands of some Jews, and had been the means of their conversion; that it had reached Trebizond, where a Jew had translated it for the Jews of that place; that it had awakened a deep interest among them; that a candid spirit of inquiry had been manifested; and that a request had been made for a missionary to be sent to them from Constantinople. Such a fact is full of meaning, a comment on the word of inspiration: "In the morning sow thy seed, and in the evening withhold not thine hand: thou knowest not which shall prosper, this or that."

Mrs. Judson, in her relation of these facts, continues, "His eyes were filled with tears when I had done reading, but still he at first spoke playfully, and in a way that a little disappointed me. Then a look of almost unearthly solemnity came over him, and, clinging fast to my hand, as though to assure himself of being really in the world, he said, 'Love, this

* At the house of Mr. Goodell, in Constantinople.

frightens me. I do not know what to make of it.' 'What?' 'Why, what you have just been reading. I never was deeply interested in any object, I never prayed sincerely and earnestly for any thing, but it came; at some time,—no matter at how distant a day,—somehow, in some shape,—probably the last I should have devised,—it came. And yet I have always had so little faith! May God forgive me, and, while he condescends to use me as his instrument, wipe the sin of unbelief from my heart.'"

"If ye abide in me, and my words abide in you, ye shall ask what ye will, and it shall be done unto you."

CHAPTER II.

ADVICE TO CANDIDATES FOR MISSIONARY LABOR — THIRD TOUR AMONG THE KARENS. — APPEALS FOR HELP — TRANSLATION OF THE BIBLE COMPLETED. — MARRIAGE TO MRS BOARDMAN.

1832-1834.

To the Foreign Missionary Association of the Hamilton Literary and Theological Institution, N. Y.

MAULMAIN, June 25, 1832.

DEAR BRETHREN: Yours of November last, from the pen of your Corresponding Secretary, Mr. William Dean, is before me. It is one of the few letters that I feel called upon to answer, for you ask my advice on several important points. There is, also, in the sentiments you express, something so congenial to my own, that I feel my heart knit to the members of your association, and instead of commonplace reply, am desirous of setting down a few items which may be profitable to you in your future course. Brief items they must be, for want of time forbids my expatiating.

In commencing my remarks, I take you as you are. You are contemplating a missionary life.

First, then, let it be a missionary *life;* that is, come out for life, and not for a limited term. Do not fancy that you have a true missionary spirit, while you are intending all along to leave the heathen soon after acquiring their language. Leave them! for what? To spend the rest of your days in enjoying the ease and plenty of your native land?

Secondly. In choosing a companion for life, have particular regard to a good constitution, and not wantonly, or without good cause, bring a burden on yourselves and the mission.

Thirdly. Be not ravenous to do good on board ship. Missionaries have frequently done more hurt than good, by injudicious zeal, during their passage out.

Fourthly. Take care that the attention you receive at home, the unfavorable circumstances in which you will be placed on board ship, and the unmissionary examples you may possibly meet with at some missionary stations, do not transform you from living missionaries to mere skeletons before you reach the place of your destination. It may be profitable to bear in mind, that a large proportion of those who come out on a mission to the East die within five years after leaving their native land. Walk softly, therefore; death is narrowly watching your steps.

Fifthly. Beware of the reaction which will take place soon after reaching your field of labor. There you will perhaps find native Christians, of whose merits or demerits you cannot judge correctly without some familiar acquaintance with their language. Some appearances will combine to disappoint and disgust you. You will meet with disappointments and discouragements, of which it is impossible to form a correct idea from written accounts, and which will lead you, at first, almost to regret that you have embarked in the cause. You will see men and women whom you have been accustomed to view through a telescope some thousands of miles long. Such an instrument is apt to magnify. Beware therefore of the reaction you will experience from a combination of all these causes, lest you become disheartened at commencing your work, or take up a prejudice against some persons and places, which will imbitter all your future lives.

Sixthly. Beware of the greater reaction which will take place after you have acquired the language, and become fatigued and worn out with preaching the gospel to a disobedient and gainsaying people. You will sometimes long for a quiet retreat, where you can find a respite from the tug of toiling at native work — the incessant, intolerable friction of the missionary grindstone. And Satan will sympathize with you in this matter; and he will present some chapel of ease, in which to officiate in your native tongue, some government situation, some professorship or editorship, some literary or scientific pursuit, some supernumerary translation, or, at least, some system of schools; any thing, in a word, that will help you, without much surrender of character, to slip out of real missionary work. Such a temptation will form the crisis of your disease. If your spiritual constitution can sustain it, you recover; if not, you die.

Seventhly. Beware of pride; not the pride of proud men, but the pride of humble men — that secret pride which is apt to grow out of the consciousness that we are esteemed by the great and good. This pride sometimes eats out the vitals of religion before its existence is suspected. In order to check its operations, it may be well to remember how we appear in the sight of God, and how we should appear in the sight of our fellow-men, *if all were known*. Endeavor to let all be known. Confess your faults freely, and as publicly as circumstances will require or admit. When you have done something of which you are ashamed, and by which, perhaps, some person has been injured, (and what man is exempt?) be glad not only to make reparation, but improve the opportunity for subduing your pride.

Eighthly. Never lay up money for yourselves or your families. Trust in God from day to day, and verily you shall be fed.

Ninthly. Beware of that indolence which leads to a neglect of bodily exercise. The poor health and premature death of most Europeans in the East must be eminently ascribed to the most wanton neglect of bodily exercise.

Tenthly. Beware of genteel living. Maintain as little intercourse as possible with fashionable European society. The mode of living adopted by many missionaries in the East is quite inconsistent with that familiar intercourse with the natives which is essential to a missionary.

There are many points of self-denial that I should like to touch upon; but a consciousness of my own deficiency constrains me to be silent. I have also left untouched several topics of vital importance, it having been my aim to select such only as appear to me to have been not much noticed or enforced. I hope you will excuse the monitorial style that I have accidentally adopted. I assure you, I mean no harm.

In regard to your inquiries concerning studies, qualifications, &c., nothing occurs that I think would be particularly useful, except the simple remark, that I fear too much stress begins to be laid on what is termed a thorough classical education.

Praying that you may be guided in all your deliberations, and that I may yet have the pleasure of welcoming some of you to these heathen shores, I remain

Your affectionate brother,
A. JUDSON.

Journal.

February 29, 1832. Left Maulmain for the Karen villages on the Salwen, accompanied by Ko Myat-kyau, who speaks Karen, three other Taling disciples, and the two Karen assistants, Panlah and Chet-thing. The other Karen assistant, Tau-nah, I expect to meet at Chummerah, according to the arrangement of February 4. At night, reached Tong-eing, and found that the few Karens near the place had concluded to reject the gospel.

March 1. Touched at the village above Nengyan, and found that the inhabitants have come to the same conclusion, "till the next rainy season." Passed by all the Taling towns, and touched at the village below Rajah's, where we found that the people still adhere to the new Karen prophet, Areemaday. Moung Zuthee unfortunately encountered a very respectable Burman priest, with a train of novices, who, not relishing his doctrine, fell upon him, and gave him a sound beating. The poor man fled to me in great dismay, and, I am sorry to say, some wrath, begging leave to assemble our forces, and seize the aggressor, for the purpose of delivering him up to justice. I did assemble them; and, all kneeling down, I praised God that he had counted one of our number worthy to suffer a little for his Son's sake; and prayed that he would give us a spirit of forgiveness, and our persecutors every blessing, temporal and spiritual; after which we left the field of battle with cool and happy minds. Reached Rajah's late at night. He remains firm, though not followed by any of his people. His wife, however, and eldest daughter, after evening worship, declared themselves on the side of Christ.

March 2. Spent the forenoon in instructing and examining the wife and daughter. The former we approved, but rejected the latter, as not yet established in the Christian faith. After the baptism, Rajah and his wife united in presenting their younger children, that I might lay my hands on them and bless them. The elder children, being capable of discerning good from evil, came of their own accord, and held up their folded hands in the act of homage to their parents' God, while we offered a prayer that they might obtain grace to become true disciples, and receive the holy ordinance of baptism. At noon, left this interesting family, and proceeded up the river, stopping occasionally, and preaching wherever we could catch a listening ear. Entered the Mai-san, and landed at the village above Rai-ngai's, which Ko Myat-kyau has formerly visited. In the evening, had two very attentive hearers.

March 3. The two attentive hearers were up nearly all night, drinking in the truth. One of them became urgent for baptism; and on hearing his present and past experience, from the time he first listened to the gospel, we concluded to receive him into the fellowship of the church. His wife is very favorably disposed, but not so far advanced in knowledge and faith. Returned to the Salwen, and made a long pull for Poo-door's village; but late in the evening, being still at a considerable distance, were obliged to coil ourselves up in our small boat, there being no house in these parts, and the country swarming with tigers at this season, so that none of us ventured to sleep on shore.

March 4, Lord's day. Uncoiled ourselves with the first dawn of light, and soon after sunrise took possession of a fine flat log, in the middle of Poo-door's village, a mile from the river, where we held forth on the duty of refraining from work on this the Lord's day, and attending divine worship. Some listened to our words; and in the forenoon we succeeded in collecting a small assembly. After worship, the old man mentioned formerly, whose son threatened to turn him out of doors, came forward, with his wife; and having both witnessed a good confession, we received them into our fellowship. Poo-door himself absent on a journey; but his wife ready to become a Christian.

March 5. Spent the forenoon in examining and receiving another couple, and then went on to Chummerah. The disciples from Tee-pah's village have built a zayat, and two or three families, including Tau-nah's, have arrived, and are settling themselves. At night, went out to the village, four miles distant, (instead of two, as first reported,) and had a full assembly of disciples and inquirers at evening worship.

March 6. The truth is evidently spreading in this village; one inquirer after another is coming over to the side of Christ. After morning worship, left some of my people to follow up the work, and returned to the zayat.

March 7. In the forenoon above twenty disciples assembled at the zayat; and after worship we examined and received five persons more, all from Tee-pah's village. Left Zuthee in charge of the zayat, and took Tau-nah in his place. Visited Pan-choo's village, where some listened in silence.

March 8. Went several miles inland, to visit Nge Koung's village; but the people, being Boodhist Karens, would not even treat us hospitably, much less listen to the word. In the afternoon, reached Yah-dan's village, and visited the little church, chiefly to receive the confession of two female members, who have been implicated in making some offering to the demon who rules over diseases — the easily-besetting sin of the Karens. Spent the rest of the day in preaching to the villagers and visitors from different parts. Several professed to believe. Had a profoundly attentive though small assembly at evening worship, on the broad sand bank of the river, with a view to the accommodation of certain boat people. We felt that the Holy Spirit set home the truth in a peculiar manner. Some of the disciples were engaged in religious discussion and prayer a great part of the night.

March 9. Several requested baptism. In the course of the day, we held a church meeting, composed of the disciples from Maulmain, and others from the neighboring village, and received three persons into our communion, all men, formerly disciples of the new prophet Areemaday. In the afternoon, proceeded up the river, as far as Zat-zan's village, where two old women, of some influence in these parts, listened with good attention. At night several of the disciples went inland a few miles, to Laidan, where the inhabitants are chiefly Boodhist Karens; but finding Mah Kee-kah, the widow of Pan-mlai-mlo, whose death is mentioned January 12, her parents and sisters drank in the truth. Hope to visit them on my return.

March 10. Went on to the mouth of the Yen-being, and as far as the great log, which prevents a boat from proceeding farther. Providentially met with Wah-hai, of whom I have heard a good report for some time. He was happy to see us, and we were happy to examine and baptize him. We then visited the village, whence they formerly sent a respectful message, desiring us to go about our business, and found some attentive listeners.

March 11, Lord's day. Again took the main river, and soon fell in with a boat, containing several of the listeners of yesterday, among whom was one man who declared his resolution to enter the new religion. We had scarcely parted with this boat when we met another, full of men, coming down the stream; and, on hailing to know whether they wished to hear the gospel of the Lord Jesus Christ, an elderly man, the chief of the party, replied that he had already heard much of the gospel; and there was nothing he desired more than to have a meeting with the teacher. Our boats were soon side by side, where, after a short engagement, the old man struck his colors, and begged us to take him into port, where he could make a proper surrender of himself to Christ. We accordingly went to the shore, and spent several hours very delightfully, under the shade of the overhanging trees, and the banner of the love of Jesus. The old man's experience was so clear, and his desire for baptism so strong, that, though circumstances prevented our gaining so much testimony of his good conduct since believing as we usually require, we felt that it would be wrong to refuse his request. A lad in his company, the person mentioned January 30, desired also to be baptized. But though he had been a preacher to the old man, his experience was not so decided and satisfactory; so that we rejected him for the present. The old man went on his way, rejoicing aloud, and declaring his resolution to make known the eternal God, and the dying love of Jesus, all along the banks of the Yoon-za-len, his native stream.

The dying words of an aged man of God, when he waved his withered, death-struck arm, and exclaimed, "*The best of all is, God is with us*," I feel in my very soul. Yes, the great Invisible is in these Karen wilds. That mighty Being, who heaped up these craggy rocks, and reared these stupendous mountains, and poured out these streams in all directions, and scattered immortal beings throughout these deserts — he is present by the influence of his Holy Spirit, and accompanies the sound of the gospel with converting, sanctifying power. "*The best of all is, God is with us.*"

> "In *these* deserts let me labor,
> On *these* mountains let me tell
> How he died — the blessed Saviour,
> To redeem a world from hell."

March 12. Alas! how soon is our joy turned into mourning! Mah Nyah-ban, of whom we all had such a high opinion, joined her husband, not many days after their baptism, in making an offering to the demon of diseases, on account of the sudden, alarming illness of their youngest child; and they have remained ever since in an impenitent prayerless state. They now refuse to listen to our exhortation, and appear to be given over to hardness of heart and blindness of mind. I was, therefore, obliged, this morning, to pronounce the sentence of suspension, and leave them to the mercy and judgment of God. Their case is greatly to be deplored. They are quite alone in this quarter, have seen no disciples since we left them, and are surrounded with enemies, some from Maulmain, who have told them all manner of lies, and used every effort to procure and perpetuate their apostasy. When I consider the evidence of grace which they formerly gave, together with all the palliating circumstances of the case, I have much remaining hope that they will yet be brought to repentance. I commend them to the prayers of the faithful, and the notice of any missionary who may travel that way. In consequence of the advantage which Satan has gained in this village, the six hopeful inquirers, whom we left here, have all fallen off; so that we are obliged to retire with the dispirited feelings of beaten troops.

I respectfully request, and sincerely hope, that this article may be neither suppressed nor polished. The principle of "double selection," as it is termed, that is, one selection by the missionary and another by the publishing committee, has done great mischief, and contributed more to impair the credit of missionary accounts than any thing else. We in the East, knowing how extensively this principle is acted on, do scarcely give any credit to the statements which appear in some periodicals, and the public at large are beginning to open their eyes to the same thing. It is strange to me that missionaries and publishing committees do not see the excellency and efficacy of the system pursued by the inspired writers — that of exhibiting the good and the bad alike. Nothing contributes more to establish the authenticity of the writing. A temporary advantage gained by suppressing truth is a real defeat in the end, and therefore $\mu o\nu\eta$ $\theta\nu\tau\varepsilon o\nu$ $\alpha\lambda\eta\theta\varepsilon\iota\alpha$.*

Returned down the river; reëntered the Yen-being; had another interview with the listeners of yesterday; met with a Taling doctor from Kan-hlah, near Maulmain, who listened all the evening with evident delight.

March 13. Spent the day and night at Tatzan's, Se-hai's, and the village of Lai-dan, where we failed of finding Mah Kee-kah, but found her parents, who listened well. In these

---

* We must sacrifice only to truth.

parts I have a considerable number of hopeful inquirers. May the Lord bless the seed sown, and give us the pleasure of reaping a plentiful harvest at no very distant period.

March 14. Touched at Yah-dan's, and went down the west side of Kan-long, as before, to Thah-pa-nike's; (15,) proceeded to Ti-yah-bans, where we left a few hopeful inquirers; and then went on to Pa-dah's village. In the evening, had worship at the chief's house.

March 16. The opposition here is violent. The man who was baptized on my last visit has been obliged to remove to the outskirts of the village, but he remains steadfast in the faith; and to-day another man came out, and having witnessed a good confession, was received into the fellowship of the persecuted. At night, ran down to Poo-door's village, about five miles, found him at home, and spent the evening in persuading him to forsake all for Christ. His language is that of Agrippa, — "Almost," &c. I have great hopes and great fears for his immortal soul. Three of the disciples went several miles inland, to a village where there are some hopeful inquirers.

March 17. Returned up the river to Chummerah. In the evening, had a considerable assembly of disciples preparatory to the administration of the Lord's supper.

March 18. Administered the Lord's supper to thirty-six communicants, chiefly from villages on the Salwen.

March 19. Left Tau-nah and Moung Tsan-lone in charge of the zayat and boat, and set out with the rest of my people, and two or three new followers, on a journey over land to the Dah-gyne. In the evening, after marrying a couple at Tee-pah's village, had an interesting assembly, with whom we enjoyed religious discussion till near midnight. Two opposers came over, I trust, to Christ.

March 20. Went on our way, and in two hours and a quarter, not including stops, reached Kwanbee, on the east of the Leing-bwai. Two hours and a quarter more brought us to Mai-pah, where the people, being prejudiced against the gospel, gave us a poor reception.

March 21. In a neighboring village, found a few who listened well. After spending the morning in instructing them continued our journey eastwardly, and after two and a half hours' hard walking, reached a small village near the Dahgyne, where the people received us hospitably, but, being Boodhists, listened with no good disposition.

March 22. Reached the new place selected January 9, which we call Newville, about forty miles distant, I conjecture, from Chummerah. Found two families only settled here, but others are about joining them. Some of the disciples went to the neighboring villages to give information of my arrival.

March 23. Most of the disciples visited me in the course of the day. In the evening, had a pretty full room. Received and baptized one couple, who applied for baptism on my first visit, but were rejected.

March 24. Having removed Moung Doot from this station, — who, though a good man, has grown cold and inactive, — appointed Pan-lah in his place, and selected a few individuals for the adult school, we set out on our return to Chummerah, and at night reached Mai-pah, twenty miles distant, being half way between the two stations.

March 25. In the morning, had a small, attentive assembly, from one of the neighboring villages. Then went on to Tee-pah's village, which we reached in season for evening worship.

March 26. Three lads from Tee-pah's village, two of them baptized, joined our company, with a view to the adult school at Maulmain. Took the boat at Chummerah, and went down the river. Spent the night at Rajah's village. Some begin to listen.

March 27. Ran down the river without touching at any place by the way. At night, reached Maulmain, after an absence of nearly a month, during which I have baptized nineteen, making eighty Karen Christians in connection with the Maulmain station, of whom one is dead, and two are suspended from communion. Am glad, yet sorry, to find that brother Bennett arrived a fortnight ago from Calcutta, with a complete fount of types, and yesterday sent a boat to call me, which, however, passed us on the way. Must I, then, relinquish my intention of making another trip up the river before the rains set in? Must I relinquish for many months, and perhaps forever, the pleasure of singing as I go, —

> "In these deserts let me labor,
> On these mountains let me tell?"

Truly, the tears fall as I write.

March 30. Corrected the first proof sheet of the New Testament in Burman. Moung Sanlone has recommenced his school, with about a dozen adults and children, mostly Karens.

April 1. Brother and sister Wade have touched here, on their way from Mergui to Rangoon. They have laid the foundation of a little church in Mergui, and left Pastor Ing in charge of that station, assisted, for the present, by Ko Manboke and wife, from this place.

April 6. Despatched Ko Myat-kyau in the mission boat, with instructions to proceed up the Salwen, touch at Chummerah, take in the three Karen assistants who are waiting there, and then follow the course of the Yoon-za-len, to the residence of the new Karen prophet Areemaday, distant about ten days from Maulmain.

May 16. The party sent up the Yoon-za-len have just returned. They were well received by the prophet, an extraordinary young man of twenty, who, while he pretends to hold communication with the invisible world, professes also to be desirous of finding the true God, and becoming acquainted with the true religion. Our people remained with him three days, during which time they were surrounded with a crowd of his followers, and were obliged to preach day and night. They also visited several places on their return, where the gospel was never preached before. One young man accompanied them to this place, and requests to be baptized. We shall recommend him to enter the school, and wait until he becomes better acquainted with the new religion.

June 25. Two of our neighbors have lately been baptized, and one Karen, Pan-mir by name, the chief of Tee-pah's village. He is now accompanying some of the Karen assistants on a tour round the Island of Ba-loo.

Moung Tsan-lone's school numbers about twenty. Some occasionally leave after learning to read, and new scholars take their place.

Since my last date, brother Wade, having had a violent attack of disease, has been obliged to come hither in haste, for medical aid; and I have succeeded in persuading him to stay, for the following reason: finding that I should be confined to this place for several months, for the purpose of superintending the printing of the New Testament, I was led to turn my attention again to the Old, one third only of which is yet done; and on making a calculation, I found that I could finish the whole in two years, if I confined myself exclusively to the work; otherwise it would hang on four years or more. Considering the uncertainty of life, and the tenor of numerous letters lately received from home, I concluded that it was my duty to adopt the former course; in order to which, however, it was necessary that one of my brethren, acquainted with the language, should be stationed here, to take charge of the church and people of Maulmain, and the Karens in this region. On stating these things to brother and sister Wade, they concluded to remain, though nothing was farther from their minds when they first came round. I have, therefore, retired to a room which I had previously prepared, at the end of the native chapel, where I propose, if life be spared, to shut myself up for the next two years; and I beg the prayers of my friends that, in my seclusion, I may enjoy the presence of the Saviour, and that special aid in translating the inspired word which I fully believe will be vouchsafed in answer to humble, fervent prayer.

To the American Baptist Board for Foreign Missions.

MAULMAIN, March 4, 1832.

RESPECTED FATHERS AND BRETHREN: At our monthly concert this morning, it was unanimously agreed that a joint letter should be addressed to you, on the importance of sending out more missionaries to this part of the heathen world. Being every one of us exceedingly pressed for want of time, we cannot stop to prepare an elaborate statement, but must come at once to the point in hand.

We are in distress. We see thousands perishing around us. We see mission stations opening on every side, the fields growing whiter every day, and no laborers to reap the harvest. If each one of us could divide himself into three parts, happy would he be, not only to take leave of his native land and beloved connections at home, but of still nearer and more intimate connections. We want instantly to send aid to the Tavoy station, where brother Mason is laboring, almost alone. We want instantly to send a missionary to Mergui, a pleasant, healthful town, south of Tavoy, where a small church has been raised up, and left in charge of a native pastor. Our hearts bleed when we think of poor Mergui and the Karens in that vicinity, many of whom are ready to embrace the gospel and be saved. But how can we allow ourselves to think of that small place, when the whole kingdom of Siam lies in our rear, and the city of Bangkok, at once a port for ships and the seat of imperial government? We want instantly to despatch one of our number to Bangkok. One? There ought, at this moment, to be three, at least, on their way to that important place. Another ought to be on his way to Yah-heing, a large town east of Maulmain, from which there is a fine river leading down to Bangkok: there are many Karens at Yah-heing. The Christian religion is creeping that way, by means of our Karen disciples. North of Yah-heing and the Thoung-yen River, the boundary of the British territory on that side, lies the kingdom or principality of Zenmai. There have been several communications between the government of Maulmain and Lah-bong, the present capital of that country. Moung Shway-bwen, one of our disciples, formerly with brother Boardman at Tavoy, is a nephew of the prince, or deputy prince, of that country, and is anxious to return thither. But how can we send him, a very young man, without a missionary? If we had a spare missionary, what a fine opportunity for introducing the gospel into that central nation! It would open the way to other neighboring nations, not even mentioned in foreign geographies, and even to the borders of China and Tartary. Between Maulmain and Zenmai are various tribes of Karens, Toung-thoos, Lah-wahs, &c. The former are literally crying out aloud for a written language, that they may read in their own tongue the wonderful works of God. From the banks of the Yoon-za-len, on the north-west, the celebrated prophet of the Karens has repeatedly sent down messages and presents to us, begging that we would come and instruct his people in the Christian religion. But how can we think of supplying that quarter, when the old kingdom of Arracan, now under British rule, and speaking the same language with the Burmese, is crying, in the whole length and breadth of her coast, for some one to come to her rescue? In that country are one or two hundred converts, and one country-born missionary, from the Serampore connection, who is laboring without any prospect of reënforcement from Bengal, and desirous that one of us should join him. Kyouk Phyoo, lately established by the English, is esteemed a healthy place. The commandant is disposed to welcome a missionary, and afford him every facility. Our hearts bleed when we think of Kyouk Phyoo, and the poor inquirers that one of our number lately left there, ready to embrace the Christian religion, if he would only promise to remain or send a successor. From Kyouk Phyoo, the way is open into the four provinces of Arracan, namely, Rek-keing, Chedubah, Ramree, and Sandoway; and what a grand field for our tracts, and the New Testament, now in press! Of all the places that now cry around us, we think that Kyouk Phyoo cries the loudest. No; we listen again, and the shrill cry of golden Ava rises above them all. O Ava! Ava! with thy metropolitan walls and gilded turrets, thou sittest a lady among these eastern nations; but our hearts bleed for thee! In thee is no Christian church, no missionary of the cross.

We have lately heard of the death of poor Prince Myen Zeing. He died without any missionary or Christian to guide his groping soul on the last dark journey. Where has that journey terminated? Is he in the bright world of paradise, or in the burning lake? He had attained some knowledge of the way of salvation. Perhaps, in his last hours, he turned away his eye from the gold and silver idols around his couch, and looked to the crucified Saviour. But those who first taught him were far away; so he died and was buried like a heathen. It is true that the one of our number who formerly lived at Ava would not be tolerated during the present reign; but another missionary would, doubtless, be well received, and, if prudent, be allowed to remain. Two missionaries ought, at this moment, to be studying the language *in Ava*.

O God of mercy, have mercy on Ava, and Chageing, and A-ma-ra-poo-ra. Have mercy on Pugan and Prome, (poor Prome!) on Toung-oo, on the port of Bassein, and on all the towns between Ava and Rangoon. Have mercy on old Pegu and the surrounding district. Have mercy on the four provinces of Arracan. Have mercy on the inhabitants of the banks of the Yoon-za-len, the Salwen, the Thoung-yen, and the Gyne. Have mercy on all the Karens, the Toung-thoos, the Lah-wahs, and other tribes, whose names, though unknown in Christian lands, are known to thee. Have mercy on Zen-mai, on Lah-bong, Myeing-yoon-gyee, and Yay-heing. Have mercy on Bangkok, and the kingdom of Siam, and all the other principalities that lie on the north and east. Have mercy on poor little Mergui, and Pah-lan, and Yay, and Lah-meing, and Nah-zaroo, and Amherst, and the Island of Baloo, with its villages of Talings and Karens. Have mercy on our mission stations at Tavoy, Maulmain, and Rangoon, and our sub-stations at Mergui, Chummerah, and Newville. Pour out thine Holy Spirit upon us and our assistants, upon our infant churches and our schools. Aid us in the solemn and laborious work of translating and printing thine holy, inspired word in the languages of these heathen. O, keep our faith from failing, our spirits from sinking, and our mortal frames from giving way prematurely under the influence of the climate and the pressure of our labors. Have mercy on the board of missions; and grant that our beloved and respected fathers and brethren may be aroused to greater effort, and go forth personally into all parts of the land, and put in requisition all the energies of thy people. Have mercy on the churches in the United States; hold back the curse of Meroz; continue and perpetuate the heavenly revivals of religion which they have begun to enjoy; and may the time soon come when no church shall dare to sit under Sabbath and sanctuary privileges without having one of their number to represent them on heathen ground. Have mercy on the theological seminaries, and hasten the time when one half of all who yearly enter the ministry shall be taken by thine Holy Spirit, and *driven* into the wilderness, feeling a sweet necessity laid on them, and the precious love of Christ and of souls constraining them. Hear, O Lord, all the prayers which are this day presented in all the monthly concerts throughout the habitable globe, and hasten the millennial glory, for which we are all longing, and praying, and laboring. Adorn thy beloved one in her bridal vestments, that she may shine forth in immaculate beauty and celestial splendor. Come, O our Bridegroom; come, Lord Jesus; come quickly. Amen and Amen.

(Signed)   C. BENNETT,
OLIVER T. CUTTER,
JOHN TAYLOR JONES,
A. JUDSON,
J. WADE.

ORIGINAL AND SECOND-HAND TRANSLATION.

To the Rev. Dr. Sharp.

MAULMAIN, June 28, 1833.

REV. AND DEAR SIR: I ought to have written you long ago; but necessity has no law. I have lately entered upon a plan by which I hope to finish the translation of the Old Testament in two years. I find by experience that I can dispose of twenty-five or thirty verses per day, by giving all my time to the work. One third of the whole is already done. You may, perhaps, wonder why I make such a tedious work of translating, when some persons despatch the whole New Testament, and perhaps part of the Old, within a year or two after entering their field of labor. There are two ways of translating — the one original, the other second hand. The first must be adopted by a missionary whose lot falls in a section of the globe where there is no translation of the Scriptures in any cognate language, or in any language known to the learned men of the country. In that case, he must spend some years in reading a great many books, and in acquiring a competent stock of the language; that, like as the spider spins her web from her own bowels, he may be able to extract the translation from his own brain. The other mode may be advantageously adopted by a missionary who has in his hand the Bible, already translated into some language known by learned natives of the country. In that case, he has only to get a smattering of their vernacular, enough to superintend their operations, and then parcel out the work, and it is done by steam. There have been but few original translations. That by Ziegenbalg and his associates, in Tamil, has served for all the dialects in the south of India. That by Carey and his associates, in Sanscrit and Bengalee, has been the basis of all the other translations which they have conducted. Morrison's Chinese translation will probably be transferred into all the cognate languages; and the Taling, Karen, and Lah-wah, together with the Siamese, and other Shan translations, will be obtained more or less directly from the Burman. I mention the above as specimens merely; not intending to imply that they are the only *original* translations that have been made. Nor would I be understood to speak disparagingly of second-hand translations. If the partners employed are faithful, a second-hand translation may be superior to an original one. At any rate, it will probably be more idiomatic, and in all cases, when practicable, it ought undoubtedly to be attempted as a first essay; and as the missionary advances in the language, he can gradually raise it to any degree of perfection.

But I sadly fear that, if I prolong this letter, it will leave my to-day's task of twenty verses in the rear. So I beg leave to subscribe myself

Yours faithfully,

A. JUDSON.

To the Baptist Churches in the United States of America.

MAULMAIN, November 21, 1832.

DEAR BRETHREN AND SISTERS: I send this line by brother Wade, who, having had ten attacks of his disease within a year, the last of which reduced him to such a state that his life was despaired of, is obliged, at the urgent advice of his physician, to take a long voyage, as the only means of prolonging his life.

Brother Boardman has left us altogether, having obtained an honorable discharge from this warfare. Brother Jones has gone hence to Siam. In suffering him to go, we cherished the hope that in us would be fulfilled that saying, "There is that scattereth and yet increaseth." Brothers Kincaid and Mason, though indefatigable in their application to the language, are yet unable to afford much efficient aid. Brothers Bennett and Cutter are necessarily confined to the printing house. Permit us, therefore, in these straitened circumstances, with all Burmah on our hands, once more to approach your numerous and flourishing churches, sitting every man under his vine and under his fig tree, laden with the richest fruit, and to beseech you to take into compassionate consideration the perishing millions of Burmah, ignorant of the eternal God, the Lord Jesus Christ, and the blessed way of salvation;

and, in consideration of the ruin impending on their immortal souls, and in remembrance of the grace of the Saviour, who shed his blood for you and for them, to send out a few of your sons and daughters to accompany brother and sister Wade, on their return to this land.

I would add, as a very powerful inducement to embrace the present opportunity, that it will not only insure the company and instructions of brother and sister Wade, but the instructions of two native converts, in consequence of which those who now volunteer their services will be able, especially if the study of the language be immediately commenced, to proclaim the glad tidings almost as soon as they land on these shores.

We have now five native churches, and above three hundred communicants; and a spirit of religious inquiry is spreading in all directions. Who will come over into Macedonia and help us?

Your brother and fellow-laborer in the kingdom and patience of Jesus Christ,

A. JUDSON.

The following note was sent to Mrs. Bennett, while weeping in her room, after Mr. Bennett had gone on board ship, with her children, Elsina and Mary,* who were about to sail for America.

> "Sovereign love appoints the measure
> And the number of our pains,
> And is pleased when we take pleasure
> In the trials he ordains."

Infinite love, my dear sister, in the person of the Lord Jesus, is even now looking down upon you, and will smile if you offer him your bleeding, breaking heart. All created excellence and all ardor of affection proceed from him. He

---

* The younger of these daughters sailed for Burmah in company with her mother and missionary husband, in January of the present year [1853.]

loves you far more than you love your children; and he loves them also, when presented in the arms of faith, far more than you can conceive. Give them up therefore to his tender care. He will, I trust, restore them to you under greater advantages, and united to himself; and you, who now sow in tears, shall reap in joy. And on the bright plains of heaven they shall dwell in your arms forever, and you shall hear their celestial songs, sweetened and heightened by your present sacrifices and tears.

Yours,
A. JUDSON.

To the Corresponding Secretary.

MAULMAIN, December 19, 1832.

REV. AND DEAR SIR: As proposed in my last, I have spent several months in prosecuting the translation of the Old Testament; and I made such progress that I hoped to finish it by the end of 1833. But brother Wade having lost his health, and been obliged to leave us for a time, I find myself under the necessity of changing my plan. The New Testament is out of press to-day, and to-morrow I leave this for the Karen wilderness, where I expect to spend the next four months. It is not my intention, however, to travel about as formerly, but to remain at Chummerah, on the Salwen, and in the intervals of receiving company, to go on with the translation, though not so rapidly or to so good advantage as hitherto. During my absence, the Digest of Scripture made by brother Boardman, and remade by me, the Epitome of the Old Testament, a separate edition of Luke and John, the Three Sciences, (revised,) and sundry tracts, Burman, Taling, and Karen, as they are required, will be carried through the press; and on my return next May, we hope to commence printing the Old Testament.

Since my last date, there have been nine natives baptized, three of them Karens, and eleven Europeans. We have also just heard of two more baptized at Rangoon.

A. JUDSON.

PROVIDING ASSISTANTS FOR TAVOY.

To the Rev. Francis Mason of Tavoy.

MAULMAIN, December 30, 1832.

DEAR BROTHER MASON: We received your letters of the 15th this morning, and late this evening have just heard that the Fortune will leave early to-morrow morning. And I hasten to advise you to send two of your best Karen converts by return of the Fortune. On their arrival here they will be despatched to Chummerah, fifty miles up the river, whither I expect to go in a very few days. In two months they will have finished the spelling book, and by that time I think I shall be able to send back with them one, at least, who will be qualified to teach his countrymen. At present, though there are several who have just learned the spelling book, there are only two men, Chet-thing and Pan-lah, who are capable of writing the language according to rule, and therefore competent to instruct. Chet-thing, the best, has gone with brother Wade. If Pan-lah should leave us, we should be unable to move a step, for I myself know nothing of the matter. Tau-nah, one of our three Karen assistants, was unfortunately prevented joining the school till after brother Wade was taken with his last illness, subsequent to which he was unable to superintend their proceedings. There are two other men only who have learned their spelling book.

It is quite impossible for me to comply with your request to send you down two of our best men. For we have but *one* who is qualified to instruct; and he is now up the country. Even him I should be unwilling to trust alone. He would probably fall into some sad mistakes. But by assembling all our little strength, and *holding together* for the next two or three months, I hope that we shall make a little advance, so as to be able to send you help, as specified above. Do not fail to send us two of your best men as soon as possible, and I will do the best I can for them. As to coming yourself, I should think it not advisable. You would spend your time here to very great disadvantage, and I do not see, judging from your statements, how you could possibly be spared from the work in your parts. I suppose you have heard that the Maulmain padre has gone down to convert the Karens between Tavoy and Mergui, and is now, I hear, at Pah-lan. Is it so?

Please to tell Mrs. Boardman that I could not to-day do any thing about her bills, even if I had heard before of the Fortune; but I shall endeavor to comply with her wishes as soon as possible. I know not how I shall succeed. We have all been without money for some time. I have lent my last fifty to Bennett to keep the pot boiling, which is, you know, a cause *sine qua non*.

Journal.

December 31, 1832. Still detained in Maulmain by a variety of circumstances, and do not expect to leave for the Karen wilderness till the middle of next month.

During the past year there were baptized at Rangoon, three; at Maulmain, seventy; at Tavoy, sixty-seven; at Mergui, three — in all, one hundred and forty-three, of whom one hundred and twenty-six are natives of this country, the majority of them Karens, and seventeen are foreigners. The whole number of natives baptized in this mission is three hundred and eighty-six, of whom seven have been finally excluded, and about as many remain suspended from communion. The whole number of foreigners baptized is one hundred and thirty, of whom about ten remain excluded, not counting a few who were rather hastily excluded, and subsequently restored. Total, since the commencement of the mission, five hundred and sixteen.

January 1, 1833. Brother Simons and friends have just arrived, and brought us a multitude of letters and most interesting publications from our own beloved native land. On many topics I could write all day and night, from a full heart, but must employ myself in more pressing work. I will only say, May God bless the Temperance Societies! May he bless the Tract Societies! May he bless the efforts made to save the valley of the Mississippi, and the efforts made to restore the poor Africans to the land of their forefathers, and to settle the tribes of American Indians together, and unite them in the bond of Christian love! But where shall I stop? May God bless every soul that loves the Lord Jesus Christ and may we all labor, to our latest breath, in making known that love to all who know it not, that ere long the whole earth may be filled with the knowledge of the Lord, as the waters cover the sea.

January 10. Mrs. Bennett set out for the Karens on the Dah-gyne, about eighty miles from Maulmain, accompanied by Tau-nah, one of the Karen interpreters. Expects to be absent about a fortnight. May the power of the Holy Spirit go with her!

January 12. Brother Kincaid, in Rangoon, writes, "We have just got a letter from Moung Nyen, who was sent to Pegu, and there imprisoned, fined, and whipped, in a savage manner. He is becoming more bold, and is almost ready to be baptized. He writes that in the midst of his sufferings Christ was his refuge, and he is now prepared to suffer all that may come. We have many inquirers from a distance, but the fear of government makes them timid." Query: Would not a little of that same discipline that poor Moung Dan and Moung Nyen have received be attended with some salutary effects?

MAULMAIN, January 1, 1833.

1. Rise at light, (in general.)
2. Pray at morning, noon, and night.
3. Read nothing in English that has not a devotional tendency.
4. Never speak an idle word.
5. Check the first risings of anger.
6. Deny self at every turn, so far as consistent with life, health, and usefulness.
7. Embrace every opportunity of doing any favor to a child of God.
8. Learn to distinguish and obey the internal impulse of the Holy Spirit.

Renewed May 5; also the 10th; also July 2.

To the Corresponding Secretary.

Maulmain, January 12, 1833.

Rev. and dear Sir: It is with regret and consternation that we have just learned that a new missionary has come out for a limited term of years. I much fear that this will occasion a breach in our mission. How can we, who are devoted for life, cordially take to our hearts and councils one who is a mere hireling? On this subject all my brethren and sisters are united in sentiment. We should perhaps address a joint letter to the board; but such a measure might not appear sufficiently respectful. May I earnestly and humbly entreat the board to reconsider this matter, and not follow implicitly in the wake of other societies, (I beg pardon,) whether right or wrong.

I have seen the beginning, middle, and end of several limited term missionaries. They are all good for nothing. Though brilliant in an English pulpit, they are incompetent to any real missionary work. They come out for a few years, with the view of acquiring a stock of credit on which they may vegetate the rest of their days, in the congenial climate of their native land. Do not a man and woman who cohabit for a time quarrel and part the first opportunity? And is it not one end of the marriage tie for life to promote harmony and love? Just so in the case before us. As to lessening the trials of the candidate for missions, and making the way smooth before him, it is just what ought not to be done. *Missionaries need more trials on their first setting out, instead of less.*

The motto of every missionary, whether preacher, printer, or schoolmaster, ought to be, "*Devoted for life.*" A few days ago, brother Kincaid was asked by a Burmese officer of government how long he intended to stay. "*Until all Burmah worships the eternal God*," was the prompt reply. If the limited term system, which begins to be fashionable in some quarters, gain the ascendency, it will be the death blow of missions, and retard the conversion of the world a hundred years.

Excuse my freedom of speech, and believe me to be,
With all faithfulness and respect,
Your "devoted for life,"
A. JUDSON.

To the Rev. F. Mason.

CHUMMERAH, January 31, 1833.

DEAR BROTHER MASON: Your boys have just arrived, and, the boat leaving on return to-morrow, I write a line to be forwarded to you. The box of books about which you inquire arrived a few days before I left Maulmain. I believe that the people who brought it threw it down on the upper wharf, or at the post office, and thereabouts it remained I know not how long. At length somebody, seeing our names on it, picked it up, and delivered it to one of our servants.

As to allowances to the Karens, we hit upon the same rate that you did, and adhered to it for a long time; that is, about six [rupees] per month. But we at length concluded to raise it to eight, in case of a full assistant missionary, if he has a wife and family to support, and engages, like ourselves, to devote himself entirely to missionary work, refraining from all trade, and all worldly means of supporting himself. We intend, in general, that this shall cover travelling expenses, building houses, &c.

But I can assure you, from long experience, that you can seldom, if ever, satisfy Burmans, Talings, or Karens, by giving them stated, specified, known wages. However much it be, they will soon be murmuring for "more 'bacco," like their betters. Few of the natives that I pay know how much they get. No word on the subject ever passes between me and them. I contrive, at unequal intervals, to pop a paper of rupees — five, ten, or fifteen — into their hands, in the most arbitrary way, and without saying a word. But I take accurate note of every payment, and at the end of the year, or of the period for which they are employed, I manage to have paid them such a sum as amounts to so much per month, the rate agreed upon with my brethren. This plan occasions less trouble than one is apt to think at first; at any rate, not so much trouble as to be in hot water all the time about their "*wages.*" However, I only show you my anvil. Hammer your tools on it, or on another of your own invention, as you like.

There were seventy baptized at the Maulmain station during the past year; forty-seven Karens, seven Burmans or Talings, and sixteen Europeans.

I am now occupying a zayat at this place, but confining myself chiefly to the translation of the Old Testament, without being able to pay much attention to the poor Karens. A few live around me who attend daily evening worship, which is conducted in Burmese and Karen; and a considerable number of the converts live within a few miles, who attend Lord's day worship; but there does not seem to be much religious inquiry among them at present. Three are suspended from communion, and I hear bad accounts of three or four more. The learning to read also drags very heavily. The fact is, I am a mere nothing, as a Karen missionary, for not one in fifty of these people understand Burmese; the Wades have gone, and there is nobody to do any thing.

Yours ever,

A. JUDSON.

To Mrs. Bennett.

CHUMMERAH, March 7, 1833.

DEAR SISTER BENNETT: I thank you for the last supply; think we have a sufficiency on hand for the ensuing month. Expect to be in Maulmain between the 7th and 14th of April. Please to purchase two pa-tsoes for the Tavoy students,* who have now no change. Let them be the best of the common kind; that is, about a rupee and a half apiece. Please to

---

* These two students, Kaula-pau and Sau Quala, were, in 1851, the only ordained Karen preachers at Tavoy.

send them up by the first safe opportunity; and if no opportunity occurs, keep them till I arrive with the said students. We have sixteen boarding scholars, and eight applicants for baptism; half of them will probably be received next Sunday. But appearances, on the whole, are not very encouraging. Multitudes appear to have taken a decided stand against Christianity. Our boat, with four assistants, has been absent up the river eleven days. We are daily expecting their return, and hope they will bring some good news. Next Sunday is sacrament season. Pray for the poor little church around me. They are literally a flock of sheep in the wilderness. The first man baptized in these parts died lately of a violent fever. He was removed here a few days before he died. His end was rather peaceful and happy. Speaking of fever, mine has left me for above a fortnight.

As to Mrs. Wade's letters and the news from Bengal, so many things crowd for utterance, that I am afraid to make a beginning, and must defer them to the happy meeting that I anticipate a month hence. However, it will not be a very happy one; for you and brother Bennett will be about going off. What a miserable world is this! No sooner does the heart's pulse begin to take a little hold, than snap it goes! How many times more shall I have to sing that melancholy ditty, —

> "Had we never loved so kindly,
> Had we never loved so blindly,
> Never met, or never parted,
> We had ne'er been broken-hearted"!

Even those poor culprits, Elsina and Mary, do so frequently squeeze out the tear, that it is painful to think of them. I don't wonder that you say your heart is ready to break. I almost wonder how you can breathe. And I don't think that Mrs. Wade's sweet, but cruel letters have helped the matter at all. But be patient, poor soul! Heaven will be sweeter for all this, though you may be unwilling to believe it. And we have every reason to pray and to hope that the dear absent ones will be with you to all eternity.

I am glad to learn that the church difficulty is a little relieved. If it had not been, I thought of advising Moung Dway to give up conducting worship, and let it come on the deacons, who shou'd be obliged, from their office, to do it, without calling to their aid some one whom no church or teacher has yet called to preach. This would soon bring them to terms. It was the deacons who formerly urged Moung Dway to relieve them, because they were incompetent themselves.

Yours,   A. JUDSON.

To the Corresponding Secretary.

MAULMAIN, April 12, 1833.

REV. AND DEAR SIR: I left this on the 18th of January, and returned on the 9th instant. The intervening time I have spent at Chummerah, three days' journey up the Salwen, where we had previously built a zayat and rooms for the occasional residence of any of the mission who might visit that place, which is our principal station among the Karens, north of Maulmain. This visit to the Karens has not, like my former visits, been devoted to laboring among the people; but, according to a determination made some time ago, to suffer nothing to interrupt the translation of the Old Testament until it was done, I took my books with me, and sat down to my studies the same as if I had been in this place. I have, therefore, done but little for the poor people, beside conducting daily evening worship, and the usual Lord's day worship, through interpreters. Eight only have been baptized, and, at the same time, eight stand suspended, out of ninety-one. A spirit of solid inquiry is extending through the whole wilderness, but no signs of a great change are yet visible. The boarding school for teaching them to read and write their own language, according to the elements given them by brother Wade, has averaged about twelve, chiefly adults and young people, not small children. Several have learned to read, and left school to make way for others. The two most important students have been a couple of young men from Tavoy, whom brother Mason sent up to learn to read, and become qualified to teach their countrymen in that province. They have come down with me, and will return to Tavoy by the first opportunity. The school is now left under the superintendence of Miss Cummings, who has selected the Chummerah station, with the intention of devoting herself to the Karen people. Our two excellent assistants, Tau-nah and Pan-lah, also are stationed there, to conduct worship, receive inquiring visitors, instruct the school, and prepare elementary works in the Karen language. Ko Myat-kyau also, and one or two others, are prosecuting their itinerant labors in these parts. Brother Kincaid having left Rangoon for Ava, brother and sister Bennett are about proceeding to Rangoon, for a time, to supply the vacancy. Ko Thah-byoo also, the first Karen who embraced the Christian religion, and his wife, a poor Karen woman, whom we formerly supported on charity, having both accompanied brother Boardman to Tavoy, and been instrumental, in the hand of God, though the man is uncommonly stupid and unamiable, of opening the way among the Karens in that quarter, have now returned to this place, and having learned to read and write their own language, are preparing to go to Rangoon, with a view to the numerous population of Karens in Burmah proper, whence they both originally came.

To the Bennetts in Rangoon.

. . . I never had a *tighter fit* of low spirits than for about a week after you had gone. I sometimes went, after dinner, to take a solitary walk in the veranda, and sing, with my *harmonious* voice, "Heartless and hopeless, life and love all gone." However, I am rallying again, as the doctors say. But I have not yet got the steam up in the Old Testament machine. "Toil and trouble," &c. Heaven must be sweet after all these things. I have no more to say.

Yours ever,

A. JUDSON.

To Mrs. Bennett.

MAULMAIN, May 14, 1833.

MY DEAR SISTER: I thank you for your good long letter, which I am going to repay with a poor short one, as you see from the paper I have taken. But it is near ten o'clock, and I am worn out with the day's work. I really think I felt as much relieved to hear your head was better, as if it had been my own. I fear, however, that your relief was only temporary. I had a somewhat remarkable instance of divine guidance last Friday, in a private case of conscience, which had troubled me for some time. It was as if I had seen with my bodily eyes my own adorable Saviour pointing out the particular passage, and shedding a flood of light on the sacred page. And yet, alas! must I add, that though I retain that guidance, and trust I shall through life, I am in other respects the same prayerless, heartless creature as ever. There was one time, however, since you left here, in which I prayed a few moments for Elsina and Mary; and I thought it was the only time that I had ever been enabled to *pray* for them, and I had a momentary feeling that they would receive some saving impression before they reached home. . . . May you both be blessed in body and soul, and be burning and shining lights in Rangoon and throughout Burmah; and you will be if you venture to follow Christ throughout, and be holy, as he is holy.

Your ever affectionate brother,

A. JUDSON.

To the Corresponding Secretary.

MAULMAIN, June 29, 1833.

REV. AND DEAR SIR: I have not made one minute in my journal since the last number, dated April 12, and forwarded. During the last six months, three have been added to the Karen church north of Maulmain, the main stock of which is at Chummerah, with one principal branch at Newville. Of the ninety-one baptized Karens, two are dead, and eight suspended from communion, leaving eighty-one communicants.

There have been no additions to the Burman church in Maulmain; but one member, Mee Tan-gan, a young woman formerly belonging to the female boarding school, has been finally excluded, for pertinacious neglect of worship and clandestine marriage, according to native custom. Some cases of restoration have taken place, so that there remains at present not one member under censure in the Maulmain church. The whole number of native communicants is sixty-three.

I have received your letters of December and January, and heartily approve of all your suggestions, and hope that we shall be more particular and definite in reporting events that transpire in our respective departments.

I am toiling on in the Old Testament. Am now in the sixteenth chapter of Ezekiel. The minor prophets, and the historical books from 1 Kings to Esther inclusive, still remain. Should I escape the fall fever, of which, however, I have no reasonable hope, and encounter no other interruption, I should certainly finish by the end of the year.

Yours faithfully,
A. JUDSON.

MAULMAIN, September 24, 1833.

REV. AND DEAR SIR: I enclose a number of notes from Ava. The Cutters embark this day for Rangoon, with a press and several thousand tracts, for distribution on the way; besides which we are putting up ten thousand tracts for brother Bennett, to meet an extraordinary festival in Rangoon, just at hand.

Since the last of June, fifteen natives have been baptized here, six of them girls from the Chummerah school, and two from the Maulmain school. In the latter school there are about fifty in daily attendance. On the departure of Mrs. Cutter, the whole devolves on Mrs. Hancock, aided a little by Mrs. Brown.

I have lost a month through a complication of ailments, but am now better. Have no remaining hope of finishing the translation of the Old Testament by the end of the year, but shall do as well as I can.

Yours faithfully,

A. JUDSON.

A Fragment — probably a Scrap torn from the Close of a Letter.

Leaving one party to prove that the standard of Christian morality is lowered since the days of the apostles, and another party to assert and expect the restoration of miraculous powers, let us adopt a middle course, the golden medium, — HOLY AS THE APOSTLES, WITHOUT THEIR POWER, — and then " the glory of this latter house shall be greater than that of the former."

Yours affectionately,

A. JUDSON.

To the Corresponding Secretary.

MAULMAIN, October 11, 1833.

REV. AND DEAR SIR: The Karen people are scattered all over Burmah and the neighboring Shan provinces. The main body stretches away to the north. The Karens in the Tavoy district are a small, struggling colony, separated by a wide waste from the Karen nation, with whom they have no communication. They have consequently lost, in some measure, their national language, and come to speak a corrupt dialect, a mixture of Karen and Tavoyan, which again is a corrupt dialect of the Burmese. Many of these facts I learned from the two Tavoy students that I had under my care a few months at Chummerah.

It was so ordered that our first Karen convert, Ko Thahbyoo, accompanied brother Boardman to Tavoy, and was diligent in bringing his countrymen to hear the gospel; and hence it has been supposed that there is some peculiar connection between Tavoy and the Karens. But all of us here well know that there is no other of our stations so remote from the Karen nation; none where a missionary must inevitably labor among that people to so great disadvantage. In the Tavoy district, it is impossible for him to acquire the language properly; and he is completely insulated from the great body of the Karen nation; and lastly, he is cut off from almost all intercourse with the handful of Karens in the district, during six months of the year, in consequence of the intervening country being flooded, and there being no river communication.

I do not mean to intimate that the Tavoy station is not a very important one. A glorious work is begun there. A church is founded which will never become extinct, but will grow, and fill the whole region. The Tavoy station must be supported at all events. And if it should be left vacant, and none other of the brethren be willing to go there, I am ready to volunteer my services. But I have now some hope that brother ———— will remove to that station. I am corresponding with him on the subject.

Yours faithfully,
A. JUDSON.

To Mrs. Bennett.

MAULMAIN, November 29, 1833.

DEAR SISTER: Here are Pallah, Tau-nah, Pah-boo-to, and Pah-boo.* If Mr. Bennett wants any more, let him say so. I hope you will take good care of these disciples. They are all good creatures. Pah-boo-to has improved very much of late. Pah-boo is a fine steady fellow, and an excellent scholar. Mah Tee and Mah Heen are inquiring about a passage in the same vessel, but it is doubtful whether they go. . . . Great care ought to be taken in receiving the first Karen converts, in any place. The best outward test is to have refrained from rum, nat worship, &c., and to have kept the Lord's day, and all this for a few months, *on the testimony of their Christian neighbors*. And perhaps it is best to make them ask for baptism several times. The first time asking they may not know their own minds. In all these matters

---

* Karen assistants.

Boardman has proceeded more wisely and judiciously than I He has laid a safer foundation. The consequence is, there are fewer suspensions in that quarter, and his successors will have much less trouble than mine.

Yours ever,
A. JUDSON.

To the Bennetts.

MAULMAIN, December 9, 1833.

DEAR BROTHER AND SISTER BENNETT: Here are Ko Man-boke, and Moung Ouk-moo. Do you want any more? The latter has settled his old transgression very properly. . . . A principal man from the village at the mouth of the Houng-ta-ran, where there are several inquirers, is here, and asking for baptism. He appears pretty well, and will be baptized, I suppose, next Sunday. I have taken old Rajah, the evangelist of the said village, into the number of the Karen assistants. He is full of the matter, and intends to march forthwith upon the north pole, and clear away all the intervening darkness. Toon-no will probably compose his tail. We have nobody to send back with aunt Sarah, except Ko Myat-kyau, who also wants to act the comet. The Karen assistants ought to come back as soon as they can be spared. Can't you find some good one, like Tau-nah and Pan-lah, well acquainted with the Burmese language, who would come here and qualify himself to be used as other assistants? . . .

Yours ever,
A. JUDSON.

MAULMAIN, December 28, 1833.

DEAR BROTHER AND SISTER BENNETT: . . . I am anxiously waiting to hear the next news from Rangoon, and whether the storm has gone over. Moung En and Moung Zoothy have gone with Miss Cummings to Chummerah. I expect them back to-night. I don't think the former will return to Rangoon at present. He will be wanted here, especially if I step out any where; for there is no other person that the church and I could agree to have conduct public worship evenings and Lord's days. Better let his pay in Rangoon stop with the month of November. I shall pay him twelve rupees a month, beginning with the 1st instant. I am seven hundred and eighty verses in debt; but it is one comfort that the debt cannot increase after the 31st instant. I am pretty free from fever when I pour down the quinine. Several letters from home, but none worth sending you, except the two accompanying. . . . I almost wish you were here, in the little triangular corner, which forms a little compound by itself, being fenced off from the school house, and containing nothing but a cook house at the extreme angle. At any rate, I wish Mrs. Bennett was here to take care of the women, who now run wild, except that Mrs. H. does as well as she can. The government has promised us fifty rupees a month if we will get up an English and Burmese school. We thought to have employed Delaney as an assistant; but he is bent on going home. To-day Mr. M. mentioned you, and says that, though he is going away, Mr. B. will do any thing in this line. Mrs. Boardman has got a letter of thanks from "his lordship;" and the government here is authorized to expend five hundred rupees per month on schools in these provinces. See some notice of schools in the November and December numbers of the Calcutta Observer. I have been in an error on this subject. The mismanagement and little success of schools have led me too hastily to condemn the system altogether. What if you should *both* think of things generally, and particularly, and abstractly, and conjointly, and all other ways? and believe me,

In haste, yours ever,

A. JUDSON.

To his Mother and Sister.

MAULMAIN, December 29, 1833.

MY DEAR MOTHER AND SISTER: I wrote you last by Mr. Wade, and have just received yours in reply, dated 9th of July, mentioning Mrs. Wade's visit to Plymouth, which was very kind in her. There is hardly a person in the world whom I love so much as Mrs. Wade. You could not know her many excellences in so short an interview. She writes me a very interesting account of her visit, and relates many things of you, my dear mother and sister, that are very gratifying to my heart.

I have also received your other letter, of October 12, last year, and the articles marked by your own hand, which I value beyond any clothes obtained from another quarter. Mrs. Wade's letter brought many things fresh to my mind, and made me long once more to visit Plymouth, and the old mansion house, and the only near and dear relatives that remain to me in this world. But the sea is too wide, and my work too great and pressing, to be relinquished or deferred for any worldly consideration.

I still live alone, and board with some one of the families that compose the mission. After the Wades left, I boarded with the Bennetts. After the Bennetts left for Rangoon, I boarded with the Cutters. After the Cutters left for Ava, I boarded with the Hancocks, where I now am. I have no family or living creature about me that I can call my own, except one dog, Fidelia, which belonged to little Maria, and which I value more on that account. Since the death of her little mistress, she has ever been with me; but she is now growing old, and will die before long; and I am sure I shall shed more than one tear when poor Fidee goes.

So Elnathan has gone, and all his family! I hope they are in paradise; but as to little Anne, I know not what evidence she gave of having her heart touched with the love of the Saviour. God does all things well — infinitely well.

About the time of your receiving this, the Wades and a number of new missionaries will be coming out. I hope you will send me a long letter. I have no time to write much, being overwhelmed with work of some sort or other. I hope you will daily pray for me.

Yours ever,

A. JUDSON.

To the Corresponding Secretary.

MAULMAIN, December 31, 1833.

REV. AND DEAR SIR: The only noticeable change that has occurred during the last six months among the members of the mission at this station is the removal of brother and sister Cutter to Rangoon and Ava. We are daily expecting to hear of their arrival in the capital. Brother Kincaid will inform you that the series of Christian baptisms at that place, which will continue, we hope, to the end of the world, commenced last month in the persons of two converts — one the wife of Ko Hlai, an old Rangoon disciple, the other a respectable inhabitant of Ava. Glory be to God!

During the said period ten have been admitted to the native church in this place, of whom five are young men of some promise, two are women whose husbands are unconverted, one is a widow, by birth a Karen, and two are girls from the school. The church now consists of seventy-three communicants. None have been excluded, and none suspended from communion; but there are two cases which would probably be pronounced censurable, did not circumstances, at present, preclude proper investigation.

Eight have also been added to the Karen church at Chummerah, making ninety-nine who have been baptized from among the Karens north of Maulmain. Of the said eight, two are men, and six are young women or girls from the Chummerah boarding school.

I did hope, at one time, to have been able to insert, under this date, a notice of the completion of the Old Testament; but, though I have long devoted nearly all my time to that work, I have found it so heavy, and my health (as usual this season) so poor, that, though near the goal, I cannot yet say I have attained.

Yours faithfully,

A. JUDSON.

P. S. January 31, 1834. Thanks be to God, I can *now* say I have attained. I have knelt down before him, with the last leaf in my hand, and imploring his forgiveness for all the sins which have polluted my labors in this department, and his aid in future efforts to remove the errors and imperfections which necessarily cleave to the work, I have commended it to his mercy and grace; I have dedicated it to his glory. May he make his own inspired word, now complete in the Burman tongue, the grand instrument of filling all Burmah with songs of praise to our great God and Saviour Jesus Christ. Amen.

P. S. 2d. The following tables may afford some satisfaction:—

Table of Persons baptized in Burmah previous to the Year 1833.

Stations.	Burmans.	Karens.	Foreigners.	Total.
Maulmain,	68	83	129	280
Tavoy,	7	174	1	182
Mergui,	3			3
Rangoon,	50		1	51
Total,	128	257	131	516

Table of Persons baptized in Burmah in the Year 1833.

Stations.	Burmans.	Karens.	Foreigners.	Total.
Maulmain,	10	16	18	44
Tavoy,	2	14	3	19
Rangoon,	5	5	1	11
Ava,	2			2
Total for 1833,	19	35	22	76
Add Table 1st,	128	257	131	516
Total,	147	292	153	592

N. B. Of the Burman converts, eight have been excluded — two in Rangoon, two at Tavoy, four at Maulmain, besides three or four in Rangoon on whom the sentence has not been formally pronounced. Of the Karens, two have been excluded in this district, and a few others remain suspended. Of the foreigners, most of whom are removed to other countries, and are destitute of proper pastoral supervision, many, it is said, have fallen into sin, but not many cases of actual apostasy have been ascertained.

N. B. I respectfully request that, in publishing my communications, discouraging statements may not be suppressed. Let the truth, the whole truth, be known, and let us put our trust in God.

To the Bennetts.

MAULMAIN, January 16, 1834.

DEAR BROTHER AND SISTER BENNETT : . . . I return your letters, with one of mine that happened to be out of the way when I sent you my last. I know not when I have enjoyed letters more than those from the children's grandparents. I have read them over several times. But I am sadly afraid that, handed about among their fond, flattering relatives, they will suffer for want of constant, faithful supervision.

I have no particular thought of going to Rangoon at present. I have no idea what I ought to do, after finishing the translation. I believe there is a great deal to be done in these parts. I think a good deal of Mergui, if an opportunity should occur at the right time. I know not what the Karens about Rangoon will do. I should suppose it would be exceedingly imprudent for a foreign missionary to visit their villages just now. It would be known at once to the Rangoon government, and be the very thing to induce such examinations and persecutions as would put a stop to all their religious inquiries. If the Karen assistants need money, let them have what is proper, keeping a minute of the same, that I may arrange it hereafter. If Thah-byoo is refractory, and threatens to perpetrate any enormities, such as baptizing and the like, his allowance must be cut off. This will make him exceedingly reasonable. If the Karens will not come to Rangoon to be baptized, they may stay at home. Ko Thah-a must never be allowed to go to their villages and baptize by the dozen, nor must he baptize in Rangoon, only on the conditions specified in my letter to him. There have been so many apostasies in the south of India, that the Bishop of Calcutta has positively forbidden even the *missionaries* under his jurisdiction from baptizing any natives without previously sending in their names, and notifying the Bishop or Archdeacon of Madras. If Thah-a is refractory, there is a way of taming him. Indeed, I am doubtful whether he ought to baptize any Karens at all. He is pastor of the Burman church in Rangoon. If he baptizes any Karens, it must be by special dispensation from some missionary on the ground. . . . .

Yours most affectionately,
A. JUDSON.

MAULMAIN, February 9, 1834.

DEAR BROTHER AND SISTER BENNETT: To yours of the second I reply that, in my opinion, it is best for you to remove to this place, because, —

First. Brother Webb is competent to do the needful in Rangoon, viz., to keep some assistant at work, to distribute tracts, and to be a medium of communication between this and Ava. He can also baptize, if Ko Thah-a is afraid to, and he will be ready to proceed to Ava when the way is open.

Secondly. You may succeed in schools. . . .

Thirdly. If you come, I shall be able to go among the Karens, and hither and thither, until the rainy season, and leave you to take care of the native church, now numbering seventy-three communicants, and to superintend the printing of the Old Testament, beginning with the first of Samuel, the commencement of the second volume, which I am now revising for that purpose. However, this work will not probably last long, for I shall not be able to travel during the rains. Still it is possible I may want to go to Mergui or Rangoon, and if you are here I can do so.

Fourthly. There is work enough for brother Bennett up stream, and down stream, and athwart stream, among all the villages on the river and in the interior.

Fifthly. There is work enough for Mrs. Bennett up street, and down street, among her old friends, who have all gone to sleep since she and Mrs. Wade left the place. Alas! I am going wrong, for I see a slight cloud of dissatisfaction gathering on a certain fair forehead; so we had better strike out this article, and make a new fifthly, to wit: Mrs. B. will be able to take her old place among the female disciples, which cannot, of course, be filled by any person here, though possessed of the best intentions. . . .

Better bring all the Karens who want to come; for after my tour, any of them can be sent back to Rangoon for the rains.

Yours ever,

A. JUDSON

To the Corresponding Secretary.

MAULMAIN, February 10, 1834.

REV. AND DEAR SIR: There is a strange, unaccountable reluctance among my missionary brethren to leave this place. Not a soul will look towards Tavoy, though poor Mrs. Mason has been here, and spent a week with us, imploring our aid. Not a soul will look towards Arracan, though my last from Mr. Fink, dated 30th November, implores our aid, and mentions three stations — Kyouk Phyoo, Ramree, and Sandoway, all occupied by British magistrates and troops, and all proving to be healthy places. Not a soul will look towards any part of the empire of Burmah.

The European church has been continually receiving accessions under successive missionaries. It may be well for a new brother to take his turn of a few months at the English chapel, while acquiring the rudiments of the language; but it pains me to see a brother, who has been here above a year, wholly absorbed in the concern, and evidently determined never to leave it, when there are so many openings for missionary labor among the heathen, on every side. Perhaps, however, the board may be pleased to employ him permanently in that department. If so, I have not a word to say. The general reply which I get from the brethren is, "We must stay and get the language." But look at dear Boardman. In eleven months after landing at Amherst, he was in Tavoy. And what a light he kindled up during his short life! Secondly, this language can be got just as well at other places as at this; much better indeed at such places as Rangoon and Ava. The few books we have are ever passing to and fro among the stations. And as for the assistance which an elder brother can afford, it is not worth much. The language is best acquired from native books and native teachers. The chief service that predecessors can afford is in the way of dictionaries and elementary works.

As to the seminary for instructing young men of promise, as suggested by the board, *this is a department which requires more acquaintance with the language than any other.* With the New Testament in hand, and tracts and prayers all prepared, a young missionary can begin to preach and exhort very soon. He can live by retailing stock furnished by others. But to instruct a seminary, like Poor at Ceylon, or Carey and his coadjutors at Serampore, *a man must be able to create his own stock*, especially when nothing scarcely has been done in that department. How much better for a young missionary to dash into Toung-oo, or some other place, get the language from the living sounds, build up a church, kindle up a bright light that will never go out! And when, after a few years' service, he shall be needed to take charge of a seminary, he will be qualified at all points. How much better than to be rusting here in Maulmain!

Now, since it is expected generally that brother Wade, having devoted himself to the Karen language, will, on his return, be chiefly employed among that people, and that, consequently, I shall be under the necessity, at least for a few years, of being more or less at or about this place, chiefly with a view to writing and printing work, any attempt to urge my brethren to a distance comes with a very bad grace from me. It is like saying to them, I wish to get rid of your company. But indeed there is not a single one that I want to get rid of; not one that it would not cost me a bitter pang to have to consign to the grave. May God safely bring back my dearest, best beloved brother and sister Wade.

I remain, with every sentiment of love and respect,

Your affectionate friend and faithful servant,

A. JUDSON.

P. S. Perhaps you may have the curiosity to know what disposition I would make of the present unoccupied forces. I would advise brother ——— to proceed forthwith to Rangoon; keep company with brother Webb, assist one another a short time, and then one proceed to Prome, make a beginning there, and be ready — that is, one of them — to join the party at Ava as soon as the door is open. I would prefer sending brother ——— to Rangoon rather than Tavoy, that he may retain the pure Burmese, and be better qualified, in due time, for the professor's chair. One of the new ones I would despatch from Amherst to Tavoy, without hardly allowing him to come up to visit Maulmain. Another I would mark for Mergui; but he might spend a year at this place or Tavoy, before taking a new station. Two more I would instantly send to Kyouk Phyoo, that they might get the Arracanese dialect, which differs considerably from the Burmese, from the very first. And as there is but one more, I should not know whether to advise him to take some new station or strengthen some old one. At any rate, he might stay at some old station one year. In this plan I have not mentioned the Karens, partly for want of men, and partly because I expect that brother Wade and brother Mason will be the great Karen missionaries. . . .

Journal.

NEWVILLE, March 12, 1834.

I have spent a few days in this place, where, on my arrival, I found the church consisting of fifteen members only, several having removed to the vicinity of the Chummerah church, which, though of later origin, is now five or six times larger than the Newville. Day before yesterday, and to-day, nine new members have been received at this place, and there are five or six others with whom I feel satisfied, but, for various reasons, their baptism has been deferred. In the number received, the most noticeable case is that of Lau-sau and wife. He is a petty chief, and possesses more personal influence than any Karen yet baptized in these parts. He has been considering the Christian religion with approbation for three years, but has had great difficulties to encounter, resulting from his family connections, and from his inveterate habits of temperate drinking. Until the present time, he could never resolve on adopting the principle of entire abstinence; but I trust that conviction of truth, and love of the Saviour, have enabled him to gain the victory.

March 16. On leaving Newville, it was my intention to go up the Patah River; but not finding sufficient water this season, I turned into the Houng-ta-ran, and, having visited a village where there are several inquirers, returned to Maulmain.

April 1. Have been closely engaged in revising a few books of the Old Testament for the press, the regular printing of the whole being now commenced. I say commenced, for the edition of the Psalms, which is out of press, we do not consider as forming a part of the present edition of the Old Testament, for it will probably be expended before long, and have to be reprinted in course with the rest of the work.

To-day, despatched Pan-lah and three younger Karen assistants to the aid of Ko Thah-byoo, in the vicinity of Rangoon, intending to proceed thither myself before long.

Tavoy, April 10. I arrived here on the evening of the 6th. Am delighted with this station, and every thing about it. The few native Christians whom I have seen, and the schools, appear excellently well. But the glory of this station, the two hundred Karen converts, and their village of Ma-tah-myu, I found myself not at leisure to visit. Indeed, I have hardly found time to step out of the mission enclosure since my arrival; and to-day, having received the benediction of the Rev. Mr. Mason, I embark for Maulmain, accompanied by Mrs. Judson,* and the only surviving child of the beloved founder of the Tavoy station. Once more, farewell to thee, Boardman, and thy long-cherished grave. May thy memory

---

* Dr. Judson was married at Tavoy, April 10, 1834, to Mrs. Sarah H., widow of the late Rev. George D. Boardman.

be ever fresh and fragrant, as the memory of the other beloved, whose beautiful, death-marred form reposes at the foot of the hopia tree. May we, the survivors, so live as to deserve and receive the smiles of those sainted ones who have gone before us. And at last may we all four be reunited before the throne of glory, and form a peculiarly happy family, our mutual loves all purified and consummated in the bright world of love.

CHAPTER III.

TREVELYANISM. — VIEWS RESPECTING THE METHOD OF CONDUCTING MISSIONS. — REVISION OF THE OLD AND NEW TESTAMENTS. — GROWTH AND RESULTS OF THE MISSION. — FIRST TWENTY-FIVE YEARS OF MISSIONARY LABOR.

1835-1839.

WHILE Dr. Judson was engaged in revising his translation of the Scriptures, a proposition was submitted to the missionaries of different denominations in India for abandoning the native alphabets of the country, and uniting in the formation of a new one upon the basis of the Roman. The author of this plan was Mr. Trevelyan, a most intelligent and active friend of missions, at that time holding an important office in the civil service. For a time it was received with considerable favor, especially by missionaries of more limited experience, who hoped that, in this manner, the difficulties of printing would be materially diminished. They seem, however, to have forgotten that improved facility in printing can be of but small consequence, unless what we print is intelligible to our readers, and that to the hundreds of millions of India our volumes would be sealed, until we had taught them to acquire an alphabet which, for several generations, they would naturally consider inferior to their own. The subject has, I believe, now passed out of notice. It is only alluded to here for the purpose of directing attention to the letter referring to it in the early part of the present chapter. It seems to me to present an admirable specimen of clearness of judgment and strong common sense, arriving at once at the truth in a practical matter, when many able and benevolent men had been decidedly misled.

To the Corresponding Secretary.

MAULMAIN, June 30, 1834.

REV. AND DEAR SIR: During the last six months nine persons have been added to the baptized Karens north of Maulmain, as noticed in my last, and seven to the Burmese church in this place. In the latter number is Mah Yay, wife of the Moung Shway-moung who accompanied brother Wade in his late visit to America.

I hoped that, after finishing the translation of the Old Testament, I should have a little leisure; but the endless labor of revising it for the press, — about one quarter is now printed, — the care of the Burmese church in this place, which now consists of eighty members, and the various avocations incident to missionary work, keep me so closely engaged that I have no time even to make such communications to the board as I am in duty bound to do.

Yours faithfully,

A. JUDSON.

MAULMAIN, October 3, 1834.

REV. AND DEAR SIR: As you will probably hear more or less about Trevelyanism, I wish to contribute my quota towards bringing the subject fairly before you, and therefore enclose you the documents which I have received from Mr. Trevelyan. Mr. T. is an assistant secretary to government in Bengal, a pious man, and much devoted to the improvement of the natives. He has projected a plan to print school books, the Scriptures, &c., in the Roman character, adapted to the various languages of the East, in hope that the eastern nations will gradually adopt that character, and have but one alphabet, like most of the nations of Europe. Mr. Duff, of the Scotch mission in Calcutta, is his most powerful supporter, and Mr. Pearce has undertaken to prepare types and print for the concern. The Calcutta School Book Society has, I understand, furnished some funds, and Mr. Duff has just now gone to Europe to raise more. Two of our brethren have entered into the plan with more ardor than, I think, its merits demand, and have proposed to procure at once a set of types and commence printing the Scriptures on Trevelyan's plan, at the expense of the board, they engaging, at the same time, to turn all the schools under our influence into the new channel, put down the native character as fast as possible, and teach the children to read their own language in the Roman letter. Some of us, however, hesitated at embarking the mission funds in this undertaking without the sanction of the board.

As to myself, I object to the plan as in all probability quite impracticable. And though it should prove to be practicable in some degree, by means of united, untiring efforts, made from one generation to another, which its warmest advocates admit to be indispensable, — though at the commencement of the twentieth century it should appear that the end was gained, — what *great* benefit, after all, would result? *Some* benefit, I admit, would be realized, particularly in the article of printing. But is that sufficient to prompt and sustain such a mighty effort? What *great* benefit results to the people of England and Spain, for instance, that their respective languages are written in the same character? Something we should gain, it is true, by compressing the Scriptures into a smaller compass, and rendering them less voluminous. But when we see that Dr. Carey has brought his Bengalee Bible into the compass of a single octavo, why should we despair of doing the same thing to the Burmese Bible? Brother Hancock is of opinion that, by improving and diminishing the types, it may be done. If, indeed, we could carry forward the Trevelyan plan to such a state of perfection as to be able to dispense with printing in the native character within a few years, it might be well to make the effort. But how many years, yea generations, must pass away before we could hope for such a dispensation? And all the intervening time we must be printing in both characters! Suppose that the plan should succeed in Maulmain; must we not continue to furnish Bibles for Burmah proper? And suppose that the children of Maulmain should learn to read their language in the new character; would that relieve them from the necessity of learning the native character also? Could we dismiss a scholar from our schools without being familiar with that character in which alone he could communicate with his countrymen throughout Burmah?

But what I most regret is, that a man like brother ———, so good and talented, with all Burmah perishing before him, and several grand central stations unoccupied, should think of devoting the ardor and energy of his mind to an object of comparatively small importance, and of very dubious attainment.

I would not be understood to be a decided opposer of Trevelyanism. The thing is yet in embryo; its merits and demerits not yet developed; and I should hesitate to pledge prematurely either personal labors or pecuniary supplies in support of an untried enterprise, which I cannot but view as highly chimerical. But if the great directors of missionary concerns in both hemispheres should, on full consideration, see reasons sufficient to induce them to join their efforts in support of the undertaking, I trust that the same reasons would have a similar effect on my mind.

Yours faithfully, A. JUDSON.

P. S. I would add that I write this letter merely as a private individual, and not requesting any official reply.

MAULMAIN, December 31, 1834.

REV. AND DEAR SIR: Since last June, four members have been added to the Maulmain Burmese church, which now consists of eighty-four communicants, two to the Newville Karen church, and one to the Chummerah Karen church. There are two cases of suspension from communion in the Burmese church, and several in the Chummerah, some of which will, I fear, terminate in final exclusion as soon as a missionary can investigate them on the spot. There are a few applicants for baptism at all the stations.

In April, 1833, Ko Thah-byoo, the missionary pioneer among the Karens at Tavoy and this place, was sent to Mau-bee, a Karen district north of Rangoon, and in the course of the year reported about thirty hopeful inquirers, five of whom received baptism at the hands of Ko Thah-a, pastor of the church in Rangoon. At the close of the year, we sent Tau-nah, Pan-lah, and two younger assistants to the aid of Ko Thah-byoo. They returned, after a stay of about three months, and gave a still more encouraging account of the state of religious inquiry in that quarter. Soon afterwards, we despatched Pan-lah and three younger assistants. Tau-nah was obliged to remain with Miss Cummings, in charge of the Chummerah station. Pan-lah and his company spread themselves over the district of Mau-bee, and each one acted as schoolmaster and preacher in his own circle, for the space of seven or eight months. On their return, they reported several hundred hopeful inquirers, out of whom two hundred and ten had made the three several applications for baptism, being examined and approved by Pan-lah and company, in council with the previously baptized; but were obliged to wait for want of an administrator of the ordinance, Ko Thah-a, in Rangoon, having become so timid, in consequence of being imprisoned, fined, and otherwise abused, as not to venture to appear so publicly as once, in the character of a propagator of the new religion. On receiving this report, we at first thought of ordaining Pan-lah pastor of the churches in Mau-bee; but considering again that brother Webb was in Rangoon, and a missionary to the Rangoon Karens daily expected, we concluded to defer that measure, and advise those who desired baptism to come down to Rangoon, a few at a time, and solicit baptism at the hands of brother Webb. Some of them have taken this advice, and the whole number of baptized Karens, north of Rangoon, including the first five, is thirty-three. Brother and sister Howard have just sailed for that place; and to his communications and brother Webb's I must refer the board for further information from that most interesting department of missionary labor.

As for myself, I have been almost entirely confined to the very tedious work of revising the Old Testament. The revision of about one half is completed, and the books from 1st Samuel to Job, inclusive, have been printed in an edition of two thousand. We should have put the first volume to press some time ago, had we not been obliged to wait for paper, the London paper not matching the American; and now, though paper has arrived, brother Hancock contemplates going to America for new founts of types, in several languages, and brother Cutter has gone on another visit to Ava, so that we shall not probably recommence printing the Old Testament till his return. I am the more satisfied with this arrangement from having just received a complete set of Rosenmüller on the Old Testament, and some other valuable works, in studying which I am very desirous of going over the whole ground once more.

The Chummerah station has been left vacant by the lamented death of dear sister Cummings, of which I have already given some account in a letter to her former pastor, the Rev. Mr. Butler. Brother and sister Vinton intend to depart for that station in a few days. The Mergui station has also been left vacant by the death of Pastor Ing, one of our most faithful, most beloved assistants. None have been baptized there since brother Wade left. Though Ko Ing was faithful and laborious until death, it did not please the Lord to give him any present success. Mergui, however, has been well sown with gospel seed, and I have no doubt the seed will spring up and contribute to the abundance of some future harvest, and the mutual joy of all the laborers, when the sower and the reaper shall rejoice together.

None of the dear brethren and sisters, whose arrival gladdened our hearts the first part of this month, contemplate remaining here, except brother and sister Osgood, who are attached to the printing department. Besides those already mentioned, brother Wade is just leaving for Tavoy, and brother Comstock will take the earliest opportunity for commencing a mission on the Arracan coast, southern division. Having been required by the board to select another missionary for the Arracan coast, we have advised brother Simons to take the northern division for his share. We have done this the more readily, because Mr. Fink, the country-born missionary from Serampore, stationed at Akyab, has been obliged to accept a situation under government for his support, and cannot, therefore, devote so much time as formerly to missionary labors.

On subjects connected with the printing department, and the mission schools, and the European church, you will doubtless receive communications from other pens.

During the last year of his life, Ko Ing was supported from the donations of Mr. Colgate of New York. But at the close of October, 1833, he wrote, that, on account of his unworthiness and want of success, he declined receiving any further allowance; that his wife — of whose conversion he had been the means — was able, by keeping a small shop, to support the family; but that he intended, however, to devote himself the same as before to the work to which he had been called. Accordingly, the same letter reports his labors and states his plans for future operations. Such communications he continued to make till his death. In order, however, to square our accounts, we requested him to receive the usual allowance for the remaining two months of that year. He did so, and in acknowledging the receipt of the money, said that he regarded it as a special gift from Heaven. We then determined that, though he declined any stated allowance, we would occasionally make him presents; and brother Mason has sent him money two or three times, amounting, I believe, to about one third of his usual allowance. The following is an extract from the letter of a pious sergeant in the detachment, stationed at Mergui, dated December 7, 1834.

"I was with Ko Ing several times during his illness, and commonly took an interpreter with me; but on account of his extreme weakness and deafness, I could say but little to him. Being anxious, however, to know his experience, I asked him a few questions, as follows: *Q.* Do you wish to die or not?

Ans. I wish to die, if it is the will of God. *Q.* Why do you wish to die? *Ans.* I shall go to heaven and be happy. *Q.* How do you know that you shall go to heaven? *Ans.* I have read in the word of God, that those who serve him will go there, and my own breast tells me of it, (placing his hand on his breast and looking up.) *Q.* How have you served God? *Ans.* By forsaking my wicked ways, and praying to him for forgiveness. *Q.* Do you think all this will take you to heaven? *Ans.* Jesus Christ came down from above, and died for sinners; and those that are sorry for and forsake their sins shall be saved, because Christ died for them. *Q.* You don't think, then, that your works and your own goodness will take you to heaven. *Ans.* No. All my works are but filthy rags. He was so much exhausted that I asked him no more questions. I think I told you, in a former letter, that he had his coffin made some days before his death; that our lads carried him to the grave; and I read the funeral service over him."

Table of Persons baptized in Burmah previous to the Year 1834.

STATIONS.	Burmans.	Karens.	Foreigners.	Total.
Maulmain,	78	99	147	324
Tavoy,	9	188	4	201
Mergui,	3			3
Rangoon,	55	5	2	62
Ava,	2			2
Total,	147	292	153	592

Table of Persons baptized in Burmah during the Year 1834.

STATIONS.	Burmans.	Karens.	Foreigners.	Total.
Maulmain,	11	12	7	30
Tavoy,	2	4	1	7
Rangoon,		28		28
Ava,	8		1	9
Total,	21	44	9	74
Add Table 1st,	147	292	153	592
Total,	168	336	162	666

Eight of the Burmese converts have been excluded, and two of the Karens; and several of both classes remain suspended.

Yours faithfully,

A. JUDSON.

P. S. It may be gratifying to the friends of the mission to have a correct idea of the population of the province of Maulmain; that is, the country under British rule, north of Yay and Tavoy. A new census has just been completed, and the second member of government has communicated to me the result, as follows: Town of Maulmain, 15,000; surrounding country, 30,000, of which 7,000 are Karens. He added, that, on account of the difficulty of taking a census of the Karen population, the real number might be fairly estimated at 10,000, but that the other results of the census might be depended on as correct.

Card.

A. Judson desires to present, through the American Baptist Magazine, his thanks to the many kind friends of himself and the mission, who have sent him, by the hands of brother and sister Wade, and their associates, various donations of wearing apparel, books, stationery, &c. Some of the articles are of great value, and all of them are very acceptable, being such as he requires for daily use. The faces of the donors he knows not; but many of their names he has marked, and the notes and letters accompanying the presents have repeatedly called forth the tear of gratitude and love. The acquaintance thus commenced, though not personal, he expects will be perfected in that world where there is no sea to separate friends, no barrier to impede the interchange of mutual love. And he rejoices in the belief that every distant expression and recognition of fraternal affection here below will form an additional tie, binding heart to heart, in the world above; that every cup of cold water given to a disciple will become a perennial stream, flowing on from age to age, and swelling the heavenly tide of life and gladness.

He would take this opportunity of saying to the friends of the mission, that no presents would be more acceptable than medicines — those of the most common kind. He would respectfully suggest to pious physicians and apothecaries, that any package or box of medicines, however small, would ever be highly prized. And as he expects to be stationed for the present in Maulmain, he would be most happy to be their almoner, and enjoy the privilege of dispensing their bounty to his brethren and sisters at the several stations, who sometimes suffer in their own persons, and more frequently see the natives, particularly the poor Karens, suffering around them for want of the simplest, cheapest medicines.

MAULMAIN, January 3, 1835.

To the Corresponding Secretary.

MAULMAIN, January 3, 1835.

. . . My ideas of a seminary are very different from those of many persons. I am really unwilling to place young men, that have just begun to love the Saviour, under teachers who will strive to carry them through a long course of study, until they are able to unravel metaphysics, and calculate eclipses, and their souls become as dry as the one and as dark as the other. I have known several promising young men completely ruined by this process. Nor is it called for in the present state of the church in Burmah. I want to see our young disciples thoroughly acquainted with the Bible from beginning to end, and with geography and history, so far as necessary to understand the Scriptures, and to furnish them with enlarged, enlightened minds. I would also have them carried through a course of systematic theology, on the plan, perhaps, of Dwight's. And I would have them well instructed in the art of communicating their ideas intelligibly and acceptably by *word* and by *writing*. So great is my desire to see such a system in operation, that I am strongly tempted, as nobody else is able to do any thing just now, to make a beginning; and perhaps after brother Wade, who is excellently well capacitated for this department, has settled the Karen language with brother Mason, he will carry on what I shall begin, having both Karen and Burmese students under his care. . . .

Yours faithfully,
A. JUDSON.

To his Sister.

MAULMAIN, January 6, 1835.

MY DEAR SISTER: I wrote you a line lately, enclosing the quitclaim deed, signed and attested. I hope it will reach you safely. Your letters of October 15 and June 20 came together by the hand of brother Wade. My last to you was dated December 29, 1834, about a year ago, since when I have received none, till brother Wade arrived the other day. The articles which you and mother sent by the same opportunity, I accept as refreshing tokens of that love which no lapse of years nor intervention of wide seas can destroy or weaken. It is a love not merely founded on natural relationship, but sanctified, and elevated, and destined to perpetuity by our common union to the glorious Saviour.

Mother is now in her seventy-sixth year. I hope and pray that, as she gradually draws nearer and nearer to the grave, her faith will become stronger and stronger, and her views of heaven more and more animating. It is a privilege which neither of your brothers has enjoyed, to support the declining state of our parents. May this privilege be especially blessed to your soul.

You will have heard of my marriage to Mrs. Boardman of Tavoy. She says she remembers seeing you in Salem, when she was Miss Hall. Perhaps you will remember her. She saw our father a little before he died; and he took her by the hand, and talked to her some time. I am very happy with her. She is possessed of a very affectionate, amiable, pious spirit; is well acquainted with the Burmese language, and is a great help to me in all respects. We keep house by ourselves, and shall probably remain in Maulmain for the present, perhaps all the rest of our lives. I have a church of eighty-four converted natives under my care, and am also revising and superintending the printing of the Old Testament. Brother and sister Wade and Miss Gardiner have gone to Tavoy. The other new ones and some of the old ones are gone or going in different directions. I am now in my forty-seventh year; and as we cannot expect to live so long in this climate as at home, I begin to feel that my work is mostly done, and to look upwards to that blessed world where I trust we shall all meet before the throne. You may have heard of the death of Dr. Carey and of Dr. Morrison. There are now only three missionaries in the East who have been out longer than myself — Marshman, Robinson, and Moore. One after another fills up, as a hireling, his day, and then passes away in the darkness of the night of death, thence to emerge and ascend to the bright regions of everlasting day. I am always glad to get a letter from you, and hope you will write often; and if mother would add a line or two, it would be a great gratification to me. At any rate, we can pray for one another. Let us continue to do so as long as we live. Your most affectionate brother,

A. JUDSON.

In the following pages the views of Dr. Judson respecting the proper method of conducting missions are more fully developed. After some hesitation, I have resolved to insert every thing in his writings with reference to this subject that could be of use to missionaries and the directors of missions. Dr. Judson was, by universal consent, one of the ablest missionaries of his time, of remarkable singleness of purpose and large opportunities of observation. It has seemed to me that all the matured opinions cf such a man on the subject to which his whole life was so exclusively devoted should be spread before the public. The cause of missions is, at present, arresting the attention of Christians in a remarkable manner. Every denomination is coming forward to bear its part in the work of evangelizing the world. It is of inconceivable importance that all possible light be thrown upon the counsels of those who direct these efforts. It behooves all our societies maturely and earnestly to inquire for the manner in which the labors of their brethren abroad will be most successful. The same remark may be made in respect to missionaries themselves. They have devoted their lives to this noble and most Christian undertaking. They will naturally desire to see every plan thoroughly canvassed, and to learn wisdom from the experience of those who have enjoyed the largest opportunities for accurate observation.

It will be seen that Dr. Judson, after mature reflection, was decidedly opposed to large missionary stations. He believed them to be adverse to that spirit of self-denying effort without which missions must soon become a nullity. He believed that they served to divert the attention of missionaries from their proper work — the preaching of the gospel — to indirect, subsidiary, and questionable modes of effort, such as in-door labor, school teaching, English preaching, book making — things in themselves good, but not distinctively missionary. Instead of *concentrating*, he was for *scattering* missionaries, and sending them in every direction to establish new stations. Nor was he alone in this opinion. The most cautious and efficient conductors of missions with whom I am acquainted are coming to the same conclusion. After trying a variety of plans themselves, and observing carefully the plans of others, they have been convinced that the New Testament itself is the great directory for missionary labor, and that he is likely to be the most successful propagator of Christianity who follows most carefully the examples recorded for our instruction in this matter in the Acts of the Apostles.

It will be seen that it was the preaching of the gospel which Dr. Judson considered the great business of his life. He became a translator because he seemed called to this work by the providence of God and the directions of the board. But his chosen field was the jungle or the zayat. While engaged in translation, he labored among the natives as far as he was able; and, as soon as his in-door work intermitted, he turned to preaching with the whole energy of his character. This continued until the failure of his voice deprived him of the power of public speaking. It was not until this affliction rendered him useless as a preacher that he could be brought to listen to the proposal to undertake the Burman dictionary. It was a work for which he had no love, and which he considered as aside from his missionary calling. Indeed, when he could no longer preach, he believed his appropriate labor completed, and looked forward with increasing earnestness for the day of his release.

To the Corresponding Secretary.

MAULMAIN, April 7, 1835.

I enclose two letters from Kyouk Phyoo, and beg to call your attention again to the important coast of Arracan. The district of Ramree itself contains, according to brother Comstock's letter, a population nearly or quite as great as all these southern provinces. Mr. Fink, from the inadequacy of the Serampore funds, has been obliged to accept a sub-collectorship under government. *The whole country is thrown into the hands of the American Baptist Board of Foreign Missions.* If they take immediate possession, it is theirs; but if the present "tide of fortune" is suffered to pass unimproved, it will probably never be recovered. If I were not tied to the press and the native church here, and had not, I must confess, the habit of keeping an eye always towards Ava, I would be off for Arracan by the first ship. I do not mean to say that the country is so important as Burmah proper; but in Burmah the prospect at present is very dark.

Mergui also is a valuable little station, the population of the town itself being nearly six thousand, and including the surrounding villages, above eight thousand by census. O that one of the brethren would take possession of Mergui, and do there what Boardman did at Tavoy! But whatever disposition of men the board shall be pleased to make, or whatever other orders to issue, I beg that nothing of importance be left discretionary with us, at least so far as I am concerned. We shall all obey orders from home; but if left to ourselves, I fear, from past experience, that we shall sometimes manage to help one another to do that which is most pleasing in our own eyes.

Since beginning this letter, I have received yours of October last. I have very little hope of the practicability of an overland route to China, but have not yet received an answer from brother Kincaid.

As to the subject of schools, and the preparation of young men for the ministry, my views are the same with those you have expressed. But I doubt the practicability of a "seminary" all of a sudden. In looking at the subject in its various bearings for a considerable time, I see but one way; and I would respectfully propose that instructions be issued to every missionary, at every station, to collect around him a few boys and young men who may appear promising, and give them such instruction as may be consistent with his other duties; with a view of obtaining, in the course of a year or two, a contribution from each station of at least two or three students, who shall be sent to Maulmain, or Tavoy, or some other station, and thus gradually form a seminary, which shall continue to be sustained by supplies from the several stations, in the same way it was commenced.

Yours faithfully,

A. JUDSON.

MAULMAIN, May 6, 1835.

REV. AND DEAR SIR: At the general meeting of the brethren in December last, I was appointed a committee to correspond with brother Kincaid on the subject of an overland route to China. I have lately received an answer, the contents of which it is not necessary for me to communicate, as he says in the same, that he has already made a full communication to the board, in answer to an application made direct to him. I have only to say, therefore, that, as the route appears to be practicable, it remains for the board to send out a man for that express purpose. . . .

Formerly, having spent many years alone, I felt desirous of missionary society, and was disposed to encourage a few to stay together, not doubting but that we should all find enough to do. But I have now learned that one missionary standing by himself, feeling his individual responsibility, and *forced to put forth all his efforts*, is worth half a dozen cooped up in one place, while there are unoccupied stations in all directions, and whole districts, of thousands, and hundreds of thousands, perishing in the darkness of heathenism. You will perhaps wonder that I am frequently writing in this strain. But when I think of seven families, — eight when the ——— s are here, which will probably be every rainy season — my spirit groans within me. I feel that I cannot spend my time to better purpose than in endeavoring to effect some change in our present arrangements. I have seen this subject more clearly, from month to month, ever since my marriage. Mrs. Judson says, that at Tavoy she was obliged to be ever on the alert, and sometimes had to run away to Ya-lah, to get leisure to write a few letters. But here there are so many in the way of one another, that she can hardly find enough to do. I can truly say that all the real missionary work done by all the sisters at this station, from day to day, might and would be done by any two of them, if left to themselves; and this not because they are disposed to indolence or self-indulgence, but simply because there are so many together. Place any one of them in a station by herself, with her husband, and she would become a new creature. In a letter just received from brother Jones, he says, "I want to see a chain of missions proceeding from Rangoon, by Bassein, Cape Negrais, Kyouk Phyoo, Chittagong, Kathay, Asam, through the Shan and Laos country into China." O that all the brethren felt as he does, or had the missionary ardor which characterizes ——— and ———! It is not for me to dictate. But I would respectfully suggest that one of the printers be ordered to join the mission at Bangkok; that one of the missionaries, beside brother ———, be ordered to Arracan or Bassein.

Bassein is the only port besides Rangoon in the Burman empire. It has a European collector of duties, appointed by the king, who annually visits Ava. With Ava Bassein communicates by one branch of the Irrawadi, as Rangoon does by another. The only advantage that Rangoon has over Bassein is, that it has, of late years, become the principal resort of foreign shipping. There is no other reason whatever why a missionary should not settle at Bassein, and make such a beginning there as has been made in Rangoon. However, Arracan has perhaps stronger claims to *immediate* attention. The whole country is ripe and ready for us. And the Khyeen nation is contiguous, bearing the same relation to Arracan that the Karens bear to Burmah. After a long conversation with Mrs. Judson, this morning, we are ready to say that, if it be thought best for us to remain in Maulmain, we feel competent, while life and health are spared, to take charge of this station, with those that remain after the above deductions are made; and indeed we could afford to make some further deductions. I have now five native assistants, who spend an hour with me, every morning, in reporting the labors of the preceding day, in receiving instructions, and in praying together. These men penetrate every lane and corner of this place and the neighboring villages; and since I have adopted this plan, — about four months, — there are some very encouraging appearances. As soon as I get through with the Old

Testament complete, I want to double their number, and devote part of my time to instructing them systematically. Now, ten such persons, half students, half assistants, cost no more than one missionary family; and for actual service they are certainly worth a great deal more. This is the way in which I think missions ought to be conducted. One missionary, or two, at most, ought to be stationed in every important central place, to collect a church and an interest around him; to set the native wheels to work, and to keep them at work. Very few native assistants will hold out well unless well instructed, and kept under rigid supervision. An additional missionary would doubtless do good; but nearly all the good he would do would probably be done if he were away, laboring in some other place, which, but for him, would be unoccupied, and where, of course, all that he should effect would be so much net gain to the cause.

But if, on the other hand, it be thought best for ———, and ———, and the rest to remain here, pray let me remove. If no one else is willing to go to Arracan, I am. It is true, there are some plans which I should like to carry into execution at this place, where I have my work before me, and some things that I should be glad to prepare for the press; but other brethren will, in time, be competent to do these things. I am, therefore, ready to obey orders. And may God give the board wisdom to direct aright.

Yours faithfully,
A. Judson.

Maulmain, June 11, 1835.

The letters of Pearce, Trevelyan, and Jenkins, copies of which have been forwarded to you from Bengal, have opened to us a new missionary field, blessed with a very healthful climate, and the protection of English government.

Brother Brown embraced the proposal with instant enthusiasm, not merely because of the above advantages, for Asam presents a splendid opening for missionary efforts, and brother Brown is excellently well qualified to take the lead in that great and important mission. My heart leaps for joy, and swells with gratitude and praise to God, when I think of brother Jones at Bangkok, in the southern extremity of the continent, and brother Brown at Sadiya, in Asam, on the frontiers of China, immensely distant points, and of all the intervening stations, Ava, Rangoon, Kyouk Phyoo, Maulmain, and Tavoy, and the churches and schools which are springing up in every station, and throughout the Karen wilderness. Happy lot to live in these days! O, happy lot to be allowed to bear a part in the glorious work of bringing an apostate world to the feet of Jesus! Glory, glory be to God!

MAULMAIN, June 30, 1835.

REV. AND DEAR SIR: Since the beginning of the year, we have received six into the Maulmain native church. One has been removed by death, and one has been finally excluded; so that the present number is ninety-two. The state of the Chummerah and Newville churches, which I have hitherto included in my report, I leave to be reported by brother Vinton. I have lately adopted the plan of employing several native assistants to itinerate in the town and the neighboring villages, for the purpose of making known the gospel and distributing tracts. They meet every morning in my study to pray, and to report the labors and successes of the preceding day. This gives me an excellent opportunity for correcting their mistakes, and furnishing them with new topics of argument and exhortation. I have never adopted a plan which pleased me so much, and appeared to be fraught with so many benefits both to the assistants and the people at large. I judge, from the daily reports I receive, that a spirit of inquiry and a disposition to listen are gradually gaining ground in this uncommonly stupid, obstinate place. As to myself, I am never at leisure to go out, being closely employed in revising the translation of the Old Testament, and reading proof sheets of Scripture and tracts. The first volume of the Old Testament was completed, in an edition of two thousand, on the 4th instant, the second volume having been previously done. The third and last, from Psalms to Malachi, will, we hope, be completed, in an edition of three thousand, before the end of the year. Besides the Old Testament, the presses have been employed in printing our standard tracts, in editions of thirty and forty thousand. I hope, as soon as the whole Bible is out of press to be at leisure to add a few new tracts and elementary works to our present scanty stock, and also to attend to the more systematic instruction of the assistants, particularly the younger ones.

The translation of the New Testament into the Taling language has proceeded to the end of the 2d Corinthians. The principal tracts also are translated. Mrs. Judson is endeavoring to prepare herself to assist in that department. And as soon as the new Taling types are ready, we intend to commence printing tracts and portions of the New Testament, for the use of the numerous population in this place, and all the country east of Rangoon, very few of whom can read any other language.

Yours faithfully,

A. JUDSON.

Resolutions renewed September 26, 1835, the Era of finishing the Revision of the Old Testament. — Resolved, —

1. Strictly to observe the three seasons of prayer.
2. To read no useless thing.
3. To consult the internal monitor on every occasion.
4. To live under a constant sense of the presence of God.

From Mrs. Sarah B. Judson to Dr. Judson's Mother.

MAULMAIN, October 30, 1835.

MY DEAR MOTHER: There are four mission families in Maulmain, besides the one devoted to the Karens, in the vicinity. Mr. Hancock has charge of the printing establishment, and prints in Burman, Taling, and Karen, for all the different stations. Mr. Bennett has charge of the government school. Mr Osgood, lately arrived, is studying the language, and meanwhile is occupied a part of the time in preaching to the Europeans. Thus you perceive that the native work devolves upon your son and myself. Mr. Judson preaches *every* Lord's day to a crowded assembly, and *every evening* to a congregation averaging thirty. We find our old chapel too small, and are about having a new one erected. The native assistants go about the town every day preaching the gospel, and Mr. Judson holds a meeting with them every morning before breakfast, when he listens to their reports, prays with them, gives them instruction, &c. Besides this, the care of the Burman church, ninety-nine in number, devolves upon him, as does all the revision, superintendence of the press, &c., &c., &c. He has lately baptized eighteen persons—seven English soldiers, five Indo-Britons, three Burmans, one Hindoo, one Arracanese, and one Mahometan. The latter is faithful old *Koo-chil*, the Hindoo cook mentioned in Mrs. Judson's "Narrative." The poor old man resisted long and stubbornly the truth, and we were sometimes almost discouraged about him. But divine grace was too mighty for him, and on last Lord's day we saw him bow beneath the Salwen's yielding wave, and rise, I trust, to "newness of life." Two others have applied for baptism, and there are many hopeful inquirers both among Europeans and natives.

To his mother and Sister.

MAULMAIN, November 1, 1835.

DEAR MOTHER AND SISTER: Since I have attained, in some measure, the great objects for which I came out to the East, and do not find it necessary to be so exclusively and severely engrossed in missionary labors as I have been for a long course of years, my thoughts and affections revert more frequently, of late, to the dear home where I was born and brought up; and now especially, after having been childless many years, the birth of a daughter, and the revival of parental feelings, remind me afresh of the love with which my dear mother watched over my infancy, and of all the kindness with which she led me up from youth to man. And then I think of my earliest playmate, my dear sister, and delight to retrace the thousand incidents which marked our youthful intercourse, and which still stand, in the vista of memory, tokens of reciprocated brotherly and sisterly affection. Surely, I should have to call myself a most ungrateful son and brother, had I abandoned you forever in this world, as I have done, for any other cause than that of the kingdom of the glorious Redeemer.

It is a great comfort, however, that, though separated in this world, we are all interested in the covenant love of that Redeemer, and can therefore hope that we shall spend our eternity together, in his blissful presence. It is my particular object, in writing at the present time, to engage your prayers for our little Abigail, that she may become early interested in the same divine love, and be one of our happy number in the bright world above. Her mother and myself both hope that the little circumstance of her being your namesake will tend to bring her more frequently to your remembrance at the throne of grace, and secure your prayers in her behalf.

I alluded above to the attainment of the great objects of my missionary undertaking. I used to think, when first contemplating a missionary life, that, if I should live to see the Bible translated and printed in some new language, and a church of one hundred members raised up on heathen ground, I should anticipate death with the peaceful feelings of old Simeon. The Bible in Burmese will, I expect, be out of the press by the end of this year; and — not to speak of several hundred Burmans and Karens baptized at different stations — the Burmese church in Maulmain, of which I am pastor, contains ninety-nine native members, and there will doubtless be several more received before the end of the year. Unite with me, my dear mother and sister, in gratitude to God, that he has preserved me so long, and, notwithstanding my entire unworthiness, has made me instrumental of a little good.

Do write, and without *waiting* for an opportunity, send your letters to the care of Dr. Bolles.

Yours ever, affectionately,
A. JUDSON.

To the Corresponding Secretary.

MAULMAIN, December 31, 1835.

REV. AND DEAR SIR: During the last six months, we have received into the native church in this place nine by baptism, and two by removal from Rangoon, and lost one by death; so that the present number is one hundred and two. Among the number baptized is Koo-chil, the Mahometan servant who was so faithful to us at Ava during the late war. He came from Bengal with the first Mrs. Judson, on her return to this country, in the year 1823, and since that time has been in the employ of some one of the mission families. Though a faithful, good servant, he persisted for years in rejecting all religious instruction, and maintained his allegiance to the false prophet. His wife, a Burmese woman, was baptized a year and a half ago, and that circumstance probably combined with all he saw and heard to bring his mind over to the Christian religion. But the process was slow, the struggle strong; he felt deeply the responsibility of changing his religion, and when he made his formal request for baptism, he trembled all over. Poor old man! he is above sixty; his cheeks are quite fallen in; his long beard is quite gray; he has probably but a short time to live. May he prove to be a brand plucked out of the fire at the eleventh hour! He affectionately remembers his old mistress, and frequently sheds tears when speaking of the scenes of Ava and Amherst, where he saw her suffer and die. I hope now that they will have the pleasure of meeting again and of renewing the old acquaintance under happier auspices.

The printing of the whole Bible was finished on the 29th instant. I am now revising the Psalms for a second edition, the first edition, which was printed long ago, being nearly expended; and as we intend to bind up the new edition with the last volume of the Old Testament, we shall have no copies for distribution until the whole is completed. A large edition (thirty thousand) of the Epitome of the Old Testament revised has also been lately issued. Tracts, &c., as usual. Three presses constantly at work, besides one employed in taking proof sheets. The Taling types not yet finished, and no printing, therefore, done in that language. The translation of the New Testament is advanced to the end of Hebrews.

More preaching has been done in Maulmain and the vicinity, during the past year, than all the previous years together which we have spent in the place. Five or six native assistants have been kept constantly at work. They have brought in several converts, and excited more religious inquiry and disposition favorable to the reception of truth than we have ever known before. Thousands and thousands of tracts also have been distributed through the town, chiefly by some of the newly-arrived brethren, during their morning walks.

Table of Persons baptized in Burmah previous to 1835.

Stations.	Burmans.	Karens.	Foreigners.	Total.
Maulmain,	89	111	154	354
Tavoy,	11	188	5	208
Mergui,	3	....	....	3
Rangoon,	55	33	2	90
Ava,	10	....	1	11
Total,	168	336	162	666

Table of Persons baptized in Burmah during the Year 1835.

Stations.	Burmans.	Karens.	Foreigners.	Total.
Maulmain,	15	7	27	49
Tavoy,	2	61	3	66
Rangoon,	....	2	....	2
Yat-toung,	1	....	....	1
Ava,	2	....	....	2
Total,	20	70	30	120
Add Table 1st,	168	336	162	666
Total,	188	406	192	786

Yours faithfully,

A. Judson.

To Mr. Amariah Joy, Waterville, Maine.

Maulmain, February 8, 1836.

My dear Brother: I have received two letters from you, of July, 1833, and May, 1834. I proceed at once to answer the questions proposed in your last, not knowing how much time I shall have to write. The grand means of converting the heathen world is to preach the glorious gospel of our great God and Saviour Jesus Christ, in the vernacular language of the people; avoiding, as much as possible, all literary and scientific pursuits, to which missionaries have a strong temptation; resolving, in a word, with the great apostle of the Gentiles, to know nothing but Jesus Christ and him crucified.

"The prospect of usefulness in travelling throughout Burmah, preaching and distributing tracts," is rather dubious at present, owing to the intolerance of the government; but in the ceded provinces, on the south and west, there is no obstruction to be feared.

I should certainly think it exceedingly desirable that a person contemplating a missionary life should pursue a regular course of theological study, though he had received a collegiate education; for the better his mind is disciplined and stored with knowledge, the more efficient workman he may humbly hope to become; but I do not know that I can mention any particular branch of study to which, as a general rule, it is desirable to devote special attention. It is difficult, also, to mention the average time requisite to acquire the Burmese language; but it may be safe to say that, *with the Bible and tracts*, a young missionary will be able to labor effectively within two years.

I should be unwilling to say a word to encourage private individuals to come out to *Burmah* " as schoolmasters, mechanics, or farmers." Without the language, their lives would be almost thrown away. But in regard to single females, who intend to acquire the language and instruct their own sex and the rising generation, if they are as good as those who have already come, I can only say, the more the better.

I am rejoiced to hear that there are so many at Waterville

who are considering the subject of missions. I hope, if it is the will of God, to welcome you and many others to these shores. We have Newtonians, and Hamiltonians, and Andoverians, but no Watervillians. We had one, but he is gone. Perhaps Waterville thinks that in sending him she did all her duty.

If this finds you in Waterville, please to present my affectionate respects to your excellent president, and to S. F. Smith, better known by that name than any other, who is officiating, I believe, as tutor in your college, and please to give my love to all your fellow-students who love the cause of Christ and the cause of missions.

Yours affectionately,
A. JUDSON.

To the Rev. James M. Haswell, of Amherst.

MAULMAIN, July 4, 1836.

DEAR BROTHER HASWELL: I hear that there is a boat just going off to Amherst, and as I have lost two opportunities of writing, by not being apprised in season, I drop a hasty line, just to say, How do you do? and to wish you every blessing in your soul, family, and work, that a gracious God can bestow.

You inquire about the advisableness of setting up a school at Amherst. If practicable, every thing in that line is to be encouraged, taking care, however, to avoid the rock that many missionaries have split upon — suffering school keeping to eat up all their time and energies. If you intend a Peguan school, I have a man ready for you; not the best in the world, but the best that I can find for you at present. He is a Peguan, and was employed a little while by Mrs. Judson in teaching a few Peguan women. . . .

Your affectionate brother,
A. JUDSON.

To George D. Boardman.

MAULMAIN, August 23, 1836.

VERY DEAR GEORGE: I send you a little idol, that you may not forget what sort of gods they worship in this country, and your mother is sending you another. But, what is better, I send you a little book, called the Only Son, which I took so much pleasure in reading that I want to have you read it through two or three times. I am afraid you will forget how much your mother loves you. This book will help you to remember. I am not much afraid that you will ever become like poor Jonah, whose history you will find in the book. But when any companions shall attempt to persuade you to join them in doing some bad thing, remember poor Jonah, and remember his poor mother, and remember how dreadfully your own mother would suffer, and how she would go down to the grave in sorrow, if you should become a bad boy. You cannot tell how much she loves you. She talks about you every day; and we never pray together without praying for you. And though it cannot be that I should love you as much as your mother does, yet I love you very much, my dear George. And I am always sorry that I was so closely engaged in study, that I was able to spend but very little time with you, after we came up from Tavoy. When I think of that last pleasant, sad afternoon I carried you down to Amherst, and left you on board the Cashmere, I love you very much, and want to see you again. Perhaps we shall live to see you come out a minister of the gospel of the Lord Jesus Christ. We sometimes pray that, if it be the will of God, it may be so.

Your little sister Abigail is a sweet, fat baby. You would love her very much if you were here. Pray for her, that she may live, and may become a child of God.

Your affectionate father,

A. JUDSON.

Prayer for Little George.

Remember, Lord, my mother dear,
   Who lives in distant heathen land;
By day and night wilt thou be near,
   To guard her with thy powerful hand.

And since another babe is come,
   To fill the place which once was mine,
In mother's arms to find a home,
   And soft on mother's breast recline, —

O, listen to me from thy throne,
   And let a brother's prayer prevail,
To draw the choicest blessings down
   On little sister Abigail.

To the Rev. Professor Knowles.

MAULMAIN, December 25, 1836.

DEAR BROTHER KNOWLES: Yours of April last is before me, and we have also received the first two numbers of the Christian Review, and are highly gratified by the perusal of the work. I sincerely hope that you will be well sustained in this important undertaking. Whether I or any of my brethren will find time or ability to contribute our mite, time must show. My "practised pen" is sadly unpractised in English. A missionary who would become familiarly acquainted with a foreign tongue must, in a great measure, sacrifice his own.

After finishing the revision of the Old Testament, and spending a few months in preparing and revising some smaller works, I, last May, commenced the revision of the New, in connection with the Life of Christ, two hundred pages, 8vo., and hope to finish it in about six weeks. The Life is printed in an edition of about fifteen thousand; and the whole New Testament is being printed in an edition of ten thousand, which we should double, but for want of paper.

When I get free from my present engagements, I intend, *Deo volente*, to attempt to do a little missionary work; for there has been none done in this place for several years, — that is, since the

Wades left, — except by the native assistants; and there are but few of them left, most of them having gone to other stations.

In regard to our treatment of infants, concerning which you inquire, it was formerly my custom, and that of some of my brethren, to invite the parents, and relatives, and particular friends of a new-born child to hold a prayer meeting, for the purpose of commending it to God, and imploring his blessing upon it. A name was sometimes given when particularly requested, but not generally. The meeting was sometimes held in a private house, and sometimes in a place of public worship; but we endeavored to avoid holding it before a public assembly, lest it should degenerate into a *church rite*. Finding, however, that the practice became troublesome as the converts multiplied, and not perceiving so many good results as we expected, and fearing that in future hands it might be misunderstood and perverted, we agreed, two or three years ago, to discontinue it; and the recognition of it, which had been attached, by way of appendix to the marriage service, was in the next edition omitted. I never, however, until your letter arrived, knew that any one of my brethren had made the least objection to the practice.

In regard to the mode of baptizing, some of us bow the person forward, instead of laying him down backwards. We do not recommend kneeling, unless the water is very shallow. How I came to adopt this mode, and my reasons for preferring it, I should like to state, but neither paper nor time allow. Perhaps at some future time I shall be able to gratify you.* I say *gratify*, because I am pretty sure that my statement would afford you more gratification than you expect. In the mean time, let us remember that it is the glory of the Baptists not to contend about modes and forms. Give us the thing, they say, and we are content. — See Ripley's Christian Baptism, page 120, line 11.

I beg you will write me again, though I am but a poor cor-

---

* Dr. Judson's views on this subject may be found at the close of his sermon on baptism.

respondent, and freely mention any thing which you think will be beneficial to me or any of my brethren. I frequently feel the need of faithful, impartial advice. I am sometimes placed in circumstances where I would give any thing for one hour's free conversation with the members of the board. And if I could occasionally meet with the Newton professors, how many points of biblical criticism, and some of theology, I should want to hear discussed! But "if any man lack wisdom, let him," &c.

To the Corresponding Secretary.

MAULMAIN, January 31, 1837.

REV. AND DEAR SIR : The revision of the New Testament, on which I have been closely employed about seven months, is just finished. The printing is advanced to the end of 2d Corinthians, and will be finished in about two months.

The following tables exhibit the number baptized at the several stations, at the close of last year :—

Baptized previous to 1836.

STATIONS.	Burmans.	Karens.	Foreigners.	Total.
Maulmain,	104	118	181	403
Tavoy,	13	253	8	274
Rangoon,	55	35	2	92
Ava,	12		1	13
Scattering,	4			4
Total,	188	406	192	786

Baptized in 1836.

STATIONS.	Burmans.	Karens.	Foreigners.	Total.
Maulmain,	9	29	16	54
Tavoy,	3	88		91
Rangoon,		206		206
Ava,	7			7
Total,	19	323	16	358
Add Table 1st,	188	406	192	786
Total,	207	729	208	1144

Miscellaneous Resolutions.

March 22, 1837.

1. Use no intoxicating liquor as a beverage.
2. Indulge in no foreign — that is, English or American — newspaper reading, except a regular course of some one religious paper, and sometimes an occasional article from other papers.
3. Observe the seasons of secret prayer every day, morning, noon, and night.
4. Embrace every opportunity of preaching the gospel to every soul.
5. Endeavor to keep the "resolution for promoting brotherly love."
6. Read a certain portion of Burmese every day, Sundays excepted.
7. *Go* and *preach* the gospel, every day.

Second vow, August 6, Lord's day, 1837.
Recollected and renewed, July 12, 1838.

To the Corresponding Secretary.

Maulmain, March 29, 1837.

Rev. and dear Sir: I thought that I had finished the revision of the New Testament above a month ago; but there is no end to revising, while a thing is in the press; so I continued working at it, until I went to Dong-yan, and even later; for it was not till the 22d instant that the last proof sheet went to press.

At Dong-yan, Miss Macomber's residence, I baptized three; so that the little church which she has been instrumental of raising up in that place consists of ten; and though the opposition is extremely violent, there are some hopeful inquirers.

On my return, I was taken very ill, in consequence of imprudent exposure to the sun, and was hardly able to participate in the joy diffused through our little society by the arrival of the Rosabella, or to contribute to entertain the new missionaries during their transient visit.

I am now writing in a zayat by the wayside, not far from the mission house, where I daily sit to receive company. I have some hopeful inquirers, and a few applicants for baptism. It is my earnest desire to spend the rest of my days in more direct missionary work than my studies for many past years have permitted. May the Lord grant my desire, if it accord with his blessed will, and fit me to be a faithful missionary.

Yours, &c.,

A. JUDSON.

MAULMAIN, April 18, 1837.

REV. AND DEAR SIR: We have, for some time, understood that it is a general rule of the board not to appoint any single women to missionary work, and as *a general rule*, it is probably a good one. But on conversing with my brethren of the Tavoy station and others in this place, we have thought that if any station, or individual missionary, should point out some particular sphere in which a single female could be placed to advantage, and at the same time could recommend some individual from personal acquaintance, or the testimony of others, the board would probably approve of such an application.

From what I have observed in the cases of Miss Cummings and Miss Macomber, I am persuaded that I could locate two or three such persons to very great advantage. You know what Miss Macomber is doing among the Pwo Karens. The Toung-thoos are a small people in this neighborhood, similarly situated. In the present paucity of missionaries, we could scarcely think of giving them a missionary and family. The labors of a single woman might be blessed to introduce the gospel among them. The northern suburbs of Maulmain, called Oo-bo, and the southern suburbs, called Moung Gnan's village, each about a mile and a half or two miles from the mission establishment, are both excellent situations, where, though we could not afford to place missionaries, single women might occupy houses, in connection with some of our best assistants and their families, set up schools, instruct their neighbors, furnish a place where missionaries could occasionally resort and hold meetings, and thus become valuable auxiliaries to the main station. Another situation for a single female will probably be furnished by brother Hancock's boarding school, which, in the female department, will require more labor than Mrs. Hancock, with her large family and other cares, will be able to bestow.

If *well qualified* persons could be found, I should not object to three or four. But they must not come with the expectation of finding snug quarters in some family, and all things ready to their hands. They must come expecting, yea, desiring, to occupy some solitary, perhaps remote post, destitute of all resources for daily comfort but such as they shall find in God and their work.

Yours faithfully,
A. JUDSON.

MAULMAIN, June 30, 1837.

REV. AND DEAR SIR: We have received eight members into the Burman church by baptism since the beginning of the year; three of whom, being young men of some promise, have been sent to the Tavoy seminary.

The last sheet of the revised New Testament, for an edition of ten thousand, was sent to press, on the 22d of March. We are also reprinting the Life of Christ, in an edition of forty thousand, two hundred pages, 8vo. A Father's Advice, a tract written in English by Mr. Boardman, and lately translated into Burman by Mrs. Judson, and four of our standard tracts, translated into Peguan, have also been carried through the press, in editions of ten thousand each. Bible Questions, which will make a voluminous work, prepared by Mrs. J., are gradually printed as fast as required for Bible classes and Sunday schools.

My days are commonly spent in the following manner: the morning in reading Burman; the forenoon in a public zayat, with some assistant, preaching to those who call; the afternoon in preparing or revising something for the press, correcting proof sheets, &c.; the evening in conducting worship in the native chapel, and conversing with the assistants, and other native Christians or inquirers.

Yours faithfully,
A. JUDSON.

MAULMAIN, October 6, 1837.

REV. AND DEAR SIR: We have just returned from the new-made grave of our dear sister Osgood, who closed her mortal pilgrimage last evening, after suffering above a year and a half with pulmonary consumption. She arrived here in December, 1834; so that the greater part of her missionary life has been a scene of suffering and gradual decline. But so quietly and sweetly did she accept the will of her heavenly Father, that no one of us seemed to pass time more pleasantly, or contribute more to the general happiness of our little circle. And this, in connection with her unwearied diligence and rapid proficiency in acquiring the language, makes us feel her loss most deeply. She has certainly left no one behind her, who is more universally beloved, or whose death would be more tenderly regretted. The equanimity of temper and quietness of spirit, which peculiarly distinguished her, shone out with uncommon beauty and brilliancy during the closing scene. Though her mind, for a few of the last days, was much deranged, we were sure, whenever a lucid interval occurred, to find her in the same place, trusting in Jesus, resigning all into the hands of God — no clinging to life, no impatience to depart. Her will seemed to be lost in the will of God, and she enjoyed in an unusual degree that peace which passeth all understanding. I do think that no person ever descended the banks of Jordan with a more even step; none ever felt the cold waves dashing higher and higher, with less shrinking from the chill, less apprehension of being lost in the gulf beneath. The last sentiments which I am aware she made intelligible to us, were, *that her mind was happy, and that she was ready to go.* How sure we all feel that, the moment her mortal eyes were closed in death, the eyes of her spirit were opened to behold the face of Jesus in the paradise of the blessed!

Dear sister! we feel sad to leave thee remote and lonely in yonder burial ground. But we know that thou sleepest in Jesus, and that when the night of death is passed away, and the resurrection morn appears, thou also wilt again appear, blooming in celestial beauty, and arrayed in thy Saviour's righteousness, a being fitted to love and to be beloved, throughout the ever-revolving hours of an eternal day.

A. JUDSON.

MAULMAIN, December 31, 1837.

REV. AND DEAR SIR: We have received seven by baptism since June, making fifteen through the year, but, in the mean time, have been obliged to exclude three from communion; and some of them will probably become excluded from the church. A few also have removed to Tavoy, and some have died; so that the present number of native communicants is only one hundred and fifteen.

My principal work in the study, beside correcting a part of the Old Testament, has been a Digest of Scripture, consisting of Extracts from the Old and New Testaments, partly taken from Brown's Selection, Boardman's Digest, and other similar Works. Upon this Digest I have spent nearly four months, intending, according to the best of my ability, to make it an elaborate work, containing the most important passages of Scripture, arranged under successive heads, beginning with "The Scripture of Truth," and closing with "The Retributions of Eternity." I trust this work will be as valuable as the Life of Christ, and perhaps more useful, as a book of reference.

The Life of Christ, in Peguan, Mrs. Judson has nearly carried through the press; first edition, five thousand copies. It would have been done by the end of the year, had not both the Peguan compositors been taken ill. We have had no other work in press for a long time, for want of paper.

Brother and sister Hancock have removed to Mergui. They had both become so well versed in the language, that it seemed desirable to them, and to us all, that they should commence operations in a new place, where they might have full scope for their exertions. We exceedingly regretted to part with them; but we did not come out to this country to enjoy one another's company. Brother Osgood in the printing office, brother Howard in the school department, and brother Ingalls in the English chapel, and beginning to preach in Burmese, are, at present, with myself, the only resident members of the Maulmain station. We have six assistant preachers, viz., Ko Shway-ba, Ko Shwai, Moung Shway-moung, Moung Shway-gnong, Moung Shway-goon, and Moung Ouk-moo. Some other assistants are employed in revising our publications, copying for the press, and reading proof sheets in Burmese and Peguan.

Brother Vinton, who may be said to belong to this station, though here occasionally only, is employed among the northern Karens, his residence being New Chummerah, as much perhaps as any place; Miss Macomber resides chiefly among the Pwo Karens, at the foot of the Zwai-ka-ben Mountain; and brother Haswell, beginning to preach in Peguan, has his house at Amherst.

Table of Persons baptized in the Maulmain Mission.

	Previous to 1837.	During 1837.	Total.
Burmese and Peguans, ..	113	15	128
Karens, ...	147	42	189
Pwo Karens, ...		15	15
Foreigners, ...	197	19	216
Total, ...	457	91	548

Yours faithfully,

A. JUDSON.

To his Mother and Sister.

MAULMAIN, March 16, 1838.

EVER DEAR MOTHER AND SISTER: I remember you in my prayers every day, and hope that you do not forget me, my wife, and dear little Abby and Adoniram. Yours of October 15, 1837, I received on the arrival of Mr. and Mrs. Stevens in the Rosabella, the 19th of last month. They gave me an account of their visit to Plymouth, and their interview with you both, and how you looked and what you said, and he remembered the exhortation to "preach the three R's." He remarked, that my mother was the very picture of the venerable, and *she* observed that every thing about the house was kept in remarkably nice order. And they both thought that, from your appearance and remarks, you were in the enjoyment of much religious feeling. How I wish I could see you once more! I send you a copy of the Burman New Testament, which may be a gratifying curiosity, if nothing more.

We have just carried Adoniram through the small-pox by inoculation. He had it very lightly, and is now quite recovered. He is one of the prettiest, brightest children you ever saw. His mother says that he resembles his uncle Elnathan. Abby is growing fast. She runs about, and talks Burman quite fluently, but no English. I am not troubled about her not getting English at present, for we shall have to send her home in a few years, and then she will get it of course. She attends family and public worship with us, and has learned to sit still and behave herself. But Fen, or Pwen, as the natives call him, when he is brought into the chapel, and sees me in my place, has the impudence to roar out Bah, (as the Burmans call father,) with such a stentorian voice, that his nurse is obliged to carry him out again.

Many thanks, dear sister, for your last present of fifty dollars, which I have received. I am obliged to look after the rupees a little more carefully now than when I had no little ones to provide for.

I suppose you take the Magazine; so I do not introduce missionary affairs into my private letters.

Yours ever, affectionately,
A. JUDSON.

To the Corresponding Secretary.

MAULMAIN, March 19, 1838.

REV. AND DEAR SIR : . . . I am accused of being a discourager of schools, and perhaps the charge is partly just. . . .

In regard to a dictionary, I do not see how I can possibly undertake it. And if you consider my situation a moment, you will, I am persuaded, be of my opinion. Brother ——— is wholly employed in the printing office, and in a great variety of work resulting from our connection with the other stations; and if not, his voice has so failed him, that he is able to do nothing in English or Burmese preaching. Brother ——— is, or ought to be, absorbed in the school, if he wishes to make it a prosperous, efficient establishment. I have to spend the greater part of my time in preparing manuscripts, revising former editions, reading proof sheets, &c. Must this population of twenty thousand be left to perish without any effort to save them, except what is made by a few very inefficient native assistants? Ought there not to be a preaching missionary in this great, growing place? Circumstances have essentially changed within a few years. The population has doubled, and is increasing in an accelerated ratio. Is it not important that, since an encouraging beginning is made, our efforts should keep pace with the increasing population, lest soon we be swallowed up and lost? For a few months past, having some respite in the printing department, for want of paper, I have been able to set up evening meetings all over town, five or six in a week, and to do some zayat preaching also. Brother Ingalls now assists in the chapel, in evening meetings, and in zayat preaching; and if I have a preaching colleague, I can prosecute my labors in the book line; but if not, how can I think of devoting my time to making books, as I have done for some years past? How can I think of leaving this population to perish before me, while I am poring over manuscripts and proof sheets? I must not do it; I cannot do it, unless the board expressly order it; and then I will obey, believing that *vox senatus vox Dei*. But before they order the only preaching missionary in the place to spend his time in making books, and above all a dictionary, I beg they will deeply consider the propriety of appointing him a preaching colleague.

As to my health, the annual fever, which I have had for nine years in succession, from November to March,—except the year I spent in Burmah,—has been gradually growing lighter; but it still hangs on, and deprives me of a good deal of time. And if there should be some opening in Burmah or Arracan, where I could labor away from this coast, I should be glad to have the liberty of doing so, at least as a temporary arrangement.

Yours faithfully,
A. Judson.

Maulmain, June 30, 1838.

Rev. and dear Sir: Since my last, my time has been chiefly employed in revising parts of the Old Testament, for a new edition of the whole Bible, to be comprised in one volume quarto. This work will employ all my time for a year to come. I am anxious to make a thorough revision of the Psalms and the prophets, with the help of the latest exegetical works that I have been able to procure.

The usual worship has been conducted in the native chapel every evening, and in the forenoon of Lord's days. For a few months I attended evening meetings in different parts of the town, the native chapel being supplied by other members of the mission. But as the rainy season approached, and work also increased in the printing office, I found it necessary to return to my old routine.

The church is slowly increasing. About twelve a year is the small allowance which God grants us; and this, I suppose, must be taken as the measure of our scanty faith. Lord, increase our faith! I am sorry to have to add, that we have no less than eight members excluded from communion; and some of them will probably come to be excluded from the church altogether. Several have been dismissed to join other churches; so that the whole number of communicants at present is one hundred and eighteen, including five foreigners.

Yours faithfully,

A. JUDSON.

P. S. I have three preaching assistants only in my employ — Ko Shway-ba, Moung Shway-gnong, and Moung Ouk-moo. The first is the oldest Christian in the church, having been baptized in 1820. He is a good, steady man, not very talented or active; but being, I trust, a man of some prayer, his labors have been rather blessed. The second is a Burmo-Chinese, the best extempore preacher we have, very active and useful. The third is very energetic and enterprising, for a native, distinguished by a bold, proselyting spirit; but he has not been long employed, and I do not recollect much fruit. Ko En is my assistant in the book line, and Ko Man-boke Mrs. Judson's. The assistants in the employ of other brethren, either here or at other stations, among the Karens, I am not so competent to give an account of as those who employ them.

Rev. Solomon Peck, Corresponding Secretary, to Dr. Judson.

BAPTIST MISSIONARY ROOMS,
Boston, July 14, 1838.

DEAR BROTHER: The inquiry is sometimes made, Why have we so few communications from Mr. Judson in the Magazine? I need not assure you that any thing you may find time to prepare for the Magazine would be read with lively interest, and tend, doubtless, to foster the spirit of missions, while it would remove the necessity of giving explanations, as if some *coolness* could have found place between yourself and the conductors of the missions at home. Of the desirableness of such communications I could say much, and, from your intimate knowledge of Burmah, and of the establishment and prosecution of the mission, their authenticity to *us* would be only equalled by their facility of preparation to you. At the same time, I would not encroach on time sacred to strictly missionary work. All we could reasonably ask would be results of occasional fragmentary efforts.

In this my first communication to you, I cannot deny myself the pleasure of a personal introduction. Your beloved companion will have some remembrance of me, as a friend and correspondent of the lamented Boardman. Shut out by irremovable hinderances from participating in your labors in the foreign field, I esteem myself happy in contributing, in any measure, to your efficiency and comfort from here. The cause, the object, is one, however diverse and distant our spheres of operation; and whether it suffer, we both suffer with it, or be honored, we rejoice together.

We send by this conveyance Robinson's Hebrew Lexicon and Ripley's Notes, for the mission library, with other books ordered by individuals of the mission, and periodicals, &c.

I should be glad to write to several of them, but the ship sails to-morrow, (Sunday,) and it will be impracticable.

To his Sister.

July 20, 1838.

I have lately had the happiness of baptizing the first Toungthoo that ever became a Christian. I hope he will be the first fruits of a plentiful harvest. God has given me the privilege and happiness of witnessing and contributing a little, I trust, to the conversion of the first Burmese convert, the first Peguan, the first Karen, and the first Toung-thoo. Three of them I baptized. The Karen was approved for baptism; but just then, brother Boardman removing to Tavoy, I sent the Karen with him, and he was baptized there.

There are now above a thousand converts from heathenism, formed into various churches throughout the country. And I trust that the good work will go on, until every vestige of idolatry shall be effaced, and millennial glory shall bless the whole land. The thirteenth day of this month finished a quarter of a century that I have spent in Burmah; and on the eighth of next month, if I live, I shall complete the fiftieth year of my life. And I see that mother, if living, will enter on her eightieth year next December. May we all meet in heaven.

Yours ever, affectionately,

A. JUDSON.

MAULMAIN, November 18, 1838.

MY DEAR SISTER: I wrote you last July, since which I have received yours of April 2. I have also received one hundred dollars last year, and one hundred dollars this year, from mother and you, through the treasurer of the board. These sums were very acceptable indeed, not, I trust, because I have grown avaricious, but because I have an increasing family of dear little ones, for whom it is my duty to provide; and you will readily suppose, too, that money is more acceptable, coming from the only two individuals who, with my present family, constitute the dearest society that remains to me on earth. O that we may all be so blessed as to form one happy family in the world above! . . . If it were not for my missionary obligations, and duty to the perishing heathen, how happy I should feel if we were all settled with you in the old mansion house at Plymouth! I feel more desirous than I did formerly to do something to express my gratitude to dear mother for the love she felt, and the pains she took for me when I was a little one. But I can do nothing but pray that her last days may be illuminated by the light of God's countenance, and that an abundant entrance may be administered to her into the kingdom of our Lord. As for you, dear sister, I cannot help thinking that we shall yet meet in this world. But God knows, and his will be done. It seems an unnatural thing that families should be broken up and scattered, as ours has been. This missionary work, though a blessed work, is attended with severe trials and sacrifices, especially of a domestic kind. These dear children I shall have to part with, I suppose, and send to America, to be educated; and what a heart-rending trial that will be!

You observe that you look in vain for my journal. I have been employed, for some time, in revising the translation of Scripture, and in the ordinary details of pastoral duties, without itinerating or doing much missionary work, properly speaking; so that I have but few materials, and less inclination, for journalizing, especially as there are so many younger missionaries, who, I observe, are very handy with their pens; and therefore I only write a short semiannual letter to the board, just to let them know what I am doing, and satisfy them that I am not eating up my allowance for nothing.

I hope you will write me at least as often, and let me know how you live, and what you are doing from time to time, and all about your and mother's health and circumstances. You must believe that the minutest items are interesting to me, your only brother and son. Dear wife sends her best love, and begs you will daily pray for the children, that they may early obtain divine grace.

Ever yours,
A. JUDSON.

To the Corresponding Secretary.

MAULMAIN, December 21, 1838.

. . Modern missions have been distinguished from the Roman Catholic, and indeed from all former missions, since apostolic times, by patronizing and honoring the word of God. And I do believe that those missions which give the highest place to the divine word will be most owned of God, and blessed. There is only one book in the world which has descended from heaven, or, as I tell the Burmans, there is only one golden lamp which God has suspended from heaven to guide us hither. Shall we missionaries throw a shade around it, or do ought to prevent the universal diffusion of its life-giving rays? O that one complete volume of the Bible, and not merely the New Testament, — for the word of God, though not such a book as human philosophy and logic would have devised, is doubtless, in the eye of infinite Wisdom, *a perfect work*, and just fitted to answer the great end which God has in view, — O that one copy of the Burman Bible were safely deposited in every village where the language is understood! Burmah is now shut against us; but it will not be so always, and where there is a will there is a way. And Arracan, with her two thousand villages or more, is open for the reception and deposit of two or three thousand Bibles.

I would not be understood to depreciate the preaching of the gospel, the grand means instituted by Christ for the conversion of the world. But all our preaching must be based on the written word; and when the voice of the living preacher is passed away from the village, the inspired volume may still remain to convict and to edify. I would say, therefore, that the preached gospel and the written word are the two arms which are to pull down the kingdom of darkness and build up the Redeemer's. Let us not cut off one of these arms; for the other will, by itself, be comparatively powerless, as the history of the church in every age will testify.

To the Rev. J. M. Haswell.

MAULMAIN, January 4, 1839.

DEAR BROTHER HASWELL : I send you the accompanying copy of the Articles, &c., of our English church, as affording the best reply I can give to your inquiries. The *exclusion from communion*, defined in the 11th rule, is *one act only*, though repeated and communicated to the offending party at three successive communion seasons. This, in cases where, as in the native church, we have the communion once in four months, gives the offender a whole year to repent in, and the church a whole year to labor with him. This process also makes the *final exclusion from the church* a more solemn and *dreaded* infliction. I have known several cases in which the offender would hold out under exclusion from communion declared the first, second, and even the third time, but would break down at the approach of the final exclusion from the church. In the English church, where they receive the communion every other month, the process contemplated in the said rule is confined to six or eight months. I prefer the former for a native church, but think the latter is sufficient for a European church. I do not suppose that I have attained unto perfection. But my plan is the result of some experience and trying several other plans. Nor am I a great stickler for uniformity, though I suppose that some understanding among neighboring churches, especially among the heathen, is desirable. The Articles of Faith and Covenant contained in the accompanying pamphlet, are from Professor Chase. I found them in the Christian Review; but I do not think they are near so well adapted to a native church, as those which we have adopted.

After all, one touch of the Spirit of God is worth more than all *our plans and contrivances* for the promotion of church order.

"Come, Holy Spirit, heavenly dove."

Yet we must not only partake of the feasts which Jesus furnishes, but we must also gather up the fragments, that nothing be lost.

Yours most affectionately,

A. JUDSON.

To the Corresponding Secretary, Rev. S. Peck.

MAULMAIN, January 5, 1839.

. . . I wish it was in my power to make more copious and more interesting communications for the Magazine; but what can be expected from a man who spends his days at a study table, poring over Hebrew and Greek, and Gesenius and Rosenmüller, &c., &c., and Burmese manuscripts interlined to illegibility?

I warded off the translation of the Bible for several years, thinking it would fall to Boardman, or Jones, or some other; but the providence of God, at length, laid it upon me. And seeing how some eminent missionaries divided their attention among several objects, at the risk of doing nothing well, I thought it incumbent on me, with less capacity, to aim *at more singleness of object.* And I now feel that it is one main duty of the remnant of my life to study and labor *to perfect the Burmese translation of the Bible.*

I know much of your history from Mrs. Judson, and some of my brethren who are acquainted with you, and I rejoice in the privilege of corresponding with you. May our correspondence be a mutual blessing, which we shall appreciate and thank God for in the happy world to which we are hastening.

Yours affectionately,

A. JUDSON.

MAULMAIN, January 21, 1839.

MY DEAR SIR: Allow me to suggest whether the exegetical works of Stuart, Robinson, Stowe, Ripley, Bush, Noyes, and such like, with some of the best German works, ought not to be sent out to the library, as soon as they come from the press, without waiting for an application to be made for them. I frequently see a sterling work on the cover of the Herald or Magazine, and am ready to scream, with some variations, "The book, the book! my kingdom for the book!" Yes, a kingdom, if the same ship which brought the notice had brought the work too; whereas I have to wait for letters to cross the ocean twice or three times, at least, and thus two or three years' use of the book is lost, during which time I am, perhaps, working upon that very portion of Scripture which that book is intended to illustrate.

Could a very small portion of the funds contributed to the

Bible cause be better spent than in sending such works as the above, *without the least delay*, to the several mission libraries where translations of the Scriptures are in progress? Individuals might send, at their leisure, for such of the works for their private use, as they could afford to purchase.

Yours faithfully,
A. JUDSON.

CHAPTER IV.

DECLINING HEALTH — VISIT TO CALCUTTA. — PRINCIPLES OF TRANSLATION. — MISSIONARY WORK. — REVISION OF BURMESE SCRIPTURES COMPLETED — CHARACTER OF THE VERSION.

1839-1840.

With the following letter commences the record of those attacks of pulmonary disease which followed Dr. Judson through the remainder of his life. They commenced with a loss of voice, pain in the organs of speech, and soreness in the lungs, betokening the approach of ordinary consumption. He was obliged to take several voyages for the restoration of his health, but seemed to derive from them only temporary benefit. Preaching, generally in the course of a few months, brought on a relapse; and henceforth the greater portion of his life was, from necessity, spent in solitary labor with the pen. The letters which were written during these absences from home present a lovely picture of his domestic character, and prove that his entire devotion to one object for life had dried up none of the springs of human kindness, but that his affections as a husband, father, son, and brother, instead of being chilled and stupefied, were warmed and animated by the daily labors of general Christian benevolence.

To Mrs. Judson.

Near Amherst, February 20, 10 o'clock, A. M., 1839.

My dear Love: I have felt but little disposition to cough since I have been on board; but as we are not yet out of the river, I cannot expect any special change. I conform myself to all the habits of the people on board in regard to eating and drinking, except that I do not take beer or wine. Tea did not at all prevent my sleeping. My cot is very comfortable, and my cabin, though small, answers every purpose. I think I was never, on shipboard, situated so comfortably in all respects. I spent this morning in sorting all my things, and found it as good exercise as going up the hill. There is a little lid table at the side of the cabin, used formerly as a washing stand, on which I have placed the writing desk, and the chair stands between that and the cot, and just fills up the place, so that I am quite snug and secure in case the vessel rolls; and you can judge from this arrangement of the size of the cabin. Right before me, and over the said table, is a long shelf, on which I have arranged my library and other utensils. The trunks that I don't use are stored under the cot; and the green box, containing things for the voyage, is placed at my feet, by the side of the table. Now I think you can look in and see me pretty clearly. I only wish you were sitting in another chair, for which there is just room, or lolling on the cot. I now turn my head around, and fancy how it would seem if I could see you there, and the dear children, over whom my feelings yearn.

Mrs. ——— seems to be a quiet woman, chiefly employed with her children, "Miss Polly," four years old, and Edmund, six months. Captain ——— does the talking chiefly, and is a pleasant young man. Mr. ——— is fifty years old; but certainly, if my new glass does not flatter me, I do look ten years younger than he. He is probably in an incurable consumption, but says he is infinitely better than he was before coming to sea. This is his second trip to Maulmain in the Snipe. He is very ready to enter into a detailed account of his ailments, and laughs at me for pretending to be consumptive when I have only a slight cough, *without raising any thing.* He says he has no doubt the trip will cure me. Mr. D., the chief officer, I see only on deck. No religious person in the company. Koon-gyah behaves very well, and tries to make himself useful. He is always ready, but not officious, so that I like him well. The captain expects a fortnight's passage. I hope to enjoy some religious meditation and reading, and shall perhaps write two or three letters, but intend to spend most of my time idly, on deck, snuffing in the sea air.

Some servant has been teasing this half hour to come in and wash my cabin; so that I shall not be able to write much more before the pilot leaves. We are now off Amherst. The Enterprise has just passed us, on her return from Rangoon. Tell Mrs. Hough and daughter that the vessel was under way in the morning of the 29th before we were aware; and in the hurry of getting off, I was sorry to miss taking her letters. My love to Mrs. Howard, and tell her I commenced operations on her cakes last evening, and found them most excellent. Particular love to dear brother and sister Stevens, and sweet little Edward. I had a most affectionate parting with brother Osgood. I hope you will get Na Hee-moo off to Amherst without delay. Tell Moung En that I remember him, and all the Christians, as occasion may offer, and ask them to pray for me. I hope that you and the children will enjoy health, and that we shall all live to meet again. You know I love you more than all the world beside.

A. Judson.

On Board the Snipe, bound to Calcutta, February 21, 1839.

My dear Love: I wrote you yesterday, by the pilot, and enclosed my letter, with one to brother Haswell. The afternoon we lay at anchor, outside the buoy; and though in the face of the sea breeze, my cough was rather troublesome all day and evening. Perhaps it was one of my bad days. I passed a poor night, a little sick from the motion of the vessel; and this morning put on Dr. Richardson's pitch plaster, which my fellow-consumptive assures me is the best thing in the world. I have begun this letter more for my own amusement than yours; for what can a poor invalid, in my circumstances, write that will be interesting even to an affectionate wife? We are now moving forward with a light wind. The slower the better, I suppose, for me. How did you and the children pass the night, or rather the two nights, that we have been separated? I think of you, and the house, and the chapel, and the compound, and all the scenes, and occupations, and endearments that are passed — passed, perhaps, never to return; but they will return, if not in this world, yet in another, purified, exalted, when all this mortal shall be invested with immortality.

February 22. Much better since last. Very little cough. Spent all the evening, till nine o'clock, on deck, without any inconvenience. Wished you were with me, basking under the clear moonlight, and inhaling the soft sea air.

March 3, Sunday. Have not attempted to write since the last date, in consequence of the motion of the vessel, occasioned by a light cargo and a head wind. We are now steering north, and expect to reach the pilot ground in three or four days. My cough has almost left me. But there is a soreness remaining which I feel particularly when the air is cold. I have taken off the plaster and done with licorice. I am decidedly convalescent at sea. Whether my complaint will return on land, remains yet to be seen. If I continue to get better, I shall probably return in this vessel. I hope to hear from you by a steamer, as soon as I arrive in Calcutta. It seems an age since I left Maulmain. The entire change of scene, succeeding such a monotonous life as mine has been for several years, contributes to the illusion. I have found your beautiful braid of hair; and I hunted for some further note or token, but in vain. Every thing about me reminds me of your care and love. I feel that no wife ever deserved her husband's gratitude and love more than you. May God preserve you and the children until we meet again, or prepare me to bear whatever distressing dispensation he may have decreed.

March 5. Within a hundred miles of the pilot ground. No wind. I don't care how long we lie here. Yesterday I had a slight touch of cough, which I fancied was brought on by the vicinity to land. But perhaps not. I have written letters to your parents and to George, also to Comstock and Cutter, Dr. Anderson and Mr. Peck.

March 7. A pilot came on board last night. We are not far from Saugur. The fourth and fifth I had some cough. Yesterday none, nor this morning. I feel well in body, but very low in spirits. It is sad, dull work to go to a place which you have no wish to see, and where you have no object scarcely to obtain. I hope to be on my return before long. The bosom of my family is almost the only bright spot that remains to me on earth. O that my desires were more ready to ascend to heaven! But I seem to be at the very lowest ebb in religious exercise. I shall fold up this letter, and have it ready to send by any vessel we may happen to pass.

March 8. We have passed Kedgeree, and are running up fast to Calcutta. Shall probably arrive this evening, or some time to-morrow. We expect to meet the Elizabeth on her way to Maulmain, and I shall endeavor to put this letter aboard of her. I have told Captain S. to-day that, if nothing happens, I shall return with him.

To George D. Boardman.

On Passage from Maulmain to Calcutta, March 3, 1839.

Dear George: I am taking a voyage for the benefit of my health, and being alone on board ship, separated from your mamma and her family, I thought I would write a few lines to you. I left her the 19th of last month, and then she was well, and Abby Ann, Adoniram, and Elnathan. Would you like to see them all? Every body says that Adoniram looks just like you at that age. I think there is a most striking resemblance. Elnathan has blue eyes, and looks more like his mother. I hope you will frequently pray that your sister and brothers may, as well as yourself, become partakers of divine grace. We are all, you know, born with a depraved nature, destitute of the true love of God, full of self-love, and wholly under the influence of self-will. And we are also blind, as well as depraved, and do not at first see our depravity. Perhaps this is your case, and you do not yet know how depraved and sinful you are. But you must depend on the word of God, rather than on your own poor discernment, and cherish feelings of repentance and earnest desire to put your trust in the Saviour, who has died for all of us, and will certainly save every one who puts his trust in him. Such feelings of repentance and faith in the Saviour constitute a new heart. If you get a new heart, you will, when you die, go to heaven, where your sainted father doubtless is, and where your mother and I hope to go. But if not, you will never reach our happy company, and we shall look around in vain for George. Do not forget these things; and while you are engaged in your studies, take care to secure the one thing needful. Your mother and I remember you every day in our family prayers and in our secret devotions. There is nothing we so much long to hear as that you have given your heart to the Saviour, and made a profession of religion in holy baptism.

We are glad to learn from your letters that you are happy in the family of Captain Childs. You must be very obedient and grateful for all the attentions and kindnesses you receive.

I have had an attack of the same complaint that your own father died of; but I am deriving much benefit from the sea air. If I should recover, I shall have returned to Maulmain when you receive this, and be again happy, I hope, in the society of your mamma.

Your affectionate father,
A. Judson.

Verses written for his Children.

Prayer to Jesus.

Dear Jesus, hear me when I pray,
And take this naughty heart away;
Teach me to love thee, gracious Lord,
And learn to read thy holy word.

Another.

Come, dearest Saviour, take my heart,
And let me ne'er from thee depart;
From every evil set me free,
And all the glory be to thee.

For Abby Ann.

Look down on little brother dear,
Safe may he sleep while thou art near,
Preserve his life to know thy love,
And dwell at last in heaven above.

A Morning Prayer.

My waking thoughts I raise to thee,
Who through the night hast guarded me;
Keep me this day from every ill,
And help me, Lord, to do thy will.

Duty to Others.

Love others as you love yourself;
And as you would that they
Should do to you, do you to them,
That is the golden way.

The Dying Child.

"O, grant that Christ and heaven be mine:
What can I want beside?
Hark! hear ye not that voice divine?
'My daughter, Christ and heaven are thine!'
And see! the glorious portals shine!"
She sweetly sang, and died.

To the Corresponding Secretary.

ON PASSAGE FROM MAULMAIN TO CALCUTTA, March 3, 1839.

REV AND DEAR SIR: I had been subject to a cough several months, and some kind of inflammation of the throat and lungs, which, for a time, almost deprived me of the use of my voice; and lest the complaint should become confirmed consumption, I was advised to try a voyage to sea. I left Maulmain, therefore, on the 19th of last month, and my cough is now much better. I hope that I shall sufficiently recover, if it be the will of God, that I can return in the same vessel, and not have to proceed to other places, as mentioned in the accompanying note. Indeed, I did not at at first think of taking such a voyage as the present, but proposed a trip up and down the coast to Rangoon, Tavoy, &c. It was, however, thought not sufficient, and I acquiesced in the present arrangement.

Yours faithfully,
A. JUDSON.

To Mrs. Judson.

CALCUTTA, March 9, 1839.

MY DEAR LOVE: My first business in my new lodgings is to take up my pen for you. I sent a letter on board the Elizabeth yesterday, after which the Snipe came up nearly to town, and quite, this morning. I took a palanquin, and came out to Mr. Thomas's, to whom I had written a line from Kedgeree; and he, being full, sent me to Mr. Ellis's, who has hospitably received me, and given me a room, in which I am now writing.

My cough has not returned on shore, as I feared it would. The soreness remains about the same. I expect to return in the same ship, which will stay here a fortnight or three weeks, so that you will probably see me as soon as this letter. But, as we know not what a day may bring forth, I shall occasionally minute down my adventures, that, if you should not see me again, you may get some shadow of me. And then, I take a greater pleasure in writing to you than in any thing else.

> "Where'er I roam, whatever realms I see,
> My heart, untravelled, *fondly* turns to thee" —

thee, my most beloved wife, and you, my dear children, Abby Ann, Adoniram, and Elnathan.

March 11. For two days I have had a return of soreness, accompanied with some cough. I fear that the atmosphere of this place, loaded with dust and smoke, will bring on a relapse. I have thought of you a great deal to-day, and I long to get back, though I do not entertain so sanguine hopes of ultimately recovering as I did at sea. Brother and sister Ellis are extremely kind, and all the missionaries here treat me with much more attention than I expected. Yesterday I went to the Circular Road chapel, in the forenoon, and heard Mr. Brooks, a General Baptist, from near Orissa. In the afternoon attended Mr. Ellis's native worship. A native convert preached. In the evening, staid at home, rather ill. To-day, also, I have staid at home; missionary company in the evening — the Baynes and the Parsonses, Baptist missionaries, lately arrived.

March 12, Tuesday, A. M. Went with Mr. Ellis to attend a meeting of the committee of the Tract Society; then to the auction rooms and the watchmaker's; left my watch. In the evening, missionary company. No better in health.

March 13, Wednesday. Early in the morning, saw a notice of the arrival of the steamer Enterprise. Hope to get a letter from you at night. Set off for Serampore with the Ellises and Mrs. Parsons. Just saw the Marshmans, Macks, &c. On return, visited Mrs. Wilson's celebrated girls' school. Will tell you particulars if ever I get back. In the evening, missionary company. Sadly disappointed in not finding any letter from you.

March 14, Thursday. Early in the morning, your precious letter of *five sheets* was brought in. I was just dressed, and sat down to the feast before breakfast. How much I enjoyed it, and how much I loved you, during the perusal, I cannot stop to detail. No one can tell the value of such a letter but an absent husband and father, whose heart is wrapped up in his family. I will only say that I rejoiced in your narrow escape from fire, and that I entirely approve of your invitation to the Hancocks.

Took a palanquin and went into town. Called on Mr. Roberts and Captain Spain. The Snipe is to sail on the 25th. Came home, put your letter in my pocket, and called at Yates's, Thomas's, &c. They all knew that I was expecting a letter, and was disappointed last night; gave them a peep at the *five sheets*. Showed some of the sisters the Burman writing, and explained a little what the children said. They all thought that you must be a wonderful woman to make books as you do; and they all say, particularly Mrs. Ellis, how sorry they are that you did not come with me. I almost think that if I had known all things, and what good accommodations we could have had in this house, we should have come together. I should have been *so* happy to have had you with me. If such exquisite delights as we have enjoyed with those now in paradise, and with one another, are allowed to sinful creatures on earth, what must the joys of heaven be? Surely there is not a single lawful pleasure, the loss of which we shall have to regret there. What high and transporting intercommunion of souls we may, therefore, anticipate, and that to all eternity!— intercommunion between one another, and between the "Bridegroom" and the "Bride," of which wedded love on earth is but a type and shadow. "Thanks be unto God for his unspeakable gift."

I forgot to mention, yesterday, that no sooner had I left the shores of Calcutta than my soreness of lungs and cough fled away. I was quite well all day, and have continued pretty well to-day, but have a little relapse this evening, on which account I am staying at home, while the rest have gone to the chapel.

March 15, Friday. Read your letter again this morning. I long to be once more in the bosom of my family. It seems an age since we exchanged the parting kiss. Spent the day at home. A large missionary party at tea in the evening, the Mortons, the Baynes, the Parsonses, Yates, and Macdonald. A very pleasant season. But I wanted to see you present. You would have enjoyed a debate between Mrs. Ellis and Mrs. Morton on schools. Morton, Yates, and I had a long discussion about the standard text of Scripture; while Macdonald and the rest were chiefly employed, as I occasionally overheard, in settling the chronology of the sacred records.

Not much tendency to cough; but the climate of Calcutta does not agree with me, and I intend going to Serampore to-morrow for a change of air. Farewell, until I return, which will probably be on Monday.

March 18, Monday. Here I am again. I went up in two hours, Saturday afternoon, and came down in two hours, this morning. I staid at old Mrs. Marshman's, and visited John Marshman and wife, and Mr. and Mrs. Mack. Heard Mr. Mack and Mr. Pickance preach on the Sabbath, and with Mrs. Marshman and her daughter, Mrs. Voight, visited a meeting of female converts. But the glory has departed from Serampore. Glad to return. Health pretty good. Captain and Mrs. Spain called in the evening. He says he shall sail on the 27th. Scarcely any cough nowadays.

March 19, Tuesday. Went to the Calcutta bazaars, and spent the forenoon in shopping. Mrs. Ellis has undertaken to get the shoes and the children's clothes made. Towards night and in the evening, called on all the Baptist missionaries in succession; also on Mr. and Mrs. Sykes, and saw their school, and Dr. R.'s five children.

March 20, Wednesday. I sometimes amuse myself with Mrs. Hemans's poetry, with which Mr. Ellis has furnished me. Beautiful — but to my disappointment, entirely destitute of religion! Among several pieces that I want to transcribe for you is the following: —

The Invocation.

O, art thou still on earth, *my love?*
My only love!
Or smiling in a brighter home,
Far, far above?
O, is thy sweet voice fled, my love,
Thy light step gone?
And art thou not, in earth or heaven,
Still, still my own?
I see thee with thy gleaming hair,
In midnight dreams;
But cold, and clear, and spirit-like
Thy soft eye seems.
Peace, in thy saddest hour, my love,
Dwelt on thy brow;
But something mournfully divine
There shineth now!

> And silent ever is thy lip,
> And pale thy cheek! —
> O, art thou earth's, or art thou heaven's?
> Speak to me, speak!

Two o'clock, P. M. I have spent the forenoon in visiting the "Central School," containing three hundred girls, and the General Assembly's Seminary, containing six hundred boys and young men.

Nine o'clock. Spent the whole evening at Mr. Yates's, in comparing the principles which we have respectively adopted in translating Scripture. Remarkable agreement.

March 22, Friday. Yesterday, took breakfast at Mr. Morton's, and in the evening, heard Mr. Yates preach at the Circular Road chapel. This morning, saw a notice in a newspaper that the Snipe was loading for Mauritius. Was more miserable for an hour than since I left Maulmain. But having written immediately to Captain Spain, got the following joyful intelligence: "The Snipe will leave town on Tuesday for Maulmain. Let me know if you take the same cabin back." I am so well now that I do not hesitate about returning in the same vessel. How joyfully do I hope to embark! How joyfully retrace my way, and at length see the hills of Amherst and Maulmain rising in the distant perspective! And how joyfully do I hope to see your dear face, and take you to my longing arms, and find again "that home is home."

March 23, Saturday. Breakfast at Mr. Macdonald's. Tea and evening at Mr. Bayne's. Much of my time, through the day, in thinking of "home, sweet home," and depicting joys past, not never, but soon, I hope, to return.

March 24, Lord's day. Heard Mr. Parsons in the forenoon, and Mr. Yates in the evening. Dined at Mr. Bayne's.

March 25, Monday. In the morning, called on Archdeacon Dealtry, where I saw the oldest East Indian in the country — Mrs. Ellerton, who has been out sixty years. Spent most of the day at Mr. Thomas's printing office, &c.

March 26, Tuesday. Went with Mr. Dealtry to Bishop's College, two miles down the river, on the opposite side.

Breakfasted with the bishop, and spent the forenoon in attending worship, viewing the college, &c. There are fifteen students only.

March 27, Wednesday. Called on Mrs. Locke, an American lady, from Boston, member of Mr. Stow's church, and on Captain Spain, who says the Snipe will drop down to-morrow. In the evening all the missionary brethren and sisters assembled at Mr. Bayne's, on account of my approaching departure from Calcutta.

March 28, Thursday. In the forenoon, put my boxes on board the vessel. Took tea at Mr. Thomas's, and heard Mr. Yates preach in the evening.

March 30, Saturday. Called on all the Baptist missionaries in Calcutta, and took leave of them — a lovely set of brethren and sisters. Wish you had come with me, and formed an acquaintance with them. They all say that I must bring you the next time, or send you alone. Took another run through the bazaars. At night, left town, in a boat with Captain Spain and Captain Major, the only passenger beside myself; but the tide turned against us about midnight, so that we were obliged to anchor, and sleep in the boat.

March 31, Lord's day. Reached the Snipe at daylight, near Fultah, and took possession of my old cabin.

Ever thine,
A. JUDSON.

To the Corresponding Secretary.

MAULMAIN, April 24, 1839.

DEAR BROTHER: My last informed you that I was on a passage to Calcutta for my health, by the direction of a physician and the recommendation of the brethren at the station. I derived great benefit from the voyage; and my health continued generally to improve during my stay in Calcutta of three weeks, and on the return voyage, until the Sunday preceding my arrival here, when I made trial of my voice, by attempting to conduct Burmese worship in my cabin, with the only native convert on board. And though the effort was very small, I was dismayed to find, in the course of the after noon, the old soreness of lungs and tendency to cough come on; and for three days I was rather worse than I had been for six weeks. Being at sea, however, I partially recovered from the relapse before I reached home, but am not so well as at my last date. It is a great mercy that I am able to use my voice in common conversation without much difficulty; but when I shall be able to preach again I know not. The approaching rainy season will probably decide whether my complaint is to return with violence, or whether I am to have a further lease of life. I am rather desirous of living, for the sake of the work and of my family; but He who appoints all our times, and the bounds of our habitation, does all things well; and we ought not to desire to pass the appointed limits.

During my absence the Digest of Scripture, one hundred and thirty-six pages, octavo, which I left in press, has been printed, except the Index, which is now in press; and the printing of the new edition of the Bible, which was suspended, is just recommencing, at the twenty-sixth chapter of the 1st of Samuel.

I am anxiously hoping to receive a copy of Bloomfield's Greek Testament before I come to the final revision of that part of the Bible, and whatever other helps to biblical exegesis may have been recently published.

Yours faithfully,
A. JUDSON.

To the Hon. Heman Lincoln.

MAULMAIN, May 1, 1839.

DEAR BROTHER: On the arrival of the Apthorp, a few days ago, I received the India rubber pantaloons, and felt much obliged to you for your kindness; but they have probably come too late for me, and I hardly expect to use them. My throat complaint, which seemed to be nearly removed by a voyage to Calcutta, has returned with fresh violence since the commencement of the rains, three days ago. Some advise me to take another voyage, as before; but I have no heart to do so, thinking that the benefit will be but temporary. Others suggest a voyage home to America, and a residence there for a year or two; but to this course I have strong objections. There are so many missionaries going home for their health, or for some other cause, that I should be very unwilling to do so, unless my brethren and the board thought it a case of absolute necessity. I should be of no use to the cause at home, not being able to use my voice. And lastly, I am in my fifty-first year. I have lived long enough. I have lived to see accomplished the particular objects on which I set my heart when I commenced a missionary life. And why should I wish to live longer? I am unable to preach; and since the last relapse, the irritation of my throat is so very troublesome that I cannot converse but with difficulty, or even sit at the table, as I have done to-day, and prepare copy for the press. My complaint, it is said, is very much like that of which the late Mrs. Osgood died — not common pulmonary consumption, but something in the throat, which puzzled even her attending physicians, one of whom maintained, till near her death, that she was not in a consumption, and would recover.

My present expectation is, to use medicinal palliatives, and endeavor to keep along for a few months, until I see the present edition of the Bible completed, and then be ready to rest from my labors. But the very thought brings joy to my soul. For, though I am a poor, poor sinner, and know that I have never done a single action which can claim the least merit or praise, glory is before me, interminable glory, through the blood of the Lamb, the Lamb for sinners slain. But I shrink back again, when I think of my dear wife and darling children, who have wound round my once widowed, bereaved heart, and would fain draw me down from heaven and glory. And then I think, also, of the world of work before me. But the sufficient answer to all is, *The Lord will provide.*

I remain,
Yours faithfully,
A. JUDSON.

To the Corresponding Secretary.

MAULMAIN, July 12, 1837.

DEAR BROTHER: As Mr. Malcom and myself have had some conversation and correspondence about the Burman translation of the formula of baptism, I will now give you the sequel.

Though, in the year 1836, I altered the translation to " baptizing them *in the religion* of the Father," &c., I was never well satisfied with that rendering, especially as the elder brethren, Wade and Mason, preferred retaining the old rendering, which had been objected to by some of the later brethren, and which conveyed the idea of *introducing into the religion.* So, after much correspondence with different brethren of the mission, and discussion with the best scholars within my reach, I concluded, last year, to render thus, " baptizing them in, that is, *into the name of the Father*," and thus departing from the common English version, which renders " in the name, that is, *by the authority* of the Father," &c., which is unsupported by the Greek, and unanimously discarded by all modern biblical critics, English, American, and German. Brother Mason has adopted the same in the Karen, and brother Yates in the Bengalee, Hindoostanee, &c., and it is approved by brother Comstock of Arracan and brother Stevens with me, nor have I yet heard a single objection to it from any quarter. It was so printed in the Digest of Scripture, before my late voyage to Calcutta.

I take this occasion to say that I heartily approve of the resolution of the American Baptist Board of Foreign Missions, passed April, 1833 : " That all the missionaries of the board who are, or who shall be, engaged in translating the Scriptures, be instructed to endeavor, by earnest prayer and diligent study, to ascertain the exact meaning of *the original text*, and to express that meaning as exactly as the nature of the language into which they shall translate," &c.

And I approve also of the principles on which the American and Foreign Bible Society was founded, and which are repeatedly recognized in their first annual report, particularly *that foreign translations are not to be conformed to the common English version.* See, also, the "Resignation," page 57 of the said report, beginning with, "He is bound to express;" the letter of Mr. Hinton to Lord Bexley, page 66, beginning with, "In the name of all that is honest;" and the fifth reason of the "Protest," page 31 of the Constitution of the American and Foreign Bible Society.

I would here respectfully suggest what I conceive to be the proper course to be pursued, in case of dissatisfaction with any instance of translation into a foreign language.

1. *State the objection* to the translator, and request him to reconsider the subject.

2. If he be unable to remove the objection satisfactorily, and still decline altering, call upon the missionaries who are acting in concert with him in publishing and circulating the work which contains the said controverted passage, to appoint a committee, including the translator, of course, to examine the subject, and report.

3. If the translator be still "conscientiously obstinate," and the subject be of sufficient importance, let the work which contains the obnoxious passage be suppressed. But such an extreme case, we may safely suppose, would never occur.

I remain,
Yours faithfully and affectionately,
A. JUDSON

To his Mother and Sister.

MAULMAIN, August 9, 1839

DEAR MOTHER AND SISTER: On this day I enter my fifty-second year. Fifty-one years have rolled over my head, twenty-six of which have been spent in this heathen land. I believe I write you more frequently than I used to. I am not so much driven in my studies as formerly, and the weakness and irritability of my lungs, though much better, do not yet suffer me to use my voice in public. Add to which that I have a family of young children growing up around me, so that my mind has become more domesticated, and returns with more readiness and frequency to the scenes of my own childhood. Twenty-seven years and a half have passed since we parted in Plymouth and in Boston, during which time my father and brother, and his family, and my first family, have all been swept away by death. You two only remain, and my present family, whom you have never seen. I sometimes feel concerned for my three little children, from the fact that I was advanced in life when they were born, and cannot, therefore, expect to live to see them grown up and happily settled before I shall be removed. Even if my present complaint should not terminate in consumption, I can hardly expect to hold out many more years in this climate; so that I have the prospect of leaving them fatherless in the very bloom of youth, when they will especially need a father's support and care. However, I endeavor daily to commend them to God, and trust that, when I come to die, I shall be enabled to avail myself of the command and promise, " Leave thy fatherless children; I will preserve them alive; and let thy widows trust in me." Jer. xlix. 11.

Abby Ann has begun to go to school, with Julia Osgood, to Mrs. Simons, who, with her husband, is here from Rangoon, expecting a war with Burmah, and has set up an English school. Abby attends every forenoon, and just begins to read words of one syllable. Adoniram says, "I want go school;" but he stays at home, and deports himself like a little man. Elnathan has been very ill. We thought we should lose him; but he is now better, and begins to be bright and playful.

I do wish you could call in and make us a visit. We would try to make you so comfortable that you would not wish to return to old Plymouth. However, it is of little consequence where we spend the short remnant of life. Heaven is before us. Let us pray much, and live devoted to God, and we sha.. soon be united in that happy world where there is no dividing sea.

Can't you give me some account of your house, and furniture, and neighbors, and street, so that I can form a little idea how you are situated? I have tried to glean some particulars from the Stevenses; but transient passers cannot be expected to give much satisfactory information. And when you write, leave a good place for the wafer of your letter, as you see I do; otherwise there are sometimes words which I cannot make out. My wife has been intending to write you, and would by the present opportunity, but she has been afflicted with very sore eyes for about two months. I shall be glad when any of the little ones shall be able to conjure out a scrawl to their grandmother and aunt. Pray for them, that they may be early converted to God. Perhaps mother will add a line with her own hand, when you write. Dear mother, I wish I could make you some return for all the trouble I once gave you.

Yours ever,

A. JUDSON.

Mrs. Sarah Judson, to Dr. Judson's Mother.

MAULMAIN, October 30, 1839.

MY DEAR MOTHER: . . . I have during the past year suffered deep anxiety and gloomy foreboding on account of my dear husband's health. But God has been merciful beyond our fears, and so far restored him that he was able to preach last Lord's day, the first time for about ten months. His discourse was short, and he spoke low. I felt exceedingly anxious respecting his making the attempt, but he has experienced no ill effects from it as yet. How pleased you would have been to see the joy beaming from the countenances of the dear native Christians, as they saw their beloved and revered pastor once more take the desk! He applies himself very closely to study, though he is still far from well. He takes cold very easily, and still feels a slight uneasiness in the chest and left side. But he is so much better than he was, that I am comforted with the hope that he will soon be entirely restored to health. He is now revising the Scriptures for a second edition, quarto. They have already proceeded in printing as far as Psalms. He revises as they print, and often finds himself closely driven. But God gives him strength equal to his day. With much love to sister Abigail, I remain, my dear mother

Your affectionate daughter,
SARAH JUDSON.

To his Sister.

DEAR SISTER: I avail myself of the margin of this letter to mother, to say good morning to you, across the wide world that divides us. Life is wearing away, and the time drawing on, when, I trust, we shall all be reunited in one family, enjoying together eternal life and glory. Till then I hope we shall daily remember one another at the throne of grace, and especially the little ones who have not hearts to pray for themselves. Do write often, long, and particularly.

Your affectionate brother,
A. JUDSON.

To W. Crane, Esq., Baltimore.

MAULMAIN, December 9, 1839.

DEAR BROTHER: Your kind favor of May last, with the accompanying magazines and newspapers, reached me via Calcutta, on the 28th of September, and they brought us the latest intelligence from our native land, and what is rather singular, the latest intelligence that has reached any individual of the mission to the present time! Your papers and magazines were well read, I assure you; and after they were nearly worn out, I packed them up carefully, and sent them down to Tavoy, as I was not sure that the parcel you mention as directed to Mr. Wade ever reached its destination. I recollect no parcel ever received from America, that did such extensive and lasting service to us missionaries. Only think, had it not been for your kindness, not one of us would have had the least item of intelligence, down to the present time, of the proceedings of the last annual meeting of the board, and of the other most interesting meetings in Philadelphia, in April. Several have asked me, "Have you sent a letter of thanks to Mr. Crane?" I have replied, "No, not yet; but I intend to as soon as I get time." And this is the first letter that I have written to America since the receipt of yours.

I have another letter before me of yours, dated June 12, 1834, which I ought to have answered, and thanked you for the nice and very useful articles which accompanied it, by the hands of Mr. and Mrs. Wade; but I received so many letters about that time, that I could not well find time to answer them; but I hope that I have frequently felt thankful to God for putting it into the hearts of yourself, and other dear friends of the cause, to remember us in this distant land.

It is interesting to hear of your efforts to revive the state of true religion in the great city to which you have lately removed. I used to hear formerly, from the first Mrs. Price, of the low state of the cause in that city, and the great need of faithful and persevering labors to counteract the overwhelming tide of immorality and false religion. May the Lord in infinite mercy pour out his Holy Spirit in Baltimore, and may you and your brother live to see a great ingathering of precious souls into the fold of the Good Shepherd. "Nothing is impossible to industry," said one of the seven sages of Greece. Let us change the word *industry* for *persevering prayer*, and the motto will be more Christian, and worthy of universal adoption. I am persuaded that we are all more deficient in a spirit of prayer than in any other grace. God loves importunate prayer so much that he will not give us much blessing without it; and the reason he loves such prayer is, that he loves us, and knows that it is a necessary preparation for our receiving the richest blessings which he is waiting and longing to bestow.

I have been laid aside from preaching for nearly a year, by an affection of the muscles of the voice, which threatened to terminate in pulmonary consumption. But through great mercy I have lately been allowed to recommence the delightful work. During the past year I have confined myself almost exclusively to revising the translation of Scripture, as the work is going through the press in a new quarto edition of the whole Bible. The printing is just now advanced as far as Isaiah. I hope to see the work through the press by the 13th of next July, the twenty-seventh anniversary of the Burman mission.

Yours affectionately,
A. JUDSON.

From the Corresponding Secretary.

BAPTIST MISSIONARY ROOMS,
BOSTON, December 18, 1839.

MY DEAR BROTHER: At the meeting of the board on the 2d instant, your letter to Mr. Lincoln, of May 1, having been read, it was unanimously resolved to invite you to revisit this country, with a view to the restoration of your health. The invitation was intended to extend to your wife and children, should you judge it advisable for them to accompany you.

This resolution, it gives me much pleasure to add, was adopted not only with great cordiality, but with many expressions of the kindest interest and sympathy, and with the universal desire that, if your health should continue as it was at the date of your letter, you would comply with it by the earliest opportunity. It is due not only to you, but to us, and to the general cause of missions, that all suitable means be employed to reëstablish your health, and no considerations of expense or obloquy, incurred by the frequent return of missionaries, should deter you from adopting them.

You will perceive that, in making this proposal, the board have no respect to the good which might result from your personal intercourse with them, or others who are interested in missions, but which, they trust, would be of great service to them, and to the cause at large. The *main* object would be gained, if, by a double voyage, your health should be so far restored as to enable you to continue your labors at the desk, and for at least a few years longer supervise the publication of the Scriptures, and such other works as your knowledge of Burman and of the Burmese character peculiarly qualify you to prepare.

May the God of missions guide you by his good Spirit in all your way, and of his great goodness restore and preserve your health and usefulness for a long time yet to come.

    Affectionately and truly yours,

        S. PECK, For. Sec.

To the Corresponding Secretary.

        MAULMAIN, December 31, 1839.

REV. AND DEAR SIR: For many months past, my labors have been entirely devoted to the revision of the Old Testament, as the work has passed through the press. Owing to my illness and voyage to Calcutta, and some difficulties in the printing establishment, the work has not proceeded so rapidly as I expected. We are just finishing Isaiah; and several months must yet elapse before we come to the end of the New Testament.

I began to preach again in the native chapel last October, after an interval of nearly ten months. As yet I have attempted to conduct the forenoon worship on Lord's days only; but I hope, if the present cold season passes away without occasioning a return of my complaint, to resume the daily evening worship.

During the past year, fourteen have been added to the native church by baptism, and five by letter. Seven have been dismissed to form the church in Arracan, four excluded, and one deceased. Not counting a few who stand excluded from communion, the present number of native members is one hundred and thirty-three.

    Yours faithfully,

        A. JUDSON.

To the Rev. F. Mason.

        MAULMAIN, January 16, 1840

DEAR BROTHER MASON: Brother Wade will tell you that, so long ago as when we were living together, we made sundry resolutions to preach the gospel, and *not anti-Boodhism,* and to persuade our assistants to do the same. But I have found it exceedingly difficult to keep such resolutions, either in regard to myself or others. I rather think that it is a sound principle in missions, that the degree of success is proportionate to the quantity of gospel preached.

We are in Jeremiah. Hope you will send up corrections speedily. I have finally adopted *all* your suggestions on the thirty-first of Proverbs.

I have again begun to preach a little; but my fall fever is pretty bad this year, and I lose a good deal of time. My eyes are now burning so that I can hardly see to write.

Master Henry came into notice the last day of the year; but there was no earthquake, nor any thing.

Does the bibliomania rage in Tavoy? It is very prevalent in these parts. Do you think it contagious, or is it communicated by the saliva of a rabid animal? What animal? I should define man to be, not a creature that stands on two legs, but on two extremes, one at a time. When one aches, he pulls it up, and puts down the other.

Yours affectionately,

A. JUDSON.

Memoranda of a Trip to Rangoon.

February 4, 1840. Left Maulmain in a boat, with Captain Boothby, at ten o'clock in the morning, passed the Wave at anchor, and reached Nat-mau about noon. Captain N——, Mr. H——. Went about the premises. Two vessels on the stocks — one to be launched to-morrow. Dinner at four Mrs. N——. Evening in conversation with one and another.

5. Up at five o'clock, and off with Boothby. Rainy morning. Caught the Wave off Amherst at nine or ten. Captain Venture. Out to sea. Captain Antonic passenger. A little seasick all day.

6. Court and Camp of Bonaparte. A history of infernals. Rich source of meditation. At night, sighted the Elephant.

7. Life of Bonaparte, ditto. Rangoon River. At night, landed. Slept at Captain Spiers's.

8, Lord's day. Took a stroll about town. Called on Mr.

S——. Rather pleased with him. My boys got things from the ship. Took up my residence at the old Brick, but to mess at Spiers's. Sent Ko En to inform the disciples of my arrival. P. M. Ko Thah-a came, from whom I ascertained the state of all the disciples.

9. Monday. In the morning went to the great pagoda, and through the new section of the town. Rangoon considerably improved. I should judge the place about twice as large as Maulmain. Forenoon with S——; afternoon, with some of the disciples; evening with Spiers and Brown, discussing the evidences of Christianity, and answering their objections.

10, Tuesday. Various native company. Evening at Crisp and Trill's, where Boothby puts up.

11, Wednesday. Most of the day with S ——.

12, Thursday. Began to distribute tracts at the house. People greedy to get them. After about one thousand were given out, Ko En was summoned away by the head of the district, and detained. Obliged to go to the government house to find S——, who was not at home. At night Boothby and Staig went to the ray-woon, and procured Ko En's release, and glad enough was I to see him again.

13, Friday. Looked at the Water Witch. Dined at Crisp and Trill's. Took a walk with the former and Biden, discussing the evidences. Spent the evening with the above gentlemen and Boothby in religious conversation. May God grant his blessing!

15, Lord's day. Worship with a few of the Christians, Ko Hlay, Ko Kywet-nee, and some others. Dined at Crisp's.

16, Monday. In the morning, went out towards the pagoda, on the east road. Returning, took a view of the old mission premises and the graves. Sent things on board the Susan. At night, no pass obtained. Slept on board.

17, Tuesday. Spent the day at Crisp and Trill's. At night, took departure from Staig's, and found the vessel at anchor below the town. In the evening, dropped down the river, and anchored into the Elephant.

18, Wednesday, and 19, Thursday. Stretched along the

coast. Desultory reading. Came in sight of Amherst. Hope to get up to Maulmain some time in the evening or night — but farewell till then.

20, Friday, nine o'clock, A. M. Is not this too bad? Last night, instead of getting up anchor at the turn of tide, the lubbers slept till three o'clock, in consequence of which we met the ebb tide a little below Mopoon, and came to anchor about sunrise. And here we must lie till noon, not even in sight of our home, though so near. But I hope we shall meet in a few hours. You will have learned that the Wave returned to Maulmain, instead of proceeding to Calcutta, and that Captain Boothby wrote by her. But strange as it may seem, I never heard of her leaving till some days after, or I should not have let the opportunity pass without a line to you. Boothby is much attached to his family — says they are not out of his mind an hour in the day, and I can sympathize with him in this matter. I hope to find you all well.

Yours ever,

A. JUDSON.

Mrs. Sarah Judson, Maulmain.

Extract from a Letter of Mrs. Stevens.

MAULMAIN, May 12, 1840.

We had a pleasant visit last evening from Mr. and Mrs. Judson. Mr. Judson feels sadly about the state of the church; many of the young members falling into open sin, and the older ones cold and negligent of religious duties. He is desirous of doing something for its improvement, and has thought of several plans. He has framed a covenant of eight items, taken from the New Testament, which all must sign. The quarto Bible is now complete, a copy of which Mr. Judson intends to present to each head of a family, in rather a formal manner, carrying it himself to the house, and there solemnly enjoining its daily perusal, and the habit of morning and evening family worship, which has been much neglected by the church. He intends having henceforth three services for the natives on the Sabbath, which will probably supersede the brethren's prayer meeting at Mr. Osgood's. Mr. Stevens is expecting to take his turn in preaching on the Sabbath. Conversation on this point led to an interesting discussion between Mr. Judson and Mr. Stevens upon the institution of the Sabbath, and the grounds of its obligation under the Christian dispensation. The rule about temperance gives the most trouble, from the difficulty of rightly framing it.

To the Rev. F. Mason.

MAULMAIN, May 27, 1840.

DEAR BROTHER MASON: I hear that the mail is still open, and as I have just received a letter from brother Brown, which I thought you would like to see, I enclose it, for the perusal of yourself and fraternity, which being effected, please to return it. You will see that I have some chance, though undeserving, of coming in for a share of your blushing honors.

As to "the comparative facility of writing the Roman character and the Burman," if you mean the *real* Roman character, as the term is generally taken, I should say there was little or no choice, and I should think that the one would be acquired about as quick as the other, by "a person ignorant of both;" for though there is a greater variety in the Burmese character to learn, there is a still greater variety of sounds, capriciously attached to the Roman letters, as we use them. But if you mean the Trevelyanized Roman character, according to which a hundred, and indeed many hundred letters can be made out of twenty-six, in what I conceive to be the very worst possible way of making new letters, — that is, by all manner of diacritical marks attached hither and thither, and yon, to the main letter, making confusion worse confounded to the eye and the memory of learner, reader, writer, or printer, worse in some respects than the Hebrew with points, which every printer execrates from the bottom of his soul, — if, I say, such is your meaning, you have my answer already.

I would not say, however, but that there are some simple

languages in the world which can be advantageously expressed by the Roman letters; that is, without much alteration. The language of the Sandwich Islands may be such a one. Whether this is the case with the Karen, I am not competent to judge, without some further acquaintance with the language than I possess. I suspect, however, that *fifty-four* vowel sounds would require such an *awful* alteration of the five Roman vowels, as to present, in my view, an insurmountable objection.

As to "the propriety of changing the Karen to the Roman, at this late date," I can only say that I fear it is one of the deep stratagems of the devil to destroy the Karen department of the mission, as he has nearly destroyed the Burmese department by another set of stratagems. But necessity has no law. What cannot be cured must be endured. We must learn to regard certain proceedings in the light of disease, restrictions imposed by an intolerant government, and other ills which flesh is heir to. If we cannot do all the good we would, let us do all the good we can, and not fret because our means are limited. "God is great," is a saying which they use even in Algiers. He can bless a Paul, though afflicted with a thorn in the flesh and a chain on his arm; and he can bless a tract too, though almost strangled in its protracted birth, through the self-conceit and imbecility of superintending accoucheurs.

In haste, fearing I shall be too late for the mail.

Yours affectionately,

A. JUDSON.

To George D. Boardman.

MAULMAIN, December 24, 1840.

MY DEAR GEORGE: Your letter of January 9 gave us great pleasure, as it furnished proof of your proficiency in learning, and of your affectionate remembrance. Truly we remember you every day, especially in our prayers. Every morning we come around the family altar, your mother and myself, your sister Abby Ann, and your brothers Adoniram and Elnathan — Henry is too young to attend — and it is our earnest prayer that all our children may *early* become partakers of divine grace. I hope you will never neglect the duty of *secret prayer.* Never let a morning or evening pass without going into some room or place by yourself, and kneeling down and spending five or ten minutes at least in praying to God, in the name of Jesus Christ. Pray earnestly that you may have a new heart, and become a child of God, and that you may have satisfactory evidence that such is your happy state.

You observe in your letter that you are sometimes disturbed by frightful dreams, and we hear in other ways that your health is rather delicate. I warmly recommend you to rise every morning between light and sunrise, and take a quick walk of a mile or more, and to the top of some hill, if there be one in the vicinity that will suit your purpose; and in the winter, when you may not be able to walk, get some equivalent exercise in cutting wood or some other work. This is the course that, with some intermissions and with various modifications, I have pursued for thirty-five years; and to this, under God, I ascribe the good health and the long life I have enjoyed in this unpropitious climate. Your mother frequently accompanies me over the Maulmain hills, and she enjoys much better health than she did at Tavoy, where she took no exercise, scarcely. Do, my dear George, take this matter into serious consideration. You may not like it at first. You will perhaps feel tired and sleepy for a few days, but when you become a little used to it, you will enjoy it exceedingly. You will find your appetite improving, your health becoming firm, and your repose by night undisturbed. I have now given you the two best pieces of advice in my power. The first relates to your soul, the second to your body. Follow them, and be virtuous and happy. I hope to hear that you have professed religion, and devoted yourself to the ministry. Who knows but that I shall live to introduce you into missionary work in this country, where your own father labored, and where his remains are entombed. Follow your father, my dear George; and we will all, ere long, be so happy in heaven together, even in the presence of the dear, lovely, glorious Saviour, the Friend of sinners, who died for us.

Your affectionate father,
A. JUDSON.

To the Rev. Dr. Cone, of New York.

MAULMAIN, December 25, 1840.

DEAR BROTHER CONE: By brother Hancock, who returns to America on account of his wife's health, I send copies of the new edition of the Burmese Bible. The work was finished — that is, the revision and printing — on the 24th October last, and a happy day of relief and joy it was to me. I have bestowed more time and labor on the revision than on the first translation of the work, and more, perhaps, than is proportionate to the actual improvement made. Long and toilsome research among the biblical critics and commentators, especially the German, was frequently requisite to satisfy my mind that my first position was the right one. Considerable improvement, however, has been made, I trust, both in point of style and approximation to the real meaning of the original. But the *beau ideal* of translation, so far as it concerns the poetical and prophetical books of the Old Testament, I profess not to have attained. If I live many years, of which I have no expectation, I shall have to bestow much more labor upon those books. With the New Testament I am rather better satisfied, and the testimony of those acquainted with the language is rather encouraging. At least, I hope that I have laid a good foundation for my successors to build upon.

We are now about to shut up our printing office, having a sufficient supply of books on hand, so long as Burmah is closed against missionary operations. There is no prospect of war, nor ever has been, nor any preparation for war on either side, except in the fancies of certain individuals. I regret that, in some cases, zeal has not been tempered with prudence; and we are all now suffering in consequence.

I rejoice in the formation of the Bible Translation Society

in England, and in the continued prosperity of the American and Foreign Bible Society. I verily believe that it was by the special providence of God that the old Bible societies were left to take the unjustifiable course * they did, in order that the peculiar truths which distinguish the Baptist denomination might be brought forward in a manner unprecedented, and ultimately triumphant. O the depth of the riches, both of the wisdom and knowledge of God!

Yours most affectionately,
A. Judson.

To the Corresponding Secretary.

Maulmain, December 28, 1840.

Rev. and dear Sir: Your very kind letters of December and May last, inviting me to return to America, have been received; but my health is now so far recovered that I cannot persuade myself to think of such a measure at present. On this subject I have just written more particularly to Deacon Lincoln, and to that letter I beg leave to refer you.

On the 24th of October last, I enjoyed the great happiness of committing to the press the last sheet of the new edition of the Burmese Bible. It makes about twelve hundred pages, quarto. We are sending you several copies by the present conveyance.

In the first edition of the Old Testament, I paid too much regard to the critical emendations of Lowth, Horsley, and others. In the present edition, I have adhered more strictly to the Hebrew text. In my first attempts at translating portions of the New Testament, above twenty years ago, I followed Griesbach, as all the world did then. And though, from year to year, I have found reason to distrust his authority, still, not wishing to be ever changing, I deviated but little from his text, in subsequent editions, until the last; in preparing which I have followed the text of Knapp, though not

---

* Dr. Judson's view of the course of the American Bible Society was, in my judgment, formed on an imperfect knowledge of the facts.

implicitly, as, upon the whole, the safest and best extant; in consequence of which, the present Burmese version of the New Testament accords more nearly with the received English.

As to the merits of the translation, I must leave others to judge. I can only say that, though I have seldom done any thing to my own satisfaction, I am better satisfied with the translation of the New Testament than I ever expected to be. The language is, I believe, simple, plain, intelligible; and I have endeavored, I hope successfully, to make every sentence a faithful representation of the original. As to the Old Testament, I am not so well satisfied. The historical books are, perhaps, done pretty well; but the poetical and prophetical books are doubtless susceptible of much improvement, not merely in point of style, but in the rendering of difficult passages, about which the most eminent scholars are not yet agreed.

I commend the work, such as it is, to God, to the church in Burmah, and to my successors in this department of labor, begging them not to spare my errors, and yet not prematurely to correct a supposed error, without consulting the various authors whom I have consulted, and ascertaining the reasons of my position; and especially not to adopt a plausible correction, in one instance, without inquiring whether it is admissible and advisable in all parallel and similar passages.

In prosecuting the work, I have derived valuable aid from several of my missionary brethren, formerly especially from brother Wade and brother Jones, now of Bangkok, latterly from the brethren Mason, Comstock, and Stevens. Of several hundred suggestions that have been sent me from different quarters, I have sooner or later adopted by far the greater part, though, in many cases, with some modification. Nor ought I to forget my native brother, Moung En, my faithful fellow-laborer for many years, even before the present revision was begun — one of our most judicious and devoted assistants.

We expect now to suspend our operations in the printing department, as soon as two or three small things in the press are completed; and we have requested brother Osgood to devote his attention, for the present, to preaching and distributing Scriptures and tracts. We have an ample supply of books on hand for immediate use, especially as Burmah is closed against all missionary operations.

There is no prospect of war, nor ever has been, nor any preparation for war on either side, except in the wishes and imagination of certain individuals, here called "the war party," who, having ruined their interest in Burmah, see no hope of retrieving their affairs, but by a war.

Since finishing the revision of the Bible, I have resumed the charge of the native assistants, and turned my attention to the church, which has been sadly neglected for a long time. The assistants are employed in going about the town and neighboring villages, occupying zayats, and making known the gospel to all who will give them a hearing. They meet me at the native chapel every morning, after breakfast, and report the labors of the preceding day, and pray for the divine blessing on the day before them.

The church contains one hundred and forty-five native members, eight of whom are suspended from communion. Sixteen have been received during the year past, and there are several applicants for baptism, some of whom have been approved by the church.

Yours faithfully,

A. JUDSON.

On the 26th of September, 1835, Dr. Judson finished the revision of the Old Testament; on the 22d of March, 1837, he sent to the press the last sheet of the revised edition of the New Testament; and on the 24th of October, 1840, he completed the revision of the quarto edition of the Burmese Bible. The labor which he had marked out as his life's work was finished. He had always hoped to be permitted to execute a translation of the Scriptures into a language in which they had never before been known, and to collect a church among the heathen of one hundred members. His prayer had been more than granted. The translation, in several editions, had been already published; and he found that the natives themselves considered it pure Burman, and perfectly intelligible. He had long since baptized his hundredth convert; a church far exceeding that number had been gathered around him, well supplied with native preachers, and thus capable of extending itself in all directions. It seemed as if the work to which he had consecrated himself was done, and the objects for which he desired to live had become fewer and less interesting. His love for his family was ardent, and for their sakes alone did this world possess any attractions. His thoughts, which were ordinarily fixed with unusual continuity on heaven, seemed to turn thither with a more resistless longing, now that he had accomplished the work which he believed had been appointed to him; and the condition of his lungs and throat seemed to preclude the possibility of preaching to the heathen.*

Of the translation thus completed it may be proper here to offer a few remarks.

From the incidental allusions to it in Dr. Judson's letters and journals, we may form some conception of the labor which he spent upon this work. He had enjoyed the best opportunities which this country then afforded for the study of interpretation; and his progress in this department of knowledge had awakened the highest expectations of his future success as a translator. He had made himself familiar with the

---

* I observe by the latest accounts, that the excellent Dr. Scudder, who has devoted his life so successfully and unreservedly to the heathen, is at present threatened with blindness. He, however, congratulates himself that his affliction is not the loss of his voice, since, though blind, he may yet continue, as before, to preach the gospel to the perishing idolaters around him.

Burmese language to a degree never before attained by a foreigner. He determined, if it were possible, to transfer the ideas of the Holy Scriptures, from their original languages into Burman, in such a manner that his work should need as little revision as possible by his successors. He had an intense desire for rendering perfect every labor which he undertook; indeed, he said of himself that one of his failings was "a lust for finishing." Hence he availed himself of all the means of information which the progress of biblical science, either in Germany or America, placed within his reach. As early as the visit of Mrs. Ann Judson to this country, his demand for books was large, and it was all for the very best, the foundation books. I well remember the pleasure with which I stripped my library of what I considered some of its choicest treasures, to supply a part of his most urgent necessities. Thus he continued until he had surrounded himself with a most valuable apparatus for carrying on his work in the manner which its importance deserved.

While, however, he thus sought for aid from all the sources of modern and ancient learning, it is manifest from the whole of his correspondence that he used them all with the discretion of a master mind. It was not in his power to substitute the working of other intellects for the working of his own. He weighed with critical caution every recension of the text. He adopted no interpretation unless either convinced of its truth, or else sure that it was the nearest approximation to the truth that could be made in the present state of our knowledge. In order to reach this result, no labor was too great, and no investigation too protracted. United with all this that was intellectual there was, in his case, a mind deeply impressed with its own fallibility, and turning with unutterable longing to the Holy Spirit for guidance and illumination. The importance of his work to millions of immortal souls was ever present to his view. He had been called by the providence of God to unfold to a whole nation, in their own language, the revelation of the Most High. He conceived it to be a momentous undertaking; and a heavy weight would have rested on his soul if a single idea in the Scriptures had been obscurely rendered in consequence of haste, impatience, negligence, or culpable ignorance on the part of the translator.

But after he had satisfied himself as to the meaning of the original, a most difficult labor yet remained to be accomplished. It must be now transferred into a language peculiar and strongly idiomatic, and, moreover, a language destitute of terms in which to express the elementary and peculiar ideas of the New Testament. To furnish himself in this respect was the daily labor of his life. He read Burmese prose and poetry wherever he could find it. He was always surrounded by Burmese assistants and transcribers. As fast as his missionary brethren became acquainted with the language, he was incessantly calling upon them for corrections. They cheerfully aided him in this respect to the utmost of their power. Every correction or emendation he examined with the minutest care. Many — I think he says most — of them he adopted; and none of them were rejected without the most careful and diligent inquiry.

The result of this able and indefatigable labor was such as might have been expected. Competent judges affirm that Dr. Judson's translation of the Scriptures is the most perfect work of the kind that has yet appeared in India. On this subject it will not be inappropriate to introduce a few sentences from the pen of a gentleman high in rank in India, himself a distinguished linguist, and a proficient in the Burmese language.

To Judson it was granted, not only to found the spiritual Burman church of Christ, but also to give it the entire Bible in its own vernacular, thus securing that church's endurance and ultimate extension; the instances being few or none, of that word, after it has once struck root in any tongue, being ever wholly suppressed. Divine and human nature alike forbid such a result; for, when once it has become incorporated in a living tongue, holiness and love join hands with sin and weakness to perpetuate that word's life and dominion. We honor Wickliffe and Luther for their labors in their respective mother tongues; but what meed of praise is due to Judson for a translation of the Bible, *perfect as a literary* work, in a language so foreign to him as the Burmese? Future ages, under God's blessing, may decide this point, when his own forebodings, as he stood and pondered over the desolate, ruinous scene at Pugan, shall be fulfilled.

One and twenty years after his first landing at Rangoon, Judson finished his translation of the whole Bible; but, not satisfied with this first version, six more years were devoted to a revision of this great work; and on the 24th of October, 1840, the last sheet of the new edition was printed off. The revision cost him more time and labor than the first translation; for what he wrote in 1823 remained the object of his soul: "I never read a chapter without pencil in hand, and Griesbach and Parkhurst at my elbow; and it will be an object to me through life to bring the translation to such a state that it may be a standard work." The best judges pronounce it to be all that he aimed at making it, and also, what with him never was an object, an imperishable monument of the man's genius. We may venture to hazard the opinion that as Luther's Bible is now in the hands of Protestant Germany, so, three centuries hence, Judson's Bible will be the Bible of the Christian churches of Burmah.

The following extract from a letter written in November, 1852, by a missionary in Burmah, has been placed in my hands by the friend to whom it was addressed. It expresses very fully the estimation in which this version is held by those who are daily in the habit of using it, and of commending it to the natives. "The translation of the Holy Scriptures into the Burman language by the late Dr. Judson is admitted to be the best translation in India; that is, the translation has given more satisfaction to his contemporaries and successors than any translation of the Bible into any other Eastern language has done to associate missionaries in any other parts of India. It is free from all obscurity to the Burmese mind. It is read and understood perfectly. Its style and diction are as choice and elegant as the language itself, peculiarly honorific, would afford, and conveys, doubtless, the mind of the Spirit as perfectly as can be."

Judson might well have adopted the words of the blessed Eliot, the apostle to the Indian tribes, when he had finished his translation of the Scriptures into their dialect — "Prayer and pains, with the blessing of God, can accomplish any thing."

CHAPTER V.

ILLNESS OF HIS FAMILY. — PASSAGE TO CALCUTTA. — BEREAVEMENT AT SERAMPORE. — VOYAGE TO THE ISLE OF FRANCE AND MAULMAIN. — INCIDENTS OF THE VOYAGE. — BURMESE DICTIONARY.

1841-1845.

The ensuing chapter contains little else than a record of painful illness and a succession of voyages for the recovery of health. Mrs. Judson's constitution had already begun to fail, and the disease which completed its fatal work at St. Helena, though occasionally arrested for a short time, advanced with steady and resistless progress. The children were all alarmingly sick with similar complaints. The only remedy which remained was a sea voyage. It therefore became necessary to embark the whole family on board a vessel bound for Calcutta. They left Maulmain June 26, 1841, and arrived in Calcutta on the 11th of the following month. Here their youngest child, Henry Judson, died, and was buried in the mission burying ground at Serampore. From Serampore they took passage to the Isle of France, and thence to Maulmain. They arrived at the latter port on the 10th of December, 1841. The incidents of this voyage will be found to be both interesting and characteristic.

On his return, Dr. Judson, as usual, devoted himself to preaching, as far as the state of his lungs and throat would permit, and continued his labor on the

Burmese dictionary, in compliance with the instructions of the board.

Sickness, however, soon broke up his plans, and crippled his efforts. Mrs. Judson's health sank again. She was obliged to take various short voyages along the Tenasserim coast; but they were attended with only transient benefit. The letters which follow record these sad experiences.

To the Rev. G. S. Comstock of Arracan.

MAULMAIN, June 1, 1841.

DEAR BROTHER COMSTOCK: I received thankfully yours of 28th January, accompanied by a list of corrigenda. Some of them, or rather the greater part, I have adopted. Some of them relate to some of the most knotty questions in biblical criticism; and though not satisfied with my present position, I do not feel clear in changing it for yours, but must wait for further light. I hope you will go on with your corrigenda. Life is short, and every one ought to contribute all he can to *ascertain* and *promulgate* the precious truths of the inspired word. I hear, through a native letter, that you have baptized one person in Ramree. May it be the beginning of a glorious series. I trust you will live to see a great shaking among the dry bones of that valley, and that the Burmans around you will yet flock into this church as readily and as numerously as the Karens south of you. What is the prospect among the Ke-mees? I perceive that brother Stilson is again with you. I hope that he met with so much encouragement during his late visit as to induce him to return. My family are, at present, in the enjoyment of pretty good health. My own health is poor. I am ever and anon subject to some ailment; and every cold I take touches the sore place, and breaks down my voice. I have begun to dabble at the dictionary, as you advised, for want of ability to do something better; but it is such a chaotic affair, and seems to me so unmissionary, that I am constantly hoping that something will turn up to relieve me from the work. Yes, I received a copy of Bickersteth, but without an accompanying line. I was pretty sure, however, that it came from you, and valued it highly. O that we all had more of a spirit of prayer! Your similitude just meets my ideas. It was such considerations that helped sustain my mind while laboring in Rangoon many years, almost or quite alone, and without any success. It is certain that in due time we shall reap, if we faint not. Or, which is the same thing, if we sow faithfully, we shall, in due time, rejoice together with the Reaper. Best love to sister Comstock.

Your affectionate brother,
A. JUDSON.

To the Corresponding Secretary.

AT SEA, NEAR CALCUTTA, July 9, 1841.

MY DEAR SIR: I have been in great distress for several months, and think I have not written a letter to America, except one to my mother and sister, since the beginning of the year. Early in March, Mrs. Judson fell into a decline, and became quite confined to her bed. Three of the children had been, for some months, subject to a bowel complaint, which at length terminated in dysentery; and the two eldest were repeatedly at the point of death. The physicians, missionary brethren, and all my friends in Maulmain, became clamorous that I should try a voyage, as the only remaining means of saving the lives of the greater part of my family. But, extremely reluctant to incur the expense and encounter the breaking up which a voyage would occasion, I suffered myself to be beguiled by transient symptoms of convalescence, until, having lost two opportunities, and seeing most of my family in absolutely desperate circumstances, I consented to embrace the present opportunity, and embarked on the 26th ultimo. The voyage has had a beneficial effect on all the invalids, particularly on Mrs. Judson; but the two eldest children are subject to frequent relapses, and we have many fears about their ultimate recovery. I pay four hundred and thirty rupees for the present passage, and the return will probably cost as much more. I propose remaining a few months at Serampore, as a more healthy location than Calcutta, and hope to return to my station as soon as a prudent regard to the health of my family shall permit. My own health is good, except that my voice has never recovered its natural strength and tone, and I am under the necessity of refraining from much exertion.

Yours faithfully,
A. Judson.

To his Mother and Sister.

Serampore, July 24, 1841.

Dear Mother and Sister: We have suffered a great deal of sickness since I wrote you last, in April. Wife was confined to her bed for a long time, and appeared to be in a decline. Abby Ann, Adoniram, and Henry became worse with chronic dysentery, until the two eldest were, at different times, considered past recovery. When they were very ill, no one could take care of them but me; so that I was up every hour of the night, and sometimes scarcely lay down the whole night. The doctors then ordered us to sea, as the only means of saving life; and all my brethren and friends were very urgent to have us go, though no one hardly hoped that we could all get on board ship alive. How I managed to break up housekeeping, and pack up, and get my sick family and all the things aboard, I can hardly tell, now it is passed. But it was done somehow, and the children were stowed away in a range of berths I had made on one side of the cabin, and wife on the other, while I occupied a movable cot between the parties. The motion of the vessel and the sea air soon had a good effect on all the invalids; I left off giving medicines, and they daily improved. We embarked on the 26th of June, and arrived before Calcutta the 11th of July. But as soon as we came within the influence of the hot climate of Bengal, we began to relapse; and though we came up to this comparatively healthy place, and hired a nice dry house, on the very bank of the river, at forty rupees a month, I soon began to despair of attaining any radical and permanent recovery by remaining here. While looking about and considering what to do next, a pious captain called on us, with whom we had some acquaintance at Maulmain, whose vessel was going to the Isle of France and thence to Maulmain; and he made us such a kind proposal, that we thought we could go the circuitous voyage at no more expense than we had calculated it would cost to return direct. We should then have the benefit of being at sea two months or more, and a few weeks' residence at the Isle of France, the most healthy part of the East. We expect to break up once more and embark in the course of ten days. Thus we are tossed about when we would fain be at our work; but God orders all things for the best. At present no one of the family is dangerously ill. Abby is much better; Adoniram is considerably better, though he looks very thin and pale; Henry is still very poorly; their mother is sometimes better, sometimes worse. I dread going to sea next month, in the Bay of Bengal, it being a very dangerous month; but there seems to be no alternative. May God preserve us safely, and give me the pleasure of writing you from Port Louis, the place, you may recollect, to which I once repaired when driven away from Bengal, nearly thirty years ago.

Is it possible that my last from you is June, 1839, above two years ago? Yet so it is, by my record. And how many have I written you since that date? Four! and this is the fifth! When you see Mrs. Stevens again, don't complain to her how seldom you get letters from me, will you? I suppose, however, that you have not written me lately, expecting that if I was not better, I should accept the invitation of the board, and come home. My health is now good. I am astonished at what I have gone through the last four months. Frequently I have hardly known what sleep and regular meals meant; only my lungs are still weak, and I am obliged to be careful how I use them in public. I want very much to hear from you. The latest indirect intelligence is the fol lowing line from the Mission Rooms, dated June 11, 1840: "We have the pleasure to inform you that Mrs. Abigail Judson sent to the rooms, in cash, seventy-five dollars for your personal benefit, which sum is passed to your credit, in our books of date May 22, 1840." You may depend we take great care of such presents, spending only what is necessary, and laying by the remainder for a rainy day. And there has been no scarcity of such days lately. However, we have quite a sufficiency of the good things of this life, and beg you will never embarrass or stint yourselves to help us. We sometimes feel anxious about the poor children, in case they should be left orphans; but we endeavor to commit them to the care of our and their heavenly Father. May they, and all our posterity to the latest time, belong to Christ, and be devoted to his service. I should be glad to see your faces once more in the flesh, but it will probably never be. May God dwell in your house and your hearts; may he bless you by day and by night, in body and in soul, in time and in eternity. Wife desires to be kindly remembered, and I remain, as ever,

Your affectionate son and brother,

A. JUDSON.

SERAMPORE, August 1, 1841.

DEAR MOTHER AND SISTER: I wrote you on the 24th ultimo. Perhaps this letter will go by the same conveyance. Wife went down to Calcutta, for a few days, to do a little business, leaving the two younger children with me. On the 27th dear little Henry's disorder took an unfavorable turn. He had derived less benefit from the voyage and change than the other children, being too young to have his mind engaged and diverted, which greatly contributes to bodily recovery; and being considered less dangerously ill than the others, had, perhaps, less attention paid him than was desirable. His disorder had continued to hold on, though at times greatly mitigated. On the 28th he grew worse, and I wrote down for his mother and in the evening began to despair of his life. On the 29th the doctor gave him up, and we ceased from giving him any more medicine, for he could keep none on his stomach a single minute; and my only prayer was, that he might not die before his mother arrived. O, what heavy hours now passed! She arrived with the other children in the night, about two o'clock, and sprang to the cradle of the little sufferer, and could not think that he was really in a dying state. I let her take her own way, and she contrived to give him a little wine and water, which, however, could be of no avail; and when morning came, the marks of death on the countenance were too visible for even the unwilling mother to refuse to acknowledge. We spent the day hanging over our dying babe, and giving him some liquid, for which he was always calling, to relieve his burning thirst. When I said, "Henry, my son," he would raise his sinking eyelids, and try to stretch out his little arms for me to take him; but he could not bear to be held more than a moment before he would cry to be laid down again. O, how restless did he spend his last day, rolling from side to side, and crying out, "*Nahnee*," his imperfect pronunciation of *naughty*, by which term he was in the habit of expressing his disapprobation or dissatisfaction. In the afternoon he became convulsed for a few moments, and our hearts were rent to witness the distortion of his dear little mouth and face. After that he was more quiet; but towards evening he probably had some violent stroke of death, for he suddenly screamed out in great pain. In the evening he had another turn of convulsion. His mother lay down by his side, and, worn out with fatigue, fell fast asleep. About nine o'clock I had gone into another room, and was lying down, when a servant called me. He began to breathe loud, indicative of the closing scene. I let the mother sleep — sat down by his side, and, presently called, as usual, "Henry, my son;" upon which he opened his eyes, and looked at me more intelligently and affectionately than he had been able to do for some time; but the effort was too great, and he ceased to breathe. I instantly awoke his mother; he then gave two or three expiring gasps, and it was all over. I stripped the little emaciated body, and washed it, while his mother, with the help of a servant, made a suitable gown; and by eleven o'clock he was laid out in the same cradle in which he died. For a few days Elnathan had been ill with a severe cough and fever, and my attention had been divided between the two. After poor Henry was quiet, we turned all our attention to the others. The two elder children were much better. Next morning we had a coffin made, in which we placed our dear child; and sometimes, when other avocations permitted, looked at him through the day. And O, how sweet was his dead face! though there was an expression of pain lurking in some of the features. At night, a few of our friends came together, and we carried the coffin to the mission burial ground, where, after a prayer by Mr. Mack, the body was deposited in its final resting-place. Farewell, my darling son Henry. While thy little body rests in the grave, I trust that thy spirit, through the grace of Jesus Christ, is resting in paradise. We intend to order a small monument erected with this inscription: "The grave of Henry Judson, youngest son of the Rev. A. Judson, of Maulmain, who died July 30, 1841, aged one year and seven months."

Elnathan was very ill last night, and is not much better to-day. We tremble for him. The vessel in which we are going to the Isle of France, we hear, is to remain a few days longer, so that I will add a further line before leaving.

Calcutta, August 6. We have come down to this place with a view to embarking; but the vessel is still detained. Elnathan appears to be very ill, with a complication of complaints. We are in great distress about him. The two elder children continue better.

In haste, yours affectionately,

A. JUDSON.

August 13. We are still waiting the moving of the vessel, but shall positively go on board the 16th. Elnathan is much better, so that we hope the danger of losing him is past.

The other children continue to improve. Farewell for the present.

P. S. I enclose a small lock of poor dear Henry's hair. We are very sad whenever we think of that bright, sweet boy. It was the will of God that he should be taken from us; so we must be resigned, and I hope that he is now waiting to welcome us to the paradise where, we trust, he has safely arrived. Two vessels have just come in from America, but we have got nothing from you. Perhaps there may be a letter or some box which will be forwarded to Maulmain.

To a Friend.

OFF SAUGUR, August 22, 1841.

DEAR MRS. H.: We are on board the Ramsay, pitching most fearfully. We have been lying several days waiting for the weather, and have now got up anchor, so that I am writing a line or two to send back by the pilot.

The three surviving children are getting better, though Pwen is still far from well. We received the greatest kindness at Serampore, and became much attached to them all. At Calcutta, we lived with Mr. S., a young missionary who has succeeded to the place of Mr. E. He and his wife were indefatigable in their endeavors to make us comfortable. We became acquainted also with Mr. Mackay, one of the most estimable men in Calcutta; but he is in a most miserable state of health. Mrs. Judson looks as thin and pale as ever; but I hope the long voyage before us will restore her and the children to perfect health.

A. JUDSON.

To his Mother and Sister.

PORT LOUIS, ISLE OF FRANCE, October 18, 1841.

DEAR MOTHER AND SISTER: My last was dated on the eve of embarking at Calcutta, which we did on the 16th of August, and arrived here on the first instant; so that we were six weeks on the passage; and it was one of the most stormy voyages I ever experienced. At one time we lost half our masts and sails, and the rolling and pitching of the ship were dreadful. We, however, refitted, though at sea and suffering under very rough weather, and came at last into port in good condition. In other respects we were very comfortable on board. The captain was a pious man, and we had worship every Lord's day and every evening. Most of the crew, who were Europeans, attended worship; and I hope that some good was done. Sixteen, besides the captain and myself, solemnly subscribed their names to a resolution to serve the Lord; and though they have been exposed to some temptations since their arrival in port, I do not hear that a single one has fallen. In the early part of the voyage, Abby Ann and Elnathan recovered from the complaint with which they had been ill; but poor Adoniram remained the same, suffering under chronic dysentery, unaffected by any course of medicine or change of climate. A few days before our arrival here, some favorable symptoms began to appear; but latterly he has had some severe relapses, so that we are still trembling for the result. The poor boy has been ill so long, that he seems to have stopped growing. . . . Elnathan, on the contrary, who has had but little illness, is nearly as thick as long, has a broad back and face, is actually stouter and stronger than his elder brother. . . . Adoniram has lately improved in reading. May he be spared to grow up and become a true Christian and a minister. You see I still harp upon the children when writing to you. But, in fact, I have little else to harp upon in this place. Port Louis contains about thirty thousand inhabitants — a French place, though now under English government, and a very wicked place; very few religious people, not more than eight or ten that speak English. We are living in the house of Mr. Kelsey. We have a small room, and board at his table. Every article of food and clothing is most exorbitantly dear. A fowl is one dollar, and a common pair of shoes three dollars, and every other article almost in the same proportion. I hope we shall get away before long, for we have been at so much expense the past year, on account of sickness and travelling, that I expect, at the end of it, we shall be pretty deeply in debt. However, poor Henry is gone, so that we have not him to provide for. And yet how gladly should we undertake to provide for him, if he could only be restored to us! But no. He is gone forever. The far-distant burial ground of Serampore contains his precious remains. May the three remaining ones be spared to us! How could we sustain another and a severer bereavement? The ship in which we are sailing will leave this for Maulmain in about ten days. There is one vessel here bound to New York, and expected to sail in three or four days; so I will keep this letter open, in hope of adding a further line, before she sails.

October 20. I hear that the New York vessel sails to-day; so that I have but little more to add, except that Adoniram seems to be really getting better. His symptoms are certainly better, for a few days, than they have been since he was first taken. We trust the return voyage will effect his complete cure.

We expect head winds most of our way back, and shall not be in Maulmain much before the end of the year. I hope to find letters from you waiting me there. My last from you was dated June 17, '39, and received December 11, nearly two years ago! Is not that too bad? Whereas this is my *sixth*, since I received your last! Do pray write oftener, without reference to opportunities of sending, and forward your letters to the care of Mr. Peck, and they will reach me in due time.

Farewell once more. It is so long since I heard from you, that I know not whether you are both living. May we all meet at last in heaven. Pray for the children, that they may be early converted, and meet us there. Abby Ann shows much tenderness of feeling on the subject of religion.

Your ever-affectionate son and brother,

A. JUDSON.

To the Corresponding Secretary.

Port Louis, Isle of France, October 18, 1841.

My dear Sir: The complaint to which most of the members of my family became subject in Maulmain has proved most obstinate. But during our long and tedious voyage to this place, which we accomplished on the 1st instant, about six weeks after embarking, we all recovered our health, except Adoniram, the eldest son, who seemed to derive no benefit from any course of medicine or change of climate until we were near this island, when some favorable symptoms began to appear. Still he is subject to severe relapses, and we almost despair of his final recovery. Mrs. Judson has quite recovered from the dreadful prostration she suffered in Maulmain; and I hope that, whatever may be the fate of some of the children, we shall be able ere long to return to our station, and resume our labors with renewed strength, during the period that may yet be allowed us to labor on earth.

Yours faithfully,
A. Judson.

Maulmain, December 17, 1841.

Rev. and dear Sir: My last was dated October 18, at the Isle of France. We left that place the 1st of November, and arrived here the 10th instant, the health of my family greatly improved, though the eldest son is yet subject to severe relapses. Still, we hope that he is decidedly convalescent.

Captain Hamlin, of the ship Ramsay, has declined taking any compensation for our passage from Calcutta to Port Louis and thence to this place. The double passage would have cost above two thousand rupees, if he had made a fair charge. Indeed, we should not have thought of attempting such a circuitous and expensive voyage, though necessary to save life, had he not given us to understand that it should cost the board little or nothing. On arriving here I sent him four hundred rupees, the sum which it would have cost us to have returned direct from Calcutta, saying that I considered it no adequate compensation, but a small expression of gratitude. He, however, sent it back, saying that he considered it a privilege to have been able to show some kindness to the servants of Christ. His kindness to us has, indeed, been unwearied; and I feel wholly unable to repay the great obligation under which he has laid us. I presume, from what I have heard him say, that he would have done the same favor to any other missionary of the board. I propose, therefore, that you send him a formal letter of thanks, accompanied with what he would prize more than money — some valuable religious books, say a set of the Comprehensive Commentary, or such other as you shall think suitable. If you think proper to adopt my suggestion, please to address to "Captain Thomas Hamlin, *Jr.*, Greenock, Scotland," and oblige me with a copy of the letter, which I should like to show to my friends here. He will leave this in about a month, with a cargo of timber, on his way home, touching at the Isle of France; so that your communication would probably reach him before leaving Greenock on another voyage.

It afforded me much gratification, last Sunday, to lead him into the Maulmain baptistery, with the first officer of the ship and two of the seamen. A native woman also, who had just been received by the church, made one of the party. Several other officers and seamen of the ship are hopefully pious There are nineteen of us in all, who have affixed our names to a covenant in the ship's great Bible, to serve the Lord; but two of the number who signed, on the passage out, yielded to temptation at Port Louis. Many of them have been converted, or had previous impressions deepened, through the faithful dealing of Captain Hamlin. He is, indeed, one of the most consistent, zealous, devoted Christians I have met in this part of the world.

You will readily conceive how happy we are on finding ourselves once more in the bosom of the mission — the society of our dear missionary associates, and the native Christians. We are only sad when we remember the sweet little one, whom we were obliged to leave behind, in the burial ground at Serampore.

I have but little to add in regard to the native church. Two persons have been added during my absence, and a few individuals have misbehaved and been suspended from communion; but the church, as a body, have behaved well, and the assistants have been diligent and faithful.

Yours affectionately,
A. JUDSON.

The following account of Dr. Judson's labors during his voyage to Port Louis and Maulmain is extracted from a pamphlet published in Greenock, entitled " A Brief Narrative of the last Voyage of the Ship Ramsay, of Greenock; illustrative of the Beneficial Effects of Total Abstinence, and the Success of the Gospel in the Conversion of a Number of the Crew, the Formation of a Church on Board, &c., &c. Compiled by John Simpson, Minister of the Gospel. Greenock." I have inserted only that part of this narrative which refers to the labors of Dr. Judson. It illustrates most forcibly the steady bias of his mind, and his incessant labor for the salvation of his fellow-men. Whether on land or at sea, surrounded by his family at home or watching over their sick beds on shipboard, he was ever striving to win those around him to Christ. In this, as in other cases, he seems to have labored with remarkable success; and the Lord graciously gave him many of the souls of those who sailed with him.

After remaining about four weeks in Bombay, the Ramsay sailed for Maulmain, in Burmah, and from thence to Calcutta. During these passages, some favorable impressions seemed to have been produced in the minds of the crew; and on their arrival at Calcutta they conducted themselves with greater propriety than at any of the former ports: here they regularly attended the floating chapel. Whilst the ship was at Calcutta, the captain paid a visit to the Baptist missionary establishment at Serampore. There he fell in with the indefatigable missionary, Dr. Judson, from Burmah, who was at Serampore with his family, for the improvement of their health. As the Ramsay was shortly to sail for the Island of Mauritius, and from thence to Maulmain, — Dr. Judson's residence, — Captain Hamlin kindly offered them a passage, in the hope that it would be conducive to the object they had in view. Having accepted the offer thus generously made to him and his family, Dr. Judson felt a strong desire to be useful to the seamen, in whose dangers he was about to share. He made it a matter of prayer to God that he might be instrumental in turning some of them from the error of their ways; and, before going on board, expressed a conviction that God had heard him, and that he would answer him in communicating his grace to some, if not to all, of the crew. After putting to sea, worship was conducted by Dr. Judson and the captain alternately; but on the Sabbaths the whole of the services were conducted by the doctor. Possessing all his mental vigor, and his ardent love for souls having suffered no abatement, he availed himself of these opportunities, in addition to private instruction, to promote the great end he had in view, and for which he had so earnestly prayed, previous to his embarking on board the Ramsay. His manner of address was of the most touching description, and seldom failed in making the big tear roll down the weather-beaten cheeks of his hardy auditory. It soon became apparent that he was not laboring in vain, nor spending his strength for nought. Before their arrival at the Mauritius, three of the seamen gave pleasing evidence of being converted to God. During their stay at the Mauritius, public worship was held on board every Sabbath, and was well attended, both by seamen and landsmen. Religion was in a languid state amongst the inhabitants generally. There were, however, a few who seemed concerned for the advancement of Christ's kingdom, and by them it had been in contemplation to fit up a seaman's chapel. They had even gone so far as to make application to the late benevolent governor,

Sir Lionel Smith, for the use of an old ship lying there, belonging to government; the application had been favorably received; still nothing had been done towards effecting the object they had in view, till the captain of the Ramsay, hearing how matters stood, set about raising subscriptions towards fitting up the said vessel as a Bethel: he likewise presented another memorial to the governor, but was obliged to leave at this time, without seeing the work accomplished.

Leaving the Island of Mauritius, their next port of destination was Maulmain, in Burmah. On the passage, the usual religious services were attended to; and, in addition to the ordinary meetings, an extra one, for prayer and exhortation, was held every Wednesday evening, and conducted by the seamen who had professed the name of Christ. This meeting was the means of effecting much good. Amongst other things which came before their minds was the subject of baptism. By a diligent perusal of the word of God, and the instructions of Dr. Judson, the new converts were convinced that baptism by immersion was the scriptural mode, and that it was their duty, as believers in Christ, to be baptized in his name. Hence they determined, with the captain, — who had doubts regarding the truth of infant baptism, before his leaving home, — to be baptized on the first convenient opportunity after reaching Maulmain. Accordingly, on the first Sabbath after their arrival, the captain, mate, and two of the seamen, together with a Burmese female, were " buried with Christ by baptism," in presence of a large assemblage of natives and others, who appeared to take a deep interest in all the solemn services that were attended to. The ordinance was administered by Dr. Judson.

At Maulmain there are two Baptist churches — one for the natives, which is supplied by Dr. Judson; the other for Europeans, &c., which is supplied by assistant missionaries. Both churches were in a flourishing condition. The missionary work was being zealously prosecuted, and many of the heathen were renouncing their idols and embracing the Saviour. The labors of the missionaries had been eminently successful among the Karen tribe. Whilst at Maulmain, the captain and mate paid a visit to one of the villages of these interesting people. On their arrival they found the chief, — who acts also as their spiritual teacher, — with nearly the whole of the villagers, busily engaged in their rice fields. On the *gong* being sounded, which was the signal for the arrival of the missionaries, they flocked into the native chapel; and, after greeting affectionately their teachers, they turned to the captain and mate, and asked their chief, " Do these men love Christ ? " Being answered in the affirmative, they received them with much cordiality, and, on their departure, loaded their boat with fruit, &c., &c.

The Ramsay remained at Maulmain eight weeks, during which time the intercourse of the crew with the Christians on shore was of the most pleasing description. The evening before they sailed from this place, Dr. Judson delivered a farewell address on board the Ramsay, which produced a deep and solemn impression. All were melted into tears, as was the case with Dr. Judson himself. He alluded to the providential manner in which he had been brought amongst them, the many happy and profitable hours he had spent in their society, the converting grace of God which they had all been privileged to witness, and some to experience; and those who professed the faith he exhorted "that with purpose of heart they would cleave unto the Lord;" and those who had still held out against the entreaties of melting mercy he besought to be reconciled to God. After engaging in solemn prayer for all on board, and giving them his parting blessing, he retired, whilst, like Paul's Christian brethren at Ephesus, "they sorrowed most of all for the words which he spake, that they should see his face no more."

The following is a copy of the engagement entered into by the persons on board the Ramsay, to whicn reference is made in the preceding letters.

We, the undersigned, on board the ship Ramsay, agree with

one another, and promise before God that we will endeavor to live as sincere Christians ought to live, avoiding all known sins so far as possible, and striving to keep all the commands of God, in humble dependence on the grace and strength which he may be pleased to impart unto us.

THOMAS HAMLIN,	JOHN CHARLEY,
A. JUDSON,	DONALD MCINTYRE,
JOHN NEVIN,	JAMES STEPHENSON,
JOHN LAING,	ALEXANDER KIDDOCK,
JOHN RENNIE,	DAVID MORRISON,
ROBERT ANDERSON,	GEORGE WILLIAMS,
ALEXANDER BOWERS,	GEORGE JOHNSON,
ARCHIBALD SUTHERLAND,	GEORGE CRADDIE,
JAMES FARQUHAR,	HUGH MCKENYAN,
JAMES SMYLIE,	——— BROADHEAD,
DUNCAN GRAY,	——— KELLY.
DAVID CARBET,	

To his Mother and Sister.

MAULMAIN, December 26, 1841.

DEAR MOTHER AND SISTER: My last to you was dated October 20, at Port Louis. We left there on the 1st of November, and arrived here on the 10th instant. Adoniram is, we trust, really convalescent, though subject to relapses. Whether he will ever perfectly recover in this climate, is somewhat doubtful. It is now the cold season, and he is generally pretty well; but unless he gets perfectly well, so that the disorder is quite eradicated before the hot season, which comes on in March and April, we fear for the result. The other children are quite well, and their mother, except that she is not so stout and strong as formerly. Abby can read any easy reading, and delights to commit verses to memory, and is very careful to pray morning and evening. Adoniram can read a little, but on account of his illness his education has been very much neglected. Elnathan can boast of no great proficiency in literature, being only three and a half years old. . . I don't know which we love the most. We were all most happy to get back to our old home, after nearly six months' wandering. We found all well. The church remained in a pretty good state. Two had been added by baptism, and one more I baptized the next Sunday after my arrival. At the same time I had the pleasure of leading into the Maulmain baptistery the pious captain of the Ramsay, his first officer, and two of the crew. Several others, also, of the officers and crew of the ship are, I hope, partakers of divine grace. Captain Hamlin has declined taking any compensation of the board for our circuitous passage. Was not this very kind? He is truly one of the most devoted, excellent Christians I have ever met in this part of the world.

I was disappointed not to find any letter from you on my arrival here. It is now a long time since I heard even indirectly from you. When I remember mother's great age and feeble state of health, I should not be surprised any time to hear that her probation was passed, and that she had gone to paradise. And what would become of you, my dear sister, if you should be left alone? I should wish you were with me. Could you not come out? The board would pay your passage with that of their missionaries who might be coming out; and you might always depend on a room and a place at my table, and all such necessaries and comforts of life as I can obtain myself, in this foreign land. And my dear wife would be happy to welcome you, and the children would run to see their aunt, of whom they hear so frequently. But still I hope that mother may yet live many years to diffuse a salutary influence around her, and grow more mature for that blessed world to which she is hastening, and where, I trust, we shall all meet, when the trials and troubles, the separations and bereavements, of this life are passed forever. I wonder whether I should know you if we met? I think I should know mother. Probably neither of you would know me. How long it is since we parted! Thirty years next February, on the 31 of the month, I took leave of my parents, in

Plymouth, and on the 7th of my sister and brother, in Boston; and on the 19th embarked for the East. Farewell, my dear mother and sister. If we are not to meet in this world, may we have a happy meeting in eternity, to part no more.

Your ever affectionate son and brother,
A. JUDSON.

MAULMAIN, May 8, 1842.

DEAR MOTHER AND SISTER: Since my last to you, dated December 26, 1841, I have received yours of July 21, 1841, containing many interesting items concerning yourselves and townspeople and distant relatives. You remark that you delayed writing for want of information from Boston. You never need wait a day for such information. You have only to direct your letter thus, "Rev. A. Judson, care of Rev. S. Peck, 17 Joy's Buildings, Washington Street, Boston," and put it into the post office at Plymouth. Mr. Peck will erase the latter part of the direction, and re-direct to Maulmain, and forward with other letters, which are always accumulating at the Mission Rooms.

It is very trying weather with us at present. The rains, which commonly commence the 1st of May, still hold off, except an occasional shower; and in the intervals it is melting hot, and sometimes dreadfully oppressive.

The house which we occupied has been removed, to form, with other materials, a house for Mr. Stevens, on an adjoining lot; and we have moved into his old house, considerably improved, and find it much more cool and comfortable than the other. At the corner of the house we now occupy, I have put up a small one, containing a bed room, and small bathing room adjoining, partly with a view to accommodate company, and partly in the hope that dear sister, if left alone, will think of coming out to see us. So, if the people of Plymouth get tired of you, you may be sure of a home with your most affectionate brother.

My cough still troubles me. I was lately obliged to stop preaching entirely; but I am now better, and preach half the time — that is, one sermon on Sundays, and conduct worship every other evening in the week. The other half is taken by brother Osgood, assisted by some of the other brethren. There have been very few additions to the church lately. It stands at about one hundred and sixty.

Once more farewell. How happy it will be to meet safe in heaven at last!

Your affectionate brother,

A. JUDSON.

To the Corresponding Secretary.

MAULMAIN, June 28, 1842.

. . . But the board does know that Burmah proper has been long abandoned, and abandoned in such circumstances as renders it impossible even to circulate tracts, or employ a native assistant; nor do I see any prospect of the country's being reoccupied, unless there should be an opening for me to make an attempt, of which I entertain some faint hope. I request, therefore, that the board would say whether they think such an attempt advisable, and whether they would encourage me in making it or not. I should be glad if they would take the subject into immediate consideration, and let me have an answer as early as possible; for I know not how soon an opportunity may occur, though I have no definite expectation, nor, indeed, any but the faintest hope. And such being the case, I wish no *public* expectation to be excited.

I received your kind letter of February 1. Your sympathizing wishes are realized in the restoration of my family to health, after a long year's continued illness. We lost but one out of the number, though there were times when I expected to lose them all.

The complaint of my throat and lungs is much better. I have had but one relapse, and that comparatively slight, since my return; so that I can preach with but little difficulty, though, from prudence, I preach but once on Lord's days, and conduct worship every other day in the week.

Yours faithfully and affectionately,
A. JUDSON.

Rules of Life.

August 9, 1842.

1. Be more careful to observe the seasons of secret prayer.
2. Never indulge resentful feelings towards any person.
3. Embrace every opportunity of exercising kind feelings, and doing good to others, especially to the household of faith.
4. Sweet in temper, face, and word,
    To please an ever-present Lord.

Renewed December 31, 1842.

December 31, 1842. Resolved to make the desire to please Christ the grand motive of all my actions.

To George D. Boardman.

MAULMAIN, April 7, 1843.

MY DEAR GEORGE: You cannot tell how rejoiced we have been, and thankful to God, on hearing that you have professed religion and given yourself to the Saviour. Your fond mother has shed many tears of joy over this happy event. May you be a growing Christian, and become a faithful minister of the gospel, and follow the footsteps of your sainted father, as he followed Christ. Perhaps I shall live to introduce you into the missionary field. Who knows but that you will yet be my colleague and successor in the pastorship of the Maulmain church?

I think we have not written you since the birth of your youngest brother, which took place the 8th of July last. We have named him after the one that died at Serampore. The names of your sister and brothers now stand thus: Abby Ann, Adoniram, Elnathan, and Henry Hall. I hope that, since you now know the way to the throne of grace, you will pray for them, that they may all, in early life, become acquainted with the Saviour's dying love, and be prepared to meet you in heaven.

Your mother sends you herewith a copy of her translation of the first part of the Pilgrim's Progress. If you have not yet read the work in English, you will find it a most interesting and profitable book.

Give our warmest love to your dear and excellent friends, Mr. and Mrs. Newton. You cannot love, and esteem, and revere them too much. Yet we hope you will not bestow *all* your love upon them; but remember that you have an own mother in this remote land, who thinks of you, her eldest son, every day; and do write us a letter on every returning birthday.

Do you remember how I carried you down to Amherst, and put you on board the ship that took you far away?

Your affectionate father,
A. JUDSON.

To the Corresponding Secretary.

MAULMAIN, July 13, 1843.

DEAR BROTHER: I never think, without some uneasiness, of the infrequency of my communications to the board; and if I had not an apology at hand, I should feel self-condemned. A person employed in direct missionary work among the natives, especially if his employ is somewhat itinerant, can easily make long and interesting journals. The first epithet, at least, may be applied to some of my earlier communications. But it has been my lot, for many years past, to spend most of my time over the study table; and my itinerating has scarcely extended beyond the limits of my morning walks and the precincts of the mission enclosure. Several years were spent in translating the Bible, and several more in revising it and carrying the last edition through the press. After which, in May last year, I commenced a dictionary of the language, a work which I had resolved and re-resolved never to touch. But it is not in man that walketh to direct his steps. The board and my brethren repeatedly urged me to prepare a dictionary the one printed in 1826 being exceedingly imperfect; and as Burmah continued shut against our labors, and there were several missionaries in this place, I concluded that I could not do better than to comply.

We are apt to magnify the importance of any undertaking in which we are warmly engaged. Perhaps it is from the influence of that principle, that, notwithstanding my long-cherished aversion to the work, I have come to think it very important; and that, having seen the accomplishment of two objects on which I set my heart when I first came out to the East, the establishment of a church of converted natives, and the translation of the Bible into their language, I now beguile my daily toil with the prospect of compassing a third, which may be compared to a causeway, designed to facilitate the transmission of all knowledge, religious and scientific, from one people to the other.

It was my first intention to make a single work, Burmese and English; but as I proceeded, I discovered many reasons for constructing a double work, in two parts, the first English and Burmese, the second Burmese and English. I hope, by daily, uninterrupted labor, to have the whole ready for the press by the end of 1845. Not, indeed, that I count on living so long. Above thirty years spent in a tropical climate — to-day is the twenty-ninth anniversary of my arrival in Burmah — leaves but little ground to build future plans upon. But I feel it my duty to plod on, while daylight shall last, looking out for the night, and ready to bequeath both the plodding and the profit to any brother who shall be willing to carry on and complete the work, when I shall have obtained my discharge. I try thus to make out an apology for my apparent delinquencies, which I beg the board to accept; and believe me

Yours faithfully,

A. JUDSON.

P. S. Your favor of the 23d March has been duly received. In regard to the subject mentioned, I shall be ready to do whatever the board and my brethren, to whom you have referred the subject, shall recommend.

To his little Daughter, at Mergui.

MAULMAIN, March 9, 1845.

MY DEAR DAUGHTER: Your letters to me and your brothers, together with the shells from Mergui, arrived this afternoon in the Burmese box, which mamma sent by the steamer. The boys are delighted with the shells, and Henry has picked out some for his own; and they have agreed to give me for my share the large coral shell. They have already written some letters to you, and mamma, and Charlie, which I shall send by return of steamer; and perhaps they will add some more, as this is such a favorable opportunity. It is now between eight and nine o'clock in the evening. I have had a little meeting with Adoniram and Elnathan, and now they are asleep. Edward has become a fat little fellow; I am sure you would not know him again. He begins to look pleased when he is played with. But he has not yet made any inquiries about his absent mother and sister. Indeed, I doubt much whether he is aware that he has any such relatives. Or if he ever exercises his mind on such abstruse topics, perhaps he fancies that black Ah-mah is his mother, since she nurses him, and does not know what a fair, beautiful, fond mother he has at Mergui, who thinks of him every day. However, when he gets larger, we will tell him all about these matters.

I am getting the carpenters to make a new cot for you, longer than your old one. That I have given to Adoniram, and his to Elnathan. Both the kittens are dead, and the old yellow cat has been missing for several days. She was very thin, and apparently very ill, when we last saw her. So I suppose she crept away into some secret place, and lay down and died. Alas! poor pussy!

I pray every day that somewhere during your travels with dear mamma, you may receive a blessing from God, so that you will return a true Christian, and set such an example before your brothers as will induce them to try to follow your steps. Think of the dear Saviour every day, and frequently lift up your heart in fervent prayer to God, that he will give you his converting, sanctifying grace, and make you his own child. Try to subdue every evil passion, and avoid all bad conduct. *If you trust in the Saviour and try to be good, he will make you good.* In your daily deportment and intercourse with others, remember these two lines: —

" Sweet in *temper, face,* and *word,*
To please an ever-present Lord."

Your affectionate father,
A. JUDSON.

Love to dear Charlie.

To Mrs. Judson, at Tavoy.

MAULMAIN, March 23, 1845.

MY DEAREST LOVE: Your short letter from Goodrich's Plains came in this afternoon most unexpectedly. I am sorry that your short account of yourself is unsatisfactory. My first impression was to go down in the steamer, fearing what the result of another relapse may be, and hoping to be some comfort and use to you in your weak state. But since worship at the English chapel, I have sought an interview with Captain Briggs; and from his account, and from the fact that the steamer expects to leave Tavoy, next time, almost immediately on rearriving, I have concluded not to go; especially as the nurse, though she does well by the baby, is frequently quarrelling with A-moo and others, and threatening to quit. I don't think she really will quit; but I should be most unwilling to leave the baby under these circumstances. Captain Briggs confirms what you write, that you think your disease is really checked, so that I have now sanguine hopes of your speedy recovery. Whether we conclude to spend a month at Amherst or not, I think you had better come up at once in the steamer. We can arrange all things more comfortably, and provide a house, and go down in boats at any time. We cannot, however, pursue the boat system half so well at Amherst as here, on account of the difficulty of landing. And if you do not return pretty well, I have all along thought that that course would be the most beneficial to you. However, we must be guided by circumstances. At any rate we must do that which will be most conducive to your recovery. I am afraid that Charlie's eye teeth will pull him down lower. Glad to hear such good accounts of Abby Ann. I am sure she has been a great comfort to you.

March 24. Captain Russell has just kindly called on me — says I had better send letters on board this afternoon, as he expects, though not certain, to leave to-morrow morning. He thinks he shall be back next Monday. I have given out that you may be expected at that time, and the news occasions general joy. I am still dreadfully anxious about your health. I fear that Briggs and Russell show me the fair side to keep me quiet. Captain Russell admits that you are *thinner* and *weaker* than when you left here. But if your complaint is actually subdued, you will soon recover. We are all well. Miss Lathrop teaches the children during Miss Newlove's visit at Amherst. We hear that Tremenheere has now a better appointment at Calcutta, which he will accept. The pious officers are all gone, and the 84th regiment is going off as fast as vessels are ready for them. No new troops yet arrived.

I have nothing in particular to say to Abby, only that I hope she will return improved in every respect, and set a good example before her brothers, who have not had her advantages. My love to the dear Masons, with whom I suppose you are living.

Ever most affectionately,

A. JUDSON.

CHAPTER VI.

ILNESS OF MRS. JUDSON. — VOYAGE TO THE UNITED STATES. — DEATH OF MRS. JUDSON. — BURIAL AT ST. HELENA. — OBITUARY NOTICE. — RECEPTION AND ADDRESSES IN THE UNITED STATES.

1845.

THE health of Mrs. Judson, which had been for some time declining, had now become so thoroughly prostrated that a protracted sea voyage to a northern climate offered to her the only hope of restoration. She had become so weak that Dr. Judson was obliged to accompany her. Strong as were his domestic affections, he would have remained at Maulmain prosecuting his missionary work, if she had been able to undertake the voyage alone. As, however, this could not be done, he was unwilling to allow his labor to be suspended. He therefore took with him two of his assistants, by whose aid he could pursue the work of the dictionary, either on shipboard or in the United States, and embarked with his wife and three of his children for England in the ship Paragon, April 26, 1845.

They arrived at Port Louis, Isle of France, on the 5th of the following July. Here the health of Mrs. Judson appeared so much improved that Dr. Judson and she determined to separate, he to return to Maulmain, and she, with the children, to prosecute her voyage to this country. A more marked example of self-sacrificing adherence to principle than this can scarcely be conceived. They were most tenderly attached to each other, and had both known the pains of lonely missionary labor; but if she was able to prosecute the voyage alone, much as he yearned once more to behold his native land, and much as he wished to accompany her, he did not feel himself at liberty to leave his post of duty. A distinct voice of Providence had placed him there, and the same voice, unmoved by his own likes or dislikes, must recall him, before he felt himself at liberty to move.

These appearances, however, proved deceptive. Mrs. Judson's complaints returned with renewed violence within a few days after their arrival at Port Louis; and it became necessary for her husband to accompany her. At this juncture the ship Sophia Walker, of Boston, touched at the Isle of France, and her commander, Captain Codman, very kindly invited them to take passage with him directly for the United States. They accepted his proposal, and embarked on the 25th of July for Boston.

Mrs. Judson continued to decline very rapidly, until they arrived at St. Helena, where she expired on the 1st of September, 1845. A brief account of the life and labors of this talented and accomplished woman, from the pen of Dr. Judson, will be found in the following pages.* On the evening of her burial, Dr. Judson and his motherless children sailed from St. Helena, and arrived in Boston on the 15th of October following.

To the Corresponding Secretary.

MAULMAIN, April 13, 1845.

MY DEAR BROTHER: The hand of God is heavy upon me. The complaint to which Mrs. Judson is subject has become so violent, that it is the unanimous opinion of all the

---

* A most interesting Memoir of Mrs. S. B. Judson has been written by Mrs. E. C. Judson.

medical men, and indeed of all our friends, that nothing but a voyage beyond the tropics can possibly protract her life beyond the period of a few weeks, but that such a voyage will, in all probability, insure her recovery. All medical skill has been exhausted. She has spent six weeks with our commissioner and his lady in a trip down the coast, touching at Tavoy and Mergui, and returned weaker and nearer the grave than when she set out. She is willing to die, and I hope I am willing to see her die, if it be the divine will; but though my wife, it is no more than truth to say that there is scarcely an individual foreigner now alive who speaks and writes the Burmese tongue so acceptably as she does; and I feel that an effort ought to be made to save her life. I have long fought against the necessity of accompanying her; but she is now so desperately weak, and almost helpless, that all say it would be nothing but savage inhumanity to send her off alone. The three younger children, the youngest but three months and a half old, we must leave behind us, casting them, as it were, on the waters, in the hope of finding them after many days. The three elder, Abby Ann, Adoniram, and Elnathan, we take with us, to leave in their parents' native land. These rendings of parental ties are more severe, and wring out bitterer tears from the heart's core, than any can possibly conceive, who have never felt the wrench. But I hope I can say with truth that I love Christ above all; and I am striving, in the strength of my weak faith, to gird up my mind to face and welcome all his appointments. And I am much helped to bear these trials, by the advice and encouragement of all my dear brethren and sisters of the mission.

It is another great trial to leave my dear church and people. I never knew till now how much I loved them, and how much they loved me.

> "And 'tis to love, our farewells owe
> All their emphasis of woe."

But I leave them in the hands of my dear brethren, and there are no persons in the world to whom I should be so willing to commit so dear a charge.

Another great trial, not so much as it regards feeling as it regards the anticipated result of long-protracted labor, is the interruption which the heavy work of the Burmese dictionary, in which I have been engaged for two or three years, must sustain; and such is the state of my manuscripts, that if I should die before this work is completed, or at least carried forward to a much more advanced stage, all my previous labor would be nearly or quite lost. But I am endeavoring to obviate this difficulty in some degree, by taking with me my two assistants in that department, whose hearts God has graciously inclined to leave their families and accompany me. They are both Christians, the one a settled character, a convert of long standing, formerly a government writer in Rangoon; the other a nephew of the late premier of the court of Ava, a person of noble extraction, and though not a tried Christian, I hope a sincere one. And it is my purpose to devote some hours every day, whether on the sea or land, to the work mentioned. I shall be induced to persevere in this purpose while in America, from the fact that I am unable to travel about the country as an agent, and preach in the English language. The course that I have uniformly pursued, ever since I became a missionary, has been rather peculiar. In order to become an acceptable and eloquent preacher in a foreign language, I deliberately abjured my own. When I crossed the river, I burned my ships. For thirty-two years I have scarcely entered an English pulpit, or made a speech in that language. Whether I have pursued the wisest course, I will not contend; and how far I have attained the object aimed at, I must leave for others to say. But whether right or wrong, the course I have taken cannot be retraced. The burned ships cannot now be reconstructed. From long desuetude, I can scarcely put three sentences together in the English language.* I must therefore beg the board to allow me a quiet corner, where I can pursue my work with my assistants, undisturbed and unknown.

This request I am induced to urge from the further consid

---

* That is, I presume, in a public address.

eration, that my voice, though greatly recovered from the affection of the lungs, which laid me aside from preaching nearly a year, is still so weak that it can only fill a small room; and whenever I attempt to raise it above the conversational tone, the weak place gives way, and I am quite broken down again for several weeks. I hope, therefore, that no one will try to persuade me to be guilty of such imprudence while in America; but since there are thousands of preachers in English, and only five or six Burmese preachers in the whole world, I may be allowed to hoard up the remnant of my breath and lungs for the country where they are most needed. . . .

Your affectionate brother,
A. JUDSON.

To his Sister.

MAULMAIN, April 13, 1845.

MY DEAR SISTER: I write a line in the greatest hurry and confusion. Mrs. Judson returned from her trip down the coast, weaker and nearer dying than when she set out. Nothing more can be done for her in this country; but the doctors say decidedly that a voyage to a cold climate will cure her. The only opportunity that we can avail ourselves of, before it be too late, is a ship bound to London, which sails in about a week. All say that she is too weak, and in too precarious a state, to go alone; so I have concluded to accompany her, and once more see my native land, and you, my dear sister — the only surviving near relative that remains to me on earth.[*] We leave the three younger children with our friends here. The three elder, Abby Ann, Adoniram, and Elnathan, we shall take with us, intending to leave them in America, when we return. It is said that we shall have a five months' voyage to England. There I shall not make any stay, but embrace the first opportunity of passing over to the United

---

[*] Dr. Judson's mother, Mrs. Abigail Brown Judson, died at Plymouth, Massachusetts, January 31, 1842, at the advanced age of eighty-two years.

States. I send this over land; and when you receive it, I shall probably be half way on my passage.

Your affectionate brother,
A. JUDSON.

To the Corresponding Secretary.

BARQUE SOPHIA WALKER, AT SEA, September, 1845.

MY DEAR BROTHER: I wrote you the 13th of April, and the treasurer on the 1st of May, just before sailing from Amherst. The first part of the voyage was very rough; we suffered a good deal from seasickness; and my time was much occupied in taking care of Mrs. Judson. Having my assistants, however, I endeavored to make some progress in my work, though under great disadvantages. During the second month, Mrs. Judson began to improve, and I had the most sanguine hopes of her recovery. After crossing the line, the ship sprung a leak, and the captain determined to put in at the Isle of France. Before reaching the island, Mrs. Judson became so decidedly convalescent, that it appeared clearly to be my duty to return to Maulmain, and leave her to proceed alone. On our arrival, we found a vessel bound to Maulmain; and though I was unwilling to leave her until I should see her fairly on her way, I was so sure of returning myself, that I sent off the assistants by that vessel, and partially engaged my own passage in another, which would sail for Calcutta in two or three weeks.

In the mean time we met with Captain Codman, of the Sophia Walker, who invited us to take passage with him, and kindly offered such terms as induced us to leave the Paragon. The change furnished also an additional encouragement for me to return; as the Sophia Walker would take Mrs. Judson to the very doors of her friends, where also she would arrive a month earlier than if she went by the way of England. But all our plans were frustrated by an unforeseen event. Mrs. Judson experienced a dreadful relapse, which reduced her lower than ever before, and soon convinced me that it would be impossible for me to leave her; so that, though I bitterly regretted the loss of my assistants, I felt obliged, after having remained three weeks at Port Louis, to reëmbark with her; and we finally sailed on the 25th of July. After a time she again appeared to be recovering, and in the cold weather off the Cape of Good Hope, my hopes became again very sanguine. But she never really recovered from her last prostration, and, though sometimes better, continued, on the whole, to decline, until we neared St. Helena, when I gave up all hope of her recovery. She lingered a few days, while the vessel was detained in port, until the 1st instant, when, at three o'clock in the morning, she obtained her release from further suffering, and entered, I trust, into the joy of her Lord. She was buried in the afternoon of the same day; and in the evening we were again at sea.

Had Mrs. Judson lived to reach home, and especially if my assistants had been with me, I should have expected to remain some time in America, that her health might become confirmed. But since the object is lost, I am desirous of returning as soon as possible. I hope that no objection will be made to my leaving before the winter sets in. I dread the effects of a northern winter, not so much on my general health as on my lungs. An attack of my complaint in the winter season would probably prove fatal. And though I refuse not to die, I have so much desire, in submission to the will of God, to finish my work in Burmah, that I must confess I am unwilling to expose my poor life, though in other respects of no worth, to any unnecessary hazard.

I remain yours affectionately,

A. JUDSON.

To Mr. Anderson Port Louis, Isle of France.

ON PASSAGE FROM ST. HELENA, September 2, 1845.

MY DEAR FRIEND: I shall have no opportunity of sending this till after my arrival in the United States; so that you will probably have heard of Mrs. Judson's death before receiving this line. I was so overwhelmed with my distress while at St. Helena, that it never occurred to me to write a line to any of my friends. My dear wife continued to decline after leaving the Isle of France. Neither the best medical advice, nor the most careful nursing on my part, nor any change of climate, seemed to have much salutary effect. When we reached St. Helena, I had given up all hope of her recovery. That took place on the 26th of August. The vessel remained a few days. She lingered along till the first, that is, yesterday, at three o'clock in the morning, when her spirit took its final flight. The body was carried on shore in the afternoon, and interred in the public burial ground, by the side of Mrs. Chater, long a missionary at Ceylon, who died on her passage home. The funeral was attended by a crowd of friends, though we were entire strangers in the place. We were surprised to find several pious persons under the pastoral care of the Rev. Mr. Bertram, an excellent, zealous missionary. They took me and the children to their houses and their hearts, and their consoling conversation and sympathizing prayers, in the hour of my distress, afforded wonderful relief. Would you believe that these pious friends and the captain of our ship defrayed all the expenses of the funeral? They even had mourning suits made for the children, and sent off to the ship! But I was obliged to leave them all the same evening; and this morning, the rock of the ocean, where reposes all that is mortal of my dear, dear wife, was out of sight. And O, how desolate my cabin appears, and how dreary the way before me! But I have the great consolation that she died in peace, longing to depart and be with Christ. She had some desire, being on her passage home, to see her parents, and relatives, and friends, after twenty years' absence; but the love of Christ sustained her to the last. When near dying, I congratulated her on the prospect of soon beholding the Saviour in all his glory; and she eagerly replied, " What can I want beside ? " I have no doubt she is now leaning on her Saviour's bosom, in company with the first Mrs. Judson. I hope I feel thankful to God that he has granted me, during my pilgrimage, the society of two of the most excellent women and best of wives that ever man was blessed with. Heaven seems nearer, and eternity sweeter, when I think of them and of other dear friends who have gone before. May we who remain have grace to follow those who, through faith, inherit the promises.

I remember with gratitude your and your wife's kindness to the dear departed, and especially that of dear Mr. Kelsey. I should write to him, but presume he will have left the island. If you should be writing to him, please to mention some of these things, and give him my warmest love. Give my love also to Mr. and Mrs. Lebrun, and to Mrs. Ledo, and to Mr Chevalyay.

May God bless you, my dear friend, through life; may he give you a peaceful and joyful death; and may we have a happy meeting in his blissful presence, is the fervent prayer of
    Your affectionate friend and brother,
        A. JUDSON.

Obituary of Mrs. Sarah B. Judson.

The subject of the following brief obituary notice, Sarah Boardman Judson, was born at Alstead, in the State of New Hampshire, November 4, 1803. She was the eldest child of Ralph and Abiah Hall, who still survive her, and are at present living at Skaneateles, in the State of New York. While Sarah was but a child, her parents removed from Alstead to Danvers, and subsequently to Salem, in the State of Massachusetts. In the latter place she received her education, and continued to reside until she was married to the Rev. George Dana Boardman, July 4, 1825, with whom she embarked in the same month for the East Indies, to join the American missionaries in Burmah. After residing some time at Calcutta and at Maulmain, they settled at Tavoy, April 1, 1828. During her residence in Calcutta and Tavoy, she had three children, of whom one only, George Dana Boardman, Jr., born August 18, 1828, survives her. She lost her husband February 11, 1831, and was married again to Adoniram Judson, of Maulmain, April 10, 1834. At Maulmain she became the mother of eight children, of whom five survive her. After the birth of her last child, in December, 1844, she was attacked with chronic diarrhœa, from which she had suffered much in the early part of her missionary life. When, in the progress of the disease, it became evident that nothing but a long voyage and an entire change of climate could save her life, she embarked, with her husband and three elder children, for the United States, April 26, 1845. The voyage was at first attended with encouraging results, but finally proved unavailing, and she departed this life on shipboard, in the port of St. Helena, September 1, 1845.

Like multitudes in the highly-favored land of her nativity, the subject of this notice was blessed with early religious advantages, and in her youth became the subject of serious impressions. When about sixteen years of age, during a revival of religion in Salem, she entertained a hope, received baptism at the hands of her pastor, the Rev. Dr. Bolles, and became a member of his church. Her religious attainments, however, were not of a distinguished order, and though her amiable disposition and her deep interest in missions, especially after her acquaintance with Mr. Boardman, gave her an elevated tone of character, she subsequently felt that at that period she hardly deserved the name of a sincere Christian. And it was not until she was called to part with her eldest child, at Tavoy, in 1829, and to pass through scenes of great danger and suffering during the Tavoy rebellion, that she was enabled to live a life of faith on the Son of God.

"Sweet affliction, sweet affliction,
That brings near to Jesus' feet."

In regard to her missionary qualifications and labors, I may state, that she applied herself with great assiduity to the study of the Burmese language, in which, in conversation, prayer, and writing, she acquired an uncommon degree of correctness, fluency, and power. She was in the habit of conducting a prayer meeting of the female members of the church every week, and also another meeting for the study of the Scriptures.

Her acquaintance with and attachment to the Burmese Bible were rather extraordinary. She professed to take more pleasure and derive more profit from the perusal of that translation than from the English, and to enjoy preaching in the native chapel more than in any other. Her translation of the Pilgrim's Progress, part first, into Burmese, is one of the best pieces of composition which we have yet published. Her translation of Mr. Boardman's Dying Father's Advice has become one of our standard tracts; and her hymns in Burmese, about twenty in number, are probably the best in our Chapel Hymn Book — a work which she was appointed by the mission to edit. Besides these works, she published four volumes of Scripture questions, which are in constant use in our Sabbath schools. The last work of her life, and one which she accomplished in the midst of overwhelming family cares, and under the pressure of declining health, was a series of Sunday cards, each accompanied with a short hymn, adapted to the leading subject of the card.

Besides her acquaintance with the Burmese language, she had, in past years, when there was no missionary in the Peguan department, acquired a competent knowledge of that language, and translated, or superintended the translation of, the New Testament and the principal Burmese tracts into Peguan. But when a missionary was appointed to that department, she transferred her work to him, and gladly confined herself to the Burmese.

Something, also, might be said with regard to her labors in the Karen wilderness east of Tavoy, especially during the years of her widowhood, when she made toilsome journeys among the mountains, sometimes amid drenching rains, and always with many privations, and where, notwithstanding that she was wholly opposed to the principle of females acting the part of ministers, she was frequently obliged to conduct worship in the Karen assemblies.

Her bereaved husband is the more desirous of bearing this testimony to her various attainments, her labors, and her worth, from the fact that her own unobtrusive and retiring disposition always led her to seek the shade, as well as from the fact that she was often brought into comparison with one whose life and character were uncommonly interesting and brilliant. The memoir of his first beloved wife has been long before the public. It is, therefore, most gratifying to his feelings to be able to say, in truth, that the subject of this notice was, in every point of natural and moral excellence, the worthy successor of Ann H. Judson. He constantly thanks God that he has been blessed with two of the best of wives; he deeply feels that he has not improved these rich blessings as he ought, and it is most painful to reflect that, from the peculiar pressure of the missionary life, he has sometimes failed to treat those dear beings with that consideration, attention, and kindness, which their situation in a foreign heathen land ever demanded.

But, to show the forgiving and grateful disposition of the subject of this brief sketch, and somewhat to elucidate her character, he would add that, a few days before her death, he called her children to her bedside, and said, in their hearing, " I wish, my love, to ask pardon for every unkind word or deed of which I have ever been guilty. I feel that I have, in many instances, failed of treating you with that kindness and affection which you have ever deserved." * "O," said she, " you will kill me if you talk so. It is I that should ask pardon of you; and I only want to get well that I may have an opportunity of making some return for all your kindness, and of showing you how much I love you."

This recollection of her dying bed leads me to say a few words relative to the closing scenes of her life. After her prostration at the Isle of France, where we spent three weeks,

---

* "I always regretted that this paragraph should have been written, because it is calculated to mislead the reader. To my mind it seems utterly impossible that Dr. Judson could ever have spoken, much less acted, unkindly, or even thoughtlessly, to his wife. I never saw any one so constantly considerate and so unreservedly devoted."— E. C. J.

there remained but little expectation of her recovery. Her hope had long been fixed on the Rock of Ages, and she had been in the habit of contemplating death as neither distant nor undesirable. As it drew near, she remained perfectly tranquil. No shade of doubt, or fear, or anxiety, ever passed over her mind. She had a prevailing preference to depart and be with Christ. "I am longing to depart," and, "What can I want beside?" quoting the language of a familiar hymn, were the expressions which revealed the spiritual peace and joy of her mind; yet, at times, the thought of her native land, to which she was approaching, after an absence of twenty years, and a longing desire to see once more her son George, her parents, and the friends of her youth, drew down her ascending soul, and constrained her to say, "I am in a strait betwixt two — let the will of God be done."

In regard to her children she ever manifested the most surprising composure and resignation, so much so that I was once induced to say, "You seem to have forgotten the little ones we have left behind." "Can a mother forget?" she replied, and was unable to proceed. During her last days she spent much time in praying for the early conversion of her children. May her living and her dying prayers draw down the blessing of God on their bereaved heads.

On our passage homeward, as the strength of Mrs. Judson gradually declined, I expected to be under the painful necessity of burying her in the sea. But it was so ordered by divine Providence, that, when the indications of approaching death had become strongly marked, the ship came to anchor in the port of St. Helena. For three days she continued to sink rapidly, though her bodily sufferings were not very severe. Her mind became liable to wander; but a single word was sufficient to recall and steady her recollection. On the evening of the 31st of August, she appeared to be drawing near to the end of her pilgrimage. The children took leave of her, and retired to rest. I sat alone by the side of her bed during the hours of the night, endeavoring to administer relief to the distressed body, and consolation to the departing soul. At two o'clock in the morning, wishing to obtain one more token of recognition, I roused her attention, and said, "Do you still love the Saviour?" "O, yes," she replied, "I ever love the Lord Jesus Christ." I said again, "Do you still love me?" She replied in the affirmative, by a peculiar expression of her own. "Then give me one more kiss;" and we exchanged that token of love for the last time. Another hour passed, life continued to recede, and she ceased to breathe. For a moment I traced her upward flight, and thought of the wonders which were opening to her view. I then closed her sightless eyes, dressed her, for the last time, in the drapery of death; and being quite exhausted with many sleepless nights, I threw myself down and slept. On awaking in the morning, I saw the children standing and weeping around the body of their dear mother, then, for the first time, inattentive to their cries. In the course of the day a coffin was procured from the shore, in which I placed all that remained of her whom I had so much loved; and after a prayer had been offered by a dear brother minister from the town, the Rev. Mr. Bertram, we proceeded in boats to the shore. There we were met by the colonial chaplain, and accompanied to the burial ground by the adherents and friends of Mr. Bertram, and a large concourse of the inhabitants. They had prepared the grave in a beautiful, shady spot, contiguous to the grave of Mrs. Chater, a missionary from Ceylon, who had died in similar circumstances on her passage home. There I saw her safely deposited, and in the language of prayer, which we had often presented together at the throne of grace, I blessed God that her body had attained the repose of the grave, and her spirit the repose of paradise. After the funeral, the dear friends of Mr. Bertram took me to their houses and their hearts; and their conversation and prayers afforded me unexpected relief and consolation. But I was obliged to hasten on board ship, and we immediately went to sea. On the following morning no vestige of the island was discernible in the distant horizon. For a few days, in the solitude of my cabin, with my poor children crying around me, I could not help abandoning myself to heart-breaking sorrow. But the promises of the gospel came to my aid, and faith stretched her view to the bright world of eternal life, and anticipated a happy meeting with those beloved beings whose bodies are mouldering at Amherst and St. Helena.

I exceedingly regret that there is no portrait of the second, as of the first Mrs. Judson. Her soft blue eye, her mild aspect, her lovely face, and elegant form have never been delineated on canvas. They must soon pass away from the memory even of her children, but they will remain forever enshrined in her husband's heart.

To my friends at St. Helena I am under great obligation. I desire to thank God for having raised up in that place a most precious religious interest. The friends of the Redeemer rallied around an evangelical minister immediately on his arrival, and within a few months several souls were added to their number. Those dear, sympathizing, Christian friends received the body of the deceased from my hands as a sacred deposit, united with our kind captain, John Codman, Jr., of Dorchester, in defraying all the expenses of the funeral, and promised to take care of the grave, and see to the erection of the gravestones which I am to forward, and on which I propose to place the following inscription: —

"Sacred to the memory of Sarah B. Judson, member of the American Baptist mission to Burmah, formerly wife of the Rev. George D. Boardman, of Tavoy, and lately wife of the Rev. Adoniram Judson, of Maulmain, who died in this port, September 1, 1845, on her passage to the United States, in the forty-second year of her age, and in the twenty-first of her missionary life.

> "She sleeps sweetly here, on this rock of the ocean,
>   Away from the home of her youth,
> And far from the land where, with heartfelt devotion,
>   She scattered the bright beams of truth."

To the Editor of the Mother's Journal, New York.

MY DEAR SISTER: I send you the accompanying lines by my late beloved wife, written on board ship, near the Isle of France, when she was so decidedly convalescent that it appeared to be my duty to return to Maulmain, and leave her to prosecute the voyage alone. After we arrived, however, at the island, she became worse, and I was obliged to relinquish my first purpose. She continued to decline until we reached St. Helena, when she took her departure, not for the " setting sun," but the sun of glory that never sets, and left me to pursue a different course, and under very different circumstances from those anticipated in the lines.

> We part on this green islet, love, —
>   Thou for the eastern main,
> I for the setting sun, love,
>   O, when to meet again !
>
> My heart is sad for thee, love,
>   For lone thy way will be ;
> And oft thy tears will fall, love,
>   For thy children and for me.
>
> The music of thy daughter's voice
>   Thou'lt miss for many a year,
> And the merry shout of thine elder boys
>   Thou'lt list in vain to hear.
>
> When we knelt to see our Henry die,
>   And heard his last, faint moan,
> Each wiped the tear from other's eye :
>   Now each must weep alone.
>
> My tears fall fast for thee, love :
>   How can I say, Farewell !
> But go ; thy God be with thee, love,
>   Thy heart's deep grief to quell.
>
> Yet my spirit clings to thine, love ;
>   Thy soul remains with me,

And oft we'll hold communion sweet,
  O'er the dark and distant sea.

And who can paint our mutual joy,
  When, all our wanderings o'er,
We both shall clasp our infants three
  At home, on Burmah's shore!

But higher shall our raptures glow,
  On yon celestial plain,
When the loved and parted here below
  Meet, ne'er to part again.

Then gird thine armor on, love,
  Nor faint thou by the way,
Till Boodh shall fall, and Burmah's sons
  Shall own Messiah's sway.

And so, God willing, I will endeavor yet to do; and while her prostrate form finds repose on the rock of the ocean, and her sanctified spirit enjoys sweeter repose on the bosom of Jesus, let me continue to toil on all my appointed time, until my change, too, shall come.

Yours affectionately,
A. JUDSON.

Dr. Judson arrived in Boston on the 15th of October, and remained in this country until July of the following year, or a little less than nine months.

Of the manner of his reception here it is hardly necessary to speak. His sufferings at Ava, and his labors as a missionary for more than thirty years, had made the world conversant with his history. In the United States his name had become a familiar word. He was the only missionary remaining in a heathen land of those who had first left America for India, and, with a single exception, the only one of that number now living. But of the millions here who had known of his labors, and revered his character, probably not fifty had ever seen him. A new generation occupied the places of those venerated men who were the active supporters of missions at the time of his embarkation. Hence the desire to see him was intense. The largest houses of public worship were thronged long before the usual hour of divine service, if it was known that he was to be present. Men of all professions and of all beliefs were anxious to make his acquaintance. His movements were chronicled in all the papers, both religious and secular. In a word, a spontaneous tribute of homage, love, and veneration awaited him in every village and city that he visited.

But never was a man more completely out of his element on occasions of this kind. The manner of his reception was wholly unexpected to him. When he arrived in Boston, before coming on shore, he was much troubled with the apprehension that he should not know where to look for lodgings. The idea that a hundred houses would at once be thrown open to him, and that as many families would feel honored to receive him as a guest, never entered his mind. He had, but six weeks before, buried a beloved wife amid the rocks of St. Helena. His own health was exceedingly delicate, and our rough autumnal winds brought back, with renewed violence, the disease of his throat. Public speaking greatly aggravated his complaint. Simple attendance upon the evening meetings which were summoned to welcome his return agitated his nervous system painfully, and frequently deprived him of quiet rest for the whole of the following night. Nor was this all. He shrunk with instinctive delicacy from crowded assemblies where he himself was the theme on which every speaker dilated. He seemed to himself to stand up, for he could not speak, merely to be exhibited. In this matter he appeared to me a little nervous, and somewhat to err in judgment. When earnest Christian men sought to make his acquaintance, — men who would never have done it but because they honored his services for Christ, — his manner of receiving them was sometimes chilling, if not repulsive. He seemed to himself to have done nothing that called for any special token of respect; and he therefore too readily concluded that he was only looked at as a somewhat unusual specimen. I witnessed myself some instances of this kind, and regretted to perceive that he had, as I thought, mistaken the motives of those who really honored him as a man who had borne hardness for the sake of Christ.

The real explanation of cases of this kind is to be found, I believe, in the feeling of self-depreciation, which was habitual to him, combined with a nervous shrinking from being made an object of general observation, and not unfrequently of excessive praise. Of his humility no one who observed the tone of his religious sentiments could entertain a doubt. He was my guest during his brief visit to Providence; and conducted family worship on the evening after a meeting to welcome his return had been held in the First Baptist Church. His prayer on that occasion can never be forgotten by those who heard it. So lowly abasement in the presence of unspotted holiness, such earnest pleadings for pardon for the imperfection of those services for which men praised him, so utter renunciation of all merit for any thing that he had ever done, and so entire reliance for acceptance with God only on the merits and atonement of the gospel sacrifice for sin, I think it was never my happiness to hear on any other occasion. Such, I believe, was the habitual temper of his mind, that the more his brethren were disposed to exalt him, the more deeply did he seem to feel his own deficiencies, and the more humble was his prostration at the foot of the cross.

On several occasions, he addressed his brethren in public assemblies through the medium of some individual, who, standing by his side, would repeat to the audience the sentiments which he uttered almost in a whisper. On one or two occasions, he wrote out in full the address, which was read by another. Several of these addresses will be found in the following pages. They all breathe the same spirit. They are the words of a man whose efforts are all in one direction, and who is living in simplicity of heart for no other purpose than to advance the interests of the kingdom of Christ, and to advance them by saving souls from eternal death. The sentiment of the apostle expressed the feeling which seemed ever uppermost in his mind — " For me to live is Christ, and to die is gain."

On the evening of October 17, the second day after his arrival, a meeting, verbally notified, was held in the Bowdoin Square Church, Boston, to extend to him a public welcome. The word passed so rapidly from one to another, that at an early hour the edifice was crowded. After appropriate devotional exercises, the Rev. Dr. Sharp arose with Dr. Judson before the congregation. The following report of the addresses and incidents of the occasion is taken from contemporary journals.*

* Christian Watchman, and Christian Reflector, October 23, 24, 1845.

"There are some feelings," said Dr. Sharp, "which are too sacred for public utterance. There are sentiments of respect and regard which, when whispered to the ear, or spoken in the privacy of confidential intercourse, are pleasant and refreshing as the breath of spring, but which lose their fragrance in the atmosphere of a public assembly. Were I to express my own feelings towards yourself, — my admiration, my confidence, my gratitude, my regard, — I should say many things that in this assembly would seem out of place. I may, however, without violating Christian propriety, speak *in behalf* of the public in the *presence* of the public.

"I may say, without the semblance of flattery or adulation, the denomination have cherished a deep, and affectionate, and grateful interest in your labors. They have wondered at your steady and unfaltering perseverance; they have admired your disinterested and self-denying course; and they have tenderly sympathized with you, and prayed for you, when they heard of your personal sufferings, your imprisonment, and loss of personal liberty, and when they have heard of those greater losses, to which, in the death of loved and cherished ones, you have been subjected. And they have rejoiced with you, not, indeed, that *all* your work was done, but that a glorious work was done, when, in humble prostration before the beneficent Author of revelation, you devoutly thanked him that you had completed the translation of the Holy Scriptures in the Burman language. That was a memorable day, not only in the history of your own life, but in the history of missions.

"We can only pray, dear brother, that, after a still more extended and critical knowledge of the Burman language, the result of patient and laborious study and research, your life may be prolonged to revise and amend your translation of those soul-sanctifying and soul-comforting truths which tell with wondrous power in any language in which a version of them is given. Your prosecution of that other great work, to which your mind, and pen, and days are given, — a Burman dictionary, — at the completion of which you may well rest from your labors, will aid you greatly in giving your last correcting touch to the Burman Scriptures. Our prayer will be, in submission to God's will, that you may live until you have sent out to the world the volumes which will not only shed their radiant light on the Scriptures, but will quicken and elevate the common mind of India.

"And now, dear brother, withdrawn as you have been, by an afflictive dispensation of Providence, from your chosen and loved labors, allow me to say, in behalf of your ministering brethren, and other brethren and friends, We welcome you to your native land; we welcome you to the scenes of your early and manly youth; we welcome you to our worshipping assemblies; we welcome you to our hearts. As the representative of the ministers and private Christians present, I give to you this hand of cordial welcome, of sympathy, of approbation, and of love. And I believe, could all our denomination be collected in one vast assembly, they would request and empower some one to perform this service for them; or, rather, each one would prefer to give this significant token of love, and respect, and good wishes, for himself. Were it possible, and could your strength hold out, and your hand bear the grasp and the cordial shake of so many, I could wish that every one who loves the Bible and missions might be his own representative, and give to you, as I do, the hand of an honest, unchanging, and cordial good will."

Dr. Sharp, having thus concluded his welcome, in which all heartily participated, turned to the congregation, and continued as follows: —

"I trust I shall not be regarded as violating any rule of propriety, if, in accordance with the suggestion of my brethren, I give a brief review of the facts which the return and sight of our brother has called up to my recollection. Well do I remember the emotions which filled my own bosom, when, in the month of October or November, 1812, we heard that our respected brother, then a young man, had attached himself to our denomination. The pleasure in my own mind was not so much that he had become a Baptist, as that the event would be the means of inducing the denomination to engage in the cause of missions among the heathen. A conference of brethren was immediately held, and there was not a moment's hesitation to sustain our brother, should his connection with another respectable body of Christians be dissolved. This fact being ascertained by correspondence with the American board, he was adopted by brethren in this city and a neighboring town as their missionary, so far as to sustain him. But whether it would be best to form a foreign missionary organization here, or simply to request the English Baptist Missionary Society to receive him, he being supported by us, was for some time an unsettled question."

Dr. Sharp then read two letters written by himself in the spring of 1813; the first to the Rev. Andrew Fuller, in behalf of the Baptist Society for propagating the Gospel in India and other Foreign Parts, then recently formed in Boston, soliciting that Mr. Judson, whose change of views on the subject of baptism, and desire to be supported by a Baptist society, had just become known in this country, might be taken into the society of the English Baptist brethren in India, under the direction of Carey, Marshman, and Ward; a plan which was afterwards abandoned, and a separate mission was undertaken, under the care and patronage of the Baptists in this country. The second letter was addressed to Mr. Judson, welcoming him as a member and a missionary of the Baptist denomination in America, and giving some suggestions respecting his plans of proceeding.

Rev. Mr. Hague now arose with Dr. Judson, and said that, as the voice of the beloved brother would not permit him audibly to address the congregation, he would, by request, act for him somewhat as an interpreter, repeating his remarks so that all should be able to hear them.

Dr. Judson then said, "Through the mercy of God I am permitted to stand before you here, this evening, a pensioner of your bounty. I desire to thank you for all your sympathy and aid, and I pray God's blessing to rest upon you. . . . All that has been done in Burmah has been done by the churches, through the feeble and unworthy instrumentality of myself and my brethren. . . . It is one of the severest trials of my life not to be able to lift up my voice, and give free utterance to my feelings before this congregation; but repeated trials have assured me that I cannot safely attempt it. And I am much influenced by the circumstance that it was a request of my wife, in her dying hour, that I would not address public meetings on my arrival. . . . I will only add, that I beg your prayers for the brethren I have left in Burmah; for the feeble churches we have planted there; and that the good work of God's grace may go on until the world shall be filled with his glory."

Mr. Hague continued, in a strain of highly appropriate and impressive remarks, to give a brief view of some of the striking events connected with the history of Mr. Judson's mission, and his return to his native land, where a new generation had risen up since his absence, and the places and scenes familiar to his youth had so entirely changed.

While Mr. Hague was speaking, a gentleman was making his way from the farther part of the house towards the pulpit. He was welcomed there with surprise and delight, and was immediately introduced to the congregation by Dr. Sharp, as the Rev. Samuel Nott, the only survivor, excepting Dr. Judson, of the five missionaries who first went out to India from America, and the very man, who, when Judson became a Baptist, stood up and shielded him with the mantle of Christian love. "For this," said Dr. Sharp, "I have always respected him, and I am sure you will be glad to hear him."

It is hardly possible for us to describe the scene which followed. For thirty-three years Nott and Judson had been separated. They met at this moment for the first time since that separation; and as they now embraced each other with deep affection and grateful joy, tears started from many an eye Mr. Nott proceeded to speak with much emotion. More than thirty years ago he gave his brother the right hand of fellowship, and when he became a Baptist it was not withdrawn One reflection most solemnly impressed him — of the five who went out to India, three are dead. The grass withereth, the flower fadeth, but the word of our God shall stand forever. In a little while they would all be gone, and every agency now employed pass away; but God's word will stand fast, and prevail over all the earth. Mr. Nott referred to the small beginning of the American Board, as well as the Baptist, their trust in God, and the present great and glorious work which is exhibited to us in contrast. The missionary movement in this country originated simultaneously in different hearts; the spirit of the Most High, and not human influence, gave it birth. He deemed it a very trifling question whether Adoniram Judson or Samuel J. Mills was the originator of foreign missions. Samuel Nott, Jr., certainly was not. They were all mere boys, but with God's blessing on their puerile efforts, they had begun an influence which is spreading over the world.

It was now discovered that Mr. Bingham, a pioneer missionary to the Sandwich Islands, was unexpectedly present; and another thrill of pleasure went through the congregation as his name was also announced by Dr. Sharp. He addressed the assembly, congratulating his missionary brethren, referring to his own early toils and to the great success of the Sandwich Island mission, and exhorting the people generously to sustain the glorious cause of missions.

Special Meeting of the Acting Board.*

A special meeting of the Acting Board was called at the Missionary Rooms, Boston, October 20, the Hon. Richard Fletcher, one of the vice presidents, in the chair. The meeting was opened with prayer, after which the Corresponding Secretary, the Rev. S. Peck, announced the arrival of the Rev. Dr. Judson, on the 15th instant, in the ship Sophia Walker, and also the death of Mrs. Judson, on the 1st of September, at St. Helena. The following resolutions were unanimously adopted: —

Whereas the Rev. Dr. Judson, the earliest missionary of

* Macedonian, November, 1845.

this board, has been led by divine Providence to revisit his native country, after the lapse of more than thirty-three years, and is expected to be present with us this morning, —

Resolved, 1. That it is a fit occasion to record our sense of the goodness of God, and of his claims to our devout and fervent praise. Through all the scenes of that eventful period, — in toil, in solitude, in manifold privations, in sickness, in imprisonments, in bereavements, — God has been ever with and around his servant; has sheltered, rescued, strengthened, comforted him; has given him the desire of his heart in completing a revised translation of the Bible in the Burmese language, now multiplied and circulated by thousands has enabled him to gather a church of Burmese converts — believers in Christ, the seal of his apostleship to the heathen; and having filled up more than twice the ordinary term of missionary service, allows him to cherish the hope of prosecuting to its completion the great work in which he is now engaged — the preparation of a dictionary, the first attempted, of the Burmese language.

Resolved, 2. That, in the afflictive circumstances which more immediately occasioned the return of Dr. Judson, this board are conscious of a personal and deeply painful interest; and especially do we sympathize with our bereaved brother under the visitation of God which has separated from him helper and friend, the partner of his life and the mother of his children, and assigned a resting-place to her remains in a solitary island of the sea. But we sorrow in hope. She was almost twenty years a diligent and honored laborer in the missionary field; and many a Karen and Burman, saved through her instrumentality, will rise up in the judgment and call her *blessed*.

Resolved, 3. That it gives us an unwonted joy to see the face of our beloved brother Judson in the flesh, to take him by the hand, to mingle our mutual congratulations, to bow with him in prayers and thanksgivings before the Lord of missions, both his Lord and ours. We welcome him to this our common native land, to our places of religious concourse, to our council boards and our altars; we welcome him to our homes and our hearts.

Resolved, 4. That the president be requested, on behalf of the board, to communicate the above resolves to Dr. Judson, on his presentation.

Dr. Judson was then introduced to the board, and the foregoing resolutions were read. He made a brief reply, expressive of his feelings towards the board — feelings of gratitude, confidence, and love. The president followed, assuring him, in behalf of the board, that his sentiments were fully and cordially reciprocated.

A free conversation ensued, in which Dr. Judson made many interesting statements.

To the Corresponding Secretary.

BRADFORD, October 28, 1845.

MY DEAR BROTHER: I came here from Salem, in the stage coach, yesterday forenoon. My throat is getting much worse, not so much, I hope, from continual conversation, as from a severe cold, which I increase every day, and especially every evening that I go out to meetings. Last night I suffered a good deal through the night, and thought I should be quite disabled to-day; but now I am a little relieved. I dread the meeting this evening at Haverhill; but as it has been appointed, I suppose I must attend. My chief object in writing is to beg that I may be excused from attending any more such meetings, until I get a little better. I expect to be in Boston to-morrow, and shall want two or three days for some necessary business, and propose to go to Worcester Friday or Saturday; and if I could spend the next Sabbath alone in some chamber, I should feel it a great privilege, both as a refreshment to the soul and a relief to the body. And I should then, perhaps, be better able to prosecute my journey westward. May the Lord bless and direct us in all our ways.

Yours most affectionately,

A. JUDSON.

Visit to Providence and Brown University.

In N vember Dr. Judson visited Providence, and spen a day in Brown University, the place of his early education. The following notices of his visit are taken from the papers of the day.

PROVIDENCE, November 17, 1845.

The presence of Dr. Judson in our city has thrilled many a Christian heart with gratitude and joy. It is good, indeed, to behold the face, and listen to the voice, though it be only in whispering tones, of one whose name and worth have long had a cherished place in our hearts, and whom the whole Christian world reveres and loves. The missionary meeting that was held here on Sunday evening, on the occasion of Dr. Judson's presence, will long be remembered by all who were there. It was not the least interesting feature of the occasion, that it was a union missionary meeting of all the evangelical denominations; and, though it was held in the First Baptist Church, you will not be surprised to learn that at a very early hour every part of that large house was crowded to overflowing. Not a pew in any part of the house, not a place in all the aisles, not the remotest corner, above or below, remained unoccupied. After an appropriate anthem from the choir, selections from the Scriptures were read, and prayer was offered by Rev. Mr. Granger. Dr. Wayland then addressed the audience. He gave a rapid and interesting sketch of the life and labors of Dr. Judson, and of the origin and progress of the Burman mission, and then, with words of welcome and congratulation, introduced Dr. Judson to the audience. Dr. Judson arose, and, as his voice would not allow him audibly to address the congregation, the Rev. Dr. Caswell stood by his side and acted as an interpreter. The first wish of his heart on this occasion, Dr. Judson said, was to express, in behalf of himself and his missionary brethren, his deep sense of gratitude to the church usually worshipping in that house, as one of the foremost of the Baptist churches in the work of missions, and especially for their contributions to the support of the pastor of the native church in Rangoon. In the early part of his residence in Rangoon, he went on to relate, a Burman philosopher, attended by his pupils, on their way to a neighboring pagoda, was wont to pass the place where he lived, and from which he instructed the people. On one occasion, the philosopher was stopped by the crowd gathered about Dr. Judson, and his eye accidentally fell upon the first tract that was published in the Burmese language, the opening words of which announced the existence of a *living, eternal God.* These significant words arrested his whole attention, and he stood a long time, as in profound thought, his whole soul absorbed with the great truth which they taught. To himself, as well as the whole nation, this was a new idea, and it led to a long course of study and investigation, which finally resulted in the renunciation of the religion of his country, and the adoption of Christianity.

He was baptized, and commenced a course of zealous labor as a Christian teacher. He soon became obnoxious to the government, and was tried and condemned to death. But before the day of execution came on, he effected his escape, and fled from the city. Since that time Dr. Judson had never seen him, nor learned any particulars of his life, but had frequently heard of him, through persons who came a long distance from the interior, in search of tracts and Bibles, having been awakened to inquiry, and converted to the Christian faith, by his instructions. The native pastor, to whom reference had been made, was once a pupil of this Burman philosopher, and afterwards his disciple in the better school of Christian truth. After this interesting allusion to this signal instance of the effect of Christian missions, Dr. Judson observed that for more than thirty-three years he had been living in the midst of a people of practical atheists, whose sole object of worship was the image of a being called Gaudama, who had lived some two thousand years ago.

The image of this being they were taught to worship from their earliest infancy; mothers bringing to it their little children in their arms, and teaching them to clasp it with the affection ot infantile devotion. Through the blessing of God much good had been done, multitudes converted, and churches formed; ar d nothing but the toleration of government seemed wanting to give the blessings of Christianity to the whole nation. On returning to his native land after so long an absence, he saw on all sides much to admire and love; but he must confess that the conversion of one immortal soul on those heathen shores awakened within him deeper emotion than all the beauty of this glorious land. The greatest favor he could ask of his Christian friends was, to permit him to return as soon as possible to his home on the banks of the Salwen; those banks from which he had led so many happy converts into the baptismal waters; those banks which had so often resounded with the notes of a baptismal song, composed by her whom he had so lately lost, who had now left her task of making hymns on earth for the higher and better one of singing with angels and ransomed spirits that " new song of Moses and the Lamb." " May it be ours," were the last words of the speaker, " to meet her there at last, and join that holy throng whom no man can number, who rest not day and night, saying, Holy, holy, holy, Lord God Almighty!"

Addresses were then made by Dr. Caswell, Rev. Mr. Jameson, and Rev. Mr. Leavitt; and the exercises of the meeting were closed by prayer, and the singing of the Missionary Hymn.

On Monday Dr. Judson visited Brown University. The return of this distinguished man to this seat of learning, in which he was graduated in 1807, and from which he has been absent in a heathen land more than thirty years, awakened the deepest interest in all the members of the university. The students assembled in the library room, and, after being introduced, were addressed by him in a few words, expressing the thoughts and feelings which thronged in upon him on revisiting the place of his education. He expressed his admiration at the improved condition of all that he saw around him in the external condition of the college, as well as its internal arrangements, its increased means of education, and the quiet and gentlemanly deportment of the students, and in closing paid a high compliment to the distinguished president of the university, who was known, he said, as a scholar and a friend of missions, wherever American missionaries had gone.

Dr. Judson was also present at a special meeting of the Philermenian Society, of which he was a member when an undergraduate. On being introduced by one of the officers of the college, he was welcomed in an appropriate speech by the president of the society. The secretary then read the records of the meeting in 1804, at which time Mr. Judson joined the society. The reading of this record awakened many old associations of Dr. Judson's college life, and rising under the influence of deep emotion, he said a few earnest and affectionate words, expressive of his continued interest in the society, and his warm wishes for the intellectual and spiritual welfare of all its members.

The society was also addressed by Rev. Thomas Williams, who was well acquainted with Dr. Judson when in college. He spoke with deep feeling of the early character of Dr. Judson, and after adverting to his subsequent life and labors, exhorted the members of the society to place before them for imitation his bright Christian example. The whole occasion was one of the deepest interest, and will long be remembered by all who were present.

The following comprises the substance of Dr. Judson's address to the Society for Missionary Inquiry, in Brown University, during his visit : —

Dr. Judson, accompanied by Dr. Wayland, met the members at the society's room, where he was apprised of the object of the association, the general character of its meetings, and of the provision in its constitution which requires from every member a pledge that he will make it a matter of serious inquiry and earnest prayer, to ascertain whether it be not his duty to go in person as a missionary to the heathen.

On the table before him lay the " Holy Bible in Burmese."

He held in his hands the book containing the constitution and the names of members, some of whom are now in the missionary field. He examined it for a moment, and then in a low voice, but with a most impressive manner, expressed himself in language very nearly as follows:—

My dear young Brethren: There is one, and only one, right path for every man,—for each one of you to follow, in order to insure the full approbation of God, and the greatest success in your efforts to do good and glorify him. Seek that one path. There may, indeed, be some other path, not very far from the right one, in which you can accomplish something for the cause of truth; but nowhere can you do so much as in that one. Do not, my brethren, content yourselves with any thing short of finding *the one* path marked out for you by the will of Heaven; and when you have found it, walk in it, straight forward, and let nothing turn you aside.

But to find that path: that is the question, and one not to be settled without diligent inquiry. To determine this point in your own case, in the first place, try all your schemes by the unerring word of God. Reject, at once, whatever has not a firm basis there. Let this blessed word be to you the golden lamp of heaven, hung out to guide you into and along the pathway of duty, and do not for a moment turn your backs upon this glorious light, to follow the feeble tapers of your own lighting. But you are not to suppose that this of itself, independent of all other considerations, will decide you to your particular sphere of labor. Next, then, look for the developments of God's providence in your own characters, and in the circumstances in which you are placed. Watch for the expression of his will in the opinions and advice of your most pious and judicious brethren respecting you, and by all means humbly and earnestly pray for guidance from above.

Finally, seek for a deep and abiding conviction of duty. Do not act from the impulse of mere feeling. There is great danger here. Feelings often mislead us. Good men sometimes mistake transient impressions, or the whisperings of their own vain imaginations, for a sense of duty, and follow some satanic influence, instead of the Spirit of truth. You must be very cautious here. I well recollect when I and other young men stood before the association in Bradford, to petition that body for aid in prosecuting our missionary scheme. Inquiry was made respecting the motives which prompted us to engage in this work. Samuel J. Mills replied, with great emphasis, "I feel myself impelled to go — *yea, woe is me if I preach not the gospel to the heathen.*" It is this settled conviction of duty to Christ, a feeling that necessity is laid upon him, and this only, that will sustain a man under the severe trials and labors of the missionary life. Without this he will soon be discouraged, and faint by the way. But with the assurance that, having humbly submitted himself to the divine teaching, he has the approval of Christ, he is prepared for any event. With this he can labor; by this he can die. If brought into difficulties, from which there seems no escape, he feels that he has gone thus far in obedience to his Lord's command; that he is doing his Master's work; and that, whatever befalls him, all is well: it is the will of Christ.

If you can have this unwavering conviction, my dear brethren, that God requires you to go as missionaries to the heathen, go. But do not go without it. It is indispensable to your success. I have known more than one missionary break down for want of this assurance.

If it be the will of God, may many of you go, constrained by the love of Christ, and lead many more to love him; and when our work is done on earth, may we all be raised to heaven, where we shall know more of his love to us, and love him more.

A short but fervent prayer by Dr. Judson closed this deeply interesting interview; and I doubt not all present felt, as the man of God turned to depart, what it was to live and labor for Jesus Christ, as they never felt it before.

A special meeting of the Triennial Convention was held in the city of New York, on the 19th of

November, 1845. At this meeting, the following resolutions, prefaced with a brief and eloquent address, were offered by the Rev. Dr. Cone, of New York:—

Resolved, That this convention regard as a special occasion of gratitude to the God of all grace, that he has so long preserved the life of our senior missionary, the Rev. Adoniram Judson, D. D., and has strengthened him to perform services of inestimable value to the perishing heathen.

Resolved, That the president be requested to express to our brother Judson assurances of the pleasure with which we welcome him to his native land, and of our heartfelt sympathy with him in the painful circumstances which have withdrawn him, as we hope, only for a season from the field of his missionary labors.

The resolutions having been unanimously adopted, Dr. Judson rose, in the presence of a deeply-affected assembly, when the president addressed him as follows:—

It is with no ordinary feelings, my beloved brother, that I rise to discharge the duty imposed upon me by the resolution which you have this moment heard. My own heart assures me that language is inadequate to express the sentiments of your brethren on the present occasion.

Thirty-three years since, you and a few other servants of the most high God, relying simply upon his promises, left your native land to carry the message of Christ to the heathen. You were the first offering of the American churches to the Gentiles. You went forth amid the sneers of the thoughtless, and with only the cold and reluctant consent of many of your brethren. The general voice declared your undertaking fanatical, and those who cowered under its rebuke drew back from you in alarm. On the voyage your views respecting Christian ordinances became changed, and this change gave rise to the convention now in session before you.

When at length you arrived in India, more formidable obstacles than those arising from paganism were thrown in your path. The mightiest empire that the world has ever seen forbade every attempt to preach Christ to the countless millions subjected to her sway, and ordered you peremptorily from her shores. Escaping from her power, you took refuge in the Isle of France, and at last, after many perils, arrived at Rangoon, where, out of the reach of Christian power, you were permitted to enter upon your labors of love.

After years of toil you were able to preach Christ to the Burmans, and men began to inquire after the eternal God. The intolerance of the government then became apparent, and you proceeded to Ava, to plead the cause of toleration before the emperor. Your second attempt was successful, and permission was granted to preach the gospel in the capital itself. But how inscrutable are the ways of Providence! Your labors had just commenced when a British army took possession of Rangoon, and you and your fellow-laborer, the late Dr. Price, were cast into a loathsome dungeon, and loaded with chains. For nearly two years you suffered all that barbarian cruelty could inflict; and to the special interposition of God alone is it to be ascribed that your imprisonment was not terminated by a violent death. On you, more than any other missionary of modern times, has been conferred the distinction of suffering for Christ. Your limbs have been galled with fetters, and you have tracked with bleeding feet the burning sands between Ava and Oung-pen-la.

With the apostle of the Gentiles you may say, "Henceforth let no man trouble me; I bear in my body the scars of the Lord Jesus." Yet even here God did not leave you comfortless. He had provided an angel to minister to your wants, and when her errand was accomplished, took her to himself, and the hopia tree marks the spot whence her spirit ascended. From prison and from chains, God, in his own time, delivered you, and made your assistance of special importance in negotiating a treaty of peace between these two nations, one of whom had driven you from her shores, and the other had inflicted upon you every cruelty but death.

Since this period, the prime of your life has been spent in laboring to bless the people who had so barbarously persecuted you. Almost all the Christian literature in their language has proceeded from your pen; your own hand has given to the nation the oracles of God, and opened to the millions now living, and to those that shall come after them to the end of time, the door of everlasting life. That mysterious Providence which shut you out from Burmah proper has introduced you to the Karens — a people who seem to have preserved, from remote antiquity, the knowledge of the true God, and who were waiting to receive the message of his Son. To them you, and those who have followed in your footsteps, have made known the Saviour of the world, and they by thousands have flocked to the standard of the cross.

After years spent in unremitted toil, the providence of God has brought you to be present with us at this important crisis. We sympathize with you in all the sorrows of your painful voyage. May God sustain you in your sore bereavement, and cause even this mysterious dispensation to work out for you a far more exceeding and eternal weight of glory.

How changed is the moral aspect of the world since you first entered upon your labors! Then no pagan nation had heard the name of Christ from American lips; at present, churches of Christ, planted by American benevolence, are springing up in almost every heathen nation. The shores of the Mediterranean, the islands of the sea, the thronged cities and the wild jungles of India, are resounding with the high praises of God, in strains first taught by American missionaries. The nation that drove you from her shores has learned to foster the messenger of the cross with parental solicitude. You return to your native land, whence you were suffered to depart almost without her blessing, and you find that the missionary enterprise has kindled a flame that can never be quenched in the heart of the universal church, and that every Christian and every philanthropist comes forward to tender to you the homage due to the man through whose sufferings, labors, and examples, these changes have, to so great a degree, been effected. In behalf of our brethren, in behalf of the whole church of Christ, we welcome you back to the land of your fathers. God grant that your life may long be preserved, and that what you have seen may prove to be but the beginning of blessing to our churches at home and to the heathen abroad.

Dr. Judson briefly expressed his thanks for the kind manner in which he had been uniformly welcomed since his return, and earnestly hoped that all this would be overruled and blessed to promote his humility, and the more faithful discharge of his duty among the heathen.

The following addresses were delivered by Dr. Judson on several occasions during his visit to the United States.

Address at a Missionary Meeting in Philadelphia.

Be ye imitators of me, as I am of Christ, is a divine command. There is one Being in the universe who unites in himself all the excellences of the human and divine nature — that being is Jesus Christ. To become like Jesus Christ, we must be like him, not only in spirit and character, but in the whole course and conduct of life; and to become like him ought to be our whole aim. In order to this, it is necessary to ascertain the leading characteristics of that glorious Being. It appears from the inspired writings, that one leading characteristic of Christ was, that "he went about doing good." To be like him, we must go about — not merely *stay* and do good, but *go* and do good. There is another characteristic which we should consider. He led the life of a missionary. In order, therefore, to be like him in this particular, we must endeavor, as far as possible, to lead the life of missionaries. Before my arrival in Burmah, there were about seven millions of men, women, and children, who had no knowledge of the true God, and of salvation through Jesus Christ. They did not believe in the existence of an eternal God. They believed that when they died they would be changed into beasts, or be annihilated. Their only object in worship was to obtain some mitigation of suffering. They never expected to meet their friends again after death. Imagine yourselves, my Christian friends, in their state without a knowledge of God. Suppose, while in that state, you heard that in some isle of the sea were those who had received a revelation, informing them that God had sent his own Son to open a way to everlasting life; would you not rejoice, if some one should come to show you that way to heaven? Would not some of you believe? Would you not leap with joy, and kiss the feet of those who brought you the good tidings? Would you not, under these circumstances, desire that a messenger should come to you? "As ye would that men should do to you, do ye even so to them." I should rejoice to address the assembly at large, but my physicians have forbidden me, and I must commit this duty to others who are to follow. But allow me to say, that I regard the office of the missionary as a most glorious occupation, because the *faithful* missionary is engaged in a work which is like that of the Lord Jesus Christ; and a missionary who is *unfaithful* sinks the lowest of his species in guilt and ignominy. Happy are they who can in this respect follow Christ. But the Lord Jesus is not now a missionary. He has retired from this employment, and now employs himself in sustaining his missionaries, with the promise, "Lo, I am with you alway, even to the end." If you cannot, therefore, become a missionary, sustain by your prayers, your influence, and your property, those who are. In these ways Jesus Christ now sustains them. By his *prayers*, as Advocate and Intercessor with the Father; by his *influence*, as he is vested with all power in heaven and earth; by his *property*, by pouring out fresh supplies of his Spirit, and opening the hearts of his children to contribute. In order, therefore, to be like Christ, *go about* doing good; and if it is not in your power to give yourselves to this work, give your prayers, your influence, and your property. So far as we are like Christ in this world, so far shall we be like him through eternity So far as we sustain this cause, which is peculiarly the cause of God, so far shall we be happy through endless ages.

Remarks before the Boardman Missionary Society at Waterville College.

At the appointed hour the society, together with the faculty and the remainder of the students, assembled in one of the recitation rooms, where ensued a scene of such solemn interest as has seldom occurred among us.

The crowded room was hushed into the most death-like stillness, in order that not a syllable should be lost to any ear; and as the low, earnest and melodious tones fell upon us, it seemed hardly sacrilegious to be reminded of the "still small voice" that addressed the prophet Elijah. Copious notes of his remarks were taken by some of the brethren, which may be read with interest by those who love to treasure up every word that drops from the lips of this modern apostle.

He began, with manifest signs of deep feeling: "Upon an occasion like this, dear brethren, a multitude of thoughts crowd upon me, so that I know not where to begin or what to select. Probably many of you have the ministry in view, and some perhaps look forward to a missionary life. You will expect me to speak of missions and missionary life. I have seen so much of the trials and responsibility of missionary labors, that I am unwilling to urge any one to assume them. *The urging must come from a higher source.* One important thought just occurs to me. You have but *one* life to live in which to prepare for eternity. If you had four or five lives, two or three of them might be spent in carelessness. But you have one, only. Every action of that one life gives coloring to your eternity. How important, then, that you spend that life so as to please the Saviour, the blessed Saviour, who has done every thing for you!

"If any of you enter the gospel ministry in this or other lands, let not your object be so much to 'do your duty,' or even to 'save souls,' though these should have a place in your motives, as to *please the Lord Jesus.* Let this be your ruling motive in all that you do. Now, do you ask *how* you shall please him? How, indeed, shall we know what will please him, but by *his commands?* Obey these commands, and you will not fail to please him. And there is that 'last command,' given just before he ascended to the Father, 'Go ye into all the world, and preach the gospel to every creature.' It is not *yet* obeyed as it should be. Fulfil that, and you will please the Saviour.

"Some one asked me, not long ago, whether *faith* or *love* influenced me most in going to the heathen. I thought of it a while, and at length concluded that there was in me but *little of either.* But in thinking of what *did* influence me, I remembered a time, out in the woods back of Andover Seminary, when I was almost disheartened. Every thing looked dark. No one had gone out from this country. The way was not open. The field was far distant, and in an unhealthy climate. I knew not what to do. All at once that 'last command' seemed to come to my heart directly from heaven. I could doubt no longer, but determined on the spot to obey it at all hazards, for the sake of pleasing the Lord Jesus Christ.

"Now, my dear brethren, if the Lord wants you for missionaries, he will set that command home to your hearts. If he does so, *you neglect it at your peril.*"

Dr. Judson spoke, in a most impressive and glowing manner, of the reward laid up on high for those who endeavored to please the Saviour, and then offered a prayer which I can only describe by saying, it was one of *Judson's* prayers. I had enjoyed a previous opportunity of uniting my petitions with his before the throne of grace, and can say that the repetition of the privilege caused me to admire yet more the exceeding simplicity and humility which adorn this great man's character.

Address before the American and Foreign Bible Society.

Go ye into all the world and preach the gospel, or rather proclaim the good news, to every creature. The word *preach* has in modern usage acquired a meaning rather too specific for the original. Oral communication may be the first and most obvious, but is certainly not the exclusive meaning of the original word. It is more faithfully represented in English by the word *proclaim*. If a messenger from a king or superior government should be sent to a rebellious province, to proclaim pardon to the inhabitants, he would evidently be fulfilling his commission, whether he communicated the intelligence by addressing the people in his own person, or by inserting notices in the public prints, or by circulating handbills, or by distributing authentic documents from the sovereign, declaring the terms of pardon. The apostle Paul did as really and certainly, as effectually and extensively, proclaim the gospel, when he penned the Epistles to the Hebrews and the Romans, as when he addressed the Jews in their synagogues, or received company in his own hired house at Rome. The earlier communications of a missionary, sent to impart the gospel to an unenlightened people, will probably be of an oral kind; but he will have very imperfectly fulfilled his commission, if he leave them without the written word. The mischievous consequences also of such neglect are abundantly manifest in the missions conducted by the man of sin. Protestant missions have patronized the translation and distribution of the Scriptures; but of late years there has appeared, in one or two instances, a tendency to promote the oral communication of the gospel, not indeed to an undue preëminence, but in such a manner as to throw a shade over the written communication, by means of tracts and Scriptures. In examining the annals of modern missions, it is difficult to ascertain which mode of communicating the gospel among a reading nation has received the greatest share of divine blessing, and been instrumental of bringing most souls to the knowledge of the truth. And however the preaching of the gospel, in its common acceptation, and the distribution of tracts, may secure earlier effects, and be regarded as more popular, all missionary operations, to be permanently successful, must be based on the written word. Where that word is most regarded and honored, there will be the most pure and permanent success.

The word of God is the golden lamp hung out of heaven,

to enlighten the nations that sit in darkness, and to show them the path that leads from the confines of hell to the gates of paradise. The Bible, in the original tongues, comprises *all* the revelation now extant which God has given to this world. It is, in all its contents, and parts, and appendages, just *the book*, the one book, which infinite wisdom saw best adapted to answer the end of a written revelation. It may not be reducible to the rules of human philosophy or logic, for it transcends them all. It is just as clear and obscure, just as copious and scanty, has just as many beauties and blemishes, is replete with just as many difficulties and apparent contradictions, as infinite wisdom saw necessary, in order to make it, like all the works of God, perfect and unique. This one perfect book is the sacred deposit in the hands of the church. It has been deposited with the injunction, "Freely ye have received, freely give." Woe be to that man who withholds the treasure from his neighbor. Woe be to him who attempts to obscure the light of the lamp of heaven. It is the peculiar glory of the last half century that the Christian world has awaked to the duty and importance of giving the sacred word "to all lands." Praised be God for Bible and Missionary Societies, the peculiar institutions of modern times. May their efforts be continued and enlarged a hundred fold, until their work is consummated — until the Bible is translated and published in every language under heaven, and a copy of the sacred volume deposited in every palace, and house, and hut inhabited by man.

In this momentous era, can any believer in the Christian religion hope to lie down in the grave, and pass quietly to paradise, without having made some effort to diffuse the light of the Bible throughout the world? Before he cherishes such a hope, and makes up his mind for such repose, let him consider how many millions there are who have never seen so much as one leaf of the sacred volume, never tasted so much as one drop of the water of that well from which he is drawing and drinking every day. Let him consider how much money must be expended, how many toilsome efforts made, and how many lives sacrificed, before the book can be translated, printed, published, and distributed, before the well can be unsealed, and the water of life drawn and presented to all mankind. And then let him inquire of his conscience what he has done towards accomplishing this great work, during the years that have passed since he ventured to hope in the Saviour. He will then be unable to refrain from lifting up his cry, God of mercy, have mercy on me, and help me from this moment to spring forward to the work, with such alacrity, and resolution, and self-devotement, as will secure the approving smile of the Saviour, and afford my own soul satisfaction on the great day.

Address at a Meeting in Utica, New York.

When mingling in scenes like the present, and like that in which he participated on the preceding evening, at which he believed some then listening to him were present, he was led into trains of meditation which excited the most deep and subduing emotions. At such times he involuntarily recalled many spots memorable in his history. One of these was the prison at Ava, to which allusion had already been made. In that gloomy place, on one night when he was more heavily fettered and was enduring more suffering than usual, he rose from the painful posture in which he reclined to lean, for an interval, against the wall. As he cast his eyes around upon the mass of wretchedness before him, he was able, by the dim light which was always kept burning in the prison, to observe the condition of the miserable beings among whom he was confined. It was an appalling sight. About a hundred condemned felons were before him, some sentenced for murder, all for atrocious crimes. While looking on that spectacle, he felt that if ever, by God's mercy, he should obtain his freedom, he would endeavor to bear without repining the ills he might be called to endure. Another spot brought to his recollection was that where he stood to witness the worship of the Bengalee Juggernaut, — not the great Juggernaut of Orissa, — for there are several in India, — but one in the province of Bengal. The idol car moved onward. Before him, extending as far as the eye could reach, was a vast expanse, a sea of human heads. The whole concourse of deluded worshippers were shouting as with one voice. Again his mind reverted to a scene that fell under his observation, not many years since, in the Karen jungles. It was one of the festivals of the Karens. He saw three hundred persons, prostrate upon the earth, men, women, and children, promiscuously mingled, covered with filth, in a state of brutal intoxication — a spectacle not to be described to a Christian audience. Scenes like these forced themselves upon his recollection, in view of our places of worship and happy homes. When coming among us, and seeing the contrasted comfort, elegance, and refinement, that make our dwellings so inviting and their inmates so happy, the question spontaneously arose, What is the cause of all this difference? O, it is the gospel — the gospel! While surrounded with these manifold blessings, we could but very imperfectly appreciate the sole cause of them all.

It was to a world suffering under such wretchedness as had been spoken of, that the Lord Jesus Christ, in compassion for mankind, descended in the reign of the despotic and abandoned Herod. Amid such scenes he mingled, till he expired on the cross. If his gospel is able to effect all that we have seen, to transform the ignorant, sensual, and degraded heathen, and to elevate a nation to such a height of dignity and enjoyment, and all this in a world still so full of sin, how will its power appear in the world to which we are advancing? If here, where sin yet reigns, so great a contrast can be wrought, how much greater the contrast between this imperfect state and heaven, free from every defilement!

In Burmah, after all that has been done, there is still the same prison at Ava, with its manacled convicts. The same Bengalee Juggernaut is still surrounded by its countless worshippers. The same orgies are still celebrated in the Karen jungles; and scenes innumerable, as revolting as these, are witnessed in all heathen lands. O, let us pray for the millions who know nothing of a God or a Saviour, a heaven or a hell.

Address at Washington, D. C.

It has been said that human praise to human ears is always sweet; but to me, as a missionary of the cross, it is only so when offered through me to my Lord. I feel that I am a miserable sinner, and desire that my brethren here will unite and pray for me, that all my past unfaithfulness may be pardoned. What was the missionary's work? Some of its responsibilities, and the encouragements we had to prosecute it, Dr. Judson said, had been declared to us in the discourse to which we had listened this evening.* When he first visited Burmah, the idea of an eternal God was not believed nor entertained by any of the Burmans; and nothing more than this idea was entertained by the Karens; but now the former had in their own language the whole word of God; and the New Testament, and parts of the Old, had been translated, by American missionaries, into several other languages of the East. He spoke of our missions as *expensive,* as requiring much for the outfit of missionaries, and for sustaining them in that field; but sacrifices of a *pecuniary* character were not the only or the greatest ones to be encountered. There was the sacrifice of domestic and social comforts here enjoyed, and the sacrifice of life. He remarked that the average life of American missionaries to the East was only about five years. But we must have men and money for this work; and we must all coöperate and make sacrifices together. If men were found willing to go, the church at home should feel willing to send them out, and support them, that they might give themselves wholly to their work. Dr. Judson said that his heart was full, and it was a great privation to him that he was not able to speak out, and unburden himself, to the satisfaction of himself and of the audience; but this the providence of God prevented him from doing, and he must submit.

* By the Rev. G. W. Samson.

To his Sons.

DEAR ADONIRAM AND ELNATHAN: You know not how much I love you, and how much I think of you. I pray for you every time I pray for myself. I hear that there are revivals of religion beginning to appear in different parts of the country. It would be a blessed thing if you should both experience religion, and have the privilege of beginning a revival in Worcester. Cherish this desire in your hearts, and pray in faith that the blessing may come. If you begin to feel sorry for your sins, and afraid of the wrath to come, and begin to love the dear Saviour, because he has died to save you, and feel some desire to commit your immortal souls to him, and be forgiven and accepted, you may begin to hope the grace of God is reaching you, and that the blessed work is just beginning. Hold on, then, and cherish those impressions, until you get full light and hope.

Dear children, remember your father in his solitary wanderings, and forget not your dear mother, whom we buried at St. Helena. Pray for your sister, and your little brothers beyond the sea.

Your ever affectionate father,

A. JUDSON.

To G. D. Boardman.

WASHINGTON, January 26, 1846.

MY DEAR GEORGE: I write to say that I expect to leave this for Richmond, Virginia, in a few days; and if you write me, to the care of Mr. Archibald Thomas, of that place, I shall get your letter before proceeding farther south, or returning north. I am doubtful which course I shall take. The cold weather is moderate in these parts, and I bear it very well. My throat also is getting better, in consequence of never speaking in public. Certain medicines also have, I suppose, done me some good.

Mr. Peck writes me that there will be an opportunity of sailing direct to Maulmain, about the 1st of July. Several of us will probably go out together. On this account, I want to spend more of my time at the north.

It is my daily prayer that you may be *a growing Christian;* that your faith may become stronger, your love more ardent, and your whole soul and body more consecrated to the service of your adorable Lord.

To his Sons.

DEAR ADONIRAM AND ELNATHAN: It is most painful to reflect that I shall never, in all probability, live with you much more — only a few days, now and then — before I embark for Burmah — you, my two dear boys, that I have loved so much, and tried to take care of, by day and by night, for so many years. But this separation must take place, and I must commit you to the kind friends who now take charge of you, in hope that God will incline their hearts, as hitherto, to do all for you that is necessary and best, and in the most precious hope that you will become children of God, and be prepared to meet me and your departed mother before the throne of God, with exceeding joy. When George writes, add a few lines, each of you, that I may see your writing, though I cannot see your sweet faces.

To Mrs. Newton, of Worcester, Mass.

MY DEAR MRS. NEWTON: I thank you for the few lines that you appended to George's last letter. I need not ask you to take care of my poor boys. I know you will do so. And I only hope that they will ever be obedient and grateful.

We had splendid meetings in Philadelphia. You will see, by the papers, that above fifteen thousand dollars were raised in that city; and they will probably raise ten thousand dollars every year, perhaps more; but my nervous system became deranged again, and I passed many sleepless nights. After a few days I recovered, and am now pretty well. With love to Dr. Newton,

Most affectionately,

A. JUDSON.

To the Rev. Dr. Johnson.

RICHMOND, February 5, 1846.

REV. AND VERY DEAR BROTHER: I have heard so much of you from all quarters, and especially from my missionary associate, brother Binney, that when I received your kind letter of the 23d of December last, I felt that I *must* come on and see you and Dr. Fuller, of Beaufort. But I now find it impossible. The heavy press of business lying on me in the Northern States, which *must* be disposed of previous to sailing for the East, the prospect of which is now drawing near, the increasing complaint of my throat, and the urgent advice of the most eminent doctors that I desist from visiting new places, and continuing to aggravate the disease, which, they say, is even now ready to settle on my lungs, seem to present an insuperable barrier to my proceeding farther south than this city. This city I determined at all risks to visit, as it is the seat of the Southern Convention, in the welfare and prosperity of which I feel deeply interested. But farther south I *cannot*. I turn my face to the north with great reluctance; but the bright hope of soon turning my face to the East, my country, my home on earth, dispels all reluctance to leave any part of this country, and cheers me with the prospect of spending the remnant of life where I have spent the greater part of it.

Dear brother,
Most affectionately and respectfully yours,
A. JUDSON.

Rev. Dr. Johnson, Pres. S. Carolina Bap. State Convention, &c.

On the 8th of February, 1846, a meeting was held at Richmond, Virginia, to welcome the return of Dr. Judson to this country. At this meeting the Rev. Dr. Jeter, pastor of one of the Baptist churches in that city, and president of the Board of the Southern Baptist Convention, addressed him as follows: —

Brother Judson: I address you on behalf of the Foreign Mission Board of the Southern Baptist Convention, in Richmond, and, I may add, of the whole Baptist denomination in the south. The service is at once pleasing and painful — pleasing, because we had scarcely expected to enjoy the privilege of seeing your face and grasping your hand; painful, because your want of voice prevents you from imparting to us the instruction and encouragement which you are well qualified to communicate; and the brevity of your visit will make the pain of separation almost equal to the pleasure of meeting.

I seize the present opportunity to present a few remarks; and I do it the more readily, as the state of your health does not permit us to expect many from yourself.

It is interesting to stand at the head spring of a great river, which, traversing a continent, spreads through kingdoms fertility and all the blessings of commerce. The position awakens emotions of sublimity. It cannot be less interesting and inspiring to contemplate events which, in themselves seemingly unimportant, have produced momentous results. To such an event our attention is drawn by your presence.

When you and your honored associates, Nott, Mills, and Newell, presented to the General Association of Congregationalists in Massachusetts, assembled in Bradford, in 1810, a paper expressing your desire to engage in the work of foreign missions, and asking their advice and aid, who could have anticipated the result of the application? At that time the churches were slumbering profoundly on the subject of missions; there were no missionary societies, no plans matured for conducting missions, and no funds collected for the support of missionaries.

The application originated the American Board of Commissioners for Foreign Missions. A noble institution it is, superior to any in our own land, and vying, in the wisdom of its measures and the success of its efforts, with the best ordered and most renowned missionary organizations of the old world. Its annual expenditure is not far, if at all, short of one third of a million of dollars; and its mission stations have dotted almost the whole extent of heathendom.

Under the patronage of this board, after considerable hesitation and delay on their part, you embarked, with your companion and revered associates, in 1812, for the East. On your arrival there, an event occurred deeply affecting your own course, and the cause of missions. You, Mrs. Judson, and the lamented Rice, became Baptists. Whatever may be said or thought of the change, your sincerity in making it cannot be reasonably called in question. You abandoned a Christian denomination, wealthy, with whose members you were intimately acquainted, to whom you were tenderly attached, and from whom you expected a liberal support, and connected yourself with one comparatively poor, to whose members you were a stranger, and from whom you had no prospect of receiving assistance. The hand of God was in it. The change was the means of arousing among the Baptists of the United States the missionary spirit, and forming the Baptist Triennial Convention, under whose patronage you have so long labored.

By a remarkable train of events, among which was the breaking out of the war between this country and Great Britain, you were led, or rather driven, into Burmah. God had selected that field for you, and designed that you should accomplish a great work there.

I pass over the story of your toils and sufferings, your chains and imprisonment, and the almost superhuman fortitude of your now sainted companion. It is familiar to every American, and, indeed, every Christian reader. It forms an essential and thrilling chapter in the history of missions.

And now, my brother, — to say nothing of what has been effected by the missionaries of the Baptist Triennial Convention among the aborigines of America, in France, in Germany, in Denmark, in Greece, in Africa, in China, in Siam, in Hindoostan, in Asam, — behold what a change God hath wrought in Burmah, and in the contiguous provinces! The Bible has been translated into the Burman language, carefully revised, printed, put into circulation, and read by thousands. We watched with intense interest the progress of the translation. We prayed that your life might be spared to complete it. We saw you, when, having finished the last leaf of the precious volume, you took it in your hand, and bowing beside your desk, gave thanks to God that he had enabled you to accomplish the work. To that thanksgiving we subjoined our hearty amen! In that land, so recently enveloped in the darkness of heathenism, churches have been founded, to worship the name and keep the ordinances of Jesus. Native preachers have been raised up to proclaim, in their own tongue, and among their own countrymen, "the unsearchable riches of Christ." The Karens, a simple-hearted and singular people, are turning by hundreds and thousands to the Lord. Among them the gospel has had a success rarely equalled since the days of the apostles. On Burmah "the morning light is breaking." The time to favor her has fully come.

We cannot penetrate futurity. I pretend not to be skilled in prophetic interpretation. But in the next half century we may anticipate great accessions to Christianity. We found our hope on *past success*. Wherever the gospel has been preached plainly and faithfully, from the equator to the poles, among civilized or savage men, it has been the "power of God unto salvation." The success of the missionary enterprise has every where corresponded, in a remarkable manner, with the measures of ability, zeal, and diligence employed in its prosecution. We base our expectation on the *increasing prevalence of the missionary spirit*. When, more than half a century ago, the work of foreign missions commenced among the Anglo-Saxon Christians, led on by the immortal Carey, it was predicted that its advocates would soon grow weary, and relax their efforts. The prediction has not been fulfilled. At no previous period has it been so much the settled policy and purpose of the churches to make efforts and sacrifices in the work of evangelizing the world as it is now. And, above all, we found our hope on the *divine promises*. Unless we have misconceived their import, they point to a time of greater light, purity, and triumph in the church than the world has yet seen. This sin-darkened earth is to be filled with the knowledge of the glory of God. From the rising of the sun even unto the going down of the same, the name of Christ shall be great among the Gentiles, and in every place incense shall be offered unto his name, and a pure offering.

Henceforth, my brother, you and we shall labor in connection with different boards. Events which neither you nor we could control produced the separation; and God, we trust, will overrule it for good. One thing is certain: the southern Baptists have no thought of abandoning the missionary field. We are buckling on our armor, and marshalling our hosts for a stronger onset on the powers of darkness than we have yet made. We have selected China as our battle field; a vast, interesting, and inviting field it is. It contains one half, if not two thirds, of the heathen population of the globe. The wall which for centuries presented an insuperable barrier to the introduction of Christianity has recently been levelled with the dust; and the banner of the cross now floats in triumph in Canton.

But I must close my remarks. Brother Judson, we are acquainted with your history. We have marked your labors, have sympathized in your various sufferings, have shed many a tear at the foot of the "hopia tree," have gone, in fancy, on mournful pilgrimage to the rocky Island of St. Helena, have rejoiced in your successes and the successes of your devoted associates, and have long and fervently wished to see your face in the flesh. This privilege we now enjoy. Welcome, thrice welcome are you, my brother, to our city, our churches, our bosoms. I speak as the representative of southern Baptists. We love you for the truth's sake, and for your labors in the cause of Christ. We honor you as the father of American missions.

One thought pains us. To-morrow morning you will leave us. We shall see your face no more. You will soon return to Burmah, the land of your adoption. There you will continue your toils, and there, probably, be buried. But this separation is not without its solace. Thank God, it is as near from Burmah to heaven as from Richmond, or any other point on the globe. Angels, oft commissioned to convey to heaven the departing spirits of pious Burmans and Karens, have learned the way to that dark land. When dismissed from your toils and sufferings, they will be in readiness to perform the same service for you. God grant that we may all meet in that bright world. There sin shall no more annoy us, separations no more pain us, and every power will find full and sweet employ in the service of Christ.

And now, my brother, I give my hand in token of our affection to you, and of your cordial reception among us.

CHAPTER VII.

MARRIAGE — FAREWELL SERVICES AT BOSTON. — VOYAGE TO MAULMAIN. — RECOMMENCES LABORS AT RANGOON. — RETURN TO MAULMAIN. — REMINISCENCES OF LAST VISIT TO RANGOON.

1846-1847.

It was manifest to all the friends of Dr. Judson, that, much as he was interested in all that he saw in this country, his heart was in Burmah. He longed to escape from the whirl of even agreeable excitement, in which, from the kindness of friends, he could not but move, and resume his quiet labors for the salvation of the heathen. He therefore embraced the first opportunity that offered to return to Maulmain. This was undoubtedly unfortunate. Had he remained here for two years at least, his health might have been permanently reëstablished.

On the 2d of June, 1846, he was married, at Hamilton, New York, to Miss Emily Chubbuck, a native of Eaton, in the same state. He proceeded immediately to Boston, to prepare for his departure. On the 11th of July he embarked, with Mrs. Judson and several other missionaries, on board the ship Faneuil Hall, Captain Hallet, bound to Maulmain. They arrived there, after a pleasant passage, on the 30th of November following.

Dr. Judson, as soon as possible, resumed his labor at the dictionary. He, however, found that Maulmain was fully supplied with missionaries in both the Burman and Karen departments. No missionary had for a long time attempted to establish himself in Rangoon. He could prosecute his dictionary work as well in Rangoon as in Maulmain, and, in some respects, with greater facilities. Besides this, he could do something for the salvation of those who were in the thick darkness of paganism, without any means of religious instruction. At Rangoon, moreover, he could avail himself of any favorable opportunity that might offer for proceeding to Ava, and making another attempt to secure to the disciples some degree of religious toleration.

With these views he proceeded to Rangoon in January, 1847, explored the ground, and made arrangements for the removal of his family. As soon as these were completed, he returned to Maulmain, and reëmbarked for Rangoon February 15, 1847.

He found the government exceedingly intolerant on the subject of religion, although he, as a Protestant preacher, and maker of the dictionary, was kindly received. The governor was a member of the royal family, with whom he had been acquainted during his former residence at Ava; and he not only favored the proposal of Dr. Judson's visit to Ava, but offered him letters to the emperor himself. Encouraged thus to hope that the set time to favor Burmah had come, he commenced his preparations for a voyage to the capital of the empire.

This hope was, however, destined to a speedy extinction. Before his arrangements had been completed, he received information from Maulmain that the board had been obliged to curtail their appropriations for the Burman mission, and left it to the discretion of the missionaries there to adjust the plan of retrenchment. The missionaries did not feel themselves authorized to supply the funds needed for the support of the mission at Rangoon. Under these circumstances, but one course seemed open to him; and that was, to return to Maulmain. The hostility of the government to Christianity had greatly interfered with his efforts, and now the very possibility of laboring among them was cut off. With deep sadness of spirit he therefore bade farewell to the few disciples whom he had again gathered in Rangoon, and turned his face towards his former station. This unfortunate necessity he regretted to the close of his life. There appeared to him, at this crisis, a slight opening for further missionary effort in Burmah. Could it have been improved, he hoped that something important might have been accomplished. The opportunity, however, soon passed away, and during his lifetime it never again reappeared.

Returning to Maulmain, he continued, with his characteristic energy, the work of the dictionary; uniting with it, as his health would permit, the stated preaching of the gospel in Burmah, and the pastorship of the Burman church. In this manner the year 1848 and part of 1849 passed away, until his health began to decline, and that illness commenced which terminated in his death.

The following account of the farewell services on the occasion of the return of Dr. Judson to Burmah, is taken from one of the religious papers of the day.*

Farewell Missionary Services.

Public exercises of a deeply interesting character were held in Baldwin Place, on Tuesday afternoon, 30th ultimo, in

---

* Christian Reflector, July 9, 1846.

reference to the departure for Burmah of the Rev. Dr. Judson and a number of new missionaries. A portion of Scripture was read by Rev. Mr. Neale, and prayer offered by Professor Ripley; after which the meeting was addressed by Rev. Mr. Stow. It was not, he said, his object to glorify man, but to honor God — not to laud and magnify those Christian heralds who were about to depart for the distant East, but to commend them to the divine protection and blessing. He said his present design would be to trace some of the evidences of special divine favor manifested towards the board, in foreign lands, and particularly in Burmah.

The peculiar origin of their first mission, he said, was worthy of notice, as indicating an overruling Providence, whose ways are not as our ways. It was commenced in 1813, by Mr. and Mrs. Judson, who had been sent out by another denomination; but their views of Christian ordinances undergoing a change, their relations were of necessity changed. Proceeding to Rangoon, in Burmah, they commenced operations, and soon after were adopted by a society formed among the Baptists of this country, and, as is well known, an extensive interest was awakened in the denomination by these unlooked-for and providential occurrences.

Mr. Stow adduced the character and efficiency of the men employed, as another proof that the mission was owned of Heaven. Not one, of all the missionaries of the board, from its commencement, had, by any moral delinquency, dishonored the Christian profession.

Another proof, also, was found in the severe but healthful discipline through which the missions and the board had frequently passed. These trials had furnished abundant evidence of the approbation of Heaven — of his benevolence, as well as paternal discipline and faithfulness. In support of this assertion, Mr. Stow took a rapid survey of some of the most trying scenes in the early history of the Burman mission, and of the manner in which they had been made to contribute to the furtherance of the gospel. He also showed that these missions had been eminently successful. Every mission commenced had been sustained. More than two hundred and fifty missionaries and assistants, besides native preachers, had been appointed, most of whom had already entered the field. Upwards of nine hundred thousand dollars had been contributed and expended. The entire Bible had been translated into the Burmese language, and portions of it into other languages and dialects, spoken by hundreds of millions. Churches had been formed, and at least eight thousand pagans had been converted to Christianity, by the blessing of Heaven on the labor of this board. A large amount of work had been upon foundations, out of sight, but the *apparent* results had not been insignificant.

He alluded also to the important reflex influence of missions on the literature, piety, public spirit, and benevolence of the churches at home, and the great change of public sentiment in reference to foreign missions. Formerly, he said, the press, and, to some extent, even the pulpit, spoke of them with suspicion, distrust, and scorn; but now, respectable journals, every where, seemed cordially interested in their progress, and the community generally contemplated their success with surprise and pleasure.

He concluded with brief remarks to each of the departing missionaries; uttering, with his accustomed ardor and eloquence, the words of fraternal sympathy and encouragement.

Rev. Mr. Peck, secretary of the board, stated that Dr. and Mrs. Judson, together with Rev. Messrs. Norman Harris and John S. Beecher, and their wives, and Miss Lydia Lillybridge, an assistant teacher, were expected to leave this port, next week, in the ship Faneuil Hall, direct for Maulmain, Burmah. He then gave the committee's instructions to the new missionaries. Their designation was to the Karens of the Burman empire, among whom the Baptist missions have made great advancement during the fifteen years of their prosecution. In the neighborhood of Maulmain, in Arracan, and in Bassein, a province of Burmah proper thousands of converts to Christianity, he said, had been made, and numerous churches had been organized, and some of them placed under the care of native pastors. But the number of foreign missionaries is so inadequate, that they are in danger of falling into such heresies and corruptions as have marred the church in all ages. The special object of these new missionaries, he said, would be to have the oversight of these native churches and pastors, and to build them up in faith, virtue, and charity. He closed with a brief but very appropriate address to the venerable pioneer in these missions.

Rev. Dr. Sharp then offered solemn prayer on behalf of the departing missionaries.

Dr. Judson, unable to address so large an audience at any length, had prepared a parting address, which was read by Rev. Mr. Hague, presenting a vivid exhibition of Christian feeling in view of the many changes that had occurred since he left America, in 1812. He had increasing confidence in the wisdom and practicability of the missionary enterprise, and carried forward the immense audience in sublime contemplation of the far greater changes to be looked for during the next third of a century; exhorting all to labor on, and hope on, fully assured that, the victory, though delayed, would be certain, and the results unspeakably glorious.

Oral Remarks.

The numerous congregation experienced unusual satisfaction in hearing the following remarks from Dr. Judson, which were very distinctly and audibly uttered, and which he has kindly furnished for our columns: —

My friends are aware, that it is quite impossible for me, without serious injury to myself, to sustain my voice at such a height as to reach this large assembly, except for a few sentences. I have, therefore, taken the liberty of putting some thoughts on paper, which the Rev. Mr. Hague will do me the honor of reading to you.

I wish, however, in my own voice, to praise God for the deep interest in the cause of missions manifested by the friends of the Redeemer in this city and the vicinity, and to thank them for all their expressions and acts of kindness towards me during my brief sojourn among them. I regret that circumstances have prevented my spending more time in this city, and forming a more intimate acquaintance with those whom a slight acquaintance has taught me so much to love.

It is as certain as any future event can be, that I shall never again revisit the shores of my native land; that, after a few days, your beautiful city, this great and glorious country, will be forever shut from my view. No more shall I enter your places of worship; no more shall I behold your faces, and exchange the affectionate salutations of Christian love.

The greatest favor we can bestow on our absent friends is to bear them on our hearts at the throne of grace. I pray you, dear friends, remember me there, and my missionary associates, and our infant churches, and the poor heathen, among whom we go to live. And though we do meet no more on earth, I trust that our next meeting will be in that blessed world where "the loved and the parted here below meet ne'er to part again."

Address.

There are periods in the lives of men, who experience much change of scene and variety of adventure, when they seem to themselves to be subject to some supernatural illusion, or wild, magical dream; when they are ready, amid the whirl of conflicting recollection, to doubt their own personal identity, and, like steersmen in a storm, feel that they must keep a steady eye to the compass and a strong arm at the wheel. The scene spread out before me seems, on retrospection, to be identified with the past, and at the same time to be reaching forward and foreshadowing the future. At one moment the lapse of thirty-four years is annihilated; the scenes of 1812 are again present; and this assembly — how like that which commended me to God on first leaving my native shores for the distant East! But, as I look around, where are the well-known faces of Spring, and Worcester, and Dwight? Where are Lyman and Huntington, and Griffin? And where are those leaders of the baptized ranks who stretched out their arms across the water, and received me into their communion? Where are Baldwin and Bolles? Where Holcombe, and Rogers, and Staughton? I see them not. I have been to their temples of worship, but their voices have passed away And where are my early missionary associates, Newell, and Hall, and Rice, and Richards, and Mills? But why inquire for those so ancient? Where are the succeeding laborers in the missionary field for many years, and the intervening generation who sustained the missions? And where are those who moved amid the dark scenes of Rangoon, and Ava, and Tavoy? Where those gentle, yet firm spirits, which tenanted forms — delicate in structure, but careless of the storm — now broken, and scattered, and strewn, like the leaves of autumn, under the shadow of overhanging trees, and on remote islands of the sea?

No, these are not the scenes of 1812; nor is this the assembly that convened in the Tabernacle of a neighboring city. Many years have elapsed; many venerated, many beloved ones have passed away to be seen no more. " They rest from their labors, and their works do follow them." And with what words shall I address those who have taken their places, the successors of the venerated and the beloved, the generation of 1812?

In that year American Christians pledged themselves to the work of evangelizing the world. They had but little to rest on, except the command and promise of God. The attempts then made by British Christians had not been attended with so much success as to establish the practicability, or vindicate the wisdom, of the missionary enterprise. For many years the work advanced but slowly. One denomination after another embarked in the undertaking; and now American missionaries are seen in almost every clime. Many languages have been acquired; many translations of the Bible have been made; the gospel has been extensively preached; and churches have been established containing thousands of sincere, intelligent converts. The obligation, therefore, on the present generation, to redeem the pledge given by their fathers, is greatly enhanced And it is an animating consideration, that, with the enhancement of the obligation, the encouragement to persevere in the work, and to make still greater efforts, is increasing from year to year. Judging from the past, what may we rationally expect during the lapse of another thirty or forty years? Look forward with the eye of faith. See the missionary spirit universally diffused, and in active operation throughout this country; every church sustaining, not only its own minister, but, through some general organization, its own missionary in a foreign land. See the Bible faithfully translated into all languages; the rays of the lamp of heaven transmitted through every medium, and illuminating all lands. See the Sabbath spreading its holy calm over the face of the earth, the churches of Zion assembling, and the praises of Jesus resounding from shore to shore; and, though the great majority may still remain, as now in this Christian country, without hope and without God in the world, yet the barriers in the way of the descent and operations of the Holy Spirit removed, so that revivals of religion become more constant and more powerful.

The world is yet in its infancy; the gracious designs of God are yet hardly developed. Glorious things are spoken of Zion, the city of our God. She is yet to triumph, and become the joy and glory of the whole earth. Blessed be God that we live in these latter times — the latter times of the reign of darkness and imposture. Great is our privilege, precious our opportunity, to coöperate with the Saviour in the blessed work of enlarging and establishing his kingdom throughout the world. Most precious the opportunity of becoming wise, in turning many to righteousness, and of shining, at last, as the brightness of the firmament, and as the stars, forever and ever.

Let us not, then, regret the loss of those who have gone before us, and are waiting to welcome us home, nor shrink from the summons that must call us thither. Let us only resolve to follow them who, through faith and patience, inherit the promises. Let us so employ the remnant of life, and so pass away, that our successors will say of us, as we of our predecessors, " Blessed are the dead that die in the Lord. They rest from their labors, and their works do follow them."

The following farewell address was presented to Dr. Judson by the Executive Committee of the board, a few days before his departure.

From the Corresponding Secretary

BOSTON, June 30, 1846.

REV. AND DEAR SIR: The occasion demands, at least, a brief valediction to our beloved and honored brother who is about to return to the field of his labors. We congratulate you, dear brother, that the time of your reëmbarkation is at hand. Your heart, we know, has all the while, with a holy impatience, yearned towards the land of your adoption, and towards the people among whom, for the greater portion of your life, you have chosen to suffer and toil. But God had cast you once more upon your native shores by his own sovereign hand, and we could not justify it to our own hearts, nor to our sense of duty to your American brethren, to consent to your departure, without attesting to you, in some faint measure, our veneration for your character, our appreciation of your services, our affection for your person, and our gratitude to God, both for the grace he has bestowed on you, and for our right of participation in all that concerns you, whether of suffering or of joy. We thank God that he has given us this opportunity. And we give thanks to him that he has so directed the times and seasons of your short sojourn with us. Debarred the pleasure of listening to your voice in " the great congregation," we have still felt the delightful, the elevating influence of your presence; and we have *known* that *you were with us;* and the sight of your countenance and the pressure of your hand have given life and substance to what before seemed almost as a vision, and have brought Burmah near to us, with all its moving incidents of the last thirty years. Burmah henceforward, as it is yours, so be it ours; ours for Christ and his church. We join our hands. We pledge you our hearts and our lives. We meet not again on the earth: we shall see your face no more. But we shall meet you when your work is done; when Burmah is redeemed; when her millions of now degraded, benighted people shall have *seen* that Star in the East which has already risen upon her, and shall have come to the brightness of its rising; when a *nation* saved from sin and eternal death through the ministration of the gospel of the Son of God, by the faithful missionary, shall come up in long array, and cast their crowns of heavenly glory before the throne of God and the Lamb.

On behalf of the Executive Committee,

SOLOMON PECK, Cor. Sec.

To his Sons.

BOSTON, July 10, 1846.

MY DEAR SONS: Farewell. We embark to-morrow about noon. Many a time I shall look at your likenesses, and weep over them, and pray that you may early become true Christians. Love your brother George, and your uncle and aunt Newton. Pray every morning and evening. Your new mamma sends you her best love. Forget not

Your affectionate father,

A. JUDSON.

To his Sister.

BOSTON, July 10, 1846.

DEAR SISTER: Farewell. We embark to-morrow about noon. I have two likenesses of Abby Ann. One I take myself. The other I hand to George, that he may take it to Worcester, and keep it with the boys, until he visits Plymouth, in about a month or six weeks, when he is to give it to you. I left Abby Ann at Bradford yesterday forenoon; gave the twenty dollars, which they will place to your credit. Take care of yourself, dear sister, and spare no expense that is necessary for your health and comfort.

Emily sends her best love. Every blessing rest upon you, until we meet in heaven.

Ever most affectionately,
A. JUDSON.

To his Daughter.

BOSTON, July 10, 1846.

MY DEAR DAUGHTER: Farewell. We embark to-morrow about noon. I think the likenesses taken of your face very good. I shall take one with me, and shall many a time look at it, and weep over it, and pray that you may early become a Christian. The other I shall give to George, to keep a while at Worcester, and finally give to your aunt Judson, when he visits Plymouth.

Love your dear aunts and cousins, with whom you live; pray every morning and evening; and may we meet again on earth, and if not, O, may we meet in heaven, and be happy together. Your new mamma sends her best love.

Your affectionate father,
A. JUDSON.

Write me once in three months.

To the Corresponding Secretary.

BOSTON, July 10, 1846.

MY DEAR BROTHER: The accounts of the late revolution in Burmah are so contradictory, and the prospect of more toleration so indefinite, that no certain expectation can well be entertained. It is possible, however, that, on my arriving in Maulmain, there may be an opening for me to proceed to Ava. There is sometimes a tide in affairs, which, once lost, returns not again. Have the board sufficient confidence in me to authorize me, by an overland despatch which shall meet me on arriving in Maulmain, to attempt a mission at Ava, without waiting for further permission, or being under the necessity of debating the matter with other missionaries, who may demur, for want of something express from the board?

Yours faithfully,

A. JUDSON.

P. S. The dictionary would not be done *so soon*, if I should go to Ava; but it would be done *much better*, by means of the aids which the capital would furnish.

To the Editors of the Christian Reflector, Boston, Mass.

SHIP FANEUIL HALL,
OFF ST. HELENA, September, 1846.

DEAR BRETHREN: In the hurry of leaving America, I neglected to thank my unknown friend, who, under his initials, sent me a note, through you, suggesting some corrections in the lines prepared for inscription on the headstone of the grave at St. Helena. I received his favor just in time to avail myself of his suggestion; and the lines now stand thus: —

> She sleeps sweetly here, on this rock of the ocean,
> Away from the home of her youth,
> And far from the land where, with heartfelt devotion,
> She scattered the bright beams of truth.

The gravestones were shipped for the Cape of Good Hope about the middle of April last, and have probably by this time reached their destination. Having pen in hand, I am tempted to add a line, being, as the date indicates, "off the island," though several hundred miles distant, for it lies not in the track of outward-bound ships. The precipitous, rocky cliffs, however, that form the outline of that spot on the ocean, the narrow ravine winding between them and leading to the walled mansion of the dead, the low, overshadowing tree, and the swelling turf, marked, perhaps, by the white gravestones, are all distinctly before me. And, did the misty mythology of antiquity still obtain, I could fancy the spirit of the departed sitting on one of the cloud-wrapped peaks that overhang her grave, and pensively observing the Faneuil Hall on her circuitous route to the south-east. "Why are you wheeling away at such a distance from me and my lonely dwelling? The dear little ones that I left in your charge, where are they? And who — what slender form is that I see at your side, occupying the place that once was mine?" But the mistiness and darkness of pagan mythology have been dispelled by beams of light from those higher heights where she is really sitting. And thence, if departed spirits take cognizance of things on earth, she sees, with satisfaction, that I am *hastening* back to the field of our common labors. She sees, with delight and gratitude to God, that all her children are situated in precise accordance with her last wishes and prayers. And glad she is to see me returning, not unattended.

Farewell, rock of the ocean. I thank thee that thou hast given me a "place where I might bury my dead." Blessings on the dear friends of the Saviour who dwell there. And, if any of the surviving children of the departed should ever enjoy the privilege, which is denied me, of visiting and shedding a tear over her grave, may a double portion of her heavenly spirit descend and rest upon them.

OFF THE ISLE OF FRANCE, October, 1846.

Above thirty-three years ago, I went with my dear wife (the first Mrs. Judson) to the populous city of the dead in Port Louis, on the adjacent island, to visit the new-made grave of Harriet Newell, the first American missionary who left this world for heaven. It has been my privilege, twice since, to make a pilgrimage to the same spot. The last time, my second departed one expected to find her resting-place by the side of Mrs. Newell; but her grave was digging in another island.

It is a thought that presses on me at this moment, how little the missionary who leaves his native land can calculate on his final resting-place. Out of twenty-five missionaries, male and female, with whom I have been associated, and who have gone before me, five or six only found their graves in those places to which they were first sent. Strangers and pilgrims, they had no abiding-place on earth; they sought a permanent abode beyond the skies; and they sought to show the way thither to multitudes who were groping in darkness and saw it not.

OFF AMHERST, November 27, 1846.

The wide expanse of the ocean is again crossed; the Mauimain mountains loom in the distant horizon; the Kyaik-a-mee pagoda indicates the promontory of Amherst; and now, on the green bank just beyond, I discern, with a telescope, the small enclosure which contains the sleeping-place of my dear Ann and her daughter Maria. Like my missionary associates, the members of my own family are scattered far and wide; for the mounds that mark their graves stud the burial-places of Rangoon, Amherst, Maulmain, Serampore, and St. Helena. What other place shall next be added to the list?

Above eighteen months ago, I sailed from these shores with a heavy heart, distressed at leaving my friends and my work, and appalled at the prospect of impending death. With mingled emotions I now return. But these things suit rather the eye and the ear of private friends. I will only add my fervent wish that the Heaven-blessed land where I have been so warmly received during my late brief visit may pour forth her representatives, her wealth, and her prayers, to enlighten and enrich this my adopted land, whose shores are just now greeting my eyes.

Yours affectionately,
A. JUDSON.

To his Sister.

AT SEA, September 11, 1846.

MY DEAR SISTER: Just two months ago we sailed from Boston, and we are about half way to Burmah. I begin this letter with the intention of closing it after arriving, that I may be able to forward it by the first opportunity that occurs; for I know you will be anxious to hear from me. We have had a pleasant passage. All have enjoyed good health thus far, except Emily, who, you know, is rather delicate. But she has not suffered so much from seasickness as we apprehended, and I see no reason to doubt that she will find a warm climate congenial to her constitution.

My heart sinks within me when I think of you, living alone in the old mansion house, many of the family dead, and the rest removed to a distance. But I do not know that any better arrangement could have been made. I almost wish that I had tried more to persuade you to accompany me back to Burmah; and yet I fear that you would not have been comfortable there. It is a mercy that our times are in God's hands. Let us live prayerfully and conscientiously, and ere long we shall all meet in glory.

MAULMAIN, December 16.

We are here at last; arrived the 30th of November, a long passage — one hundred and forty days to Amherst. Found dear Henry and Edward alive and well. Charlie, you know, sleeps in the grave. . . . I have set up housekeeping in my old house; and it seems like home, notwithstanding the devastation that death and removal have made. Emily makes one of the best wives and kindest mothers to the children that ever man was blessed with. I wish you were here to make one of the family; but I suppose that cannot be. I shall now go on with the dictionary and other missionary work as usual. Your likeness is an excellent one. I keep that and the children's by me constantly. Shall I ever forget that last parting in Boston? No, never, till we meet in heaven.

Yours ever,

A. JUDSON.

To his Sons.

AT SEA, September 11, 1846.

DEAR ADONIRAM AND ELNATHAN: I begin this letter with the intention of finishing and forwarding it after arriving in Maulmain. I think of you both many times every day. I never pray for myself without praying for you; and I frequently look at your beautiful likenesses, and feel that I could not endure the thought that I shall probably never see you again in this world, were it not for the precious hope that I shall soon hear that you have become true Christians, and interested in that divine love which will not fail to bring us safely together in the future world of life and glory.

We have had a very pleasant passage, and are now half way to Maulmain. I hope to add something at my next date about your little brothers, Henry and Edward. Charlie sleeps in the grave, and you can receive no further news of him. And your own dear mamma — she is sleeping, you know, — for you saw her laid in the grave, — at St. Helena. Try to retain in your remembrance how she looked, what she used to say to you, how kind she was, and how much she loved you. Talk to one another about her and about me, and that will help you to remember us. I hope you will keep up a correspondence with your dear sister Abby Ann, at Bradford; and when you write to me, tell me all you hear about her, and give me some extracts from her letters to you.

MAULMAIN, December 20, 1846.

I can hardly realize that I am sitting in the old house, where we all lived together so long; and now your mamma, yourselves, your sister Abby Ann, and little Charlie are gone. It is now evening. I am writing in the hall where I used to sit and study when your mamma had gone down the coast with Captain and Mrs. Durand. Your new mamma has just put your little brothers, Henry and Edward, to bed. They lie in the room where you used to sleep before you removed to the corner room. Henry is singing and talking aloud to himself; and what do you think he is saying? Your new mamma has just called me to listen. "My own mamma went away, away in a boat. And then she got wings and went up. And Charlie, too, went up, and they are flying above the moon and the stars." I preach in the chapel, as I used to do, but have not yet begun to work at the dictionary; for we have been very busy seeing company and getting our house and things in order. Every thing looks as it used to when you were here. Eddy and Sarah Stevens are just so, and Emily, Mary, and David Howard. James and Julia Ann Haswell are living with their parents in Mr. Vinton's old house; so that we found Henry in this place, not at Amherst, when we arrived. My dear boys, I don't know when I shall see you again. If I ever should, you will not be the dear little fellows I left at Worcester. But I hope that as you grow larger, and change the features that are now so deeply engraven on my heart, you will also grow wiser and better, and become more worthy of my fondest love. That you will give your hearts to the Saviour is my most earnest desire. Love your dear uncle and aunt Newton. Mind all they say, and ever try to please them. I enclose a hymn that I found with Elnathan's name upon it.

Your fond father,
A. JUDSON.

To Gardner Colby, Esq., of Boston.

LAND, HO! November 27, 1846.

MY DEAR MR. COLBY: One hundred and thirty-nine days from Boston, and the mountains of Burmah appear in the horizon. None ever had a pleasanter passage than we have been favored with, though rather long, from the prevalence of head winds. The Faneuil Hall was a good sailer, an excellent sea boat, and furnished with the best accommodations. The table was well supplied, and the captain endeared himself to us, not only by unremitting kindness, but by the interchange of congenial sentiments and feelings on the subject of religion. Two services on Lord's days, the one a Bible class in the saloon, and the other, public worship on deck, with the crew, together with evening worship every day, have given the character of a Bethel to our floating home. We have all enjoyed good health, except Mrs. Judson. She suffered, indeed, less from seasickness than we had apprehended; but the cold air of the sea, during most of the voyage, has not been congenial to her temperament and constitution; yet we feel that we have as much ground as ever to hope that, once settled in a tropical climate, she may enjoy good health.

In regard to myself, I took a bad cold about the time of sailing, which increased the irritation of throat occasioned by some small attempts at public speaking, and the result was a severe cough, which continued for above a month; but since that passed away, my throat has been recovering, and now I seem to myself to be quite well. In regard to my studies, I have not much to boast of. Not having my native assistants with me, I have not ventured *to go forward* in the dictionary, but have employed myself in revising and transcribing for the press the first half of the English and Burmese part, that had been previously sketched out. This work I had hardly completed when the cry of Land, ho! saluted my ears.

I wrote you in August, and forwarded by a passing ship bound to Genoa. I hope, in my next, to give you some account of the state of the mission and the position of things in Burmah proper.

Yours most affectionately,

A. JUDSON.

Maulmain, December 15. I am once more in my old domicil, have picked up my two surviving children, and endeavored to reunite my family and recommence missionary operations.

To the Corresponding Secretary.

Maulmain, December 29, 1846.

My dear Brother : I have enjoyed the great happiness of landing once more on these shores, and meeting with my dear missionary associates and the native Christians; and it is peculiarly gratifying to find that there has been an evident advance in every department during my absence. The native church, under the care of brother Stevens, is not much enlarged, but it is much improved, in consequence of the exclusion of several unworthy members, and the admission of more promising characters, chiefly from among the children of the converts. Brother Howard's school has greatly improved both in numbers and in qualifications. Brother Binney's school, which was just beginning when I left, has attained a high degree of respectability and usefulness. The Karen missionaries and their disciples are mostly absent from Maulmain at this season; but I understand that prospects in that department of the mission were never more encouraging. The printing office and the secular business of the mission are managed by brother Ranney with promptitude and efficiency. Brother Haswell resides here at present, superintending the printing of the New Testament in the Peguan, and is preaching on all occasions. Brother Stilson is also here, making and superintending the printing of elementary books for schools in the Burman — a work for which he has a peculiar tact and *penchant.*

As to myself, I am looking towards Burmah proper. Both the dethroned kings are dead, and the eldest surviving son of the latter, who, during his father's life, acted as prince regent, has just ascended the throne. He is said to be not well disposed towards foreigners, and the present administration is thus far as decidedly unfavorable to the propagation of the Christian religion as the preceding. This is evident from the severe persecution which the Karen converts north of Rangoon are even now undergoing. But in Maulmain all the departments of labor are well supplied. In Rangoon there is not a single missionary, nor in all Burmah proper. If one can find entrance and shelter there, he may be instrumental of saving a few souls, who would otherwise be lost.

Secondly. My time for the next two or three years must be chiefly expended on the Burmese dictionary. If I am allowed to live in Rangoon without perpetual annoyance, I may as well spend the time there as here, and, indeed, should be able to carry on that work to greater advantage in a place where I could better avail myself of learned men and books than is possible in Maulmain.

Thirdly. In Rangoon, I shall be in the way of the openings of Providence into the heart of the country. It may be that the time for opening Burmah to the gospel is near. In that case it would be a pity if any delinquency on our part should retard the divine operations. My faith, however, is not very strong, nor my expectations very sanguine. The first motive is my leading one. There are some souls in Rangoon who are groping in the dark and feeling after the truth. Let there be at least one hand on which they can lay hold and be assisted in their researches. I expect to leave this place with my family in a ship which will probably sail in about a fortnight. I know not whether I shall find any footing or place of residence; but this can be ascertained in no other way than by making an attempt. I would that the friends of the mission, those dear souls with whom I so lately enjoyed sweet communion in my native land, knew what I am about, that they might aid me in this dark attempt, and pray for light to be shed down on my future pathway; but I will trust that I am not forgotten, and remain

Your affectionate brother,

A. JUDSON.

To his Sister.

MAULMAIN, January 1, 1847.

MY DEAR SISTER: The accompanying Bible was packed in a large box that was never opened till my arrival here, or I should probably have left it with you, and saved it a double voyage, to which it is now consigned, in the hope that it will find a resting-place at last in the old mansion house, and frequently meet your eyes, and be received into your heart.

Edward, my youngest, is just now sitting in a little chair to keep him still. He is just two years old. . . . A day or two ago I went out to the graveyard, and erected the gravestones that I procured in Boston, in memory of poor little Charlie — the last act of duty and kindness that I can ever do for him.

Emily loves the children as if they were her own. We should be very happy here, but the interests of the mission seem to require that we should remove to Rangoon, and endeavor to gain some footing in Burmah proper. We are now making arrangements for such a removal, and expect to leave this before long. It seems to me harder to leave Maulmain for Rangoon than to leave Boston for Maulmain. But here there are several missionaries; not one there; and doubtless there are some inquiring souls who need a missionary to take them by the hand and guide them into the paths of truth and salvation. How long we shall be tolerated there under a despotic government, we know not; but we desire to commit our future destiny into the hands of our heavenly Father, with full confidence that he will order all things well.

We are always meeting with some article of clothing, or other use, to remind us of your kindness. The two large silver spoons you gave me are the only ones on our table; but I have found half a dozen of more common metal to supply the deficiency.

I did not think of writing you a letter just now; but as I was doing up the box containing the Bible, I thought I would just write a line that will cost you no postage. I shall send the box to Mr. Colby, 22 Pemberton Square, Boston, and he will forward it to you. I have not yet heard a word from you, or the children, since I left you. Wrote you lately by overland mail.

Give my love to Mr. Harvey and family, and to other friends. My dear sister, I often think of you in your solitude. May God ever be with you, to protect and bless you. Do write me often, and tell me all about affairs in Plymouth, and the friends about you. Let us ever pray for one another. My late visit has endeared you to my heart far more than ever before.

Let me know whatever you hear about the children; and try, if possible, to visit Bradford and Worcester. You would be joyfully received at both places; and I have written to Miss Hasseltine to allow Abby Ann to visit you.

Ever your own brother,
A. JUDSON.

Emily sends best love.

To his Sons.

MAULMAIN, January 11, 1847.

MY DEAR BOYS: I send you a few books in a little box, among which are some that you particularly wanted, and I took a memorandum of, when I divided the few books you had aboard ship. I send Elnathan the toy box that I promised. It is really good for nothing; but he will, perhaps, recollect the circumstance, affecting to me, under which the promise was given; and it may afford him a moment's gratification to look at it, and remember old times. O my dear boys, how much I love you, and think of you, you can never know in your present circumstances; but perhaps you will know hereafter. In the toy box you will find two penknives; one for each of you. They are very slender, and must be used for pens only, not for whittling, or you will soon break them. We are still here waiting for a ship to take us to Rangoon. Henry and Edward are quite well. May God bless you now and forevermore.

Your affectionate father,
A. JUDSON.

To the Corresponding Secretary.

ON BOARD THE CECILIA, BOUND TO RANGOON, January 18, 1847.

MY DEAR BROTHER: At the date of my last, I expected to have been in Rangoon, with my family, by this time. But the ship in which we expected to take passage has not yet arrived, though long due; and while waiting for her, repeated news from Rangoon has been of the most unfavorable kind; so that I have concluded to go over myself, and endeavor to ascertain the state of things in Burmah more definitely, before making an attempt to settle there at once. It appears that old Rangoon, the only spot in which foreigners are allowed to reside, is more dismantled and desolate than ever; that the new king is more afraid of foreign influence than his predecessors even; and that the whole country is in a very unsettled state just at present, in consequence of all the authorities being summoned to the capital, according to custom, to attend the approaching coronation. From all accounts, it appears that the former exclusive system of the Chinese is becoming more and more prevalent in Burmah; and this will naturally have a most unfavorable bearing on the introduction of a foreign religion. But I hope I shall be able to give you more definite information after visiting Rangoon.

Yours faithfully,

A. JUDSON.

To Mrs. Judson.

OFF RANGOON, January 23, 1847.

MY DEAREST LOVE: We are just anchoring, and I write a line to be ready for any vessel that may be going out, as I go ashore. We have had a pleasant passage; but very light winds have kept us on our way till this Saturday morning, though, as you recollect, we went on board, at Maulmain, Monday forenoon. I know not what reception awaits me on shore, but shall endeavor to let you know before I close the letter.

Four o'clock, P. M. Dreadfully tired in getting my few things from the ship and through the custom house. I am now writing in Captain Crisp's brick house, who invites me to stay and make myself at home. Have yet seen no government people, nor any house that is to be let; so that I can write nothing definite about future prospects. I would not close this letter without something more satisfactory, but I hear that a vessel is just leaving for Maulmain; and I know you will be anxious to hear from me. You may be sure my heart remains in the right place; but I am too much exhausted to say how much I miss your presence, and long to see you once more.

Yours ever,
A. Judson.

Evening. I have seen a large brick house, the one we heard of in Maulmain, for the upper part of which the owner demanded one hundred rupees a month, but I beat him down to fifty. It contains six or eight rooms, some quite large; but there are but few lights, and the place looks as gloomy as a prison. It is situated in a street of Mussulmans — not a foot of ground belonging to the upper story, except a path to a spacious cook house, and a shabby horse stable, but which might be improved. I shrink at taking you and the children into such a den, and fear you would pine and die in it. But the old town — the new I have not yet seen — looks much better than I expected, though very much inferior to Maulmain. No dust in the streets, which are paved most unevenly with brick, so that it is very difficult walking or riding. To-morrow is Sunday, and I shall not go out much. Expect to have an interview with the governor, on Monday. The Portuguese magistrate, who tried to annoy the brethren last here, is absent at Amarapoora. It is after ten o'clock: you have already retired, and I am going to creep under the curtains that were dear Abby's. O my poor heart! It is torn into ten thousand pieces. How happy we shall be when we rest in the grave, and find ourselves together in paradise! Had a long discussion with ———, and hope that he will give up his infidelity. Farewell, dear love. When I turn away from all the filth and wretchedness around me, and think of you, it seems like looking from hell to heaven. How can I take you from all the comforts of Maulmain, and shut you up in this den?

Sunday morning. Have taken a stroll through the place with Crisp. Great, crowded population. Immense field for quiet missionary operation. Several of the converts are coming to see me. Unless I meet with a decided repulse from the governor to-morrow, which nobody anticipates, my mind is about made up to prosecute the "Pass of Splugen." I am going to have a little worship with the converts, but must send off this letter without further delay. Expect to take return passage in the Gyne, which sails in three, or four, or five days.

Farewell again, dearest love.

A. JUDSON.

RANGOON, January 28, 1847.

MY DEAREST LOVE: The Erwin has just come in, and I have received your sweet letter. I expected to have left to-day in the Gyne; but there is no depending on any thing you hear in this country of lies. Whether she will go to-morrow, or the next day, or the day after, I know not; and, what is worse, here are ———, and ———, and ———, who have just arrived. All want to crowd into the one only cabin of the Gyne, which I had engaged, and I cannot refuse them. I found another little vessel that is going to-morrow, by which I shall send this letter; but it has no cabin at all, nor any place where one could sustain life. But God orders all things well — the comforts and the discomforts, the bitter and the sweet, of this short, flitting life. Among the little vexations I meet with, your letter lies like a cordial in my inmost heart. I will not complain while you are alive, and well, and happy, my precious, darling wife. I am glad, too, to hear such good accounts of the children. Give my love to L. I only wish that —— was out here; but how it can be brought about, and how we could manage to have her with us in this country, I cannot tell.

Since I wrote last, I have seen the governor. He received me remarkably well — invited me to settle here — promised to give me a place for an English church, that the English might be induced to come to the place, and enjoy the " benefit of clergy "! He approved also of my prosecuting the dictionary, and spoke favorably of my going up to Amarapoora and seeking royal patronage. I have engaged the brick house I mentioned in my last; but I am afraid your spirits will sink to zero when you see it. We shall, however, be together; and we will try to keep one another's spirits up. Living here is more expensive than I thought. Two or three bottles of milk for a rupee, and eight loaves of very poor bread; but fowls and fish are cheaper. The police is well administered; and it is nearly as safe living here as in Maulmain. As to missionary efforts, nothing can be done openly. The system of intolerance is enforced more rigidly than ever. It is not as a missionary or " propagator of religion," but as a minister of a foreign religion, ministering to the foreigners in the place, that I am well received and patronized by the government. The young heir, and his younger brother, who is premier and heir apparent, are rigid Boodhists, particularly the latter. Boodhism is in full feather throughout the empire. The prospects of a missionary were never darker. But let us aim to obtain the praise bestowed upon Mary — " She has done what she could." I have been to little Roger's grave. There is room for the other children, and for either of us; and I fancy that he sleeps just as quietly here, as those who lie under the British flag.

Evening. I must put a stop to this scrawling letter, and send it to Brown's, in hope that it will reach you somehow. Farewell, my darling love. This separation has taught me more than ever how dear you are to me. May we live to be sources of happiness and promoters of holiness to each other. If we give up all to God, he will take care of us, and bring light out of darkness, and good out of evil, I do believe; and we shall praise him forever, that he led us through some dark ways in his blessed service.

How many expressions in your letter go to my heart, and take it captive! May the light of love and happiness shine around thee evermore is the prayer of

Your ever affectionate husband,
A. JUDSON.

To the Corresponding Secretary.

ON BOARD THE CITY OF LONDON, February 15, 1847.

MY DEAR BROTHER: I intended to write you a detailed account of my late visit to Rangoon; but on reëntering the mouth of the Maulmain River, we met the City of London just coming in; and as I had engaged my passage back on that ship, and had only about a week to move my family and furniture, and get on board, I was obliged to keep myself in a great hurry. We have just joined the ship, off Amherst, and have a short time before the pilot leaves us to write a few of the most necessary letters. The most rigid system of intolerance in regard to religion is maintained by the new monarch of Burmah; but a more friendly feeling towards foreigners is professed and exemplified than characterized the last reign. The governor of Rangoon, appointed by the present king, with whom I had some friendly acquaintance about twenty years ago, received me in the most kind and encouraging manner, but only in the character of a minister of the Protestant religion, coming to minister to the foreigners, English, Americans, &c., residing in the place. He approved also of my coming into the country to complete my Burmese dictionary, for which I should enjoy greater facilities than in Maulmain. He said it was a work which would promote the benefit of both countries, and which he should be willing to mention favorably to his majesty. Thus encouraged, I concluded to hire the upper story of a brick house, — for which I am obliged to pay fifty rupees a month, — and bring my family around to a place dreary indeed, and destitute of almost all outward comforts, but one which will afford an opportunity of building up the feeble church by private efforts, and of seizing the first opening for more public efforts that God in his providence may present, in answer to the prayers of his people in beloved, far-distant America.

Yours most affectionately,

A. JUDSON.

To the Rev. A. D. Gillette, Philadelphia.

RANGOON, March 2, 1847.

DEAR BROTHER AND SISTER GILLETTE: "Out of the abundance of the heart," &c.; and just as we were getting settled down in this dreary place, and counting on a little comfort in ourselves and in the work before us, we hear that the house in Maulmain where we deposited our best clothes and most valuable goods — many of them presents from dear friends that we shall see no more — has taken fire and burned down, with all its contents. We brought but few things with us, not liking to trust this rapacious government, but thought it would be better to draw our supplies from Maulmain, as they should be needed. We left our things in two places; and it has been so ordered that the most valuable assortment has gone to ashes. Half of your beautiful parting present is gone; but thankful we are that the other moiety is safe with us. So it is with human calculations. We thought our valuables safe in Maulmain; and the house was set on fire by an incendiary in the dead of night, and brother Stevens and family just escaped with their lives. And here, under this barbarous government, we have not yet been at all molested. Not a pin has been taken from us, except a few things begged and pulled away, in passing through the custom house — the most vexatious, perhaps, in the whole world.

We are living in our own hired house, without much annoyance from without, and contrive to get the necessaries and many of the comforts of life. Truly God tempers the wind to the shorn lamb. We are not allowed to make any public efforts to proselyte the natives of the country; but we can do a good deal in private, and Emily can get the language, and we can hold ourselves ready for better times. We both send you both our " heart of hearts."

Yours ever,

A. JUDSON.

To the Rev. E. A. Stevens, of Maulmain.

RANGOON, March 2, 1847.

DEAR BROTHER STEVENS: "The Lord gave and the Lord hath taken away; *blessed be the name of the Lord.*" My heart overflows with gratitude, and my eyes with tears, as I pen these precious inspired words. There are some other lines, quaint in garb, but rich in core, that are worth more than all your house and contents: —

> "Blessed be God for all,
> For all things here below;
> For every loss and every cross
> To my advantage grow."

But I sympathize with you and dear sister Stevens. Brother Bullard has also sustained a heavy loss. Brother Brayton's will not, on the whole, be any great loss. As to me — the leeks and onions that were packed up in those two valuable boxes, worth about seven or eight hundred rupees, were very bright to the eye, and soft to the feel; and many of them we shall greatly need, if we live a year or two longer; but they have gone to dust and ashes, where I have seen many bright, dear eyes go, to rescue any pair of which I would have given those boxes ten times over.

I am glad and thankful that the New Testament and the manuscripts are not wholly lost, though some are. And I am glad that so much interest has been excited in the Christian community at Maulmain. I am glad also that my house was empty, and ready to afford you immediate shelter.

We arrived here the Saturday after leaving Maulmain, and got our things through the custom house on the next Monday, a week ago yesterday. We now begin to feel a little settled, and are about commencing a routine of study, and I may add, missionary labor; for though the Burmese converts are few and timid, the Karens flock in from different parts, and occupy a good deal of my time. All the men understand Burman pretty well, and I have had some interesting meetings among them.

Yours affectionately,
A. JUDSON.

To Mr. Thomas S. Ranney, of Maulmain.

RANGOON, March 2, 1847.

DEAR BROTHER RANNEY: I thank you for your circumstantial account of the fire, which, with brother Stevens's, gives me a pretty vivid idea of the affair. It was truly a dreadful affair. My loss is probably heavier than that of any other person, except brother Stevens himself. My best clothes and wife's, together with our most valuable utensils of various sorts, were packed in the two boxes that are burned. I estimate the value about seven hundred rupees; wife says nearer one thousand. But all these things are ordered well.

The parcel of letters and papers you sent me by a native boat lay several days in a native house. Captain Crisp happened to hear from his dubash, that there were such parcels for somebody, and thinking that they might be for me, — as I had received nothing from Maulmain, and every body else had heard all about the fire, — sent me word. I sent a man to search for them, when the syrang gave them up, saying he did not know whom they were for, as he could read neither English nor Burman, in which the parcels were inscribed. Is there any objection to sending all letters and newspapers generally through the post office? Cannot the Maulmain Chronicle, after it has gone the rounds of the brethren, as usual, be regularly sent me through the post office? and the Free Press? We shall soon ascertain whether transmission through the post office can be depended on. My letter to Crisp, which you mailed while I was in Maulmain, has but just arrived! However, it *has* arrived; that is something. Perhaps the postmaster could tell how it came to be detained so long in Maulmain. Each of the brethren used to receive five or six copies of the native newspaper. Please to send mine regularly. I want to distribute them here. Let me have them from the beginning of this year. I want also two copies of the whole work from the beginning, bound together like the copy you gave me, which, however, I have been obliged to part with already.

I send you the only pair of silver-mounted spectacles that I can now boast of, with a pair of glasses. Perhaps Avung will be able to mend the frame, which is broken. If so, please to let him observe that one of the glasses has a flaw in it, and is to be so placed that the flaw may be on the upper side. If Avung is not competent, I suppose we must send the article to be mended in Calcutta.

We have had a grand bat hunt yesterday and to-day — bagged two hundred and fifty, and calculate to make up a round thousand before we have done. We find that, in hiring the upper story of this den, we secured the lower moiety only, the upper moiety thereof being preoccupied by a thriving colony of vagabonds, who flare up through the night with a vengeance, and the sound of their wings is as the sound of many waters, yea, as the sound of your boasted Yankee Niagara; so that sleep departs from our eyes, and slumber from our eyelids. But we are reading them some lessons which we hope will be profitable to all parties concerned, and remain,

Yours affectionately,

A. JUDSON.

To the Rev. E. A. Stevens.

Rangoon, March 11, 1847.

Dear Brother Stevens: Yours of the 6th has duly arrived, and I write a line in reply, to send by Ko Woon's son, and Mee Shway-yeet, who are returning to Maulmain.

I have recommenced the work of the dictionary, which has been suspended nearly two years. Why has this grievous interruption been permitted, and all this precious time lost? And why are our houses and property allowed to be burned up? And why are those most dear to us, and most qualified to be useful in the cause, torn from our arms, and dashed into the grave, and all their knowledge and qualification with them? Because infinite wisdom and love will have it so. Because it is best for us, and best for them, and best for the cause, and best for the interests of eternity, that it should be so. And blessed be God, we know it, and are thankful, and rejoice, and say, Glory be to God.

We had a good communion season last Sabbath. Ten Burmans present, one Karen, and two foreigners. The converts are very timid, but there are two or three good inquirers among the Burmans, and several among the Karens.

We have plenty to do. What with a little missionary work, and what with our studies, and what with visiting, our hands are full. For we can't get rid of company even here. Wife and I occupy remote ends of the house, and we have to visit one another, and that takes up time. And I have to hold a meeting with the rising generation every evening, and that takes time. Henry can say, " Twinkle, twinkle," all himself, and Edward can repeat it after his father! Giants of genius! paragons of erudition! With best love,

Yours affectionately,

A. Judson.

To the Hon. Heman Lincoln and Family.

RANGOON, March 14, 1847.

. . . From this land of darkness and intolerance I address a line to you, my dear, very dear friends, in blessed America, in bright, beautiful Boston and vicinity. It seems like an Elysian vision, that I have so lately seen your happy dwellings and elegant surroundings — a vision, however, dispelled instantly by a crushing nightmare feeling, on looking round upon the wretched habitations, the rude, filthy population, the towering pagodas, and the swarms of well-fed priests which every where here pain the eye and the heart. Boodhism has come out in full bloom. The few traces of Christianity discoverable in the early stages of the mission seem almost obliterated. The present king and his brother, the heir presumptive, are devoted Boodhists, especially the latter. He begs his elder brother to allow him to turn priest, that he may gratify his pious propensities; and on being refused, he does, poor man! all that he can. He descends from his prince-regal seat, pounds and winnows the rice with his own hands, washes and boils it in his own cook house, and then, on bended knees, presents it to the priests. This strong pulsation at the heart has thrown fresh blood throughout the once shrivelled system of the national superstition; and now every one vies with his neighbor in building pagodas and making offerings to the priests. What can one poor missionary effect, accompanied by his yet speechless wife, and followed by three men and one woman from Maulmain, and summoning to his aid the aged pastor of Rangoon and eight or ten surviving members of the church? But as the Mussulman says, *God is great.* He sitteth on the heavens, he setteth his foot on the earth, and the inhabitants are as grasshoppers before him. He dwelleth also in the humble and contrite soul; and the rays of indwelling glory appear more resplendent, gleaming through the chinks of the humble tenement. O for that humility and contrition, O for that simplicity of faith, which will secure the indwelling glory! May such sinners as we are hope for such a blessing?

O, help us with your prayers, ye who sit under the droppings of the sanctuary, and are sometimes allowed to approach the presence; and O Thou that hearest prayer, help thou our unbelief!

Last Sabbath was our stated communion season, occurring once in four months. No alcoholic liquor can be procured in this place, the importation of all such being strictly forbidden. Our wine was a decoction of raisins, the unadulterated juice of the grape. Ten Burmans, one Karen, and two Americans, came around the lowly, glorious board. To-day I had about the same number of disciples, and several listeners, two of whom remained long after worship, and, with two others whom I have found since arriving here, make up the small number of *four hopeful inquirers*. But all our operations are conducted in secrecy. I have been introduced to the government, not as a missionary, — though the governor and the vice-governor both knew me well from old acquaintance, — but as a minister of a foreign religion, ministering to foreigners in the place, and as a lexicographer, laboring to promote the literature of both nations! In one room, therefore, of the upper story of the brick house, — for which upper story I am obliged to pay fifty rupees a month — will the Christian public bear me out in this extra expense? — I have paraded my lexicographical apparatus, and commenced hammering at the anvil of the dictionary, which has hardly resounded with my blows for two years past; two years, alas! lost, lost, in tossing on the sea, closing dear eyes, digging graves, rending heartstrings, and feeling about for new ones. Thanks be to God. I have a sweet little family around me once more — F. F., Harry, and Eddy. God is not only "great," but good. God is love. And he can change our hard, selfish hearts, and make them full of love. Do I not love you, dear friends? Shall I see you no more? Yes, in heaven, whither we are fast hastening. Dear Mrs. Bacheller, of Lynn, has gone already. Blessings on her memory! You will have heard from brother Stevens of our sad loss by fire. All our best clothes and valuables gone. But it is doubtless for the best. Love to all of you.

I have not heard a word directly from any of you since I left, not even from my children. I should think that some one of you could drop me a line.

To the Corresponding Secretary.

RANGOON, March 28, 1847.

DEAR BROTHER : I have just returned from baptizing a Burman convert, in the same tank of water where I baptized the first Burman convert, Moung Nau, twenty-eight years ago. It is now twenty-five years since I administered baptism in Rangoon, the few converts that have been made during that period being generally baptized by the native pastor. My time has been mostly spent in Maulmain, where, having been instrumental, with others, of raising up a few Burmese and Karen churches, I have left them, since my return from America, in the care of my dear and excellent missionary brethren, and am now making a small attempt in Burmah proper.

The attempt, however, is made under very discouraging circumstances. The present administration of government, though rather more friendly to foreigners, is more rigidly intolerant than that of the late king, Tharawadi. Any known attempt at proselyting would be instantly amenable at the criminal tribunal, and would probably be punished by the imprisonment or death of the proselyte and the banishment of the missionary. The governor of this place has received me favorably, not as a missionary, though he well knows, from old acquaintance, that that is my character, but as a minister of a foreign religion, ministering to foreigners resident in the place, and a dictionary maker, "laboring to promote the welfare of both countries." Our missionary efforts, therefore, being conducted in private, must necessarily be very limited. It is, however, a precious privilege to be allowed to welcome into a private room a small company, perhaps two or three individuals only, and pour the light of truth into their immortal souls souls that, but for the efficacy of that light, would be covered with the gloom of darkness — darkness to be felt to all eternity.

Another discouraging circumstance is the very low state of the Burman church in this place. There are about twenty nominal members still surviving; but they are much scattered, and not half of them appear to be living members. I have, therefore, been making an attempt to reorganize the church, and have found four individuals who have united with myself and wife in renewing our church covenant, and establishing a new church. We have this day received one new member, and we hope to find a few more of the old members who will come up to our standard.

This is indeed a day of small things; yet, in view of the great success which attends all our efforts among the Karens, both in the provinces, and, by means of native assistants, in Burmah proper, I should be almost discouraged in regard to future efforts among the Burmans, were it not for certain considerations, some of which are contained in the following statement, which was once laid before an assembly in Brooklyn, New York, and which is now transcribed for the Magazine, in the hope that it may present to other minds what appears to me to be the true view of the case, and assist to check that discouragement in regard to the Burmese department of the mission, some symptoms of which I discovered during my late visit to the United States.

The greatest popular objection to the missionary enterprise is drawn from the small success which has attended missionary efforts among the great nations of the earth. Some progress has been made in converting the ruder tribes of man; but it must be confessed that very little impression has been made on any great and partially civilized people. The subject of missions has taken too deep hold of the public mind, and is too severely scrutinized, to allow this objection to pass without an effort to meet it fairly, and in such a way, if possible, as to encourage the well disposed, and conciliate the rest.

The nations and tribes of man that call for missionary efforts may be considered under several divisions. One division comprises those who have no religion, no literature, not even a written language, no priesthood of influence or prescriptive right, and no imposing, long-established, powerful government. Such a people will be evidently less prejudiced, their minds more open to the solicitations of our religion, and there will be fewer barriers in the way of their embracing it. In human view, therefore, success might be expected; and in the divine view, a people not crushed under the weight of idolatry, not deeply stained with the sin of hereditary enthusiastic worship of false gods, may appear less repugnant and more accessible to the influence of the Holy Spirit. These remarks seem to be justified by the success which has crowned the efforts of missionaries among the Greenlanders, the Karens, the South Sea Islanders, and the people of color in the West Indies and other parts.

Another division comprises those nations where the Christian religion once flourished, but subsequently passed away, leaving the form of godliness, without the power. Among such people we might expect that the opposition of rulers and priests to the introduction of vital Christianity would assume a ferocious, bloodthirsty character, and for a time present very formidable and appalling barriers; but that the knowledge of divine truth, extensively diffused among the people, and some hereditary reverence for the word of God, aided by the prayers of a pious ancestry, would ere long roll back the tide of opposition, and send forth judgment unto victory. Such appears to be the course of events in the northern parts of Germany, and among the Armenians; and such will probably be the course among the Greeks and the Roman Catholics.

The third division of the human family, the lowest class, that is, the last in the order of time, — the class which will tire out the wavering and the faint-hearted, and send to their homes all but the few who have put their hands to the plough with a grasp that no discouragement, not death itself, can unloose, but who bring up their children to the same work, and swear them at the same altar, — that class comprises, alas! three fourths of the family of man — all the Mahometan, the Brahminical, and the Boodhistic nations, and all those numerous tribes and subdivisions where those false religions prevail, under some modification. These nations have generally a literature erudite and extensive, closely interwoven with their religion. Their priesthood is hereditary, or invested with the most sacred, imposing credentials, and supported by all the power of the government. Their governments are monarchical, despotic, intolerant, hostile to all free inquiry, opposed to all reform, and their police well organized, and extending to almost every house and person. Shall we wonder, shall we be dismayed, shall we lose all heart, and relinquish the work in despair, because the Christian religion is not welcomed by such people? because the first missionaries cannot, within a few years, enroll thousands among their converts? Is it nothing that they have obtained entrance and foothold in almost every one of those nations? that they have acquired the languages, even the most difficult? that they have compiled grammars and dictionaries? that in the most important of those languages they have translated the New Testament, and in some cases the whole Bible? that they have prepared tracts, and hymn books, and elementary works for the purposes of education? that they have organized various orders of schools, and even theological seminaries, though yet in a quite incipient state? that they have planted churches in many parts of the Brahminical and the Boodhistic countries, containing, not indeed thousands, but yet hundreds of penitent, believing, praying souls? that angels have found their way to those long-abandoned regions, commissioned by the Saviour to gather in the first fruits, most precious in his eyes? Is it nothing that the ideas of the eternal God and of the Saviour, the Lord Jesus Christ, are daily spreading throughout those countries, commending themselves to the consciences of men, gradually undermining the reigning superstitions, and preparing the way for the triumph of truth, the full ushering in of millennial glory? Yes, the success is small; but it would have been greater if the Christian world had put forth a little more strength, and if missionaries had been more faithful. But I submit whether it has not been great enough to show us where our fault lies, great enough to prompt us to endeavor to correct it, great enough to encourage us to adopt the motto of my venerable father, as he was drawing near the grave — "*Keep straight forward, and trust in God.*"

Perhaps, finally, it will be asked whether we had better not pass by the more difficult fields, until the easier are won. I reply, Better have no plans of our own. Better that missionary societies and individuals follow the openings of divine Providence and the leadings of the Holy Spirit. All nations must be converted to the true faith, and that before long. To accomplish this, God has his own infinitely wise and eternal purpose. He will provide the instruments, he will furnish the means, he will open the way. Let us only look up to him with unwavering faith, and unreservedly commit ourselves and our services to his direction. And whether we are called to sow or to reap, whether to build the temple or only to furnish materials to our successors, his glory will be secured, the great end will be attained, and it will be well with us in time and in eternity.

Yours faithfully,
A. JUDSON.

RANGOON, May 30, 1847.

MY DEAR BROTHER: This is the first Lord's day on which I have had no regular worship. A private order of government was issued, day before yesterday, to have the house I occupy watched by police officers, in order to apprehend any who might be liable to the charge of favoring "Jesus Christ's religion." Seasonable information was communicated to me and the disciples, by "friends at court," so that they have all escaped at present. None came near me, except two from the country, and with them I had a very interesting and affecting time, in a private room; and they got off undiscovered. Four Karen lads, who had been waiting for a passage to Maulmain, decamped before light this morning for their native jungle.

The vice governor of the place, who is, indeed, the acting governor at present, is the most ferocious, bloodthirsty monster I have ever known in Burmah. It is said that his house and court yard resound, day and night, with the screams of people under torture. Even foreigners are not beyond his grasp. He lately wreaked his rage on some Armenians and Mussulmans, and one of the latter class died in the hands of a subordinate officer. His crime was quite a venial one; but in order to extort money, he was tortured so barbarously that the blood streamed from his mouth, and he was dead in an hour.

I am afraid that, while the present monster is in power, I shall not be able to convene the disciples for worship as hitherto. He is, however, only acting on the orders which are understood to be in force all over the country, proscriptive of the Christian religion. I feel the blow most deeply, for I had just succeeded in reorganizing a little church, out of old materials and some lately baptized, amounting in number to eleven, nearly all pure Burmans; and last Sunday I had an assembly of above twenty. Several new ones were expected to-day, and two would probably have been baptized. I had become so attached to the little church and assembly, and so glad on every returning Lord's day to lay aside my tedious dictionary labors, and spend all the day in obtaining and communicating spiritual refreshment, that the present interruption seems almost too hard to bear. However, I hope to do something yet, in private, to aid a few perishing souls, who are struggling, through darkness and terror, to find a way of escape from the more dread darkness and terror of eternal death. But every thing must be done in private. Not even a tract can be given publicly. That point I ascertained a few years ago, on a visit to the place, which I believe I never mentioned in writing home. In order to test the real extent and efficiency of the king's order prohibiting the distribution of books at Ava, I opened a box of tracts in the front part of the house where I was a guest for a few days. The people took them greedily; but in less than an hour my assistant,

Ko En, was arrested and placed in confinement. It cost me a great deal to get him free; and when he was released, it was on condition that he would give no more tracts. This time, therefore, I brought no tracts for distribution, and have confined myself to private conversation, except convening an assembly for worship — and that in an "upper room" — every Lord's day.

June 6, Lord's day. No formal worship; but a fine young man whom we had concluded to receive into the church, son of one of the oldest converts, spent the day with me, in company with two or three others; and just at night we repaired to the remote side of the old baptizing place, and, under cover of the bushes, perpetrated a deed which, I trust, our enemies will not be able to gainsay or invalidate to all eternity.

June 8. Yesterday morning the young man, on returning to his residence, a few miles distant, met his father under arrest, in the hands of the myrmidons of government, on their way to the court of the governor, — not, I was glad to learn, the ferocious vice governor, above mentioned. One of the converts came to give me notice; and for two or three hours I sat expecting the worst. But the blow was averted as suddenly as it was aimed. "What have you brought the man before me for?" said the officer. "To be examined on a charge of heresy and frequenting the house of Jesus Christ's teacher," said the leading accuser. "On what authority?" "Here is your written order." "What! Who? I have given no order. It must be one of my petty clerks. It is all a mistake. Go about your business." "I thought it strange," rallied the arrested, "that you should summon me on a charge of heresy, as it is well known that I worship the true God." "God," said the officer, rather nettled; "worship any God you like;" — "Or the devil," promptly added a virago sitting on an official cushion at his side; — "if you villagers just pay your taxes, what more do we want of you?"

As near as we can ascertain the truth of this strange affair, the officer, after sending off the order early in the morning, not entertaining the least doubt that the measure would be approved, as the religion of Jesus Christ is understood to be universally proscribed, stepped, however, into the government house, and reported what he had done; and the governor, remembering his pledge to me on my first arrival, quashed the proceeding. Thanks be to God!

And this is not the first favor he has done me, as I have just learned by a very private confidential communication from a sworn employé of government, a friend of mine, though not of the cause. A few days ago, one of the highest members of government represented to his excellency, that two or three years ago, under the administration of his predecessor, three of these heretical teachers came from Maulmain with the intention of effecting a settlement in the empire; that he mentioned their arrival to the then governor, who left their disposal entirely in his hands, on which he ordered them out of the country; and that the said teachers then pretended they had not come to stay, and immediately took their departure. On hearing this, the governor kept his head bent over his breakfast, and made no reply. And the officer, feeling that he had not sufficient encouragement to bring forward my case, withdrew to wait for a more convenient season. But the term of this governor's rule is drawing to a close; and it is expected by many that he will be succeeded by the ferocious vice governor.

June 13, Lord's day. Not an individual ventures to come near me. I am advised to make friends with the vice governor, by whose orders the house is watched, and whose authority is now paramount to that of the governor, a weak old man, who suffers himself to be set at defiance; but I think that an attempt of that sort would but expose the cause to greater danger.

I am persuaded, as I have been for years past, that the only way to keep footing in Rangoon is to obtain some countenance at Ava. My principal object in coming hither was to ascertain the practicability and probable advantage of proceeding to the capital. The present governor has given his permission, and the season favorable for going up the river is not far distant. But at the approaching crisis, I find myself destitute of the requisite means. The board have approved the measure, but have not been able to accompany their approval with the needful remittance. On the contrary, I learn from my last letters from Maulmain, that the annual appropriation for the Burman mission is ten thousand rupees less than the current expenses require. The brethren have been obliged to retrench in every department, instead of being able to make an appropriation for a new enterprise. My extra expense in Rangoon for assistants and house rent is eighty-six rupees a month, and they have been able to allow me seventeen and a half only. The mission secretary writes me, that for any thing beyond that sum, I must look, not to their treasury, but to the board. Instead, therefore, of entering on a new and expensive undertaking, I find myself unable to remain in Rangoon. But no; I might hope that an appeal home would provide means for remaining here; but in present circumstances, unable to remain to any advantage without making friends at Ava, and having no hope that the board will be able to commence a new station, or even sustain the old ones much longer, there remains nothing for me but to fall back upon Maulmain.

It is my growing conviction that the Baptist churches in America are behind the age in missionary spirit. They now and then make a spasmodic effort to throw off a nightmare debt of some years' accumulation, and then sink back into unconscious repose. Then come paralyzing orders to retrench; new enterprises are checked in their very conception, and applicants for missionary employ are advised to wait, and soon become merged in the ministry at home. Several cases of that sort I encountered during my late visit to the United States. This state of things cannot last always. The Baptist missions will probably pass into the hands of other denominations, or be temporarily suspended; and those who have occupied the van will fall back into the rear. Nebuchadnezzar will be driven out from men, to eat grass like an ox, until seven times pass over him. But he will, at length, recover his senses, and be restored to the throne of his kingdom, and reign over the whole earth.

Yours faithfully,

A. JUDSON.

To Mrs. Stevens, Maulmain.

RANGOON, June 30, 1847.

DEAR SISTER: I have heard Mrs. Judson say, two or three times, that she ought to write you; so I thought I would supply her deficiency. She has been very ill, with a combination of nervous complaints, and become "as thin as the shad that went up the Niagara." I was taken with dysentery two or three weeks ago, and had the hardest time that I ever knew since I have been in the mission. Henry lost his appetite, and grew thin with fever. . . . And in the midst of it, poor little Edward was seized with the erysipelas, and his eyes and face swelled so that he was not recognizable. At length several frightful sores opened, and are still discharging. Government troubles came thick upon us and the converts. The season of Lent arrived, and for four months no flesh or fowl — nothing but fish — is procurable, except by stealth, and at a great price. We had depended chiefly on fowl soup, and now it seemed as if we must die. However, we kept on breathing. . . .

Only think that next July 11, will be the anniversary of our sailing from Boston, and I shall not then have received — except two short letters from Abby Ann, and ditto from Mr. Peck — a single communication from the thousands of warm friends I left at home!

Better sing "Vive," &c., over the graves of friendship, and all things here below, except — except what? *love;* and that we will cherish in the young corner of our hearts, an oasis in the desert.

Yours affectionately,

A. JUDSON.

To Mr. Thomas S. Ranney.

RANGOON, July 21, 1847.

MY DEAR BROTHER: The accompanying heavy parcel for Colby, with the letter, is to go by the August steamer to Calcutta, with direction to be forwarded overland to the agent in London. The postage will, of course, be heavy; but the thing is the property of the board, and it is very important that it should reach home as soon as it can be conveyed by the overland.

I received your kind letter of yesterday, the missing Herald, &c. We are all creeping up the valetudinarian hill with the utmost assiduity. We had the happiness of nabbing fifty fowls by the help of a government man in the neighborhood, whose favor we propitiated; and to such a degree that he let us have them for seventy-two rupees per hundred. Three nights after we had cooped them, our friend's jackals, we know, stole twenty of them; and soon after our friend himself borrowed eight more, because he let us have them so cheap, I suppose. The rest we are bolting as fast as possible, for fear he will want to borrow them too. By we, I mean I, for wife has become a sort of Grahamite, living chiefly, or vegetating rather, on Mrs. Stevens's gingerbread, your coffee, and the scrapings of yams which we pick up now and then — the article being now out of season. O ye frequenters of Astor and Tremont! O ye shades of strawberries and ice-creams! But I will spare your feelings and my own. May you be happy in devouring and being devoured. I see you are getting up a school of shadows in Maulmain. Please tell the superioress that we are assiduously qualifying ourselves for an early admission.

I remain, that is, what does remain,

Yours affectionately,

A. JUDSON.

To Miss Lillybridge, of Maulmain.

RANGOON, August 12, 1847.

MY DEAR LYDIA: I have never written you, because I know that Emily is frequently writing you, and that you will, or ought to, take all she writes as coming from us both. For the same reason I have never written to —— —— till just now, in answer to a note from her. So, having perpetrated that anomaly, I am now venturing on another, like the monkey who, having in an unlucky hour said A, was whipped to make him say B. However, the comparison is imperfect, in that there is no whipping needed to make me write to those I love. We have frequently wanted you with us here, and once seriously thought of it, in connection with a projected school; but the folly of the thought soon became apparent in the more evident precariousness of our own situation. I hope you pass your time not sadly or unhappily, though the study of a foreign language and getting used to a new school in a foreign land are not very epicurean occupations. But we must sow before we reap; and though our whole life should prove to be but sowing time, the harvest of eternity will produce ample returns.

You are enough acquainted with Emily to know how happy I must be in her society. My sojourn in Rangoon, though tedious and trying in some respects, I regard as one of the brightest spots, one of the greenest oases in the diversified wilderness of my life. May God make me thankful for all the blessings which have hitherto fallen to my lot, and for the hope of those richer blessings which are just concealed by the cloud of sense from our spiritual vision. If this world is so happy, what must heaven be? And as to trials, let us bear up under them, remembering that if we suffer for Christ's sake, with him we shall reign.

Yours affectionately,

A. JUDSON.

Reminiscences of Dr. Judson's last Visit to Rangoon.*

While we were stopping in Boston, previous to sailing, Dr. Judson first mentioned to me the subject of going into Burmah proper, on his return. He said there was a wide difference between Maulmain and Rangoon or Ava; and until I could have some opportunity of understanding this difference, he did not wish me to decide whether I would go or not. He was thinking very seriously of the undertaking, however, and wished me to say whether I was willing that he should make such an arrangement with the board as would place him at liberty to go, provided we both thought it best, on our arrival at Maulmain. He had no great confidence in the change that had taken place in government; still, it might possibly be the "accepted time" for Burmah; at any rate, he wished to make one more effort, to present the gospel to the blinded people, leaving the result in the hands of God. His own circumstances, he said, were peculiarly favorable. His family was smaller than it had been for many years; and during his absence, the church which he had founded, and watched over so long, had become so weaned from him, that he thought he and they would be able to live without each other. He also felt the need of better assistance in completing his dictionary of the language, than he thought he could get at Maulmain; and though this was not his impelling motive, it was yet in his mind of sufficient weight to warrant the step, and much more presentable to the minds of others than the dearer object, into which even his hopeful nature could infuse but little of the enthusiasm of probable success. Thus, probably without his being aware of it, the dictionary received almost undue prominence in his general communications with others, while to me it was seldom mentioned.

* The following notes were furnished by Mrs. Judson, not for publication, but for my own personal use. They, however, possess so much interest, and illustrate so forcibly the motives of Dr. Judson in making this last attempt to carry the gospel to the interior of Burmah, that I have inserted them on my own responsibility.

When we arrived at Maulmain, we found quite a little missionary coterie gathered there, and every department well filled. An over land letter from the board awaited us, with permission to go to Rangoon; and so we went. Dr. Judson seemed to think that he was under no obligation to ask of any human government permission to preach the gospel of Christ, having probably changed his mind after his first visit to Ava; but as a matter of courtesy, and to invite protection as a resident, he did ask permission to take a house, and bring his family. The matter of the dictionary was also mentioned, and received with great respect; but from the fact of Dr. Judson's being a foreign priest, the propriety of his ministering to the religious wants of foreigners settled in Rangoon was rather tenaciously insisted on by the governor. Dr. Judson perfectly understood the implied interdiction couched under this seeming generosity, and politely abstained from a reply, while the governor returned again and again to his old position, with the evident determination of obtaining a pledge from his visitor, which the latter was as fully resolved not to give. When they parted, it was perfectly understood by the lookers-on, that the foreign teacher would be protected in his character of scholar and foreign priest, but that if he attempted the conversion of Burmans to his religion, he at once became lawful prey. He had scarcely expected more. He had known the kind governor, however, in years gone by; and there was something in the friendly glance of the old man's eye which promised as much as, in the precarious state of his own affairs, could reasonably be expected.

The first business of my husband, on arriving in Rangoon, was to collect the Christians together; but so scattered was the little flock, and so doubtful their state, that he was obliged to reorganize the church, commencing the new organization with about a dozen members. For a time every thing went prosperously with us. Frequent meetings were held at our house, and regular worship on the Sabbath. Gradually, the congregation enlarged to twenty, to thirty, and still upward, until it attracted the attention of government. It must not be supposed that these men were so imprudent as to come in of a morning, or leave the house after worship, *in a company* They came at all hours between daylight and ten o'clock, and dispersed as gradually. Some brought parcels, some dishes of fruit, some came with their robes tucked up like coolies, and some, scorning concealment, or believing it unavailing, appeared in their usual dress, as though on a matter-of-course visit to the foreigner. When they were assembled, the outer door was barred, and it was with great difficulty that any one could gain admittance afterwards. Dr. Judson sometimes smiled at these precautions; but he considered that this was the first time since the war that any missionary had been stationed in Burmah, without the protection of an English resident at Ava, and was assured that there never had been a time of such intolerance, throughout the land, as under the new king. Meantime the Karens had been apprised of our arrival, and they came down from the jungle in parties of three, four, or a half dozen, remaining at our house till one of the Burmese assistants could procure them passports thence to Maulmain. (Previously they had escaped, over land.) All this coming and going attracted attention to our house, and would have done so much earlier, but that it chanced to be on a Mussulman street.

One Saturday morning we were startled by some private intimations that the bloody ray-woon, as one of the vice-governors was called, had his eye on us; and a little before evening, the hints were fully confirmed. We learned from an undoubted source, that a police guard had been stationed in the vicinity of our house, with orders to seize every native, not known to be a servant of the house, seen coming out of it. We inferred that their policy was not to disturb *us*, at present, but the blow was first to fall on the poor Christians. Several Karens were stopping with us, and in addition to our usual company of worshippers, quite a number of invited friends and strangers had promised to be with us on the next day. The church had been making individual efforts to enlarge the congregation. I shall never forget the expression of my husband's face, as though really piercing to the invisible, when he exclaimed, "I tell you, if we had but the power to see them, the air above us is thick with contending spirits — the good and the bad, striving for the mastery. I know where final victory lies, but the struggle may be a long one." There was not much time for talking, however. He communicated the state of things, as far as he thought expedient, to his two native assistants, and sent them out to warn the nearer worshippers. In this, great caution was necessary, in order to prevent a panic; and I suppose that the Rangoon Christians have never, to this day, known the extent of their danger. As the assistants, by an especial arrangement, did not return till after our landlord's hour for closing the gate, Dr. Judson, with some difficulty, got the key into his own possession; and so, in the first gray of morning, the Karens were guided out of town, and advised to return to the jungle. The last place to which the assistants carried their warning, on Sunday morning, was a little village five miles from Rangoon, where they remained till towards evening. Dr. Judson was afraid of compromising the Christians by going to any of their houses that day; but he had advised them, through the assistants, how to hold worship, and we knew of several places where little knots of men and women were gathered for prayer.

These demonstrations on the part of government were followed up by a series of petty annoyances and insults, which effectually precluded the possibility of accomplishing much good. The governor was friendly, but weak and cowardly; and we soon found that his protection was really worthless, except as he could hold the petty officers in awe. The bloody ray-woon laughed at his authority, and once actually assembled the troops against him, when the poor governor yielded. Both Christians and inquirers, however, still came to us in private; and many a man, who refused to take even a book from the teacher's hands, would watch his opportunity, when going out, to snatch one from a box placed near the door for that purpose, and hide it in his dress, congratulating himself, no doubt, that he was unsuspected even by us.

In the mean time, the rainy season set in; and it proved a season of unusual sickliness, even for that sickly place. To add still more to the uncomfortableness of our situation, the season for the Buddhistic Lent, which continues several months, came round; and, probably for the first time in fifty years, foreigners were so far compelled to observe it as to abstain from eating flesh or fowl. If we had known of the prohibition in season, we could have been prepared; but it took us quite by surprise. A few fish were exhibited in the bazaar; but it was so disreputable to trade, even in these, that they could scarcely be found, except in a half-putrid state. The only baker in town left soon after our arrival; and we were forced to live almost exclusively on boiled rice and fruits. To the former I unfortunately took an unconquerable disgust; and the latter proved unwholesome to all of us. One child was seized with erysipelas; the other with a complication of diseases brought on, as we supposed, by the meagre diet, and exposure to the damp winds; and Dr. Judson himself had a most violent attack of dysentery, which kept him from his study table six weeks. For myself, my appetite had failed in proportion to the means of gratifying it; so, without being ill, I was so reduced in strength as often, in walking across the room, to fall, or rather slide, down on the floor, not from faintness, but sheer physical weakness. One of the assistants also took the fever; and the nurse I brought from Maulmain, the only woman besides myself in the household, became seriously ill. Of course, we had no medical adviser; and if we had desired it ever so much, we could not get away, as the monsoon was now at its height, and the small native vessels in the harbor were not only without accommodations for invalids, but too frail to be trusted with the freight of human lives.

With all the rest, the police regulations of the city were in the worst condition possible, indeed quite nugatory, and nightly robberies were taking place all over the city, often in our immediate vicinity. We learned afterwards that the captains of the band were the ray-woon, and a nephew of the governor, and that the old governor himself winked at the wickedness —

facts of which we were happily ignorant at the time. Dr. Judson, when he could keep down his groans, used to speak of our position as "the pass of the Splugen," and say he had no doubt we should find sunny vales and fruited vineyards the other side. The government was certainly very bad, and our prospects, at the best, misty; yet as soon as his health and the children's began to amend, our courage revived. We could not bear, now we had gone so far, and been through so much, to think of retreating, without an effort to get to Ava. For myself, as I believe is natural to the practical minds of women, I sat down to examine the worst features of the case in detail. We should of course be subjected to inconceivable annoyances, but we must trust Providence to give us wise thoughts. We very likely might be banished; but we could always hold ourselves in readiness to go, and the loss of the few goods we had would not be much. Possibly we should be imprisoned; but I did not think that very likely, and we should always have means of informing our friends in Maulmain. Death was the worst. We *must* endure it some time. If it came a little earlier, it would be in a good cause; and there would be faithful Christians about us, who would never rest till they had taken the children to Maulmain. The way seemed clear to me. Dr. Judson said it was scarcely possible for us to encounter the complication of troubles that we had already passed through in Rangoon. Ava, he said, was always better governed than Rangoon; and this starving of people during Lent had never occurred before in all his missionary life, and was not likely to occur again; besides, the rains were less heavy, and consequently the rainy season less sickly. In addition to this, he had a friend at court — a Burman of rank, who loved him, and was exerting himself to the utmost to gain respect for the "wise man," and to explain that Americans were not Englishmen. The plan of going to Ava really seemed, on the whole, feasible. Accordingly Dr. Judson used his first returning strength to call on the governor, to obtain permission to go. Not that we could not go without permission; but it was polite and conciliatory to ask and in the permission would be an implied exemption from annoyance in getting away, and protection — probably that of a government flag or official umbrella — on the river. The Lent was not yet over; but what with boxes of biscuit from Maulmain, bribing a Mussulman — a rascally fellow, who afterwards came and robbed us of our dearly-bought treasure — to obtain fowls for us secretly, and the improved health of some of us, we began to be quite valorous. As Dr. Judson expressed it, "our faces began to shine." Indeed, we had not been very desponding any of the time. Never, except during an occasional hour, when his illness was most alarming, did his courage falter. It was delightful to be so directly in the hands of God. Then, we had not expected much when we left Maulmain. The church in Rangoon had been aroused, a few baptisms had taken place, and several more hopeful conversions; and the *way* to Ava, if not the golden city itself, was open before us.

The letter from Maulmain with no appropriation for our contemplated expedition, and giving us only twenty rupees to cover the eighty-six rupees we were even then monthly expending, came upon us like a sudden tornado in a sunny day. Oddly enough, it had not once occurred to us that the *money* could be wanting. You will readily appreciate the one broad feature of the case, which would have made the blow heavy to any sincere Christian having much of the missionary spirit; but to my husband there was additional bitterness in the manner of his disappointment, and in the hands from which it came. "I thought they loved me," he would say, mournfully, "and they would scarcely have known it if I had died." "All through our troubles, I was comforted with the thought that my brethren in Maulmain, and in America, were praying for us, and they have never once thought of us." At other times he would draw startling pictures of missionaries abandoning the spirit of their mission, and sacrificing every thing to some darling project; and at others he would talk hopelessly of the impulsive nature of the home movements, and then pray, in a voice of agony, that these sins of the children of God might not be visited on the heathen. This was an unnatural state of excitement, — for *him* peculiarly unnatural, — and he was not long in recovering from it. He very soon began to devise apologies for every body, and said we must remember that so far as *we* were concerned, or the missionary cause itself, God had done this thing, and done it, as he always does, for good. It was not his will that we should go to Ava then, and we had no right to complain of the means he made use of to prevent it. He insisted, too, that our obedience was not to be yielded grudgingly; that it must be a cheerful acquiescence in all that God had done, and a sincere, careful study of the indications of his providence afterwards, without any suspicion that our ways were hedged by any thing harder or thornier than his love and mercy. By the time he had an opportunity to send letters to Maulmain and Boston, his mind was restored to its usual serenity. My impression, however, is, that his first letter to the board was written in a slightly discouraged tone. He wrote more hopefully to Maulmain, but I have sometimes thought that his generosity took the point from his letter, and that his meaning was not understood in saying that it was *for the best*. I think now that they mistook resignation to God for a personal willingness to abandon the enterprise. After our return to Maulmain, we remained for a half year at some distance from the chapel; Dr. Judson being desirous of keeping aloof from pastoral duties, lest he should become so entangled with the church as to make it difficult to leave. He never afterwards assumed the full pastorship.

CHAPTER VIII.

NUMBER OF MISSIONARIES IN MAULMAIN. — MODES OF MISSIONARY LABOR. — THE BURMESE DICTIONARY. — STATE OF THE MISSION.

1847–1849.

To the Corresponding Secretary.

MAULMAIN, September 25, 1847.

DEAR BROTHER: There are twenty-four missionaries, male and female, congregated in this place; eleven in the Karen department, nine in the Burmese, two in the Peguan, and one couple in the printing department.

You have one single missionary in Arracan, where there is a population much larger than in all the Tenasserim provinces, and two married missionaries in Tavoy, — the Wades being about leaving. Mergui has passed out of your hands;* so that nearly all your missionaries to Burmah and its dependencies — that is, twenty-four out of twenty-nine — are in Maulmain, where, I am sure, from being pretty well acquainted with the whole ground, that one half the number would be sufficient, and indeed work with more efficiency.

Many, who once belonged to or were intended for other missions or stations, have removed or are removing hither, and all, as they conceive, for the most substantial reasons.

If I might presume so far, I should be inclined to advise the board to send out no more missionaries to these parts, until they can devise some way of making men go where they are sent, and stay there.

The above sentiments I have frequently heard from the Burmese missionaries in regard to the Karen department, and from the Karen missionaries in regard to the Burmese depart-

---

* Mergui was occupied by a missionary of the New Brunswick and Nova Scotia Baptist Associations; but the withdrawal of the Missionary Union was temporary, and the station has been since resumed by the board.

ment, though each party is bent on increasing its own. I feel equally interested in both parties; and though I certainly find it very pleasant to enjoy such a large and agreeable society, I feel impelled to make this communication from a mere sense of duty. I request that it may be made known, in some way, to the members of the Acting Board; and if they take a different view of the subject from mine, I shall cheerfully acquiesce.

Yours faithfully,
A. JUDSON.

Mrs. Stevens to her Mother.

In a letter dated January, 1848, Mrs. Stevens writes, "Yesterday Dr. Judson gave us one of his striking discourses."

. . . In comparing labors among a people without a national religion to labors among idolaters or Mussulmans, Dr. Judson used a figure which ought to be published in the Macedonian in reply to some things which have appeared there and elsewhere, to the import that difference of success among Burmans and Karens is owing to difference of labor performed among them. He supposed a man offering to fill two jars, one of which stands empty, the other filled with earth oil. Now, the force of the illustration will not appear to you as to us, because we are so familiar with this oil; and you are not, as we are, obliged to make frequent use of it; but you can judge of its character by a translation of the Burman name for it, "stinking water." The smell of it cannot be extracted from a jar which has been emptied of it, except by burning. I should never think of using a vessel which had once contained it for any other purpose. To return to the illustration. A man goes to the owner of the empty jar, and asks if he may fill it with pure and sweet water. "O, yes, I shall consider it a favor." So the Sandwich Islander, so the Karen receives the truth, the benefits of a written language, and instruction in books, and the elevation that follows, as favors conferred; and as there are no stains of ancient superstitions, they are better Christians than converts from heathenism. When I say *no* stains, of course comparatively is meant.

Let the missionary next go to the owner of the jar filled

with earth oil. He must first empty it, which the owner considers robbery. He would say, "You are taking away my property; this is my merit, which I have been many years gathering. You wish to deprive me of my offerings. I will apply to the king and priests to uphold me in clinging to my property." But the missionary says, "If you drink that oil it will be poison to you; let me give you water, which will insure life eternal." "O, my ancestors have all drank of this, and I wish to do the same; this is good for me, and yours for you. My books are good for me, and my religion, and so yours for you." But after long argument and persuasion, he gains the man's consent to give up his earth oil, and he labors through the process of dipping it out, and cleansing the jar; he rubs and washes; the man all the while begging him not to deprive him of *all* of it; to allow him some of his former customs, and some of the practices of his worldly neighbors and relatives; and often so much of the oil is left, that the water is very offensive, and bystanders say, "We do not perceive that the water is any sweeter than the oil." Sometimes the man himself joins in, and says he does not know but the smell is as bad as before, and the change has been of no use; so he upsets the jar and apostatizes.

To the Corresponding Secretary.

MAULMAIN, May 21, 1848.

DEAR BROTHER: I have just returned from the Burmese chapel, where I have been endeavoring to do something analogous to what I suppose many ministers are doing before their respective churches on this the first Sabbath subsequent to the annual meeting of the Union. I improved the occasion to impress on my hearers their obligations to the Christians in America for having sustained this mission through the long period of thirty-five years, and not this mission only, but missions throughout the world; so that there are, at present, above a thousand American missionaries of different denominations scattered over the habitable globe. It is true that the relative position of the parties would not allow them to manifest their gratitude in such a manner as the Christians of Macedonia and Achaia manifested their gratitude to the poor brethren in Jerusalem, (Rom. xv. 26, 27;) but they could be convinced of their obligations, they could ponder on them, and converse about them, until their hearts burned with gratitude and love to their American brethren, and to the Saviour, the Lord of missions. They could, though separated by wide oceans, meet at the same throne of grace; and, though they could not extend their own hands in kindness, they could open that hand which is replete with every good and perfect gift, and cause a shower of blessings to descend on their distant benefactors. They could gladden their hearts, and the heart of their Saviour, by living according to the precepts of the holy religion which had been sent them; and is there any thing sweeter and nobler in this world than to gladden the hearts of our benefactors, especially of our great Benefactor, who laid down his life for us? And, lastly, they could second the intentions of their American brethren by making every effort to spread the gospel around them. "Freely ye have received; freely give."

I never had a more attentive audience. May God bless the feeble effort, and the efforts of my brethren during the past week, in drawing into closer union the far-separated members of Christ's body, until we become one in him forevermore.

Yours faithfully,
A. JUDSON.

To his Sons.

MAULMAIN, May 21, 1848.

MY DEAR SONS: Is it possible that I have letters from you at last? I had waited so long that I began to think it would never be. And I am so glad to hear of your welfare, and especially that you have both been under religious impressions, and that Elnathan begins to entertain a hope in Christ! O, this is the most blessed news. Go on, my dear boys, and not rest until you have made your calling and election sure. I believe that you both and Abby Ann will become true Christians, and meet me in heaven; for I never pray without praying for your conversion, and I think I pray in faith. Go to school, attend to your studies, be good scholars, try to get a good education; but, O, heaven is all. Life, life, eternal life! Without this, without an interest in the Lord of life, you are lost, lost forever. Dear Adoniram, give your heart at once to the Saviour. Don't go to sleep without doing it. You may wake up in hell. Try, try for your life. Don't mind what any body may say to the contrary, nor how much foolish boys may laugh at you. Love the dear Saviour, who has loved you unto death. Dear sons, so soon as you have a good hope in Christ that your sins are pardoned, and that Christ loves you, urge your pastor and the church to baptize and receive you into communion. They will hold back, thinking you are too young, and must give more evidence. But don't be discouraged. Push on. Determine to do it. *Determine to stand by Christ, come what will.* That is the way to get to heaven. . . . Will Elnathan tell me what little book it was that was so much blessed to him? I have forgotten what I sent him. I have sent you copies of your mother's Memoir. You will be delighted to read it, so beautifully and so truthfully is it written. Ever love to cherish the memory of your own dear mother, — how much she loved you to the last gasp; — and prepare to follow her to heaven.

Your fond father,
A. JUDSON.

To Mr. and Mrs. Bennett.

MAULMAIN, July 29, 1848.

DEAR BROTHER AND SISTER BENNETT: I do "recollect that there is a station at Tavoy," and that you and the C———s are there, and I suppose some dozen of the rising generation that I have never set eyes on. Pretty much all I recollect of the C———s is, that she is a very interesting lady, and has sisters and parents in America, whom I saw — just saw. Of you two, my recollections extend back into the misty past, and partake somewhat of the nature of the shadows with which they are blended. We did once live together in this place, and mingle with many others who are far removed, some to distant countries, and some to distant worlds, and we are in the same way. The ever-advancing, sweeping tide will soon carry us away, and the places that now know us will know us again no more. I hope I am willing to die, but was never more willing to live. My present family is all that I could wish. . . . My brethren all love me more than I deserve, and I am sure I love them. I could wish to see more success among the Burmans; but we live in hope, and try to enjoy, by way of a succedaneum, the great success which attends every effort among the Karens. If I had a little spare money, I should like to run down to Tavoy, and make you a visit, and renew my old acquaintance, and tell you how much I love and revere your excellent father, and how much I was interested in your children whom I saw at home. E——, I hear, is married to a pious person, and that is the great thing. Better so than to have married the most distinguished personage in the country destitute of religion. . . . When I get through the dictionary, if I could only get a little foothold in Burmah, I would be off at once; that is, if the board would give me assurance that they will behave better, in regard to money, than they did the last time I went there. However, there cannot be many links of my chain remaining. In ten days I step into that dim space that lies between sixty and seventy, or, in other words, I shall enter my sixty-first year. Time to set my house in order, and take leave of all further earthly aspirations.

I was very glad, by the last accounts, to learn that Mrs. Bennett is much better. May she still be spared. You are very weak in numbers at Tavoy, and her death would be an irreparable loss, not only to her family, but to the mission.

Emily has prepared a small Memoir of her predecessor, chiefly from information communicated by me. I hear it is just published, and I will send you a copy as soon as I get any.

They talk here of printing a small preparatory edition of my dictionary, — that is, the English and Burmese part, — as soon as it is done, which will be in about three months. Mrs. Judson intends to write you by this opportunity, if she is able; but she is frequently ill, and unable to fulfil her engagements.

Yours affectionately,
A. JUDSON.

To the Corresponding Secretary.

MAULMAIN, September 23, 1848.

DEAR BROTHER: The preparation of the English and Burmese part of my dictionary is so far advanced, that I hope to commence printing a small edition next month, preparatory to a larger and uniform edition of both parts, when the Burmese and English part is completed. But as I advance in the latter part, I feel more deeply the desirableness and importance of making a visit to Ava, and availing myself of the learned men and the literary works that are to be found at the capital alone. The government interpreter of Rangoon, who greatly befriended me during my visit to that place last year, lately wrote me that he hoped I would bear in mind the necessity of going to Ava before I printed the work, and that if I did not, it would be impossible for me to make it what it ought to be. I presume that no person, acquainted with the circumstances of the case, would dissent from that opinion. But the difficulty of penetrating into the country, and staying long enough to improve the dictionary, is very great, while the importance of the undertaking will appear still greater, if some view be had to the welfare of the scattered church, and the necessity of conciliating the government, and obtaining, if possible, some religious toleration.

When last in Rangoon, I lost a favorable opportunity, such as may not occur once in a hundred years. The governor of Rangoon was the very last of all my old court acquaintances; and he was ready to clear my way to Ava, by a letter of introduction, into the very presence of the king. But I had no money to buy a boat, pay the boatmen, and defray the other inevitable expenses of the undertaking, nor even to pay my house rent in Rangoon; and so I was obliged to return to this place. The committee have since kindly defrayed the debt contracted on the latter account; but that is all. I suppose they thought with me, that such a good opportunity would never occur again, and that no benefit would result from lamenting over the past, or providing for the future — a future so utterly improbable. There is, however, at the present moment, a small prospect in the horizon, which may, in a few months, disclose an open path to Ava. If such should be the case, the committee, as well as myself, would regret that my hands were still left tied, and another opportunity be irretrievably lost. I request, therefore, that they will take into immediate consideration the question of appropriating a sum — say one thousand rupees — to defray the expenses of such an undertaking as I speak of; and they may depend that I shall render, as in former times, a minute, and I hope satisfactory account of the way in which the money shall be expended.

I should endeavor to make it a point, before leaving this, not only to see one part of the dictionary out of the press, but the other part brought to such a state that it may be transcribed, and a copy left with the mission, in case of ulterior accidents.

Yours faithfully,

A. JUDSON.

To his Daughter.

MAULMAIN, November 26, 1848.

. . . We are a deliciously happy family; but we think much of the three dear absent ones, and my tears frequently fall for your dear, dear mother in her lone bed at St. Helena. And any time I enter the burial-place here, I see the white gravestone of poor little black-eyed Charlie. Ah, we had to leave the poor little fellow to die in the arms of Mrs. Osgood,

It was hard, but we could not help it. God's will be done. He is now happy with his mother. If you should die, would you go to them too? O that I could hear of your and your brothers' conversion!

You can never know how much I want to see you, how much I think of you, how much I pray for you, always when I pray for myself. O my dear daughter, my motherless daughter, meet me at the throne of grace; meet me in the bosom of Jesus, and we shall live in his blessed presence on high, together with your dear mother, lost to us for a time, but not forever; whose spirit ever watches over you, and will rejoice with joy yet unfelt, when you turn to the Saviour and give your heart to him.

Your longing, hoping father,
A. Judson.

To Mr. and Mrs. Robarts, of Philadelphia.

Maulmain, December 18, 1848.

My very dear Friends: Have I written you since the birth of little Emily Frances? I was sure I had, until looking in my letter book, I find not your name where I expected to see it. The little thing will be one year old on the 24th instant. She is a great pet of her brothers, Henry and Edward; and her mother has taken to the two boys, as if they were her own, so that we are a very happy family; not a happier, I am sure, on the broad earth. For a few months we have been occupying the same house that my late family occupied; I have the same church and chapel; I am sitting at the same study table; and I can hardly realize that I have been through such a whirl; that the strange American dream has intervened; that I am writing to certain persons of whom, before I had that dream, I had never heard, but whom I now have in my heart; and their house, and the way to the "publication office," and that office, and the Gillettes, and Philadelphia, are all before my eye, as plain as if I saw them again; and that cold winter, and your gaslights, and little Mary rigged out to go to school through the snow — ah, the snow, that curious article, drifting in at the slightest opening of a window, and that broken pane that I bumped my unlucky head against, I see it, looking at me reproachfully. O, wouldn't I give something to be able to walk into your house, and spend a day or two with you once more! But that can never be. I suppose that by this time you have our dear Utica friends with you in Philadelphia. I hope they will be appreciated; and they will, I am sure, be a great accession to your society and church. Do write me, and tell me all about my friends in Philadelphia by name. I directed copies of the Memoir of the late Mrs. Judson to be sent you, and Mrs. Gillette, and Mary Anna Longstreth, and Mrs. President Dagg, all under cover to you, which I mention, because I find that copies, which I sent to friends, have, by some accident, failed of reaching their destination.

The work of the Lord is going forward in every direction, though much slower than we desire. Scarcely a month elapses without witnessing the baptism of some Burmans, or Peguans, or Karens, or descendants of Europeans, in some of our churches in this place and vicinity. And beside the actual evident conversions, we believe that the truth is spreading and gaining ground through the country; and we expect to meet many in heaven, whom we never met on earth. And we are endeavoring to labor not only for the present generation, but for all future generations; and for this purpose are preparing a great variety of elementary books in the various departments of science and religion.

"Cheerly, cheerly ply the lever;
Pause not, faint not, falter never,"

is our song, and in that chorus we all join, with joyful hearts. Even the "young romance writer" has made a little book, completing her predecessor's series of Scripture Questions on the Historical Parts of the New Testament; and she manages to conduct a Bible class and native female prayer meetings;

so that I hope she will yet come to some good. Pray for us, my dear friends; and may we all be prepared to meet in heaven. With Mrs. Judson's love,

Yours most affectionately,
A. JUDSON.

The following letter, with two others, which will be found on subsequent pages of this chapter, was written to Dr. Judson by the then prince royal of Siam, who has since succeeded to the throne — an intelligent and learned Buddhist, who had become acquainted in Bangkok with the character of the missionary. They are mainly interesting from the indications which they exhibit of intellectual cultivation in a native prince, and of the respect in which the labors of Dr. Judson were held in every part of India.

To Rev. Mr. Adoniram Judson, the American Missionary of Maulmain.

BANGKOK, SIAM, December 23, 1848.

VENERABLE SIR: Having received very often your far-famed qualities, honesty, faithfulness, righteousness, gracefulness and very kindness to poor nation, &c., from reading the book of your's ancient wife's memoir and journal, with some newspapers, and from conversation with your missionaries, Mr. John T. Jones and Mr. Chandler, I trust that you will be glad and satisfacted to receive my correspondence, if I address to you, declaring that I am affectionate friend of Rev. Mr. J. T. Jones along during seventeen or sixteen years since he came to this country, and that I am acquired on some way, with the knowledge of English. Therefore I was brave without hesitating to write you this first letter to communicate with you, through the care of my friend, the Rahany Chief nobleman who is minister of my eldest Brother, His Majesty, the king of Siam.

I am now acquainted with several Singhalese friends of

Ceylon, some of whom are still Buddhist as I am, and respectful to their Burmese teachers whose fraternity they have had been entered, and desirous to pronounce by manner of their sound, but they do not ascertain because they did not meet with Burmese more than forty years ago. I wish therefore show them some tracts or books of pronunciation of Burmese alphabet and its division which recently and exactly printed with English and Burmese characters to let them be ascertain in manner of Burmese pronounce.

I hope you will supply me with a few books or tracts of the such account with much pleasure for sake of your missionaries in Siam who are my friends. I beg to show this my necessity please pardon me if it is not proper for you.

I desire also to be acquainted with certain gentlemen of European resident of Maulmain to correspond mutually with for know somethings and matters which perhaps sometime may be in my necessity in future, but I did not hear of any person of that place except yourself alone.

You shall direct my name by the following Siamese characters on the back of parcel or envelope of my address: if you would send to me by 'Rahany' or other northern state of Siam, then it will be reached my hand very soon, or you shall send it to care of your missionaries herein.

Siamese Direction:
To His Royal Highness, T. Y. Chaufa Mongkut, of Bangkok, Siam.

I am a Buddhist high priest, and have the honour to be your friend

PRINCE T. Y. CHAUFA MONGKUT.

Perhaps you might ever hear of my name formerly from your missionaries.

To his Sister.

MAULMAIN, January 22, 1849.

MY DEAR SISTER: My last to you was July 21, 1848, and yours of August 15, has just come to hand. I had previously received your present of one hundred dollars, sent to the treasurer of the board, about March, I believe, and forwarded by him a few months after. For this fresh proof of your kind remembrance, accept my cordial thanks, and also for your repeated kindnesses to my children in America; though, as to that matter, I fancy they are about as much your children as mine. At any rate, you can see them and hear from them much oftener than I can. I am very much concerned about Adoniram, since hearing from you of his illness; and I am so much concerned about the spiritual welfare of all three! O, if I could only hear that they are truly converted, I could lie down and sleep in peace, so far as they are concerned. But here are three others to pray for and tremble over. Poor little Emily Frances has been dangerously ill with a species of cholera; but we hope she is now better.

No change has taken place in my outward circumstances since I wrote last, excepting that, in consequence of Mr. Haswell's going home on account of his health, the care of the Burmese native church has again devolved on me, though Mr. Stevens assists me much in the preaching department, and in other ways. I may mention, also, that the English and Burmese part of my dictionary is done, and is now printing in a small edition of three hundred. It will make a volume of about six hundred pages quarto. I have now entered upon the Burmese and English part; and that will make another volume about as large. I hope to get through with this tedious work in a year and a half more — perhaps two years, if I should live so long. You don't mention receiving a copy of the Memoir of the late Mrs. Judson. I directed the publishers to send you one. Please mention whether you got it. . . . Emily is now preparing notes for a new edition of the work. And she has made some progress in the Burmese language, so as to finish the Questions on the Acts, for Sabbath schools, left unfinished by her predecessor. But the language is not, of course, equal to that of the first part of the work. I could have improved it, but thought it was best to let her hammer it out herself. She will do better by and by.

O, how I wish I could make you a visit in your solitude! I am glad you have repaired the house. Don't spare any expense to make yourself comfortable. Don't think of laying up any thing for me and mine, so as to abridge your own comforts. Emily sends you her best love.

Your ever affectionate brother,

A. JUDSON.

The following letter relates to a subject most intimately connected with the prosperity of missions, and it deserves additional consideration from the fact, that Dr. Judson did not write it in haste, but after deliberation; and, after having written it, laid it aside for several months before he finally resolved to send it to the board. It may therefore be esteemed his last testimony as to the manner in which missionary efforts should be conducted. While these pages are passing through my hands, I have received a letter from a friend in Hindoostan on this very subject, from which it appears that the worst apprehensions of Dr. Judson are likely to be more than realized in some of the most important missions in India. Good men have abandoned the preaching of the gospel, and have employed themselves in teaching, in order to *prepare* the natives to receive the gospel; and the pupils of these very schools are found to be the worst opponents of Christianity.

To the Corresponding Secretary.

MAULMAIN, March 16, 1849.

DEAR BROTHER: When I spoke of brother ———'s school, in my letter to you of the 22d November, 1847, as one of our most effective engines for the renovation of these provinces, I had not become aware of the great change which the school had gradually undergone.

. . . The propriety of bestowing much missionary labor and expense upon country-born children is very questionable, that class of the population being found throughout India to have less influence on the population at large than any other. Their influence, for obvious reasons, is generally confined to themselves. The propriety of teaching English to the natives, to the exclusion and depreciation of their own vernacular, is still more questionable.

. . . I am more and more convinced of the truth of a remark which I made some years ago, that *English preaching*, *English teaching*, and *English periodicals* are the bane of missions at the East. There are several missionaries — more, it is true, from Great Britain than from America — who never acquire the languages, except a mere smattering of them, of the countries to which they are sent, but beguile their time and expend their labors among their own countrymen and the country-born population, under the fallacious idea that through them the Christian religion will gradually reach the masses of the native population. There are, however, some symptoms of an approaching change in public sentiment throughout the East, in regard to the mode of conducting missionary operations. It begins to be found that popular English schools, containing hundreds of pupils, and instructed by great and powerful men, — but men ignorant of all native languages, — will never convert the millions of the heathen. "Such schools," as the senior missionary of the Kishnagur mission lately observed to me, on visiting this place, "are very pretty things to amuse English visitors with, and make interesting reports for people at a distance, who cannot enter into the merits of the case."

Still, some good results from every good effort, though not the most judiciously directed; and I have always endeavored to keep myself free from strong party feelings. Live and let live is not a bad motto, nor should I have written a word of the above, had I not felt for some time past that I had committed myself too far in what I had said about one of the the mission schools, and made myself somewhat responsible for what I cannot regard as the most judicious expenditure of labor and funds.

Yours faithfully,

A. JUDSON.

To Miss Anable, of Philadelphia.

MAULMAIN, March 18, 1849.

DEAR ANNA MARIA : I know not how to begin to write you. A dark cloud is gathering around me. A crushing weight is upon me. I cannot resist the dreadful conviction that dear Emily is in a settled and rapid decline. For nearly a year after the birth of baby, she enjoyed pretty good health, and I flattered myself that she would be spared for many years. But three or four months ago her appetite almost entirely failed her. Soon after, baby was taken very ill, and in the midst of it, our usual help left us, and she was obliged to undergo a great deal of severe fatigue; and I see now that she has been declining ever since. She soon became unable to take our usual walks, and I procured a pony for her, and she tried riding, but without any good effect. I next sent her to Tavoy in a steamer, on a visit to the missionaries there. She was gone ten days, and returned thinner in flesh and weaker than ever. I now take her out every morning in a chaise, and this is all the exercise she can bear. She is under the care of a very skilful doctor, who appears to be making every possible effort to save her; but the symptoms are such that I have scarcely any hope left. She is thinner than she has ever been; strength almost gone; no appetite; various pains in the region of the lungs; a dry cough, which has hung on pertinaciously for two or three months. She was preparing some "Notes," to append to the Memoir, but has been obliged to leave them unfinished, being unable to write, or even read, without aggravating her pains. I look around in despair. If a change to any place promised the least relief, I would go any where. But we are here in the healthiest part of India, and in the dry, warm season;

and she suffers so much at sea that a voyage would hardly be recommended for itself. My only hope is, that the doctor declares that her lungs are not seriously affected, and that as soon as her system is fairly brought under the influence of the course of medicine he is pursuing,—digitalis being a principal ingredient,—there will be a favorable result. I shall dissuade her from writing by this month's mail, though she has mentioned that she wants to write to you and her family. Nor does she know that I am writing to you. Her family I don't want to distress at present. She may get better. But I suffer so much myself, that I felt it would be some relief to sit down and tell you all about it. . . . When she was at Tavoy, she made up her mind that she must die soon, and that is now her prevailing expectation; but she contemplates the event with composure and resignation. Within a few months she has grown much in devotional feelings, and in longing desires to be wholly conformed to the will of Christ. She had formerly some doubts about the genuineness of her early conversion, but they have all left her; and though she feels that in her circumstances prolonged life is exceedingly desirable, she is quite willing to leave all, at the Saviour's call. Praise be to God for his love to her.

Yours affectionately,
A. JUDSON.

March 23. Glad I am that the mail is still open, so that I can add that Emily is better. The medicine seems really to have taken effect, and the crisis to have passed. But though the deadly pressure is a little removed from my heart, I do not venture to indulge very sanguine hopes, after what I have seen; for a few days may prostrate all again. Do remember us in your prayers. I feel more than ever that God heareth prayer.

The Philadelphia box has just arrived. I have opened it, and shown Emily the things. May she be able to write next month, and acknowledge the kindness of her friends.

To Mrs. Moore, of Maulmain.

April 2, 1849.

DEAR SISTER: I do sympathize with you while suffering under the loss of your little babe. It is true that it breathed the breath of life a day or two only; but your heart — a *mother's* heart — feels anguish never before conceived of; and as the coffin lid shuts out the sweet face from your longing gaze, and bars all further maternal care, the tears you shed will be, O, so bitter!

You need not my suggestion that God has done this thing in infinite wisdom and love. While, therefore, you mourn, be thankful. A part of yourself has gone before you to heaven. Yours is the early privilege of furnishing a little seraph to occupy its place in paradise. There it will wait to welcome its mother's arrival. The prayers you have frequently offered for the little creature will yet all be answered; the warm affections now apparently crushed in the bud will expand and bloom in heavenly glory; and every succeeding age of eternity will heighten your song of praise to God for making you the mother of a little immortal, and then, for some special purpose, bearing it away thus early to the grave, and to heaven.

Your sympathizing friend and brother,

A. JUDSON.

To Mrs. Bennett.

MAULMAIN, April 12, 1849.

MY DEAR SISTER BENNETT: Mrs. Judson has sent over to the office some books for you, . . . which she begs you will accept. She would be glad to write you a line, but, though much better than when at Tavoy, the doctor forbids her the use of either needle or pen. She drives out every morning in a gharry, and her appetite is greatly improved. Whether her illness before and at Tavoy will prove to be an incipient decline, destined to terminate fatally, or only the result of incautiously-increased fatigue, aggravated by a severe cold, remains yet to be seen. We and all we love are in the hands of God for life and for death. Mrs. Judson frequently speaks of the very happy acquaintance she formed with you at Tavoy; and would that it might be frequently repeated and perpetuated in a brighter and better world. Please to give our love to Dr. Van Someren, and thanks for his very kind attentions while Mrs. Judson was at Tavoy.

Yours ever affectionately,
A. JUDSON.

From Letters to his Daughter.

MAULMAIN, April 20, 1849.

When I think of you and your brothers at Worcester, O, I have such a longing to see you that it seems as if I could not always stay on the other side of the globe, "severed from you by stormy seas and the wide world's expanse." But O, if you are not in Christ, a wider expanse — even the impassable gulf — will soon lie between us, and the wide expanse of eternity itself will show no point of meeting, no spot where I and your departed mother will be able to take you to our longing arms.

MAULMAIN, October 1, 1849.

I have just received your very nice letter of 19th of July last, and am much pleased with your proficiency in all things, except that you have not yet given your heart to the Saviour. Believe me, that every year, every month, you live without grace, will occasion you a loss that will be irreparable through all eternity.

We have all been ill with a sort of influenza, but are now better. Emily Frances is the sweetest little fairy you ever saw. I hope she will one day come under your instruction and care.

From his Royal Highness, the Prince of Siam.

August 1849.

. . . I put together with my box, comprising a few artificial flowers, two passion flower, one mogneyet, or surnamed flower, and three roses, manufactured by most celebrated princess the daughter of late second king, or sub-king, who was my royal uncle, for your memorial, but are, indeed, that I don't know what would be in your necessity from me, beg to let me know without hesitation, I shall endeavor for your desire how my power would allow.

If you desire to visit Siam some time, don't come by land, as the strangers are prohibited to come by northern way from command of his majesty, and you would be tributed for coming by way of three pagodas, though traveling of strangers by it was allowed by political authority. It would be best if you embark on board the steamer for Singapore, and lodge little while at residence of my beloved friend Tan Tock Sing, whom I can request to comfort or make attention to you respectfully, and take passage by Siamese vessels that visit the Singapore almost every month to our country, and on your ascending and descending to and fro between this post and Singapore you need not expend any of your own, as I can pay or request the owners of ships for you if you let me be aware.

Whenever do you please to send me packet or letters, or to certain of your friend herein, you shall send by sea to Singapore with the direction thus: —

To His Royal Highness, T. Y. Chaufa Mongkut, of Bangkok, Siam.
Kind care of Tan Tock Sing, of Singapore.

If you have opportunity to send by land, you shall send by hand of Rahany messengers, or credible traveling tradesmen of the same, for care of my friend the Rahany chief governor, with Siamese characters in direction as follows: —

[*Here is inserted the direction in Siamese.*]

because there is none interpreter of English. I am not pleasing the Peguen, or Pegunese, or Mons messenger, who were dignified and appointed to visit Maulmein once for a year from our court, as they generally are proud in vain and ignorant of foreign custom, and wondering or surprising themselves that they are embassadors from the king improper to carry letters from others. I think if you commit your letter or pack to them, lest they might say or do any laughable.

All white race at Bangkok, both clergymen and merchant, are well during time of cholera, as the missionaries were generally prevented themselves from filling of disease by using of drinking the dissolved mixture of calomel and opium with some spirit and oil put in water, and others by generally use of brandy.

On the ninth day of the current month, eight of Roman Catholic French priests disputed away from Siamese kingdom, on account of disagreement with the king, for ordinance the annual taxes, which were ordained upon all inhabitants of district of Bangkok. You will hear exactly from letters, perhaps, of your friends. I have no time to write you more.

I wrote you so long to fulfill your desire to hear from again as you had requested, in your addressed, as I am seeming to be, your curious but little as I was just studied of some way of English 4 years ago, commencing June, 1845, during one less of which I learned from mouth of my teacher, and on rest but by reading only.

I have the honour to be your friend,
T. Y. CHAUFA MONGKUT.

To Mr. Anderson, of Port Louis.

MAULMAIN, August 5, 1849.

MY DEAR BROTHER ANDERSON: Yours of January, 1848, I received with much pleasure, and have just reperused with much interest. But I should have been more gratified if I could have perused one of later date, giving me an account of the state of things at Port Louis down to the present time. I really don't know that I have heard a word from your island since the date of your letter.

Since my return from America, with the exception of a visit of a few months at Rangoon, I have been occupying my old stand, engaged chiefly in preparing a Burmese dictionary, which is now in the press; that is, the English and Burmese part. The Burmese and English part will, I hope, be ready for the press in the course of another year. They will make two quarto volumes of five or six hundred pages each. There are three Baptist churches in this town: a Burmese church, containing about one hundred and fifty members, of which I am pastor; a Karen church, containing about one hundred members, of which Mr. Binney is pastor; and an English church, containing about twenty-five members, of which Mr. Simons is pastor. There are two other Burmese churches in these regions, and above a dozen Karen churches. I suppose there are between fifteen hundred and two thousand baptized communicants in all the churches under our supervision in these parts, besides double that number, or more, exclusively Karen, attached to the Arracan mission. There is also a flourishing little church of some thirty or forty Burmese at Akyab, on the Arracan coast, under the care of brother Ingalls. We find it impossible, at present, to penetrate into Burmah proper, though my earnest view and ardent wishes are always directed thither. But now and then we baptize an individual from the empire; so that we trust the seed is sowing there, which will finally spring up in large and flourishing churches to the glory of God. At my age, (entering my sixty-second year on the 9th instant,) I can hardly expect to see the long-desired and long-prayed-for triumph of the Redeemer's kingdom in Burmah; but I trust I shall see it from the windows of paradise. Notwithstanding the remark above, I have sometimes heard, through the religious periodicals, of the state of things in Madagascar; and I look forward to the time when that great island shall submit to Christ. We live in wonderful times. Every revolution among the kingdoms of the earth seems to be designed to prepare the way for the universal establishment of the kingdom of Christ.

I have a little family once more around me — my present wife, a worthy successor of her predecessors; two little boys, remaining from the wreck of my last family; and a little girl, a year and a half old, just the age of the little one you lost. My three elder children are in America; and I have some hope that one of them has given his heart to God, though he has not yet professed religion. I shall send you, by the first opportunity, a copy of the Memoir of my late wife, by my present one, as a small token of my affectionate remembrance of you and Mrs. Anderson. There is nothing I should like better than to revisit the Isle of France; and you may depend that, if convenient to you, I should come straight to your house, according to your kind invitation. And as I have, in a good measure, recovered the use of my voice, I hope I should be able to do a little in your *English* prayer meetings that you speak of. But this will probably never be. May every blessing rest on you, and your family, and the precious circle of praying souls around you. Truly my heart is with you.

Your affectionate brother in the Lord,

A. JUDSON.

To the Corresponding Secretary.

MAULMAIN, August 20, 1849.

DEAR BROTHER: As you see from the date, I am still at Maulmain. Before receiving yours of the 20th of February last, with the appropriation for the expenses of a journey to Ava, the "small prospect in the horizon," mentioned in mine of the September preceding, had passed away; and since that, nothing encouraging has occurred. Were it not, however, for the following reason, I should prosecute my first intention; for so far as a *mere journey* to Ava is concerned, I know of no obstacle in the way of any foreigner who wishes to proceed thither.

Just as I had finished the English and Burmese part of the dictionary, at the close of last year, and was about commencing the Burmese and English part, Providence sent me, without my seeking, an excellent Burmese scholar, once a priest at Ava, and recommended by a gentleman quite competent to appreciate his qualifications — since deceased — as " the most profound scholar he had ever met with." I took him at once into my employ, and his aid, united with that of my two other assistants, proves to be invaluable, and, in my opinion, obviates much of the necessity of going to Ava, *so far as the dictionary is concerned.*

Considering, therefore, the uncertainty of life, and the state of my manuscripts, so effaced by time, or so erased and interlined as to be illegible to any other person but myself, I have thought it was my duty to forego, for the present, what I cannot but regard as an interesting expedition, in order to drive forward the heavy work of the dictionary in the most satisfactory manner, and without increasing the hazard of any serious interruption; *provided always*, that in the mean time nothing particularly encouraging in the direction of Ava should occur.

I hope, however, that the appropriation of the Executive Committee will not be withdrawn, but that I may be allowed to consider it available at the very earliest opportunity.

Yours affectionately,

A. JUDSON.

To the Rev. Mr. Gillette.

MAULMAIN, October 21, 1849.

DEAR BROTHER GILLETTE: I hope that dear wife keeps up the correspondence with you and your family properly; if she does not, please to drop me a line, and I will see to her. However, I feel as if it would do my heart good to write you a short letter myself. How glad I should be to step into your house, and spend an evening with you and dear Mrs. Gillette! It seems to me that I should enjoy your company far more than when I was with you. I was then so taken up with certain other matters, that I cannot help thinking I never became well acquainted with you. I should like very much to have you find a spare hour to sit down and write me about your family, and church, and brother ministers, in Philadelphia, and particularly those individuals that I knew. I suppose that death has been at work there, as well as every where else. I am glad to hear that your university affairs are well settled, and that brother Kincaid is coming out again.

Emily's health is very delicate — her hold on life very precarious. Yet she may live on many, many years. She has already outlived several whose health was much more robust. And while she does live, she will be a blessing to all, whether near or remote. I never cease to thank God that I found her, accidentally as it were, under your roof.

I am still hard at work on the dictionary, and shall be for above a year to come, if I live so long. The work will make two volumes quarto, containing above a thousand pages. No one can tell what toil it has cost me. But I trust it will be a valuable and standard work for a long time. It sweetens all toil to be conscious that we are laboring for the King of kings, the Lord of lords. I doubt not we find it so, whether in Maulmain or in Philadelphia.

Love to the Robartses, and all your and their friends.

Most affectionately yours,

A. JUDSON.

To the Rev. Mr. Osgood, formerly of Maulmain.

MAULMAIN, October 21, 1849.

So the light in your dwelling has gone out, my poor brother, and it is all darkness there, only as you draw down by faith some faint gleams of the light of heaven; and coldness has gathered round your hearthstone; your house is probably desolate, your children scattered, and you a homeless wanderer over the face of the land. We have both tasted of these bitter cups once and again; we have found them bitter, and we have found them sweet too. Every cup stirred by the finger of God becomes sweet to the humble believer. Do you remember how our late wives, and sister Stevens, and perhaps some others, used to cluster around the well-curb in the mission compound, at the close of day? I can almost see them sitting there, with their smiling faces, as I look out of the window at which I am now writing. Where are ours now? Clustering around the well-curb of the fountain of living water, to which the Lamb of heaven shows them the way — reposing in the arms of infinite love, who wipes away all their tears with his own hand.

Let us travel on and look up. We shall soon be there. As sure as I write or you read these lines, we shall soon be there. Many a weary step we may yet have to take, but we shall surely get there at last. And the longer and more tedious the way, the sweeter will be our repose.

I never wanted to hear from you so much as at the present moment. I hope you will have written me before receiving this. If not, do not delay giving me a long letter, and telling me all about yourself and your children, your circumstances and your prospects.

I am still hard at work, and shall be for a year more if I live so long. I hope then to get into more congenial employ. However, I would not choose for myself. Work of all sorts must be done, and it is a great privilege to be allowed to do any thing for the King of kings, the Lord of lords.

Dear wife has comfortable health just now, but her hold on life is very precarious.

Yours ever,
A. JUDSON.

From the Prince of Siam.

To Rev. Mr. Adoniram and Mrs. Emily Judsons, of Maulmain.

DATED WAT PAWARNWEES, BANGKOK, SIAM, March 13, 1850.

SIR AND MADAM: Your's letter addressed me under the date of 15th December ultimo, together another addressed to Rev. Mr. J. T. Jones, was received on 8th March as long as it was detained at the hand of His Honor Phytuck the Governor of Rahany, who was much engaged in the great funeral service of his old mother on last month.

I have forwarded the latter to Rev. J. T. Jones on the same day, who (J. T. Jones) wrote me the note that he was suffering for the considerable fever during a week so painful as he could not write you on this opportunity, but his sickness is not dangerous, he hope he will write you on next opportunity.

On the 10th March, before this date three days, I wrote you another letter and sent by hand of my messenger who was sent to visit Arracan by our Barque "Lion," according to counsel of the principal of our partical priesthood and superintendent gentlemen of our society, to let you know the news of the same depution that we wish to negotiate or communicate with the Buddhist people of the same land as we had ever done with Singhalese a few years ago.

Please receive a copy of the Calendar for the current year, the ending part of which was prepared myself and printed by Mr. H. Chandler, at mission press.

I shall be very glad to have from you, on return of Pegunese Messengers of our country, or of Northern Siamese messenger Rahany, some newspapers relating the news of Burman Golden city, or Capital, which might be printed and published at Maulemien by which we must be very, interested in reading. I am also eagerly desirous of having a tract of pronunciation of Burman letter which you had prepared and printed longly, trusting you would be able to get one from any where, even one old book in present.

Your faithful

PRINCE T. Y. CHAUFA MONGKUT.

CHAPTER IX.

HIS LAST ILLNESS. — INTENDED VOYAGE TO THE ISLE OF FRANCE. — THE CLOSING SCENES OF HIS LIFE. — HIS DEATH AND BURIAL. — NOTICES OF THE PRESS — ANECDOTES AND SKETCHES.

1849-1850.

Our narrative now hastens rapidly to its close. Dr. Judson employed himself, without intermission, upon the Burmese dictionary, until the month of November, 1849. He then took a violent cold while engaged, during the night, in assisting Mrs. Judson in the care of one of the children, that had been suddenly taken ill. This was followed by an attack of the fever of the country of a much graver character than he had ever before suffered. He had been so much accustomed to seizures of this kind, that neither he nor his friends became alarmed until the disease had reached the springs of life. At length he was persuaded to try the effect of a trip down the coast, and sailed in the steamer to Mergui. This afforded but partial relief, and he was advised to remove, for a season, to Amherst, for the benefit of the sea air. Here he rapidly sank, and it became too apparent that the only remaining hope of his recovery would be in a protracted sea voyage. To this proposal, however, he was for a long while strongly opposed, more especially because it was impossible for Mrs. Judson to accompany him. After much deliberation, he resolved to make the trial, and engaged a passage in the Aristide Marie, a

French bark, bound to the Isle of France. He embarked on the 3d of April, 1850, accompanied by Mr. Ranney, of the Maulmain mission. Some unfortunate delays occurred in their progress down the river, and several days elapsed, after leaving Maulmain, before they proceeded to sea. Dr. Judson never rallied, but gradually sank under the agonizing distress that preceded the fatal termination. The pilot left the vessel on Monday, April 8. Baffling winds and sultry weather supervened, and the distress of the sufferer became intense. The scene was closed by death on Friday, the 12th of April; and on the same day all that was mortal of Dr. Judson was committed to the deep.

From a Missionary.

. . . I saw Dr. Judson occasionally, and have seen no man in India, or elsewhere, whom I thought riper for heaven. I was particularly impressed with his firm reliance on the promises of God. He used the word *grace* very frequently, and in a way somewhat peculiar to himself. "I am sorry," said he on one occasion, "to learn that ——— is doing so badly. Yet his evidences were clear. I think he has grace, and will go safe at last." Speaking of the dubious conduct of a native assistant, he said in substance, "My assistants think meanly of him — not that he is wholly without grace, but he is too willing to find excuses for neglecting his duty." "I think he has grace," "I fear he is without grace," were very common expressions with him.

I once, in conversation with Dr. Judson, referred to ———'s sermon, and remarked that I considered that sermon a fair sample of the author — a production full of brilliant paradox, with little sober and safe reasoning. I afterwards sent him the sermon with a letter. The following was his reply: —

MAULMAIN, July 1, 1849.

DEAR BROTHER ————: Accompanying I return ———— ———— with thanks for your kindness. I presume, from what passed in a little conversation between us, that our sentiments on the discourse and on the character of the author perfectly accord. Eccentricity and ultraism have ruined many a genius. The longer we live, the more we learn to value plain, practical common sense, in religion, in politics, and in the ordinary affairs of life.

There were some touches in your letter which called forth all my sympathy. May God bless you and your dear wife, and be your never-failing portion. You must endeavor to look away from all outward things — from the satisfactions and discomforts, the commendations and censures, which are the common lot of man, and find your happiness in your own bosoms, in your work, in communion with God, and in the joyful anticipations of that blessed state, the heavenly Jerusalem, the "happy home" to which we are travelling.

I must add that, from the little acquaintance I formed with you and Mrs. ————, I should feel very happy if our lot could have fallen in the same station. However, what we have not now we shall have, I trust, hereafter.

Yours affectionately,
A. JUDSON.

To the Corresponding Secretary.

MAULMAIN, February 21, 1850.

MY DEAR BROTHER: I cannot manage a pen; so please to excuse pencil. I have been prostrated with fever ever since the latter part of last November, and have suffered so much, that I have frequently remarked that I was never ill in India before. Through the mercy of God, I think I am convalescent for the last ten days; but the doctor and all my friends are very urgent that I should take a sea voyage of a month or two, and be absent from this a long time. May God direct in the path of duty. My hand is failing; so I will beg to remain

        Yours affectionately,

                      A. JUDSON.

From Mrs. Judson to the Children in America.

                      MAULMAIN, April 11, 1850.

MY VERY DEAR CHILDREN: I have painful news to tell you — news that I am sure will make your hearts ache; but I hope our heavenly Father will help you to bear it. Your dear papa is very, *very* ill indeed, so much so that the best judges fear he will never be any better. He began to fail about five months ago, and has declined so gradually that we were not fully aware of his danger until lately; but within a few weeks those who love him have become very much alarmed. In January we went down to Mergui, by the steamer, and when we returned, thought he was a little better; but he soon failed again. We next spent a month at Amherst, but he received little, if any, benefit. Next, the doctors pronounced our house — the one you used to live in — unhealthy, and we removed to another. But all was of no use. Your dear papa continued to fail, till suddenly, one evening, his muscular strength gave way, and he was prostrated on the bed, unable to help himself. This occurred about two weeks ago. The doctor now became alarmed, and said the only hope for him was in a long voyage. It was very hard to think of such a thing in his reduced state, particularly as I could not go with him; but after we had wept and prayed over it one day and night, we concluded that it was our duty to use the only means which God had left us, however painful. We immediately engaged his passage aboard a French bark bound for the Mauritius; but before it sailed he had become so very low that no one thought it right for him to go alone. They therefore called a meeting of the mission, and appointed Mr. Ranney, the superintendent of the press, to accompany him. It was a great relief to me, for he is a very kind man, and loves your dear papa very much; and he will do every thing that can be done for his comfort. The officers of the vessel, too, seemed greatly interested for him, as did every one else. He was carried on board a week ago yesterday, in a litter, and placed on a nice easy cot, made purposely for him. I staid on board with him all day, and at dark came home to stay with the children. The next day I found that the vessel had only dropped down a little distance, and so I took a boat and followed. I expected this would certainly be the last day with him; but it was not. Friday I went again; and though he did not appear as well as on the previous days, I was forced to take, as I then supposed, a final leave of him. But when morning came, I felt as though I could not live through the day without knowing how he was. So I took a boat again, and reached the vessel about two o'clock, P. M. He could not speak, except in whispers, but seemed very glad that I came. The natives that I had sent to fan him, till he should get out of the river, came to me, and begged to have him taken ashore again; and so small was my hope of his recovery, that my heart pleaded on their side, though I still thought it duty to do as the doctor had ordered. I came away at dark, and though his lips moved to say some word of farewell, they made no sound. I hope that you, my dear boys, will never have cause to know what a heavy heart I bore back to my desolate home that night. The vessel got out to sea about four o'clock on Monday, and last night the natives returned, bringing a letter from Mr. Ranney. Your precious papa had revived again, spoke aloud, took a little tea and toast, said there was something animating in the touch of the sea breeze, and directed Mr. Ranney to write to me that he had a strong belief it was the will of God to restore him again to health. I feel somewhat encouraged, but dare not hope too much.

And now, my dear boys, it will be three, perhaps four long months before we can hear from our loved one again; and we shall all be very anxious. All that we can do is to commit him to the care of our heavenly Father, and if we never see him again in this world, pray that we may be prepared to meet him in heaven.

Your dear little brothers and sister enjoy excellent health. They are so young that they do not understand much about their papa, though they sometimes cry when I talk to them about him. I shall write to you just as quick as I hear from your papa, and wish you to write to me, for I love you very much for his sake, though I saw so little of you at Worcester. Give love to Dr. and Mrs. Newton, and believe me

Your most affectionate mamma,

EMILY C. JUDSON.

Closing Scenes in Dr. Judson's Life, communicated to his sister, by Mrs. Judson.

MAULMAIN, September 20, 1850.

MY DEAR SISTER: Last month I could do no more than announce to you our painful bereavement, which, though not altogether unexpected, will, I very well know, fall upon your heart with overwhelming weight. You will find the account of your brother's last days on board the Aristide Marie, in a letter written by Mr. Ranney, from Mauritius, to the secretary of the board; and I can add nothing to it, with the exception of a few unimportant particulars, gleaned in conversations with Mr. Ranney and the Coringa servant. I grieve that it should be so — that I was not permitted to watch beside him during those days of terrible suffering; but the pain which I at first felt is gradually yielding to gratitude for the inestimable privileges which had previously been granted me.

There was something exceedingly beautiful in the decline of your brother's life — more beautiful than I can describe, though the impression will remain with me as a sacred legacy, until I go to meet him where suns shall never set, and life shall never end. He had been, from my first acquaintance with him, an uncommonly spiritual Christian, exhibiting his richest graces in the unguarded intercourse of private life; but during his last year, it seemed as though the light of the world on which he was entering had been sent to brighten his upward pathway. Every subject on which we conversed, every book we read, every incident that occurred, whether trivial or important, had a tendency to suggest some peculiarly spiritual train of thought, till it seemed to me that, more than ever before, " Christ was all his theme." Something of the same nature was also noted in his preaching, to which I then had not the privilege of listening. He was in the habit, however, of studying his subject for the Sabbath, audibly, and in my presence, at which time he was frequently so much affected as to weep, and sometimes so overwhelmed with the vastness of his conceptions as to be obliged to abandon his theme and choose another. My own illness at the commencement of the year had brought eternity very near to us, and rendered death, the grave, and the bright heaven beyond it, familiar subjects of conversation. Gladly would I give you, my dear sister, some idea of the share borne by him in those memorable conversations; but it would be impossible to convey, even to those who knew him best, the most distant conception of them. I believe he has sometimes been thought eloquent, both in conversation and in the sacred desk; but the fervid, burning eloquence, the deep pathos, the touching tenderness, the elevation of thought, and intense beauty of expression, which characterized those private teachings, were not only beyond what I had ever heard before, but such as I felt sure arrested his own attention, and surprised even himself. About this time he began to find unusual satisfaction and enjoyment in his private devotions, and seemed to have new objects of interest continually rising in his mind, each of which in turn became special subjects of prayer. Among these, one of the most prominent was the conversion of his posterity. He remarked, that he had always prayed for his children, but that of late he had felt impressed with the duty of praying for their children and their children's children down to the latest generation. He also prayed most fervently that his impressions on this particular subject might be transferred to his sons and daughters, and thence to their offspring, so that he should ultimately meet a long, unbroken line of descendants before the throne of God, where all might join together in ascribing everlasting praises to their Redeemer.

Another subject, which occupied a large share of his attention, was that of brotherly love. You are, perhaps, aware that, like all persons of his ardent temperament, he was subject to strong attachments and aversions, which he sometimes had difficulty in bringing under the controlling influence of divine grace. He remarked that he had always felt more or less of an affectionate interest in his brethren, as brethren, and some of them he had loved very dearly for their personal qualities; but he was now aware that he had never placed his standard of love high enough. He spoke of them as children of God, redeemed by the Saviour's blood, watched over and guarded by his love, dear to his heart, honored by him in the election, and to be honored hereafter before the assembled universe; and he said it was not sufficient to be kind and obliging to such, to abstain from evil speaking, and make a general mention of them in our prayers; but our attachment to them should be of the most ardent and exalted character: it would be so in heaven, and we lost immeasurably by not beginning now. "As I have loved you, so ought ye also to love one another," was a precept continually in his mind; and he would often murmur, as though unconsciously, "'As I have loved you'—'as I have loved you,'"—then burst out with the exclamation, "O, the love of Christ! the love of Christ!"

His prayers for the mission were marked by an earnest, grateful enthusiasm, and in speaking of missionary operations in general, his tone was one of elevated triumph, almost of exultation; for he not only felt an unshaken confidence in their final success, but would often exclaim, "What wonders — O, what wonders God has already wrought!"

I remarked that during this year his literary labor, which he had never liked, and upon which he had entered unwillingly and from a feeling of necessity, was growing daily more irksome to him; and he always spoke of it as his "heavy work," his "tedious work," "that wearisome dictionary," &c., though this feeling led to no relaxation of effort. He longed, however, to find some more spiritual employment, to be engaged in what he considered more legitimate missionary labor, and drew delightful pictures of the future, when his whole business would be but to preach and to pray.

During all this time I had not observed any failure in physical strength; and though his mental exercises occupied a large share of my thoughts when alone, it never once occurred to me that this might be the brightening of the setting sun; my only feeling was that of pleasure, that one so near to me was becoming so pure and elevated in his sentiments, and so lovely and Christ-like in his character. In person he had grown somewhat stouter than when in America; his complexion had a healthful hue, compared with that of his associates generally; and though by no means a person of uniformly firm health, he seemed to possess such vigor and strength of constitution, that I thought his life as likely to be extended twenty years longer, as that of any member of the mission. He continued his system of morning exercise, commenced when a student at Andover, and was not satisfied with a common walk on level ground, but always chose an up-hill path, and then frequently went bounding on his way with all the exuberant activity of boyhood.

He was of a singularly happy temperament, although not of that even cast which never rises above a certain level, and is never depressed. Possessing acute sensibilities, suffering with those who suffered, and entering as readily into the joys of the prosperous and happy, he was variable in his moods; but religion formed such an essential element in his character, and his trust in Providence was so implicit and habitual, that he was never gloomy, and seldom more than momentarily disheartened. On the other hand, being accustomed to regard all the events of this life, however minute or painful, as ordered in wisdom, and tending to one great and glorious end, he lived in almost constant obedience to the apostolic injunction, "Rejoice evermore!" He often told me that although he had endured much personal suffering, and passed through many fearful trials in the course of his eventful life, a kind Providence had also hedged him round with precious, peculiar blessings, so that his joys had far outnumbered his sorrows.

Towards the close of September of last year, he said to me one evening, "What deep cause have we for gratitude to God! Do you believe there are any other two persons in the wide world so happy as we are?" enumerating, in his own earnest manner, several sources of happiness, in which our work as missionaries, and our eternal prospects, occupied a prominent position. When he had finished his glowing picture, I remarked,—I scarcely know why, but there was a heavy cloud upon my spirits that evening,—" We are certainly very happy now, but it cannot be so always. I am thinking of the time when one of us must stand beside the bed, and see the other die."

"Yes," he said, "that will be a sad moment; I felt it most deeply a little while ago, but now it would not be strange if your life were prolonged beyond mine — though I should wish, if it were possible, to spare you that pain. It is the one left alone who suffers, not the one who goes to be with Christ. If it should only be the will of God that we might go together, like young James and his wife! But he will order all things well, and we can safely trust our future to his hands."

That same night we were roused from sleep by the sudden illness of one of the children. There was an unpleasant, chilling dampness in the air, as it came to us through the openings in the sloats above the windows, which affected your brother very sensibly; and he soon began to shiver so violently that he was obliged to return to his couch, where he remained under a warm covering until morning. In the morning he awoke with a severe cold, accompanied by some degree of fever; but as it did not seem very serious, and our three children were all suffering from a similar cause, we failed to give it any especial attention. From that time he was never well, though in writing to you before, I think I dated the commencement of his illness from the month of November, when he laid aside his studies I know that he regarded this attack as trifling; and yet one evening he spent a long time in advising me with regard to my future course, if I should be deprived of his guidance, saying that it is always wise to be prepared for exigencies of this nature. After the month of November, he failed gradually, occasionally rallying in such a manner as to deceive us all, but at each relapse sinking lower than at the previous one, though still full of hope and courage, and yielding ground only inch by inch, as compelled by the triumphant progress of disease. During some hours of every day he suffered intense pain; but his naturally buoyant spirits and uncomplaining disposition led him to speak so lightly of it, that I used sometimes to fear that the doctor, though a very skilful man, would be fatally deceived.

As his health declined, his mental exercises at first seemed deepened; and he gave still larger portions of his time to prayer, conversing with the utmost freedom on his daily progress, and the extent of his self-conquest. Just before our trip to Mergui, which took place in January, he looked up from his pillow one day with sudden animation, and said to me earnestly, "I have gained the victory at last. I love every one of Christ's redeemed, as I believe he would have me love them — in the same manner, though not probably to the same degree as we shall love one another in heaven; and gladly would I prefer the meanest of his creatures, who bears his name, before myself." This he said in allusion to the text, "In honor preferring one another," on which he had frequently dwelt with great emphasis. After further similar conversation, he concluded, "And now here I lie at peace with all the world, and what is better still, at peace with my own conscience. I know that I am a miserable sinner in the sight of God, with no hope but in the blessed Saviour's merits; but I cannot think of any particular fault, any peculiarly besetting sin, which it is now my duty to correct. Can you tell me of any?"

And truly, from this time no other word would so well express his state of feeling as that one of his own choosing — *peace*. He had no particular exercises afterwards, but remained calm and serene, speaking of himself daily as a great sinner, who had been overwhelmed with benefits, and declaring that he had never in all his life before had such delightful views of the unfathomable love and infinite condescension of the Saviour as were now daily opening before him. "O, the love of Christ! the love of Christ!" he would suddenly exclaim, while his eye kindled, and the tears chased each other down his cheeks; "we cannot understand it now — but what a beautiful study for eternity!"

After our return from Mergui, the doctor advised a still further trial of the effects of sea air and sea bathing; and we accordingly proceeded to Amherst, where we remained nearly a month. This to me was the darkest period of his illness — no medical adviser, no friend, at hand, and he daily growing weaker and weaker. He began to totter in walking, clinging to the furniture and walls, when he thought he was unobserved, (for he was not willing to acknowledge the extent of his debility,) and his wan face was of a ghastly paleness. His sufferings too were sometimes fearfully intense, so that, in spite of his habitual self-control, his groans would fill the house. At other times a kind of lethargy seemed to steal over him, and he would sleep almost incessantly for twenty-four hours, seeming annoyed if he were aroused or disturbed. Yet there were portions of the time when he was comparatively comfortable, and conversed intelligently; but his mind seemed to revert to former scenes, and he tried to amuse me with stories of his boyhood, his college days, his imprisonment in France, and his early missionary life. He had a great deal also to say on his favorite theme, "the love of Christ;" but his strength was too much impaired for any continuous mental effort. Even a short prayer, made audibly, exhausted him to such a degree that he was obliged to discontinue the practice.

A length I wrote to Maulmain, giving some expression of my anxieties and misgivings, and our kind missionary friends, who had from the first evinced all the tender interest and watchful sympathy of the nearest kindred, immediately sent for us — the doctor advising a sea voyage. But as there was no vessel in the harbor bound for a port sufficiently distant, we thought it best, in the mean time, to remove from our old dwelling, which had long been condemned as unhealthy, to another mission house, fortunately empty. This change was, at first, attended with the most beneficial results; and our hopes revived so much, that we looked forward to the approaching rainy season for entire restoration. But it lasted only a little while; and then both of us became convinced that, though a voyage at sea involved much that was exceedingly painful, it yet presented the only prospect of recovery, and could not, therefore, without a breach of duty, be neglected.

"O, if it were only the will of God to take me now — to let me die here!" he repeated over and over again, in a tone of anguish, while we were considering the subject. "I cannot, cannot go! This is almost more than I can bear! Was there ever suffering like our suffering?" and the like broken expressions, were continually falling from his lips. But he soon gathered more strength of purpose; and after the decision was fairly made, he never hesitated for a moment, rather regarding the prospect with pleasure. I think the struggle which this resolution cost injured him very materially; though probably it had no share in bringing about the final result. God, who saw the end from the beginning, had counted out his days, and they were hastening to a close. Until this time he had been able to stand, and to walk slowly from room to room; but as he one evening attempted to rise from his chair, he was suddenly deprived of his small remnant of muscular strength, and would have fallen to the floor but for timely support.

From that moment his decline was rapid. As he lay helplessly upon his couch, and watched the swelling of his feet, and other alarming symptoms, he became very anxious to commence his voyage, and I felt equally anxious to have his wishes gratified. I still hoped he might recover; the doctor said the chances of life and death were, in his opinion, equally balanced. And then he always loved the sea so dearly! There was something exhilarating to him in the motion of a vessel, and he spoke with animation of getting free from the almost suffocating atmosphere incident to the hot season, and drinking in the fresh sea breezes. He talked but little more, however, than was necessary to indicate his wants, his bodily sufferings being too great to allow of conversation; but several times he looked up to me with a bright smile, and exclaimed, as heretofore, "O, the love of Christ! the love of Christ!"

I found it difficult to ascertain, from expressions casually dropped from time to time, his real opinion with regard to his recovery; but I thought there was some reason to doubt whether he was fully aware of his critical situation. I did not suppose he had any preparation to make at this late hour, and I felt sure that, if he should be called ever so unexpectedly, he would not enter the presence of his Maker with a ruffled spirit; but I could not bear to have him go away, without knowing how doubtful it was whether our next meeting would not be in eternity; and perhaps too, in my own distress, I might still have looked for words of encouragement and sympathy to a source which had never before failed.

It was late in the night, and I had been performing some little sick-room offices, when suddenly he looked up to me, and exclaimed, "This will never do! You are killing yourself for me, and I will not permit it. You must have some one to relieve you. If I had not been made selfish by suffering, I should have insisted upon it long ago."

He spoke so like himself, with the earnestness of health, and in a tone to which my ear had of late been a stranger, that for a moment I felt almost bewildered with sudden hope. He received my reply to what he had said with a half-pitying, half-gratified smile; but in the mean time his expression had changed — the marks of excessive debility were again apparent, and I could not forbear adding, "It is only a little while, you know."

"Only a little while," he repeated mournfully; "this separation is a bitter thing, but it does not distress me now as it did — I am too weak." "You have no reason to be distressed," I answered, "with such glorious prospects before you.

You have often told me it is the one left alone who suffers, not the one who goes to be with Christ." He gave me a rapid, questioning glance, then assumed for several moments an attitude of deep thought. Finally, he slowly unclosed his eyes, and fixing them on me, said in a calm, earnest tone, " I do not believe I am going to die. I think I know why this illness has been sent upon me; I needed it; I feel that it has done me good; and it is my impression that I shall now recover, and be a better and more useful man."

"Then it is your wish to recover?" I inquired. "If it should be the will of God, yes. I should like to complete the dictionary, on which I have bestowed so much labor, now that it is so nearly done; for though it has not been a work that pleased my taste, or quite satisfied my feelings, I have never underrated its importance. Then after that come all the plans that we have formed. O, I feel as if I were only just beginning to be prepared for usefulness."

"It is the opinion of most of the mission," I remarked, "that you will not recover." "I know it is," he replied; "and I suppose they think me an old man, and imagine it is nothing for one like me to resign a life so full of trials. But I am not old — at least in that sense; you know I am not. O, no man ever left this world, with more inviting prospects, with brighter hopes or warmer feelings — warmer feelings;" he repeated, and burst into tears. His face was perfectly placid, even while the tears broke away from the closed lids, and rolled, one after another, down to the pillow. There was no trace of agitation or pain in his manner of weeping, but it was evidently the result of acute sensibilities, combined with great physical weakness. To some suggestions which I ventured to make, he replied, "It is not that — I know all that, and feel it in my inmost heart. Lying here on my bed, when I could not talk, I have had such views of the loving condescension of Christ, and the glories of heaven, as I believe are seldom granted to mortal man. It is not because I shrink from death that I wish to live, neither is it because the ties that bind me here, though some of them are very sweet, bear any comparison with the drawings I at times feel towards heaven; but a few years would not be missed from my eternity of bliss, and I can well afford to spare them, both for your sake and for the sake of the poor Burmans. I am not tired of my work, neither am I tired of the world; yet when Christ calls me home, I shall go with the gladness of a boy bounding away from his school. Perhaps I feel something like the young bride, when she contemplates resigning the pleasant associations of her childhood for a yet dearer home — though only a very little like her, for *there is no doubt resting on my future.*" "Then death would not take you by surprise," I remarked, "if it should come even before you could get on board ship?" "O, no," he said, "death will never take me by surprise — do not be afraid of that — I feel *so strong in Christ.* He has not led me so tenderly thus far, to forsake me at the very gate of heaven. No, no; I am willing to live a few years longer, if it should be so ordered; and if otherwise, I am willing and glad to die now. I leave myself entirely in the hands of God, to be disposed of according to his holy will."

The next day some one mentioned, in his presence, that the native Christians were greatly opposed to the voyage, and that many other persons had a similar feeling with regard to it. I thought he seemed troubled, and after the visitor had withdrawn, I inquired if he still felt as when he conversed with me the night previous. He replied, "O, yes; that was no evanescent feeling. It has been with me, to a greater or less extent, for years, and will be with me, I trust, to the end. I am ready to go *to-day* — if it should be the will of God, this very hour; but I am not *anxious* to die; at least when I am not beside myself with pain."

"Then why are you so desirous to go to sea? I should think it would be a matter of indifference to you." "No," he answered quietly, "my judgment tells me it would be wrong not to go; the doctor says *criminal.* I shall certainly die here; if I go away I may possibly recover. There is no question with regard to duty in such a case; and I do not like to see any hesitation, even though it springs from affection."

He several times spoke of a burial at sea, and always as though the prospect were agreeable. It brought, he said, a sense of freedom and expansion, and seemed far pleasanter than the confined, dark, narrow grave, to which he had committed so many that he loved. And he added, that although his burial-place was a matter of no real importance, yet he believed it was not in human nature to be altogether without a choice.

I have already given you an account of the embarkation, of my visits to him while the vessel remained in the river, and of our last sad, silent parting; and Mr. Ranney has finished the picture. You will find, in this closing part, some dark shadows, that will give you pain; but you must remember that his present felicity is enhanced by those very sufferings; and we should regret nothing that serves to brighten his crown in glory. I ought also to add, that I have gained pleasanter impressions in conversation with Mr. Ranney than from his written account; but it would be difficult to convey them to you; and, as he whom they concern was accustomed to say of similar things, "you will learn it all in heaven."

During the last hour of your sainted brother's life, Mr. Ranney bent over him, and held his hand, while poor Panapah stood at a little distance weeping bitterly. The table had been spread in the cuddy, as usual, and the officers did not know what was passing in the cabin, till summoned to dinner. Then they gathered about the door, and watched the closing scene with solemn reverence. Now — thanks to a merciful God! — his pains had left him; not a momentary spasm disturbed his placid face, nor did the contraction of a muscle denote the least degree of suffering; the agony of death was passed, and his wearied spirit was turning to its rest in the bosom of the Saviour. From time to time, he pressed the hand in which his own was resting, his clasp losing in force at each successive pressure; while his shortened breath — though there was no struggle, no gasping, as if it came and went with difficulty — gradually grew softer and fainter, until it died upon the air — and he was gone. Mr Ranney closed the eyes, and composed the passive limbs; the ship's officers stole softly from the door, and the neglected meal was left upon the board untasted.

They lowered him to his ocean grave without a prayer. His freed spirit had soared above the reach of earthly intercession, and to the foreigners who stood around it would have been a senseless form. And there they left him in his unquiet sepulchre; but it matters little, for we know that while the unconscious clay is " drifting, on the shifting currents of the restless main," nothing can disturb the hallowed rest of the immortal spirit. Neither could he have a more fitting monument than the blue waves which visit every coast; for his warm sympathies went forth to the ends of the earth, and included the whole family of man. It is all as God would have it, and our duty is but to bend meekly to his will, and wait, in faith and patience, till we also shall be summoned home.

The Last Days of Dr. Judson, as derived from a Letter of Mr. Ranney to the Corresponding Secretary.

Dr. Judson was carried on board the French bark Aristide Marie, bound for the Isle of Bourbon, with the reluctant assent of his friends, his physician having recommended such a voyage as the only possible means of restoration. It being desirable to get to sea as soon as practicable, application was made to the commissioner of the provinces, to permit the bark to be towed out of the river by the steamer Proserpine, which was that morning to proceed southward with troops. Permission was granted, and on Wednesday, April 3, by the kindness of Captain Lawford, commandant of artillery, a palanquin and bearers took Dr. Judson, then too weak to stand, and carried him on board. There they learned, with surprise and sorrow, that the steamer would not take them in tow. The commander of the troops claimed that, while employed as a military transport, the vessel was not subject to the commissioner's order, and on the ground that it might endanger the lives of the soldiers, declined to comply with it. The consequence of this collision of authorities was, that, instead of getting to sea in twenty-four hours, they were five days in reaching Amherst, and it was six days before the pilot left the vessel. How much was thus lost it is impossible to conjecture.

The delay permitted Mrs. Judson, (who would gladly have accompanied her husband, though at the hazard of her life, if he had consented,) and Mr. Stilson, and Mr. and Mrs. Stevens to visit him repeatedly, and minister to his comfort. He bore the fatigue of embarkation very well, and on Thursday took more refreshment than for several days previous. This gave hope of a favorable change; but on Friday he was not as well, and his two Burmese assistants, Ko En and Ko Shway Doke, disciples of many years' standing, who remained on board till the pilot left the vessel, requested that he might be taken back to Maulmain. They were confident he was near his end, and could not endure the thought of his burial in the ocean; they wanted his grave to be made where they and the other disciples could look upon it. But any attempt to do this would have proved fatal, and there was no choice but to fulfil their original purpose, Mr. Stilson reminding the affectionate disciples of the death and unknown burial-place of Moses.

On Saturday he was perceptibly weaker. Such was his pain that he said he would willingly die, if he could. On Sunday, being more calm and free from pain, he conversed freely and more at length than he had been able to do, describing somewhat minutely the causes of his pain. He said that no one could conceive the intensity of his sufferings. Death would have been a glad relief. The idea of death caused no peculiar emotion of either fear or transport. His mind was so affected by suffering that he could not think, or even pray. Nay, he could not think of his wife and family. He had bitter sorrow in parting with them at first; but in Mrs. Judson's subsequent visit, speech had been almost denied him; and when they parted the day before, perhaps the last time on earth, it was without a word, and almost without a thought, so entirely had pain absorbed every faculty Yet he felt he had nothing to complain of. He knew it was the will of God, and therefore right. Alluding to the swelling of his feet, he said, " The natives are frightened when they see this. They regard it as a sure sign of approaching death; but I do not. I have talked with the doctor about this, and have myself remarked, at different times, the swelling and subsiding. I still feel that there is so much of life in me that I shall recover."

On Monday, the 6th, at half past three o'clock, P. M., the pilot, with the two assistants above named, and Moung Shwaymoung, of the Amherst church, left the ship. At the request of Dr. Judson, Mr. Ranney wrote to Mrs. Judson his opinion of himself, that " he went out to sea with a strong feeling that he should recover." But on the same day the violence of his pains returned, and his left side was swollen much, from which he gained partial relief. On Tuesday morning, the Tenasserim coast being yet visible, they enjoyed a fresh and invigorating breeze; but a violent thunder storm came on, followed by a calm. For a short time Dr. Judson suffered less pain; but a hiccough increased upon him. He said, " This hiccough is killing me; can you think of any thing to do for it?" He afterwards slept considerably, and took some slight refreshment; but in the afternoon a new symptom appeared, which continued to the last — frequent vomiting and an inability to retain any thing upon his stomach.

During the night and the next day the weather was exceedingly hot. Dr. Judson refused all nourishment, and inclined to sleep, probably on account of the laudanum and ether administered. He said he should weary them but little longer. The captain gave several prescriptions without effect; on which he said, " It is of but little consequence. I do not wish any one to think I died because all was not done that could be done for me. Medicine is of no use. The disease will take its course." While suffering the acute pain which invariably preceded vomiting, he said, " O that I could die at once, and go immediately into paradise, where there is no pain!"

On the evening of Wednesday, as Mr. Ranney was sitting by his bedside, he said, "I am glad you are here. I do not feel so abandoned. You are my only kindred now — the only one on board who loves Christ, I mean; and it is a great comfort to have one near me who loves Christ." "I hope," said Mr. Ranney, "you feel that Christ is now near, sustaining you." "O, yes," he replied, "*it is all right there.* I believe he gives me just so much pain and suffering as is necessary to fit me to die — to make me submissive to his will." The captain — who spoke but little English, but took unwearied pains to make himself understood by a frequent resort to a French and English dictionary, and was a pattern of kindness and benevolence — offered another prescription; but Dr. Judson thanked him, and declined. He spoke of the invigorating influence of the wind, and expressed a fear that they would lose it during the night; which proved true. After midnight there was a dead calm, and a very oppressive atmosphere. At two o'clock his breathing became very difficult; but afterwards he breathed more freely.

On Thursday morning his eyes had a dull appearance, remained half closed while sleeping, and seemed glassy and death-like. His stomach rejected all refreshment. At ten and twelve o'clock he took some ether, which he said did him good. After vomiting, with the suffering which preceded it, he said, "O, how few there are who suffer such great torment — who die so hard!" During all the night his sufferings increased, so that it was inexpressibly painful to behold his agony — sometimes calling for water, which gave relief only while he was drinking it, to be followed by the pain of ejecting it. At midnight he said his fever had returned. His extremities were cold, his head hot. It was the fever of death. His weakness was such that he now seldom spoke, except to indicate some want, which he more frequently did by signs.

During the forenoon of Friday, the 12th, his countenance was that of a dying man. About noon he showed some aberration of mind; but it was only transient. At three o'clock he said, in Burman, to Panapah, a native servant, "It is done; I am going." Shortly after he made a sign with his hand downwards, which was not understood; drawing Mr. Ranney's ear close to his mouth, he said, convulsively, "Brother Ranney, will you bury me? bury me?—quick! quick!" These words were prompted, perhaps, by the thought of burial in the sea crossing his mind. Mr. Ranney here being called out for a moment, Dr. Judson spoke to the servant in English, and also in Burman, of Mrs. Judson, bidding him "take care of poor mistress;" and at fifteen minutes past four o'clock he breathed his last. "His death," says Mr. Ranney, "was like falling asleep. Not the movement of a muscle was perceptible, and the moment of the going out of life was indicated only by his ceasing to breathe. A gentle pressure of the hand, growing more and more feeble as life waned, showed the peacefulness of the spirit about to take its homeward flight."

It was first determined to keep the body until Saturday for burial; but Mr. Ranney was admonished of the necessity of immediate preparations. A strong plank coffin was soon constructed; several buckets of sand were poured in to make it sink; and at eight o'clock in the evening the crew assembled, the larboard port was opened, and in perfect silence, broken only by the voice of the captain, all that was mortal of Dr. Judson was committed to the deep, in latitude thirteen degrees north, longitude ninety-three degrees east, nine days after their embarkation from Maulmain, and scarcely three days out of sight of the mountains of Burmah.

Action of the Executive Committee.

The facts in the preceding statement having been communicated to the Executive Committee on Monday, September 9, the following preamble and resolutions were unanimously adopted:—

As God, in his righteous administration, has been pleased to remove, by death, the senior missionary of the American Baptist Missionary Union, the Rev. Adoniram Judson, D. D., and as the event is one of such peculiar importance as to demand of this committee a more than ordinary expression of interest, therefore, —

Resolved, That we recognize with devout gratitude the special grace of the Head of the church, in providing for us such a pioneer of our missionary enterprise; in endowing him with such eminent qualifications for the service; in preserving him so long through a series of extraordinary labors, sufferings, and perils; and in enabling him to execute so much for the glory of Christ and the welfare of the heathen.

Resolved, That, while we bow submissively to the will of Him who has thus, in a mysterious way, elevated his servant from the work of earth to the reward of heaven, we are happy to cherish a grateful recollection of the many excellences of our beloved brother, and to place on permanent record our cordial and unqualified testimony to the great purity of his personal character; to the singular uniformity with which he has exemplified the spirit of his vocation; and to the distinguished patience, perseverance, and fidelity with which, ever since the date of his appointment, May 25, 1814, he has prosecuted his appropriate work.

Resolved, That, in the absence of the Foreign Secretary, the Home Secretary be requested to address to Mrs. Judson a letter of condolence, assuring her of the tenderest sympathy of the committee in her most afflictive bereavement; of the high estimation in which they held the eminently good man of whom she has been thus painfully deprived; and of their readiness, should she so desire, to facilitate the return of herself and family to her native land.

Resolved, That the Home Secretary be requested to communicate to the mission with which Dr. Judson was connected, a fraternal expression of our sympathy with them in the severe loss which they have sustained, and of our fervent desire that this dispensation of Providence may be so graciously overruled as to subserve the advancement of that cause to which they and we are mutually pledged.

Resolved, That the secretaries be requested to take the

steps necessary to secure the materials for the preparation of a Memoir of Dr. Judson.

Resolved, That immediate arrangements be made for a public discourse, and other religious services appropriate to this afflictive occasion.

Resolved, That copies of these resolutions be forwarded to Mrs. Judson, and to the Maulmain mission; also to Miss Abigail B. Judson, the only surviving sister of the deceased.

From the Right Reverend the Bishop of Calcutta to Mrs. Judson.

MAULMAIN, December 17, 1850.

DEAREST SISTER IN THE LORD: I cannot express to you with what feelings of tender remembrance I have received this double present — the one from heaven, as it were, the other from the beloved widow of that sainted one now gone before us to glory.

I have always considered Dr. Judson as one of the most devoted, wise, learned, and truly charitable missionaries I have ever known. I rank him with Brainerd, Eliot, Schwartz, H. Martyn, D. Brown, Bishop Corrie, &c., &c.

Will you allow me to offer to your dear children two small testimonies of love?

And if any Memoir of Dr. Judson should appear, may I beg the great favor of a copy?

My time must soon come. I am ten years older than your dear husband, having been born July 2, 1778; and I am now in the fiftieth year of my ministry. May I have grace to "*end well*," as Bible Scott used to say!

I commend myself to your prayers and those of *all America*, and am

Your most affectionate

D. CALCUTTA.

From the Rev. L Ingalls, Missionary at Akyab.

AKYAB, May 18, 1852.

REV. FRANCIS WAYLAND, D. D.

MY DEAR BROTHER: I perceive, by a notice in the Macedonian, that you have been appointed to write the Memoir of the lamented Dr. Judson. I have felt anxious to make a few remarks with reference to that good man. He possessed, in an eminent degree, the missionary spirit. This I ascertained, not from his writings, but personal observation. During my first year in the mission, I was for some time connected with him at Maulmain. He was then upon the great work of his life, the Burmese Bible. If I wished to see him, I always knew where to find him — in the study. His conversation was ever upon the theme of the soul's salvation. The Burmans lay near his heart; he was accustomed to spend a portion of each day in secret prayer for them. I had the privilege of enjoying some of these seasons, and shall never forget those hallowed hours. He not only prayed, but labored; the zayat was the place of his delight, and he had a peculiar tact to arrest the attention of the Buddhists. His mild, winning manner gained an influence over them. The disciples loved and revered him; they reposed in him the confidence the child does in a father. It was thus he had a power to build and sustain a Burmese church. He was ever anxious for the salvation of souls; hence his constant desire to be preaching. It was a great self-denial to be shut up in his study, and he anticipated, with exulting feelings, the completion of the Burmese Bible. He sighed bitterly when he was required to compile a Burmese dictionary. But he is gone. Burmah's best, dearest earthly friend is removed. He will no more cheer the new missionary as he steps upon the pagan field. I doubt not but you will so bring out his peculiar traits as a missionary, that his Memoir will be the means of imparting a new and fervent missionary spirit in the rising ministry, and that thousands will enter the field of his choice, and labor, suffer, and die like the illustrious Judson.

Affectionately and sincerely yours,

L. INGALLS.

P. S. The reason I have sent you these few lines above, is, I have felt exceedingly lonely since my return, while reflecting upon the loss of brother Judson to the Burman mission. Is Burmah to have no more Judsons?

From the various notices of the public press, which the death of Dr. Judson occasioned, we select the following: —

From the Christian Register, the Organ of the Unitarians of New England.

We cannot let so great and good a man pass from the catalogue of the living without a few words of commemoration. Human history contains no more glorious records of Christian heroism than are to be found in the narrative of the Baptist missionary transactions in Burmah. We have read, over and over again, with intense and admiring interest, the story of Boardman, consciously the victim of consumption, yet toiling only with the greater earnestness as the time drew near for his departure, borne in a litter across swollen torrents and over rough mountain passes, that the closing moments of his life might not be lost for his Master's work; usurping the last energies of dissolving nature in expounding to his newly baptized converts "the way of the Lord more perfectly," his hands lifted in prayer or spread in blessing for his flock, till they grew rigid in death. With no less delight and reverence have we traced the course of his young widow, who took up he cross so dear to the departed, encountered perils from which the stoutest heart, unfortified by divine grace, might shrink — "perils of waters, perils by the heathen, perils in the wilderness, perils among false brethren;" with more than manly perseverance and more than womanly tenderness, bore about the message of redeeming love; and was personally the means of keeping from dispersion, and enriching in numbers and in spiritual gifts, numerous and widely scattered communities of native Christians. Nor are we ever made more sensible of the presence and influence of the divine Spirit than in the preternatural endurance and energy of the first Mrs. Judson, when, in the seat of war, alone and friendless, with a helpless babe at her bosom, she ministers to her husband and the partner of his horrible captivity, staves off the blind fury of their savage jailers, sustains in their hearts and her own the hope of deliverance, and at length becomes, under God, the author of their liberty, and their return to their long-suspended walk of missionary duty.

Dr. Judson was not only the pioneer in this holy work, and the father of this devoted band, but his life spans the history of foreign missions from America. He was the writer and one of the four signers of the first appeal to the churches in behalf of this work. He was then a theological student in Andover, and sailed for India under the auspices of the Orthodox Congregationalists of New England. On his outward voyage he became convinced of the scriptural validity of adult baptism by immersion as the only authorized form of initiation into the Christian church, and shortly after his arrival was baptized by one of the English Baptist missionaries. He threw himself for support on the then feeble body of American Baptists, who, in their efforts to sustain and reënforce him, were led to the surest possible means of strengthening the spirit of piety and philanthropy among themselves at home, and may date from their zeal in his behalf the dawn of their own rapid enlargement and culminating prosperity. With an iron constitution, with indomitable strength of purpose, with apostolic energy of faith and love, with devotedness as entire as ever marked a servant of Christ; he has given youth, manhood, and vigorous old age to the ministry among the heathen. Two * brief visits to his native country, absolutely necessitated by the condition of his health, and consecrated to the furtherance of his work among the churches that sustained him, have been the only intermis-

* Dr. Judson made but one visit to his native land after he first left it for India.

sion to labors as abundant, hardships as severe, sufferings as intense, as have fallen to the lot of a Christian soldier since the martyrdom of St. Paul. And now he has died with his harness on, and left a name which must be a watchword for successive ranks of the "sacramental hosts," till they have won their last victory, "and the kingdoms of this world have become the kingdom of our Lord and of his Christ."

Had the missionary enterprise only served to develop such characters, to bequeath such examples, to manifest in such strong and beautiful relief the full power of the gospel in and over the individual soul, this alone would have been a work and glory amply worth all that it has cost.

But we believe that it has done immeasurably more. We like not that its fruits should be measured by a numerical standard. That in its earlier stages reliable converts should be few, was no more than should have been expected. The kingdom of Christ could be built up over the waters of heathenism only on a sunken foundation. A vast amount of preliminary work was to be wrought which could make no statistical show.

The mastery of languages which had no grammars, vocabularies, or qualified teachers, was a sufficient labor for one generation. The translation of the Scriptures, without which no permanent benefit could be conferred, demanded a large apparatus of effort and of mind. It was no slight task to become so conversant with the characters, customs, and religions of nations previously unknown, as to devise appropriate measures for their evangelization. Taking these things into the account, we have no reason to think lightly of the results already obtained; but, on the other hand, are constrained to marvel that they should have been so substantial and so satisfying. In Burmah the chief obstacles have now been removed; the dominion of old superstitions has been effectually shaken; bands of native Christians form with the missionary stations a *cordon* of religious influence, belting the empire in every direction; and the laborer who first broke up the fallow ground could behold in death the fields already white for the harvest.

Extract from a Biographical Sketch of Dr. Judson by John Marshman, Esq., Editor of the Friend of India.

Thus lived and died the Apostle of the Burmese. To this distinguished title Dr. Judson is fully entitled by his long, arduous, and successful labors in the Burmese mission, of which he was the founder. He was the last of the great men whose name was associated with the early struggles and exertions of the Serampore missionaries, with whom he lived on terms of the most cordial sympathy and affection to the close of their respective lives. His natural genius would have rendered him eminent in any position of life. He had all that spirit of zeal and perseverance which contributes to form a truly great man. He possessed that energy of character, which a great enterprise develops, and which great difficulties serve to invigorate. He set before himself, as the one object of pursuit through life, the promotion of a sacred and animating cause, which afforded the fullest scope for the warmest affections of his heart, and the noblest efforts of his mind. On this effort was concentrated all the enthusiasm of his character, and he has left behind him an example which will long continue to stimulate others in the same noble career. His views were always elevated and comprehensive; his powers of observation very acute; and his knowledge and appreciation of character, more especially of the Burmese, singularly correct. His acquaintance with the Burmese language and literature was more complete than that of any other foreigner; and it is through his labors that the language has been unlocked to the future evangelist and philanthropist. He was exemplary in all the domestic relations of life, a fond husband, an affectionate father, and a cordial friend. Those who have enjoyed the advantage of personal intercourse with him will not readily forget his ever-cheerful disposition, his countenance always lighted with a smile, and his animated and instructive conversation. But his best eulogy is to be found in the simple enumeration of those noble and arduous labors to which he consecrated thirty-eight years of his life.

Extract from a Letter of the Rev. W. S. Mackay, of the Scotch Free Church, Calcutta, to the Editor of the Friend of India.

SIR: I have read with sincere pleasure the admirable biographical sketch of Dr. Judson in your issue of November 21. He may indeed be called, truly and worthily, "the Apostle of Burmah." He labored in that country for thirty-seven years. He mastered its language, and made it his own, and smoothed its difficulties for his successors. He translated into the language of the people the whole word of God, with such skill, patience, and judgment, that his version bids fair, in the opinion of competent judges, to be the standard Bible of Burmah. He made the first Burman converts, and gathered together the first Burman congregation of Christians; and, with full assurance that the good seed had taken root, and would spring up vigorously in the land of his adoption, he died "in his harness," young in spirit, but ripe in years and honors. To me he has always stood out as the most remarkable man in the modern era of missions. Tried by every vicissitude of humanity, he came out like pure gold: chained in a dungeon, and face to face with the executioner, or swimming on the topmost wave of popularity, the idol of all that was holy and good in his native land; in the extremes of household happiness and household bereavements; driven again and again, as it seemed, forever, from the mission field, or rejoicing over his little flock and his completed Bible; in the pulpit, on the platform, or in cheerful, social intercourse, — Adoniram Judson was always true to his own high nature, combining the warm affections of a man with the strength, simplicity, and directness of an apostle of the living God.

His name alone is a tower of strength to the missionary cause; but his name is not alone. He was the centre of a family group, to which, so far as I have read, no parallel can be found in ancient or in modern history. Ann, Sarah, and Emily Judson — all three, noble, intellectual, and Christian women, all three devoted and affectionate — sympathized with, and shared in all his labors, rose to his height, and shine even beside him.

Such a noble group warms our hearts to America, and makes us feel proud that the same blood runs in our veins.

Anecdotes and Sketches of Dr. Judson, by Mrs. E. C. Judson.

Dr. Judson used often to remark that the religion of the Romanists could not prevail very extensively in Burmah, as it is unsuited — at least as presented by the Portuguese and Italian priests — to the character of the people. It is seldom that a pure Burman enters their church, which consists almost exclusively of Portuguese half-castes. That is the reason, also, why they remain with safety under the Burmese government — proselytism being the only thing in foreign religions to which the Buddhists object. In illustration of the common misapprehension of Burmese character by Romish priests, he one day related an anecdote. In the early days of the mission, two of his native assistants came to inquire if it would be wrong for them to visit the Roman Catholic priest, and learn something of his doctrines. After ascertaining that their object was not to annoy, but really to seek information, he assured them that it would be quite right to go, and that he had not the slightest objection. The next time he met them, they declared, with some degree of mortification, that they had never been treated so like silly little children in all their lives. The priest had received them very kindly, calling them his children, and was overjoyed to learn that they wished to know something of his religion. He then retired into an inner room, and soon came out, with one hand hidden under his robe, and very softly and smilingly inquired, "What think you, my dear children, I have here?" at the same time assuring them it was something "very precious," "more precious than gold," something he would not part with for his life, &c. After a while he cautiously gave a slight peep, then a little more, and a little more, till finally the whole of some saintly relic, of which his visitors could not have the slightest appreciation, was held up before their eyes. The Burmans owned, that, uncivil as it might appear, they remained silent, uncertain whether it was not the object of the priest to insult them. Presently he discovered that something was wrong, and returned to his room. When he again appeared, he was robed anew, and with the same soft, insinuating smile, he inquired, "*Now*, my dear children, what do you think I have brought you?" The men shook their heads. "O, no," he continued, "you need not try to guess; you could never guess: it is one of the loveliest, the most beautiful things in the universe." Gradually, little by little, his robe was again opened, and the wonder permitted to peep forth, though still concealed by his hand, while he whetted curiosity by lavishing upon it the most extravagant praises. At last the treasure was fully exposed, and proved to be a small statuette of her whom the priest assured them was "the mother of God." The newly converted Christians were shocked, and still more so at being called on to *shiko* to this doll, as they called it. They went from the priest's dwelling with the conclusion on their minds, that, if they were ever left to the sin of idolatry, their own Gaudama, with the godship wrought out by his own persevering self-discipline, was a more dignified object of worship than this Jewish woman. And they used afterwards to allude not infrequently to the time when they went to inquire after grave matters of religion, and were amused by children's playthings.

A native Christian woman told me that she was at one time about to engage in something which Dr. Judson considered not conducive to her spiritual good. He sent for her, and remonstrated; but she would not give up her darling project. "Look here!" said he, eagerly snatching a ruler from the table, and tracing not a very straight line on the floor; "*here* is where you have been walking. You have made a crooked track, to be sure — out of the path half of the time; but then you have kept near it, and not taken to new roads, and you have — not so much as you might have done, mind, but still to a certain extent — grown in grace; and now, with all this growth upon your heart and head, in the maturity of your years, with ripened understanding and an every day deepening sense of the goodness of God, here," bringing down the ruler with emphasis to indicate a certain position, " *here you stand.* You know where this path leads. You know what is before you — some struggles, some sorrows, and finally eternal life and a crown of glory. But to the left branches off another very pleasant road, and along the air floats, rather temptingly, a pretty bubble. You do not mean to leave the path you have walked in fifteen years — fifteen long years — altogether; you only want to step aside and catch the bubble, and think you will come back again; but *you never will.* Woman, think! Dare you deliberately leave this strait and narrow path, drawn by the Saviour's finger, and go away for one moment into that of your enemy? Will you? *will you?* WILL YOU?"

"I was sobbing so," said the woman, "that I could not speak a word; but he knew, as he always did, what I meant; for he knelt down, and prayed that God would preserve me in my determination. I have made a great many crooked tracks since," she added, tearfully; "but, whenever I am unusually tempted, I see the teacher as he looked that day, bending over in his chair, the ruler placed on the floor to represent me, his finger pointing along the path of eternal life, his eye looking so strangely over his shoulder, and that terrible 'Will you?' coming from his lips as though it was the voice of God; and I pray just as Peter did, for I am frightened."

One of the native assistants, speaking of Dr. Judson's knowledge of Burmese character, said that it was particularly impossible to conceal a sin from him; and, while a culprit was exulting in fancied security, he would suddenly find an eye fixed upon him that was perfectly irresistible, and would be obliged, in spite of himself, to go to the teacher and confess. He also said that Dr. Judson never accused except upon an absolute certainty, never insinuated a suspicion, and never placed any reliance on a mere hearsay. He always interrupted any communication of one Christian against another with, "Have you told him his fault between you and him alone?" Most likely this had not been done; and the informer would always have some good reason for not taking up the matter himself, but he "thought the teacher ought to know," &c. Probably hints like these, never openly acted on, gave the peculiar expression to the eye which the Burman considered so very remarkable. "He knew us," the man continued, "through and through, much better than we know ourselves. If we had done any thing amiss, he called us pleasantly, talked *so*," — taking up, by way of illustration, a toy that lay upon the floor beside him, and passing his finger gently around the rim, — "talked, and talked, and talked, till suddenly, before we knew it, he pounced upon us there," — striking his finger violently on the centre of the toy, — "and held us breathless till we had told him every thing. Ah, no one will ever know us poor Burmans so again," added the old man, mournfully.

There is a class of people in the East, — soldiers and others, — who, by reason of their social position, are not amenable to the rules of society which protect, even while they embarrass, more cultivated classes. These people meet the missionary on the common platform of religion, and are very apt to make such draughts on his time as to render themselves really troublesome. Dr. Judson had one invariable rule for all who called upon him in his ministerial capacity. He appeared, as he felt, glad to see them, made a few inquiries as to their temporal welfare, ascertained in the same manner their spiritual state, read a half dozen suitable verses from the Bible, made a short but singularly appropriate prayer, and, with a cordial shake of the hand, dismissed the well-pleased visitor, without a single moment's having been wasted.

A pious officer called on Dr. Judson, one day, just as his fever was coming on.

"Why, I can't do him any good. *Must* I see him?" he said, with a deprecatory smile. "Well, show him in."

I soon discovered, however, that my husband was suffering intense pain, as he very often did during the hours of his fever, and was about to repair my mistake as well as I could, when the visitor chanced to mention the name of a common friend. Dr. Judson's countenance instantly brightened. "You knew Major ——, then?" he exclaimed, with warmth.

"Yes; one of nature's own noblemen, is he not?"

"The nobility of nature, or grace, do you consider it?" asked Dr. Judson; and then both of them smilingly agreed that there was something of both in their friend.

"I loved him like a brother," continued Dr. Judson, rather sadly; "but, poor fellow! many are the tears I have shed for him of late."

"Indeed!" exclaimed the visitor, in amazement.

"I suppose you know he has taken to certain wild courses."

"Impossible!"

"Both possible and true. You know something of the Plymouth Brethren, of course?"

Our visitor's features relaxed, though his color was very manifestly heightened — a demonstration which I understood, but was afraid my husband did not.

"Well, they got hold of poor Major ——," he continued, "and have utterly ruined him — that is, his usefulness in this world; I believe his eternal salvation is secure."

"Then you have no very high opinion of the doctrines of the Plymouth Brethren?"

"Most assuredly not. They do not believe the promises of God to his people, and their influence goes to discourage and paralyze all missionary enterprise; they do not believe in church organizations, and so the poor, ignorant soldiery, and Protestant half-castes, coming under their influence, are scattered as sheep without a shepherd."

"But there seem to me to be many good, spiritually-minded Christians among them."

"Have you never observed that when seekers after sanctification attain to a certain degree of spirituality, they are peculiarly liable to fall into errors of form? Why, it is in this way that the wildest impostors have sometimes gained their most deluded and unquestioning followers. Men long for what they have not, and instead of sitting down at the Saviour's feet, and drinking in his words, they go away to furnish themselves with swimming bladders, the work of their own invention."

"This cannot, however, be said of the Plymouth Brethren. They are especially opposed to forms."

"That is, they throw away the forms of every other sect, and adopt a new set, peculiar to themselves."

"I see," said the visitor, good humoredly, "that you have no mercy." Dr. Judson smiled. "Shall I tell you, my dear ——, at the risk of being written down a bigot, what my real, candid opinion is in the matter? When the arch enemy of souls finds a Christian so weaned from the world as to be inaccessible to all the grosser modes of temptation, he just dons this sheep's clothing of Plymouth Brethrenism, and in despair of getting this particular soul, puts a veto on the man's usefulness, to the serious detriment of hundreds and thousands of others."

"Did you know," I inquired, as soon as the visitor had withdrawn, "that —— is said to have a strong bias towards Plymouth Brethrenism, so much so that his best friends are trembling for his stability?"

"Of course I know it," came a faint voice up from the pillow, where the tired invalid had sunk down in utter exhaustion. "You do not fancy me so overburdened with strength as to throw away any in warning men who are not in danger?"

"People will call it a strange providence," Dr. Judson remarked, one day, "if I do not live to finish my dictionary. But to me it will be a strange providence if I do. Men almost always leave some work, that they or their friends consider vastly important, unfinished. It is a way God has of showing us what really worthless creatures we are, and how altogether unnecessary, as active agents, in the working out of his plans."

Some ladies were conversing one day on the subject of sailors' superstitions with regard to clergymen, and especially missionaries, and finally added it was remarkable that, among all the missionaries our board had sent out, not one had been lost at sea.

"And so you incline to the opposite superstition, I presume," Dr. Judson said, smilingly.

"I think that God exercises a peculiar care over his people," was the rejoinder.

"True," said he, with one of those beaming looks which usually broke forth and passed away with the expression of some characteristic sentiment — "true; so 'though he slay me, yet will I trust in him;' not because I have wrought myself into an unwarrantable belief that he will carry me over smooth waters. He may cast us in a burning fiery furnace, or precipitate us to the lowest depths of the sea, but his care, his tenderness, his love, are still the same."

The news of the loss of Dr. and Mrs. James, of the Southern board, in the China seas, struck us with consternation. Dr. Judson had met young James in America, and he entertained for him a tender personal regard. He was much affected, and I think wept at the intelligence, but never spoke of it as a mysterious providence, a dark dispensation, or any thing that was in the least difficult to be understood. When some one remarked that this event was likely to chill the ardor of the patrons of missions, he repelled the suggestion with great earnestness, at first; and when finally compelled to admit the possibility of such a result, he remained in sad silence for some time. "O, when *will* Christians learn," he at length broke forth, "that their puny, polluted offerings of works are not necessary to God? He permits them to work, as a favor, in order to do them good, personally, because he loves them, and desires to honor them, not because he *needs* them. The withdrawal of any man from his harvest field, however learned, and wise, and good, however well prepared, even by a life-long discipline for that particular part of the field, is no loss to *Him*. As though the omnipotent God had so few weapons in his armory, that we must tremble and faint at the loss of one! — I have thought for years," he added, "that God, in his dealings with us, aims particularly at our individual development and growth, with the ultimate object of fitting each one of us personally for the life to come; and when, in his infinite wisdom, he sees that the recast of our original natures is so filed, and rasped, and polished, as to be ready for the position he designs us to occupy, he graciously removes us thither."

Dr. Judson used often to speak of God's having honored him, through the Saviour's worthiness, with a commission to the Burmans; of Christ's having permitted him to do a little work in his name, and be the means of saving a few souls; and he always prayed most fervently, both in his own behalf and that of his children, for a long life of labor and self-denial.

Dr. Judson was not at all given to admonishing people not connected with him, or, indeed, those that were, much; but there were some things that he seldom allowed to pass without attention. If I said I disliked a person, he would inquire, "Is she a Christian?" If he got one answer, the conclusion would be, "Poor creature! you ought to pity her too much for dislike;" and if the other, he would say, "Then Christ loves her dearly — cannot you?"

I recollect one day showing my husband two different newspaper articles, in one of which he was compared to the apostle Paul, and in the other spoken of as the "beloved John." Instead of being amused, as I had expected, at the contradiction, he exclaimed, with a sorrowfulness which made me regret having called his attention to the subject, "O, how little — how little do they know me! 'Who shall deliver me from the body of this death?'" I believe he was not in the least aware of whose words he had used; and I had ample reason for wishing to divert his thoughts, for he was not strong enough to indulge in deep emotions. "It is very evident," I said, carelessly, "that they do not know you. One day you are Peter, or Paul, or Luther, and the next, gentle John, or mild Melancthon."

"And I do not want to be like any of them," he said, energetically — "Paul, nor Apollos, nor Cephas, nor any other mere man. I want to be like Christ. We have a great many aids and encouragers along the Christian path; but only one perfectly safe Exemplar — only One who, tempted like as we are in every point, is still without sin. I want to follow *him* only — copy his teachings, drink in his spirit, place my feet in his footprints, and measure their short comings by these, and these alone. It is not safe to take any man, not even an inspired apostle, for a pattern. O, to be more like Christ!"

A short time before Dr. Judson left this country, he took considerable pains to visit my native village, and the church with which I first united, though I had long since removed my membership. As the house was small, he had consented to address the congregation; and this, although the day was rainy, brought together quite a crowd. After the usual sermon was over, he spoke for about fifteen minutes, with singular simplicity, and, as I thought, with touching pathos, of the "precious Saviour," what he has done for us, and what we owe to him. As he sat down, however, it was evident, even to the most unobservant eye, that most of the listeners were disappointed. After the exercises were over, several persons inquired of me, frankly, why Dr. Judson had not talked of something else; why he had not told a story, &c.; while others signified their disappointment by not alluding to his having spoken at all. On the way home, I mentioned the subject to him.

"Why, what did they want?" he inquired; "I presented the most interesting subject in the world, to the best of my ability."

"But they wanted something different — a story."

"Well, I am sure I gave them a story — the most thrilling one that can be conceived of."

"But they had heard it before. They wanted something new of a man who had just come from the antipodes."

"Then I am glad they have it to say, that a man coming

from the antipodes had nothing better to tell than the wondrous story of Jesus' dying love. My business is to preach the gospel of Christ, and when I can speak at all, I dare not trifle with my commission. When I looked upon those people to-day, and remembered where I should next meet them, how could I stand up and furnish food to vain curiosity — tickle their fancies with amusing stories, however decently strung together on a thread of religion? That is not what Christ meant by preaching the gospel. And then, how could I hereafter meet the fearful charge, 'I gave you one opportunity to tell them of me — you spent it in describing your own adventures!'"

He acknowledged that the diffusion of missionary information was a thing of great importance, but said that the good of the cause of missions did not require a lowering of the standard of gospel preaching; and that whatever was done for missions at the expense of spirituality in the American churches, was lost on the world.

He used frequently to speak of the tendency of cultivated people to visit the house of God in search of intellectual gratification, rather than for the purposes of worship, or the promotion of their spiritual good, and mentioned it as the most dangerous snare in the path of the rising ministry.

When once asked, in private, how he liked a sermon that had just been eliciting warm praises from a parlor circle, he answered, "It was very elegant; every word was chosen with care and taste, and many of the thoughts were exceedingly beautiful. It delighted my ears so much, that I quite forgot I had a heart, and I am afraid all the other hearers did the same."

At another time, when speaking in glowing terms of a sermon to which he had listened with evident interest, he suddenly broke off with, "But such are not the sermons to arouse a dead sinner, or to feed the sheep. No man could say there to-day, '*The poor* have the gospel preached.'"

Dr. Judson could never bear to hear missions spoken of as having accomplished but little, even by the best friends of the cause, who sometimes will complain with the best intentions. A lady in India, herself a missionary, was remarking with some severity on the character of the missionary gatherings common at home, where she said a great crowd of people met to "glorify missionaries, make mutual admiration speeches, and sing millennial hymns."

Dr. Judson replied that glorifying, and even mutual admiration, in such a connection, was robbery of God, but that — thanks to his grace! — the day for millennial hymns was dawning. For his part, he thought there could not be too much rejoicing over what had been accomplished; and the very disposition to rejoice was to him a pledge of interest which would lead to future results far more glorious.

The lady was very sure the condition of things at present was any thing but glorious, and drew a ludicrous picture of missionary delving and home exultation — an ear of corn for famishing millions, &c.

"To be sure," said Dr. Judson, "our oak is a tiny sapling yet; but it is a real live oak, and well out of the ground; and when I think of that, and know that He who fashioned it will unfailingly bring it to its perfect stature, my heart thrills with joy indescribable."

"But really, candidly," inquired the lady, "do you not think the idea so prevalent among uninformed people, and indeed among many who ought to know better, that the world is almost converted, has a tendency to make them fold their hands, and think they have nothing more to do?"

"No, I do not. On the principle that a work well begun is half done, the world *is* considerably more than half converted already; and this very consideration has something in it so spirit-stirring, that, when allowed to take its proper hold upon the heart, it will bind us anew to labors, to sufferings, to sacrifices of every kind, so that life itself will seem nothing in the balance. Why, I would pour out my blood like water in such a cause; and so would you, and so would hundreds and thousands, both at home and in the mission field."

"Ah," sighed the lady, "why don't they do it then?"

"Many pour out what is much better — the incense of prayerful hearts. There is many a martyr spirit at the kitchen fire, over the wash tub, and in the plough field; many obscure men and women make personal sacrifices, beside which ours — yours and mine — will appear in the great day very small indeed. But it must be acknowledged that by far the greater part hear the command of the Saviour faintly, as in a dream, and regard it with slumberous indifference. I am always glad to see Christians so much awake to the importance of extending the Master's kingdom, as to rejoice, even though it be in the conversion of but a single soul. 'There is joy in heaven;' why not among the redeemed of earth? Look here!" He turned suddenly to a little map of the world, lying on his study table, and passing his finger rapidly from town to town, and from one continent to another, exclaimed, "See how the gospel light is girdling the world! It is base ingratitude to be blind to all these wonders."

After our return from Rangoon, Dr. Judson's missionary life was not of that settled character it had been for many years previous to his visit to America. He regarded his residence in Maulmain as a mere temporary arrangement, and said that his future prospects looked to him as Abraham's must have appeared when he went out not knowing whither. But expressions like the following were continually dropping from his lips: "We must look *up* for direction;" "If we only please Christ, no matter for the rest;" "If God has designed a work for us to do, he will arrange all the little particulars, and we have only to trust in him;" "If it be the will of God, never fear for the consequences," &c. And the way he learned the will of God, was prayerfully to look for manifestations of it; not in any wonderful way, but as an affectionate child almost intuitively seems to know what will please a parent.

CHAPTER X.

GENERAL VIEW OF HIS CHARACTER AND LABORS.

It is commonly expected that a volume of this kind will close with an estimate of the character and services of him whose life it has recorded. In order to satisfy this expectation, it is, I suppose, necessary for me to attempt a sketch of the character of Dr. Judson. I do it with diffidence, for it is a work in which I am unpractised, and for which I have but small facilities beyond the record found in the preceding pages. Sensible of the imperfections which must attach to my attempt, I will, nevertheless, present, as clearly as possible, the impression which, at the close of my labor, abides upon my own mind.

The intellectual endowments of Dr. Judson were unquestionably of a very high order. In boyhood he astonished his teachers by the rapidity of his acquisitions. In youth, during his residence at the university, he left behind him every competitor. In early manhood he never seems to have held a second place among his contemporaries; and when, in maturer years, he was called to associate with military commanders, civilians, and diplomatists in India, that cradle of great men, his talents placed him on a level with the ablest of them. I cannot recall the name of any modern missionary, the noble old Schwartz only excepted, who has occupied so great a variety of prominent positions, and has occupied them all, not merely with honor to himself, but in such a manner as to give to others the assurance that he was capable of much greater things.

The intellect of Dr. Judson was eminently clear and discriminating. It instinctively sought for precision in all that it attempted to know. He could not believe unless the reasons of his belief had been thoroughly examined; and hence he was a diligent and earnest student; but when he did believe, it was with his whole heart. His power of acquisition was great, and his memory unusually retentive. His mind, however, was as far as possible from being a mere receptacle, a storehouse of knowledge. It instinctively formed its own judgments on the opinions and reasonings of others, and carried out the truth thus purified to its generalized results. It never allowed knowledge to rest as an end, but made it ever the seed from which other and richer knowledge might be produced. It is, I think, this type of mind, which, having within itself the element of self-expansion, men have generally honored with the name of genius.

The powers of Dr. Judson seem rather to have belonged to the logical than the imaginative. His style is a model of exact and perspicuous English. I do not remember an ambiguous sentence, or one that does not express precisely what he evidently intended, in all that he has written. The almost entire absence of figurative language is remarkable, especially in a man of so strong and various impulses. It is probable that his power of imagination was more vigorous in youth, but that his labor in translation, fixing his mind exclusively on absolute distinctness of thought and perfect clearness of expression, tended to disincline him from frequent exercise of the fancy. Yet his friends describe his conversation as unusually graphic and playful, and at times poetic. In his preaching he seems to have been eminently successful, at the same time convincing the intellect by the most condensed argument, arousing the conscience by irresistible appeal, and entrancing the attention by aptness of illustration, and sometimes by splendor of imagery. A few specimens of poetry are found among his papers, which display a talent for versification, sometimes called into action by the humorous, and at other times by the devout or the pathetic. The verses written in the prison at Ava, and addressed to his babe, are exceedingly affecting.

Highly as I estimate the intellectual elements of the character of Dr. Judson, I think that its motive forces, — if I may use the expression, — were yet more remarkable. Of these, the most conspicuous in the early part of his life was the intense love of superiority. He was ever striving to do what others had not done, or could not do. Every where it was his aim, though always by honorable means, to be first. This disposition, instead of being checked, was cultivated by his father. Hence the excessive exultation which both of them felt when he received the first appointment in his class. This element of character, though modified and purified by religion, remained with him to the last. Hence his preference to preach Christ where he had never been named. Hence his desire to give to a nation that had never known of an eternal God their first version of his revealed will. Hence, too, his extreme care in the translation, and his ceaseless labor in revision. No pains seemed to him too great, if they only tended to realize his idea of a perfect version; that is, a version that conveyed, in language clearly intelligible to the people, the precise mind of the Spirit. Thus we see how those tempers of mind, which, if left ungoverned by Christian principle, tend to nothing but strife and selfish aggrandizement, when sanctified and refined by the love of God, work powerfully in promoting the interests of the most elevated Christian benevolence.

But this inherent love of excellence reposed on the basis of indomitable perseverance. When once he had deliberately resolved upon a course of action, it was a part of his nature to pursue it to the death. His spirit clung to it with a grasp that nothing seemed to relax. Difficulties did not discourage him. Obstacles did not embarrass him. Hence, when he observed that the friends of missions began to be disheartened because no converts had been made, after his residence of several years in Rangoon, the idea of failure never once occurred to him. Instead of sympathizing in the despondency of those who were merely giving of their abundance, without making a single personal sacrifice for the mission, he replied by sending back words of lofty cheer, which struck upon the ear of the churches at home like the sound of a trumpet; adding the memorable request to be permitted to labor on in the name of the Lord of Hosts, and then, perhaps, said he, "at the end of some twenty years you may hear of us again."

But it sometimes happens that great talents, even when united with a considerable measure of perseverance, fail from the want of power in other elements of character. Such men have large ideals, and they strive to realize them; but they break down before the course is completed, and arrive at the goal only to confess that they have been distanced. They are unable to concentrate their efforts on a prolonged and agonizing struggle. They never come to the full and unreserved resolution to do or die. Their will fails at the critical point, and they fall back disheartened and beaten in the warfare of life. In this respect, Dr. Judson was peculiarly favored. He was endowed with a will of the very highest order. It was capable of controlling his physical nature, so that his body would do or suffer whatever it was commanded. It subjected the material to the spiritual in a degree very rarely attained. Its power over his spiritual faculties was equally worthy of observation. It held them steadily to their work, without cessation, under every mode of discouragement, and most of all at the very moment when inferior natures would most readily yield to the pressure of difficulty. Nor was this all: it was capable of moulding the faculties themselves into any form which the exigency of the case demanded. He could have made himself a mathematician, a philologist, a diplomatist, a statesman, an impassioned orator, and perhaps a poet, by the strenuous exertion of his will. This is, I think, one of the rarest of human endowments, and it is bestowed only upon men who are eminently gifted. It has seemed to me that the highest range of human talent is distinguished, not by the power of doing well any one particular thing, but by the power of doing well any thing which we resolutely determine to do.

To this we may add, that, in common with other men of a similar character, he was capable of relying with great confidence upon the decisions of his own judgment. Satisfied that he was acting from motives with which selfishness did not intermingle, and conscious that with pure intentions he had sought for truth wherever it was within his reach, he came to his conclusions with remarkable distinctness, and he was always ready to carry them into practice at the cost of any personal sacrifice. From this element of his character it resulted that he rarely asked advice, and that he as rarely proffered it. Acting from the dictates of his own judgment, and taking it for granted that other men did, or ought to do the same, he was not forward in obtruding his opinions upon others, though perfectly willing to give to others the benefit of his counsel whenever it was desired. On this account, perhaps, it was frequently said, that he was peculiarly secretive, never revealing his plans or his counsels to his brethren. In how far this was the case I know not; but I can readily conceive that a man who was so prone to act on the decisions of his own judgment would not be forward in soliciting the opinions of others.

Such seem to me to have been some of the prominent elements of Dr. Judson's natural character. When he yielded himself, with his whole heart, as a servant of God, he became a new creature in Christ. He renounced the dominion of selfishness, and became the disciple of Him who went about doing good. The change in his character was marked, and, with Saul, his language at once became, " Lord, what wilt thou have me to do?" The answer to this question was received in the grove at Andover, where, as though an audible voice addressed him, the command reached his inmost soul, " Go ye into all the world, and preach the gospel to every creature." He " was not disobedient unto the heavenly vision," but at once consecrated himself, with all his powers, to the missionary service.

His piety was in some respects peculiar. The change that was wrought in him was so great that through life he never doubted either of its reality or of his title to a heavenly inheritance. This at all times cheered and animated him in the hours of most depressing loneliness. Never after his conversion did he look upon God as any other than a reconciled Father in Christ. Every thing that happened to him was sent in parental love, and he was content. Thus, emphatically, "the joy of the Lord was his strength."

While this, however, was true of the relation which his religion bore to the outward circumstances of his life, it was by no means true that his inner life was destitute of wars and fightings. He seems from the beginning to have labored, with a rare earnestness, to subdue every thing within him to the obedience of Christ. It was not enough that he abstained from outward transgression, and felt assurance of his adoption into the family of Christ. He labored incessantly to achieve more and more signal victories over sin and selfishness, so that neither love of ease, nor ambition, nor social affection, nor dread of pain, or persecution, or death, could, in any manner, interfere with his love to God, and his cheerful obedience to the divine will. He seemed to have ever in his mind's eye the saying of Christ, "If any man come to me, and hate not his father and mother, and wife and children, and brethren and sisters, yea, and his own life also, he cannot be my disciple;" "And whosoever doth not bear his cross, and come after me, cannot be my disciple." His inner life seems to have witnessed a struggle, in simple earnest, to realize in his moral affections an habitual obedience to this precept. And he carried on this warfare in a remarkably practical manner. If he found that any desire or appetite was usurping an undue place in his affections, he proceeded at once to effect its entire subjugation. If the love of ease and comfort was creeping over him, he would spend weeks in a cabin in the jungle. If friends were becoming so dear as to becloud his consciousness of the love of Christ, he would live for weeks alone. If the dissolution of the body distressed him, he would sit for hours by the side of a grave, in order to overcome it. Nor were his labors unsuccessful. His dearest affections seem to have been subordinated in an uncommon degree to his views of religious duty. When his first wife, whom he loved so intensely, was obliged to return home for a season, he parted with her at Rangoon, leaving her to pursue her voyage alone, because he did not dare to leave the work which God had assigned to him, so long as he was able to perform it. When the second Mrs. Judson was obliged to flee to a northern climate, he would not have accompanied her, much as he longed to see his native land once more, had she been able to go without him. And when she had apparently so far recovered as to be able to proceed without him, they had both resolved to separate, he to return to Maulmain and resume his labor; she, with the children, to pursue the voyage to America. That must surely have been successful and vigorous training which enabled a soul to achieve such moral victories as these, and attain the habit of so athletic Christian virtue.

It may be supposed that the faith of such a man was in a high degree simple and confiding. In this respect I have rarely seen it equalled. It seemed to place him in direct communication with God. It never appeared to him possible, for a moment, that God could fail to do precisely as he had said; and he therefore relied on the divine assurance with a confidence that excluded all wavering. He believed that

Burmah was to be converted to Christ, just as much as he believed that Burmah existed. He believed that he had been sent there to preach the gospel, and he as much believed that the Holy Ghost would make his labors, in some way, or at some time, the means of the salvation of the nation, as he believed that there was a Holy Ghost. During his visit to Boston, the late venerable James Loring asked him, "Do you think the prospects bright for the speedy conversion of the heathen?" "As bright," was his prompt reply, "as the promises of God." And this same spirit of unshaken confidence in God was manifested in all the affairs of life. In prayer he asked not as a duty, nor even as a pleasure, but he asked that he might receive. He acted on the assurance that his heavenly Father delighted to bestow upon him whatever was for his best good. It was a common thing for him to ask until he received in his own consciousness an assurance that his requests would be granted. Thus he prayed that he might be useful to the crew of the ship in which he sailed to the Isle of France and to Maulmain; thus he prayed and labored for the conversion of the Jews, and his prayers were, in a remarkable manner, answered. Thus he ever prayed for the early conversion of his children; and it is worthy of remark that, since his death, three of them have, as we hope, become heirs of eternal life.

In treating of his religious character, it would be an omission not to refer to his habitual heavenly mindedness. In his letters, I know of no topic that is so frequently referred to as the nearness of the heavenly glory. If his loved ones died, his consolation was, that they should all so soon meet in paradise. If an untoward event occurred, it was of no great consequence, for soon we should be in heaven, where all such trials would either be forgotten, or where the recollection of them would render our bliss the more intense. Thither his social feelings pointed, and he was ever thinking of the meeting that awaited him with those who with him had fought the good fight, and were now wearing the crown of victory. So habitual were these trains of thought, that a person well acquainted with him remarks, that " meditation on death was his common solace in all the troubles of life." I do not know that the habitual temper of his mind can in any words be so well expressed as in the following lines, which he wrote in pencil on the inner cover of a book that he was using in the compilation of his dictionary : —

> " In joy or sorrow, health or pain,
> Our course be onward still;
> We sow on Burmah's barren plain,
> We reap on Zion's hill."

But while I thus speak of his high attainments in Christian character, it is proper to remark, that they were not made without great and long-continued moral effort. The Judson of maturer life was a very different character from the Judson of youth and early manhood. At first, religion had but imperfectly conquered his fiery ambition, his love of precedence, and that confidence in his own opinions which was unbecoming a man of his limited experience. From the imperfection of his character at this period arose his unfortunate difference with the Board of Commissioners, to which I have already referred. He did not obey their instructions in his visit to England, doubtless believing that he was better acquainted with the subject of missions than they. When they justly admonished him, he thought so little of the occurrence, in the joy of accomplished purpose, that for a long time he could recall nothing which indicated any displeasure at the course he had pursued. As he advanced in years and improved in piety, these imperfections were so thoroughly subdued, that, by the testimony of the officers of the Baptist board, they have sent no missionary from this country who has yielded more implicit compliance to all their regulations.

I am aware that when I present the character of Dr. Judson in this light, some abatements on specific grounds will be suggested. I will not pass them over, but will meet them here, lest it should be said that my object has been to write a panegyric, and not a biography. I have heard it said, by way of depreciation, that Dr. Judson was eccentric. As instances of this, his modes of self-mortification above alluded to are mentioned. It is also said that at one time he wore at Rangoon a yellow robe, in apparent imitation of the Burmese priesthood, and that when he, for the first time, appeared before the emperor at Ava, he was arrayed in a white garment, like a surplice. Let us examine this subject carefully.

A man is eccentric who deviates from the ordinary or established course of conduct of those who are around him. In this sense every Christian is bound to be eccentric in his relations to the world which lieth in wickedness. " Ye are a chosen generation, a *peculiar* people." " Be ye *not conformed* to the world, but be ye transformed." " Because ye are *not of the world*, therefore the world hateth you."

Or, again: a Christian who aims at higher attainments in piety, at sterner self-denial, or at more perfect conformity to Christ than his brethren, must be, by so much, eccentric. How often is such eccentricity urged upon the members of the Jewish church by the prophets, and upon professors of religion in the later epistles by the apostles! If this be so, eccentricity is not by necessity either a fault or a failing. It only becomes either when it is assumed for the sake of oddity, or love of singularity, or a desire to attract notice.

Now, in the cases before us, I can see nothing that marks either a weak or a fanatical mind. Abstract from Dr. Judson's self-mortification what properly belongs to a nervous system shattered by nearly two years of horrible and incessant suffering in the death prisons of Ava, and then by a bereavement rendered more intensely painful by these agonizing reminiscences, and what remains but the earnest striving of a resolute soul after perfect victory over every sin of the flesh and of the spirit? What shall we discover that will not find its parallel in the lives of Edwards, Brainerd, Payson, Schwartz and Henry Martyn? It is also the fact that for a short time Dr. Judson wore a robe of the color, though not in the form, of that worn by the Buddhist priesthood, and that he appeared before the emperor in a white garment. But let us consider, in the first place, that he was a pioneer in an untrodden field, where he had no precedents to guide him. To expect that a man who is feeling his way in the dark will make no movement in a wrong direction, is a demand so unreasonable, that simply to mention it is to exhibit its absurdity.

But let us hear Dr Judson's own account of this matter. He said, in conversation on this subject, that he had reason to doubt if the character of previous missionaries, as *public teachers of religion*, had ever been known to the Burmans, and specially he believed that Mr. Carey had never been known in this character at Ava. He desired to remove all doubt on this subject, and to make himself to be distinctly recognized as a "religion-propagating teacher." For this purpose he put on in one case a distinctive dress, and at another a garment of the color peculiar to the priesthood. He found, however, no advantage resulting from the experiment; and he at once laid aside every distinction of this kind, never to resume it. The eccentricity in this case is certainly very pardonable.

But it has been said by some persons that Dr. Judson was a manager, accomplishing his purposes by indirect and tortuous measures. A word or two on this subject may not be out of place.

The accusation of management and intrigue is often and very naturally brought against far-seeing men. He who judges by general principles will, of course, anticipate coming events much sooner than his brethren. If he shapes his conduct and forms his plans with reference to what he sees must soon occur, it will be easy to imagine that the occurrences, as they transpire, were the work of his hands and the product of his contrivance. Napoleon has a remark which bears somewhat on this subject. He says that people frequently puzzled themselves to no purpose in endeavoring to ascertain his plans, and divine the hidden motive for his combinations, always supposing that he had some deep-laid scheme which governed his conduct, when, in fact, he had no plan at all. "I had," said he, "some general principles by which I was guided, some general objects which I desired to accomplish. Whenever I saw any opportunity for advancing them, I availed myself of it in any direction." I have no doubt the same may be said of men in less prominent situations.

But while it is easy to be misunderstood in a matter of this kind, I apply myself to the facts which come within my knowledge. I have read every thing that could be collected of Dr. Judson's writings, both in print and in manuscript. I have never read any record of acts and opinions more distinctly marked by directness of aim and entire simplicity of purpose. I have withheld nothing of any importance which I have found among his papers. The evidence is therefore before the world, and let the world judge of it.

With these elements of character, intellectual and moral, cultivated by internal discipline and external affliction, it might well be anticipated that Dr. Judson's career as a missionary would be worthy of observation. It has been necessary for me, in the preparation of the preceding pages, to consider this subject with attention. The impression which it has made upon me is, I will confess, somewhat unlike that which many men would expect to find in the history of one of the most able and original of modern missionaries. I perceive in his missionary life, from beginning to end, no bold strokes of policy, no train of masterly combinations, nothing that would liken a man to the statesmen and soldiers who have filled the world with their renown; but I behold something far greater — a man of decided ability, and probably capable of doing what soldiers and statesmen have done, planting the standard of the cross on a heathen shore, and esteeming his own wisdom foolishness, meekly laboring precisely as Christ and his apostles had given him an example. Though able to have struck out magnificent schemes of missionary labor, he never suggested one. Though he might have claimed the least laborious position, he always placed himself in the most laborious. Being the senior missionary of the Baptist churches, and by far the most conspicuous, he illustrated the conception he had formed by setting an example which all subsequent missionaries might most profitably follow. Old John Leland used to say, "There are many men little enough to be great — there are few men great enough to be little."

His first effort was, of course, to acquire a knowledge of the Burmese language. In this he was eminently successful. He wrote it and spoke it so much, that, in the later years of his life, he was more at home before an audience in Burman than in English. As soon as he had acquired any competent knowledge of the language, he commenced his labor as a preacher of the gospel. The view which he took of his work was that which had long before been taken by Christ and the apostles. He began by telling every one whom he met, that Christ had died for him, and now offered to him eternal life. He built a zayat by the wayside, and proclaimed these truths to every passer by. No one paid any attention to his message; but Christ had commanded him to preach the gospel to every creature, and therefore he continued preaching. The more discouraging his prospects became, the more earnestly he fasted and prayed for the coming of the Holy Spirit. He did not faint, and in due season he reaped. One and another was spiritually renewed, and thus a church of believers was formed. These he employed, according to their several gifts, in proclaiming the truth; and thus this church embraced within itself the elements of self-extension.

This was his chosen employment, and that which he considered preëminently missionary. Until the disease in his throat laid him aside from out-door labor, he steadfastly continued it, unless interrupted by the express directions of the board. When compelled to leave it for the work of translation, he did it with regret, and always returned to it with alacrity as soon as his circumstances would permit. It is true that early in the history of the mission he translated the Gospels, a few of the Epistles, and wrote one or two tracts in Burman; but he states that he always had hoped that the completion of the translation might fall into other hands. He seems to have believed most fully that the world was to be converted by the simple process of telling man after man "that God so loved the world that he gave his only-begotten Son, that whosoever believeth on him should not perish, but have everlasting life;" always relying with earnest prayer on the power of the Holy Spirit to make the truth effectual for the regeneration of men. Such was his labor in the zayat and in the jungle; and to the success which attended it the preceding pages bear ample testimony.

It is, however, only stating the truth very imperfectly to speak of Dr. Judson's ability to use the Burman language with remarkable skill. He went vastly farther, and became in that language a most eloquent preacher. Those who knew him only in this country can have, it is said, no conception of his power over a Burmese assembly. The following extract from a letter of Mr. Vinton, on his arrival in Maulmain, is said to convey a correct idea of Dr. Judson's Burman preaching: "The first Sabbath after our arrival, we were privileged to hear the man whose praise is in all our

American churches. True, he preached in Burman; but though I did not know the meaning of a single sentence he uttered, still my attention was never more closely riveted on any sermon I ever heard. Were I to fix upon any one characteristic of the preacher which, perhaps, more than any other, rendered his discourse interesting and impressive, I should say it was earnestness of manner. It was impossible for any one to escape the conviction that his whole soul was in the work. Every tone, every look, every sentence, spoke out in the most emphatic language, to tell us that the man was seriously in earnest, and himself believed the truths he uttered. But what contributed not a little to the interest of the occasion, was the appearance of the assembly. Every hearer sat motionless, every eye was fixed immovably upon the preacher, and every countenance seemed to change with every varied expression of sentiment; now beaming forth joy, as though some joyous news from the other world had just reached them, which before had never gladdened their hearts; now depicting a feeling of anxiety, as though their immortal all, or that of their friends, was at stake; and next of deep solemnity, as though standing before their final Judge."

A missionary, who knew him intimately, remarks in a private letter, " I fear that no one at home will be able to do him justice, in the biography, on the point of pulpit eloquence. People at home had no opportunity of judging, as Dr. Judson's health was so poor, and moreover his thoughts had so long run in Burman channels, that it required a Burman pulpit in which to exhibit them."

Mrs. Judson gives the following account of the manner in which he prepared for the pulpit: " He used to rise somewhat earlier on Sunday mornings than on other days, — I speak now of the time when he was able to preach only once a day, — and take his usual walk over the hill. He occupied his walking time generally in devotion, and after his return, spent some time in prayer in his study. He would then call me, and we would walk up and down the veranda together until breakfast, occupying in this manner from an hour to an hour and a half. His text was sometimes selected on the previous evening, and sometimes in the morning before he went out; but oftener several texts occurred to him while walking, and the first business on the veranda was to choose between them. Then arose quite an animated discussion, if that can be called a discussion which has the wisdom all on one side. These Sunday morning walks in the veranda were very profitable to me, for there was always matter for a dozen sermons in the suggestions of the hour. He was rather fond of speculation on these occasions, but never introduced any thing of this kind into the pulpit. He did not *plan* his sermon during the morning walks, but disentangled and sifted the text, making himself familiar with all its bearings, and possible as well as obvious applications. Afterwards the topics chosen were adapted to the congregation before him; and before I understood the language, I used to take great interest in ascertaining, by his manner and the faces of his auditors, the peculiar train of thought which he had followed out. He preached with great fervor and earnestness; but besides this, there was a touching simplicity in the matter and language, which it was long before I could appreciate. His figures, which I understood sooner, were drawn from immediately surrounding objects. Of these, in accordance with eastern taste, he made great use. He often remarked that 'Christ was the model preacher, and that *he* never preached *great* sermons.' Whether Dr. Judson preached great sermons or not, his preaching was peculiarly effective there, and I think would have been so any where."

Such was Dr. Judson as a preacher. As to his success as a translator, I have already spoken. I cannot, however, feel satisfied without quoting the following passage from the Calcutta Review; since it so well exhibits the difficulties which were to be encountered in the accomplishment of this great work. " Some languages, however, — and the Burman is one, — seem to mould themselves with great difficulty to the elimination of thought, in the intermediate stages of a continued chain of close argument. In such languages an argument, or train of reasoning, appears to advance with abrupt steps, the mind being left to trace and fill up their connection. The resulting formula has to be reached, dropping out, as it were, some of the intermediate equations. Let our readers dwell for a moment upon the difficulty, in their own powerful Saxon tongue, of discoursing upon free will, predestination, and many other such subjects, and then endeavor to realize to themselves how infinitely more difficult the attempt must be in a language of monosyllabic formation and structure; its very polysyllables being the roughest possible mosaic of monosyllables, and the genius and construction of the tongue such, that even the simple language of the Gospels — the sentences of which are in general so remarkably plain and free from complication, — is beyond its flexibility, the simplest sentences in the Gospels of

Mark or John having to be chopped up and decomposed, in order to adapt them to this peculiar language. Let our readers imagine, if they can, the wonderful command requisite of so awkward an instrument, in order to be enabled to answer an Oo Yan — ' How are sin and eternal misery reconcilable with the character of an infinitely holy, wise, and powerful God?' or to meet the subtleties of a Moung Shwa-gnong, arguing on his fundamental doctrine, that divine wisdom, not concentrated in any existing spirit, or embodied in any form, but diffused throughout the universe, and partaken in different degrees by various intelligences, and in a very high degree by the Buddhs, is the true and only God. Yet so completely was Judson master of this very difficult tongue, and of the modes of thought of its people, that he could, by his replies and arguments, impart to an Oo Yan intense satisfaction, and a joy which exhibited itself by the ebullitions natural to a susceptible temperament; and, in the end, could force a subtle Moung Shwagnong to yield to the skill of a foreign disputant."*
Such were the difficulties to be encountered in the translation of the Scriptures into Burman; and yet so completely were they overcome, that not only the natives read the version with delight, but even Americans have affirmed that they studied it with a clearer understanding, and a greater pleasure, than that in their own vernacular.

Such was Dr. Judson's success in the great work to which he had consecrated his life — the founding of a Burman church, and the translation of the Scriptures into the language of that people. To this he had

---

* Calcutta Review for December, 1850.

sacrificed every other pursuit, with a simplicity of purpose which was worthy of an apostle. He abjured English preaching, English reading, English society, and, by devoting every energy to this great purpose, accomplished a work which has few parallels in the history of modern missions. So exclusively did he consider Burmah his field of labor, that he for a long time refused to give religious instruction even to the British soldiers at Maulmain. It was not until they were really seeking the salvation of their souls that he felt at liberty to devote to them any portion of his time. Then he so far deviated from his rule as to receive them at his study for conversation; and he had the pleasure of introducing many of them into the Christian church by baptism. He, however, considered this to be aside from his legitimate work, and relinquished it at the earliest opportunity. He esteemed missionary service to be in its nature peculiar, — unlike the labor of a pastor at home, a teacher, or a general philanthropist; and with this high view he consecrated himself exclusively to it.

From the preceding pages, the views of Dr. Judson respecting the present aspect of the missionary enterprise may be pretty distinctly learned. It may be observed that there were many views which have been gradually gaining favor with which he did not cordially sympathize. "He thought that greater boldness of effort, sustained by a simple trust in God, was demanded of those who direct the missionary enterprise, rather than the study of perfect immunity from danger. It seemed to him that, in the Christian world at large, there was a lack of a proper appreciation of the missionary work as *instituted by the Saviour*, but that a higher view could be obtained only through the teachings of the Spirit, and was incompatible with a low state of piety. In the conduct of missions there seemed to him too strong a tendency to rely on human contrivances, and to waste time, and strength, and money, on inferior interests — too much whetting of the scythe and building of the granary, while the ground was yet fallow, and the seed lying useless for want of a scatterer. He used to remark that missionaries had forgotten that the earth was to help the woman, and that they kept the woman so long helping the earth, that she could not look after her own children."

These views, however, in no degree affected his appreciation of the glory of the enterprise in which he was engaged. Only let the work go on, he would say, and in time it will rectify itself. He used to speak in a tone of exultation of the wonders that had been accomplished in the midst of weakness and errors — errors that exist in every department of modern missions and under every society, and he seemed to glorify God the more that there was so much to be ashamed of in the conduct of his instruments, never failing to class himself among the most erring of all. When the Spirit of God should come down as on the day of Pentecost, men would not contrive machines, or lay wise plans for extensive school operations, or labor to Anglicize eastern nations, either in habits or language, or gather together in large stations; but they would go forth as the apostles did, and the renovation of the world would follow.

In the social relations of life, the character of Dr. Judson was eminently worthy of imitation. His letters to his family all breathe the spirit of impassioned affection. While he made every personal sacrifice to the work which occupied his whole energies, he was ever ready, at any expense of time and labor, to promote the happiness of his wife and children. In sickness he was their ever-vigilant and tender nurse, and in health their associate and playmate. A lady exceedingly well qualified to form an opinion on this subject, both from her intimate knowledge of Dr. Judson and her familiarity with the best society in India, remarks, respecting his domestic character, as follows: " I have seen something of married life, and I never saw a husband so *entirely* devoted to a wife as dear Judson. I speak from personal acquaintance. Many are loving enough in their way, who would not sacrifice an hour's ease to relieve a wife of care, or attend her in sickness. Judson would allow nobody but himself to relieve his wife in any way, and I have felt hurt at his refusing my aid, as it looked as though he thought me unequal to the duty."

There was a feature in Dr. Judson's affection as a husband, which was, I think, peculiar. He was, as it is well known, married three times, and no man was ever more tenderly attached to each of his wives. The present affection, however, seemed in no respect to lessen his affection for those for whom he mourned. He ever spoke of those that had gone before with undiminished interest. In one of his letters to his daughter, after saying that he did not believe there existed on earth so happy a family as his, he soon after adds, " My tears frequently fall for her who lies in her lone bed in St. Helena." It was at his suggestion that Mrs. Emily Judson wrote the life of her predecessor. He frequently refers with delight to the time when he, and all those whom he so much loved, shall meet in paradise, no more to part, but to spend an eternity together in the presence of Christ. Those that were once loved were loved to the end; but this did not prevent the bestowment of an equal amount of affection on a successor.

In a letter to Mrs. E. Judson he writes as follows: "Heaven will be brighter to me for thy presence. Thou wilt be with Ann and Sarah. We shall join in the same song of love and praise; and how happy shall we be in beholding each other's faces glow with heavenly rapture, as we drink in the life-giving, joy-inspiring smiles of Him whom we shall all love above all!"

As might be expected, Dr. Judson spent but little of his time in social intercourse, beyond the limits of his own home. He had no time for it, and he considered his work of far too engrossing a nature to allow of it. He was always ready to go abroad to attend a meeting for prayer among the Burmans of his church, or to visit any family in the mission that happened to be in affliction. But beyond this he did not go. Hence he was, I believe, sometimes considered unsocial. When, however, he could alleviate sorrow, or bind up the broken in heart, no one in the mission was more prompt in his attentions, or more acceptable in his sympathy. That this should have been the case, is perfectly in harmony with his character. He felt that he was doing a great work, which allowed no time for trifling or ceremony. To do good to all men, especially to the disciples of Christ, was, however, a part of that work which he above all delighted to accomplish.

His conduct while in this country was governed by the same principles. While he showed himself exceedingly indifferent to what he considered merely visits of ceremony or curiosity, he was ever ready to devote his time and attention to any person whom he could serve by his advice, counsel, or sympathy. Instances of this kind, in any number, might be mentioned, were it desirable; and although in Burmah he avoided English society, whenever it would interfere with the great object of his life, he was always ready to render to the officers of government any service in his power, when, by so doing, he could advance the best interests of the people. Says the writer above alluded to, " We have made no allusion to the very important services which he rendered to the British government, our attention being engaged by other and higher considerations; yet we should fail to convey even a faint sketch of the character and qualities of the man, were we to omit all notice of the aid he afforded, first to Sir Archibald Campbell, afterwards to Mr. Crawfurd, and subsequently to every commissioner on the Tenasserim coast who had occasion to solicit either information or advice. To the last he clung to the hope that, through the instrumentality of our influence and power, Burmah would, sooner or later, be opened as a field for the exertion of missionary labor; and to a commissioner who was leaving Maulmain, and bidding farewell to Judson, his last words were, ' In case of difficulties, or of war, arising between the British government and Burmah, I expect to see you again on this field; and mind, if ever you are sent, and you think I can be of any use to your mission to Ava, if alive I shall be happy to join you, and be of every assistance in my power.' That which had induced him to accompany Crawfurd, and to afford him invaluable aid, — the hope of securing in the treaty concluded with Burmah a proviso favorable to religious toleration, — would, to the close of his career, have led Judson again to come forward as a powerful auxiliary to a diplomatic mission, and to devote his great abilities, and thorough acquaintance with Burmah, its princes and its people, to aid in the conduct of negotiations, which, if successful on the one point he had at heart, would, he felt assured, prove for the enduring advantage of Burmah, and therefore would richly recompense him for the sacrifices which such a journey and occupation must inevitably entail. Other reward, it is needless to add, found no place in his thought. The sum of money presented to him by the British government after Crawfurd's embassy went, every farthing, into the American Baptist mission fund, but swollen in amount by the addition of what constituted the whole of Judson's private property." *

In person, Dr. Judson was of about the medium height, slenderly built, but compactly knitted together. His complexion was in youth fair; but residence in India had given him the sallow hue common to that climate. His hair, when in this country, was yet of a fine chestnut, with scarcely a trace of gray. The elasticity of his movement indicated a man of thirty, rather than of nearly sixty years of age. His deportment was, in a remarkable degree, quiet and self-possessed, and his manner was pointed out as perfectly well bred, by those who consider the cultivation of social accomplishments the serious business of life. The reviewer alluded to writes on this subject as follows: "A person overtaking Judson in one of his early morning walks, as he strode along the pagoda-capped hills of Maulmain, would have thought the pedestrian before him rather under-sized, and of a build showing

---

* Calcutta Review, Dec., 1850, p. 454.

no great muscular development; although the pace was good and the step firm, yet there was nothing to indicate great powers of physical endurance, in the somewhat slight and spare frame tramping steadily in front of the observer. The latter would scarcely suppose that he had before him the man who, on the 25th of March, 1826, wrote, 'Through the kind interposition of our heavenly Father, our lives have been preserved in the most imminent danger from the hand of the executioner, and in repeated instances of most alarming illness during my protracted imprisonment of one year and seven months; nine months in three pairs of fetters, two months in five, six months in one, and two months a prisoner at large.' Illness nigh unto death, and three or five pairs of fetters to aid in weighing down the shattered and exhausted frame, seemed a dispensation calculated for the endurance of a far more muscular build. But meet the man, instead of overtaking him, or, better still, see him enter a room and bare his head, and the observer at once caught an eye beaming with intelligence, a countenance full of life and expression. Attention could scarce fail of being riveted on that head and face, which told at once that the spiritual and intellectual formed the man; the physical was wholly subordinate, and must have been borne through its trials by the more essential elements of the individual, by the *feu sacre* which predominated in his disposition. Nor was this impression weakened by his conversation. Wisdom and piety were, as might be expected in such a man, its general tone; but there was a vivacity pervading it which indicated strong, buoyant, though well, it may be said very severely, disciplined animal spirits. Wit, too, was there, playful, pure, free from malice, and a certain quiet Cervantic humor, full of benignity, would often enliven and illustrate what he had to say on purely temporal affairs. His conversation was thus both very able and remarkably pleasing." *

Of his personal habits, Mrs. Judson gives the following account: " His predilection for neatness, uniformity, and order, amounted, indeed, to a passion. Then he had an innate sort of refinement about him, which would subject him to annoyance when a less sensitive person would only be amused — a most inconvenient qualification for a missionary. This passion for order — which I should rather consider an unconquerable love for the beautiful and elegant, studiously perverted — displayed itself rather oddly after the means for its natural gratification and development were cut off. Nobody ever luxuriated more in perfectly spotless linen, though, partly from necessity, and partly because there was a suspicion among his friends that he would wear no other, it was always coarse. The tie of the narrow black ribbon, which he wore instead of a neckcloth, was perfect, and the ribbon itself would not have soiled the purest snow, though it was often limp and rusty from frequent washing. His general dress was always clean, and adjusted with scrupulous exactness, though it often looked as if it might have belonged to some rustic of the last century; being of the plainest material, and in fashion the American idea of what was proper for a missionary, perpetuated in broad caricature by a bungling Bengalee tailor. Most people thought that he dressed oddly from a love of eccentricity; but the truth is, he was not in the least aware

* Calcutta Review.

of any thing peculiar in his costume, never seeing himself in a mirror larger than his pocket toilet glass. He could see his feet, however; and his shoes never had a spot on their polish, nor the long, white, carefully-gartered stockings a wrinkle, much less a stain. In the construction and arrangement of his unique studying apparatus, which was composed of two long, narrow boxes mounted on a teak table, there was the same mixture of plainness with neatness and order, and, what was rather conspicuous in all his arrangements, a wonderful capacity for convenience. No one ever thought of invading his study corner; for he dusted his books and papers himself, and knew so well where every thing was placed, that he could have laid his hand upon the smallest article, in the darkest night." *

I do not know that I can close these remarks, already I fear too far protracted, more appropriately than by introducing a paragraph from the review of his life and labors, to which I have already been so largely indebted. " He, [Dr. Judson,] from the dawn to the close of his eventful career, could contemplate the millions still under the yoke of Buddhist error, with the hope and assurance of ultimate victory for the cause of truth. Strong in this hope, like a good

---

* One little circumstance in his personal habits is perhaps worth recording, as it may be useful to young men. It was a great wonder to him that men should be willing to suffer inconvenience all their lives, rather than spend half an hour in mastering the simplest art in the world. He made no secret of the fact that, from the time when his mother first fitted him out with a needle book and its accessories, when he went to college, he had been independent of womankind in the matter of tapes and buttons; and he used somewhat boastingly to affirm that he could achieve a patch or darn with lady-like neatness, if circumstances should ever warrant the draught on his time.

soldier of the cross, he unfurled his standard on the enemy's ground, and, though in the contest it was at times struck down, yet the standard bearer's heart and courage were proof, and the banner, triumphing in such hands over every struggle, soon rose and floated again in the breath of heaven. We may well say with the Psalmist, 'How are the mighty fallen in the midst of the battle!' But in this instance, though the mighty are fallen, the weapons of war are not perished. A champion of the cross, and a notable one too, has, indeed, after waging a severe and thirty years' conflict with the powers of darkness, fallen at his post; but he has fallen gloriously, leaving a well-furnished armory to his seconds and successors in the fight — weapons sound of temper, sharp of edge, and gleaming brightly with the light of heaven. He was, indeed, a mighty champion; mighty in word, mighty in thought, mighty in suffering, mighty in the elasticity of an unconquerable spirit; mighty in the entire absence of selfishness, avarice, and of all the meaner passions of the unregenerate soul; mighty in the yearning spirit of love and affection; above all, mighty in real humility, in the knowledge and confession of the natural evil and corruption of his own heart, in the weakness which brings forth strength; mighty in fulfilling the apostolic injunction, ' Whatsoever ye do, do it heartily, as to the Lord, and not unto men;' mighty in the entire devotion of means, time, strength, and great intellect to his Master, Christ."

Such was the man who is known throughout the East as the Apostle of Burmah. He went forth alone, trusting simply in the promises of God, and buried himself in the thickest darkness of Buddhism, until "righteousness came forth as brightness, and salvation as a lamp that burneth." Crucified to every desire for human applause, God has given him a name that is spoken with affectionate reverence by every household in Christendom. Driven with indignity from British India, he lived to receive the thanks of the governor general in council, for the services which he had rendered to the government. That his motives might be purified from every trace of ambition, he destroyed every line within his power that might minister to posthumous fame; and God has indelibly inscribed his name on every tablet of the future history of Burmah. He left behind him all that he loved in his native land, and only asked, as his reward, that he might gather a church of a hundred members from the worshippers of Gaudama, and see the Bible translated into their language. All this, and more than this, was granted, and the Karens also were given to him — a people of whose existence no Christian had heard, whom he beheld by thousands flocking to the standard of the cross. He asked that he might redeem a few immortal souls from eternal death, and it was granted to him to lay the foundations of Christian civilization for an empire. When the kingdoms of the world shall become the kingdoms of the Lord and of his Christ; when every pagoda shall have been levelled, and every hilltop, from the Bay of Bengal to the foot of the Himalaya, shall be crowned with a temple to Jehovah; when the landscape shall be thickly studded with schools, scattering broadcast the seeds of human knowledge; when law shall have spread the shield of its protection over the most lowly and the most exalted; when civil and religious liberty shall be the birthright of every Burman, — then will the spot where stood the prison at Oung-pen-la be consecrated ground; thither will pilgrims resort to do honor to the name of their benefactor; and mothers, as they teach their children to pray to the eternal God, will remind them of the atheism of their forefathers, and repeat to them the story of the life and labors of Adoniram Judson. Such honor doth God bestow upon HOLY, HUMBLE, SELF-DENYING, AND LONG-SUFFERING LOVE.

APPENDIX.

APPENDIX.

A.

DR. JUDSON'S OPINION ON SOME OF THE TENETS OF BUDDHISM.

DR. JUDSON, from a limited examination of the ancient Pali, an extensive acquaintance with the religious literature of Burmah, and a thorough knowledge of the people of that country, arrived at different conclusions with regard to some of the principal doctrines of Buddhism from those of most writers on the mythology of the East. He thought that Buddhism and Brahminism could not be "different branches of the same religion;" for though both recognize the universal oriental doctrine of metempsychosis, they are, in almost every other particular, directly antagonistic. Which of the two could justly claim the greater antiquity, he did not pretend to decide, though quite confident that Buddhism, in some form, had existed previous to the days of Gaudama.

He thought there was sufficient evidence that Gaudama flourished as a Hindoo prince, and a great heathen philosopher, some five or six hundred years before the Christian era; and he thought it probable that a devotee so wise and so sincere as this prince must have been, purified the system, and very possibly spiritualized it, to a greater extent than appears in the Buddhistic scriptures. These scriptures (the Be-ta-gat) were not written until four hundred and fifty-eight years after the death of Gaudama, and very probably do not embody the subtler teachings of the heathen sage. Be that as it may, Dr. Judson could not discover, either in the Burmese versions of these sacred books, or in conversation with professedly rigid Buddhists, any thing to redeem the system from the charge of absolute atheism. The few semi-atheists, &c., that he occasionally met, however closely they might adhere to the practices of Buddhism, readily acknowledged the latitudinous nature of their opinions. According to Dr. Judson's views of Buddhism, it acknowledges no moral governor of the universe; and though the doctrine of future rewards and punishments is one of the great pillars of the system, it recognizes no executive power, no supreme judge, no agent or minister of justice. The whole destiny of the infinitude of souls continually passing from one state of existence to another, is adjusted by the ceaseless turnings of the "unerring wheel of fate." Hence Gaudama himself endured the punishment of sins committed in previous states of existence, — "the sixteen great results of guilt," — even during his deityship.

Dr. Judson also regarded the state of nigban as nothing less than a total extinction of soul and body. He was aware that the original Sanscrit word, nirvana, has a very different signification; but he knew also that this signification, absorption in deity, is peculiarly abhorrent to Buddhists. Buddh is their deity, and they recognize no superior. From the circumlocution incidental to the honorific language of the Burmans, it is sometimes difficult to ascertain their precise meaning. No Burman, for instance, ever says the king or the priest is dead. It would be disrespectful to say so. For the same reason, they would not say broadly, that a Buddh is extinct, that he ceases to exist. He reposes. At the same time, they readily acknowledge that he is devoid of sensation, passion, emotion, and thought; that he neither takes cognizance of the devotion of his worshippers, nor is capable of extending to them any benefit. They teach that all existence bears within itself the elements of change, suffering, disease, decay, and death; and that *therefore* nigban — exemption from these evils, these fundamental principles of existence — is the only true good. So read the books, and so the strict disciples of Buddhism in Burmah, whether learned or unlearned, believe.

It must be borne in mind, however, that there is no reliable proof of the introduction of Buddhism into Burmah earlier than A. D. 386; that it subsequently underwent some modifications, and was not fully established in its present form until about A. D. 1000. The approved translations of the Be-ta-gat are not only tediously verbal, * but always give the Pali text alongside the rendering; and there is no reason to doubt their purity, or to suspect that interpolations or alterations of any kind have been admitted; though, on the other hand, there are many portions of it which have never yet been translated into the Burmese language.

On the whole, it is fair to suppose that this system is somewhat modified by the circumstances of the different nations that have adopted it; and that, in all probability, it underwent still greater modifications during the centuries that intervened between the death of Gaudama and the composition of the Be-ta-gat. — E. C. J.

In order to present to the reader some additional information on the subject of Buddhism, I have extracted several notes from the appendix of Mrs. Emily C. Judson's Memoir of Mrs. Sarah B. Judson.

PREVALENCE OF BUDDHISM.

Buddhism took its rise, about six hundred years before Christ, in Central India, where the antiquarian still finds ample proof of its former prevalence. It was banished from India by the Brahmins, but still prevails in Ceylon, and has spread itself over Burmah, Siam, Cochin China, Tartary,

* There are, of course, many free translations, some of which are quite interesting. Among these, the ten zats, or lives of Gaudama, by Aubathah, a priest of Moksobo, who flourished about a century ago, are really elegant compositions.

and Japan. It is also, in a modified form, the religion of Thibet, the grand lama being a sort of demi-Buddh. In China, it is somewhat corrupted by Shamanism; and in Burmah, especially among the Peguan part of the population, by nat worship, from both of which Buddhism, in its original purity, is quite distinct. The system of Confucius also prevails to some extent in China; but the popular religion is the same as in the neighboring nations, *Foe,* or *Fuh,* being the Chinese pronunciation of the Pali *Buddha.*

When the populousness of the regions where this system of religion flourishes is considered, some conception may be formed of its great prevalence; and, by taking the usual estimate of other religions for data, we may arrive at still more definite conclusions. The four prevailing systems of religion, now in the world, are Christianity, in its different forms, Mahometanism, Brahminism, and Buddhism. These comprise about nine tenths of the one thousand millions, at which the population of the earth is estimated; the residue, exclusive of ten millions of Jews, being made up of wild nomadic tribes, and isolated islanders, with various local superstitions, but with no settled form of religion. Protestant Christians are estimated at sixty-five millions; nominal Christians — Romanists, Greeks, and Armenians, collectively, at one hundred and eighty-five millions; Mahometans, at one hundred and forty millions; Brahminists, nearly one hundred millions; and Buddhists, probably, number above four hundred millions, or as many as the other false systems and the corrupted forms of Christianity combined.

BUDDH.

A Buddh is a being who, by virtue of the voluntary performance of certain austerities, becomes the object of supreme adoration throughout the universe, and from that state passes into annihilation.* He has been, like all other beings, transmigrating through various stages of existence from eternity; but upon receiving, through a predecessor, some intimation of the high destiny that awaits him, he enters upon a course of sacrifices and sufferings, the duration of which it is impossible to compute. As the length of the life of man after the deluge was gradually diminished, some suppose that it will be increased as gradually, till, during the approaching millennium, it will be once more measured by centuries, instead of scores. Something like this, though on a far more magnificent scale, is the theory of the Buddhists. They believe that the common age of man has been thus fluctuating from eternity, like the ebb and flow of the sea. There is a time when the "years of his life" are only ten; but they continue swelling, gradually, till they amount to one hundred quadrillions of quadragintillions, a number designated by a unit and one hundred and forty ciphers. When man arrives at this age of longevity, which the Burmans term an *a-then-kyay*, his age decreases, with the same imperceptible slowness, until it is again reduced to the term of ten years. This inconceivable stretch of time, for which the English language has no name, and before which figures become useless, constitutes what the Burmans call an Intermediate Period. Sixty-four of these Intermediate Periods complete one Cardinal Period, and four Cardinal Periods one Grand Period or Cycle, termed a *Kam-bah*, (Sanscrit, *Kalpa*.) Gaudama, the last Buddh, toiled, to obtain his divinity, through four *a-then-kyays* of these Grand Cycles, with the comparatively trifling addition of one hundred thousand Kam-bahs at the end. He was finally born of human parents, six hundred and twenty-four years before Christ, and spent the

---

* This being must not be confounded with the Buddh of Hindoo mythology, one of the ten incarnations of Vishnu. That very disreputable incarnation, made to synchronize with the last Buddh, was, doubtless, fabricated by the Brahmins, for the purpose of degrading the divinity of their powerful rivals to a level with their own gods, the nats of Burmah.

early part of his life amid the voluptuous splendors of an eastern court, being the only son of a powerful Indian monarch. At the age of twenty-nine he renounced royalty, with all its attractions, among which a harem of eighty thousand oriental beauties was not the least. Abandoning his only son, and the wife who had accompanied him through countless ages, — being a tigress when he was a tiger, a doe when he was a deer, and the queen of heaven or hell as he wielded the sceptre of either realm, — he fled into the wilderness. There he spent six years in practising austerities of unprecedented severity, after which he found himself invested with a divine nature, and thus became the supreme object of worship. He flourished as a Buddh until eighty years of age, when he died, and attained *nigban*, or annihilation.* His claims to supreme adoration, however, extend to five thousand years after his extinction. Thus the temples and sacred groves are crowded with his images; and pagodas are every where erected over some portion of his reputed relics, which are as miraculously plentiful as the fragments of the "true cross" among the devotees of Rome.

To give a more definite idea of the nature of a Buddh, it will be necessary to enter upon a brief outline of the system of worlds. The Grand Cycle, termed a Kam-bah, comprehends one entire revolution of nature, or the age of a world. The Period begins with the destruction of the old world, by the three elements, fire, air, and water. During the first of the four Cardinal Periods, which constitute a Kam-bah, the earth is enveloped in a conflagration. During the second Period, the flames are struggling with roaring winds and dashing waters; and the third is occupied in processes of

---

* The word *nigban* is undoubtedly derived from the same root as the Sanscrit *nirvana*, which implies absorption in Deity; but the Buddhists, so far from adopting this theory of Brahminism, would regard it with horror. The idea of any being superior to a Buddh, who should receive his divine essence, would be, in their opinion, blasphemous; and the only meaning they attach to the word *nigban* is simple annihilation.

reorganization. At the beginning of the fourth Period, a little spot of earth appears in the midst of the limitless waste of waters; and the spirits congregated in the invisible regions, that have escaped the conflagration, bend their heads to gaze down upon it with intense interest. A magnificent lily springs up from the centre of the mound; and if it blossoms, they are filled with joy; for the period is to be blessed by the advent of as many Buddhs as the lily stem bears flowers. Most frequently it is barren; in which case the period is full of gloom, and all creatures are degraded and miserable. The present Kam-bah is of an extraordinarily high order, the emblematic lily having borne five blossoms. Four Buddhs — Kek-ku-than, Gau-na-gong, Kat-tha-ba, and Gau-da-ma * — have already flourished, and passed into annihilation; and another is yet to be developed. The age of man is now on the ebb, and will continue to decrease, till reduced to the term of ten years; then it will gradually rise again, until it attains the enormous height of an a-then-kyay of years. During the next ebb, when the age of man is diminished to a hundred thousand years, A-re-ma-day,† the fifth Buddh, will appear, and flourish eighty thousand years.

As the waters continue to recede, the beautiful results of processes carried on during the previous period become visible. The Myeen-mo Mount stands in the centre of the rising system, encircled by seven graduated ranges of mountains, which are separated from each other by seven broad belts of water. Beyond these, in the direction of the cardinal points of the compass, appear four large islands, around each of which cluster five hundred smaller ones; and the whole is encompassed by a wall of incalculable height and magnitude. The base of the central mountain is inhabited by five races of monsters; and above these, midway from the base, and extending thence to the summit, is the first celestial region.

---

* All accented on the first and third syllables, thus: *Kek*-ku *than*, &c.

† Accented on the second and fourth syllables: A-*re*-ma-*day*.

The summit, a beautiful plain one hundred and twenty thousand miles in extent, and surrounded by high walls, constitutes the second celestial region; and over this, ranged one above another, at unequal distances, are four similar inferior heavens, and twenty superior ones, the four highest of which are immaterial and invisible. The distance from the foot of the mountain to the highest heaven is eight hundred and sixty-four millions of miles. The Mycen-mo Mount is reared on three immense rocks, so arranged as to leave a concave space in the centre; and this place is occupied by a race of beings resembling the Titans of old, who have been banished from the celestial regions. Below this are ranged eight hells, one immediately beneath the other, and extending through a layer of earth one hundred and twenty thousand miles in depth. The earth rests on a rocky stratum of the same depth, beneath which is a continually restless flood of water; and still below this, a similar body of air, by the mighty force of whose continued action and reaction the whole structure is supported.

At the commencement of the new organization just described, several glorious beings, while gliding through the upper regions of air, inhale a delicious perfume, which they trace down to the southernmost of the four large islands. This they find, as it emerges from the waters, fresh and beautiful; and they delay their return to dally with its attractions, till, in process of time, they become so gross, that the glory which illuminated their bodies is extinguished, and they are left in utter darkness. At this crisis, the sun and moon very opportunely appear, and commence their revolutions around the central mount, on a level with the summit of the middle range of encircling mountains. The celestial visitants, having lost the power of traversing air, as formerly, are compelled to make their homes below. Here they continue to deteriorate, until they undergo important physical changes, and the propagation of the race of man commences.

Each of the four large islands is one hundred and twenty thousand miles in extent; but they vary in form, being fashioned like the faces of the beings who inhabit them. The Southern Island, shaped like the human face, is the earth on which we dwell, and the only spot where a Buddh can be developed, or from which any being can pass into annihilation. The chance of becoming an inhabitant of earth is as though a needle, tossed from the summit of Myeen-mo Mount, should strike with its point the point of some particular needle planted on the Southern Island; or as though a mass of fragments, which are cast into an ocean, drifted thousands of miles, and stranded on a hundred coasts, should, by the careless winds and tossing billows, again be brought together. There are, therefore, few greater boons in the gift of fate, than that of being born a man, on this favored isle.

Ten thousand systems of worlds, like the one above described, each with its central mount, its heavens and its hells, its mountains and moats, its islands and outer wall, are destroyed and reproduced at the same time. The influence of a Buddh can extend over a trillion; while his omniscience, when he so wills it, embraces the vast infinitude of systems, which are stretched out on a limitless plain, in as close contact with each other as their circular walls will admit.

The jurisdiction exercised by a Buddh is neither that of a lawgiver, nor a judge. He is a mere religious teacher, explaining the immutable laws of duty and destiny, and persuading men to perform meritorious deeds; but he has no power to forgive sin, or avert the suffering which is its inevitable consequence. Most of his time is passed in a species of ecstatic revery, peculiar to himself; but he will "preach," when invited, or when suitable occasions present themselves; and he frequently travels from place to place, in search of meritorious persons, who need his aid on their way to annihilation. He is insusceptible of human passions, emotions, or sympathies, though liable to physical suffering, disease, and death. Omniscience, and that of an imperfect character, is the only attribute of the true God, which is claimed for him; and with the exception of ability to perform a minor class of miracles, he has no more power than any other man. Like all beings, he is a creature of destiny; and even after he has entered upon his Buddhship, is not exempt from the penalty of sins committed in a former state of existence.

To such a system of religion, which owns no living God, and counts immortality a curse, — a system brilliant with many a glowing fragment of sin-shattered mind, and hoary with the honored rime of antiquity, — millions and hundreds of millions of our race are at this very moment clinging, as their only hope. And, in order to effect the overthrow of this system, together with Brahminism and Mahometanism, the church of Christ must awake to the employment of her highest energies, and must put forth her mightiest efforts. It is no trifling foe with which she has to contend — no light skirmishing with the unarmed few upon the outskirts of the army, which is to engage her strength; but she is to attack the very heart of the fortress, and grapple with the Prince of Darkness on his throne. Every Christian will thank God for the wonders he is performing among the Greenlanders, the South Sea Islanders, the West India Negroes, and the Karens of Burmah; but no discriminating Christian will be unduly elated when he considers that such results have been limited to comparatively small tribes, destitute of a systematic religion, a national literature, and even a written language, and therefore presenting few obstacles to Christianization. The great battle of the Lord is to be fought upon a different field. The haughty priesthood, the imposing ceremonies, the spacious temples and magnificent pagodas, that are the pride and glory of those nations on which the heavy curse of idolatry is resting, are not so easily demolished. But demolished they must be eventually; and even now is the work begun. The clang of gospel armor, from the plains of India, mingles with the noise of the battery that has commenced its daring play upon the walls of China; and the stroke of the armorer's hammer, which never ceases in the borders of Burmah and Siam, is echoed from choice citadels that are springing up beneath the curve of the Moslem crescent. From other lands, also, — lands crimsoned with the blood of martyrs, or blackened by infidelity, — from the abodes of the wandering sons of Israel, — from dark-browed Africa, and from the wilds of America, the axe of the sturdy pioneer is ringing, and the trumpet of the Lord is pealing forth a battle call. We are standing on the vestibule of a resplendently glorious era. The angel " having the everlasting gospel to preach," is already " in the midst of heaven," and we hear the rushing of his mighty wings; the church is shaking off the drowsy dust of ages, polishing her weapons, and spreading her banner to the breeze; the word of command has sounded from the walls of heaven; and there are sure indications that the immutable promises of Jehovah are hastening to their accomplishment. Already the Morning Star has risen on thousands and tens of thousands "sitting in darkness, and in the region and shadow of death;" and although the twilight is yet gray about us, there is a deepening glow upon the sky, sure usher of advancing day. Courage, lone laborer! Of the myriads who have lived and passed from earth before thee, who so blessed as thou? Courage! Each well-directed blow of thine is destined to reverberate through eternity; and every ray shed from thy gospel lamp speeds away as the mountain rill to the ocean, swelling the flood of radiance which is ere long to sweep over the entire earth. Then, at the rising of the Sun of Righteousness, shall the nations clap their hands in gladness, and the redeemed and renovated race of man burst forth in one universal shout: " HALLELUJAH! HALLELUJAH! THE LORD GOD OMNIPOTENT REIGNETH!"

KYOUNGS AND PRIESTS.

A kyoung is a Burmese monastery. Though sometimes quite plain in its style of building, it is usually profusely ornamented with minute and curious carvings, and surmounted by a graduated roof, which presents numerous gables on every side, and bristles with small gilded spires. The rank of the occupant is ascertained by the number of gradations in the roof. The Burmese, when about to erect a kyoung, choose the finest site, a rising spot of ground, sufficiently spacious to convert the noise of the busy world without into a distant, pleasing hum. The clear waters of an artificial pool sparkle in the vicinity; images of gilded wood or of alabaster are elevated on small thrones, lodged in the branches of the sacred banian, and enclosed in shrines, which are scattered, here and there, among its fruit trees; a few richly-scented flowers are allowed to bud and blossom in the cool shadows; and the whole scene is overlooked by a neighboring pagoda, whose little gilded bells, kept in motion by the air, create a continual, low, murmuring music. The numerous small pagodas, which cluster around the large one, are interspersed with temples and shrines of various descriptions; and here and there towers a tall flagstaff, with a group of fabulous monsters near the top, and beneath them a long gauze cylinder, glittering with tinsel, streaming out upon the air. When a Burman draws near one of these quiet and beautiful places, he reverently bares his feet, for to him it is holy ground.

The priests of Buddh practise the strictest celibacy; and thus their system differs essentially from that of the Brahmins, whose priesthood is hereditary. Brahminical priests, by observing the sanctity of their caste, and keeping aloof from other men, are regarded as a superior order of beings; but though this practice is calculated to inspire the greater awe, the Buddhistic priesthood, from having its roots in almost every family of respectability throughout the empire, has a far stronger hold on the affections of the people. The priests in Burmah are supported by voluntary contributions. It is customary for them to go out every morning, each bearing his own rice pot, which, as they pass from house to house, never looking in at the door, except as they are invited, grows heavy with the liberality of their worshippers. On great festival days, each district prepares an artificial tree, which, being laden with gifts, is carried at the head of a long, gayly-dressed train of persons, each bearing a well-filled vessel, lavishly ornamented with flowers and tinsel. The priests are also the schoolmasters of the nation; and the gifts which they receive from their numerous pupils contribute essentially to their support. Every rainy season the boys flock to the kyoungs for instruction; and nearly every man of respectability in the empire has worn the yellow cloth through a novitiatory term of two or three seasons. Thus the religion of the Burman enters deeply into all his early and more pleasing associations, and in process of time becomes entwined with the very fibres of his nationality, so that he literally *forsakes all* when he embraces Christianity.

B.

LETTER FROM RANGOON IN 1826.

The following is the letter alluded to in the article from the Calcutta Review, to which frequent reference is made in the last chapter of the Memoir.

To the Corresponding Secretary.

RANGOON, March 25, 1826.

REV. AND DEAR SIR: Through the kind interposition of our heavenly Father, our lives have been preserved, in the most imminent danger, from the hand of the executioner, and in repeated instances of most alarming illness, during my protracted imprisonment of one year and seven months — nine months in three pairs of fetters, two months in five, six months in one, and two months a prisoner at large. Subsequent to the latter period, I spent about six weeks in the house of the north governor of the palace, who petitioned for my release, and took me under his charge, and finally, on the joyful 21st of February last, I took leave, with Mrs. Judson and family, of the scene of our sufferings — sufferings which, it would seem, have been unavailing to answer any valuable missionary purpose, unless so far as they may have been silently blessed to our spiritual improvement and capacity for future usefulness. Let me beg your prayers that it may not be in vain that we have been afflicted. Dr. Price remains in the service of his Burmese majesty. My intention, on leaving Ava, was to proceed to Mergui or Tavoy, ports south of Rangoon, and ceded by the treaty to the British government; but since arriving, I have found it advisable to wait a little, previous to the evacuation of this place by the British troops, with a view to settling at a new town about to be established in the neighborhood of Martaban, on the dividing line between the British and Burman territories.

It is supposed that all Martaban will remove to the new place on the other side of the Salwen River. The emigration also from all the southern districts of Burmah will doubtless be great, so that the native population will far exceed that of the places first mentioned. Add to which that it is much more centrical, and from the superior productiveness of the adjacent country, and the facility of communication with Siam, will probably become a place of much greater trade. The matter, however, is yet quite uncertain, and the first report we have from a party who have just gone to survey the new place and make a beginning, may be decidedly unfavorable. At any rate, I intend to leave this for some place under British government within a month.

The disciples and inquirers have been dispersed in all directions. Several are dead; several I found on my passage down the river, and gave them notice of my plans, in case they might wish to follow; and several are in this place waiting for some movement. Moung Shwa-ba has been in the mission house through the whole, and Moung Ing with Mrs. Judson at Ava. Moung Shwa-gnong I have been unable to find, but understand he is alive somewhere in the interior. We had a pleasant meeting with Mah Men-la and her sister, Mah Doke, who were living in boats at Prome, and instantly resolved to accompany us. I long for the time when we shall be able to reërect the standard of the gospel, and enjoy once more the stated worship and ordinances of the Lord's house. I feel a strong desire henceforth to know nothing among this people but Jesus Christ and him crucified; and under an abiding sense of the comparative worthlessness of all worldly things, to avoid every secular occupation, and all literary and scientific pursuits, and devote the remainder of my days to the simple declaration of the all-precious truths of the gospel of our great God and Saviour Jesus Christ.

Very affectionately yours,
A. JUDSON, JR.

C.

DEPOSITION OF DR. JUDSON.

The following deposition was made by Mr. Judson before Mr. Commissioner Crawfurd, at the close of the war in 1826, at Rangoon. As it illustrates in a striking manner the character of the Burmans and their government, and the thoroughness of Dr. Judson's knowledge of both, it is here inserted.

Question. What is your name, and of what country are you a native? — *Answer.* My name is Adoniram Judson, and I am a native of Massachusetts, in the United States of America.

Q. How long have you resided in the Burman dominions? — *A.* I arrived at Rangoon in the month of July, 1813, and have resided in the Burman dominions ever since, with the exception of two short visits made to Bengal and Madras.

Q. How have you been generally occupied during that time? — *A.* For the first six years of my stay, I was entirely occupied in studying the Burmese language, and framing a dictionary of it; and for the next four, in preaching the gospel to the natives, translating the New Testament into the Burmese language, with the other duties of the mission. For twenty-one months I was a prisoner, out of which I was seventeen in irons.

Q. Have you resided any time at the Burmese court? — *A.* I have visited Ava, or Amarapura, three times, and resided there in all near three years.

Q. Had you, during that time, any intercourse with any of the members of the royal family, or the principal officers? — *A.* In my second visit to Ava, in 1822, I had frequent intercourse with the palace, knew almost every member of the royal family, and both the public and private officers of state, the wonghees * and attawuns. I have spent whole days at

---

* Mr. Crawfurd's orthography of proper names is retained in this article.

the palace, and five or six times attended the morning levees, which is considered a matter of especial privilege. I arrived at Ava, the third time, in the beginning of 1824. I then visited the palace, and renewed my acquaintance with the chiefs, but was received coldly by his majesty. I continued, as in my former visit, however, to call at the houses of the king's brothers and sisters, the queen's brother, and other principal officers.

Q. What, according to your opinion, was the cause of your being coldly received by his majesty, during your third visit to the court? — A. I conceive that the principal reason was, the approaching rupture between the British and Burman governments.

Q. Was there any distinction made between American and British subjects by the court of Ava? — A. Before the war commenced, it was fully explained to the Burmese government, that the American missionaries were not subjects of Great Britain; and under this impression, I thought it safe to visit the court in 1824, although then of opinion that war was impending. The imprisonment of the American missionaries, after the commencement of the war, now convinces me that they made no distinction. The Burmese, in fact, are of opinion that all white men, except the French, are subjects of the King of England. Since the overthrow of the Emperor Napoleon, they even believe that France has become part of the King of England's dominions. The Americans are peculiarly liable to be confounded with the English, from speaking the same language.

Q. On your way from Rangoon to Ava, in 1824, did you observe any hostile preparations making? — A. I observed none until reaching Prome, when I heard that troops were levying in all the provinces above that place. As I advanced, I saw in several places the conscripts quitting the villages where they had been raised. Between Sembeguen and Pugan, I met Bandula proceeding in state to take command of an army assembled at the former place. I was told that the destination of this army was the British frontier.

Q. Did you see the army which you have now mentioned? — *A.* No; I did not; I passed on the opposite side of the river; and at all events, Sembeguen, where the troops would be assembled, is several miles distant from the bank. I saw only the troops in the immediate suite of Bandula, probably not above one thousand.

Q. Were you told, and by whom, that the army of Bandula intended to attack the British dominions? — *A.* I was told that such was the intention, but I cannot specify any particular authority for this opinion: the impression was general among the people: no secret was made of it.

Q. Had you any personal intercourse with Bandula, on the occasion of meeting his fleet on the river? — *A.* No; I did not see Bandula, but my boat was stopped and examined by his orders. I stated that I was proceeding to the capital by orders from the king, and was allowed to pass.

Q. Do you know what became of the army of Bandula, to which you now allude? — *A.* Soon after my arrival in Ava, I heard that Bandula, with his army, had arrived at the place of his destination, and had sent the Burmese government a plan of some meditated attack on the British territory. This was stated to me by a person who had heard the king mention this circumstance at one of the morning levees. I cannot recollect the person who gave me this information, but think it was Dr. Price, who was then more in habits of visiting the palace than myself.

Q. During your residence at the court, have you ever observed any disposition on the part of the officers of government to enter into a war with the British? — *A.* From the first visit I made to Ava, such a disposition has always been manifested whenever an occasion presented itself to express it. I heard such sentiments expressed by the principal officers of government, but more particularly by the members of the royal family.

Q. Did such a disposition exist during the late reign? — *A.* I have understood that it did; but cannot speak from personal experience on this subject, not having, although in the country, visited the court of Ava until the accession of the present king.

Q. What, according to your opinion, led to the late war between the British and Burman governments? — *A.* A jealousy of the British power on the part of the Burmans, confidence in their own prowess on account of the recent conquests of Cassay and Assam, and a desire to extend their territory.

Q. What opinion did the Burmese court entertain of the military character of the British nation and power in India, previous to the war? — *A.* They thought the British power formidable to the Hindus only, but considered themselves a superior order of men, whom the British could not withstand in battle, on account of their personal courage, skill in stratagem, and the practice of desultory modes of warfare, which would fatigue and destroy a British army.

Q. Did you hear what was thought at court when news arrived of the capture of Rangoon? — *A.* It was considered a mere marauding incursion, similar to that which the Siamese frequently made on the province of Martaban — an example quoted at the time. The king frequently expressed his anxiety for the speedy march of his troops, lest the English who had landed at Rangoon should escape.

Q. Who were the persons about the court that most frequently expressed, in your hearing, a desire for war with the British government in India? — *A.* The Prince of Sarawadi, brother to the king, a favorite, and the person next to him in rank; the Princess of Taungdwen, the eldest sister of the king, and on that account unmarried, according to immemorial usage; a person of great intelligence, and perfectly well acquainted with the feelings of the court; and the seah wonghee, the king's tutor, and amongst the courtiers next in influence to the queen's brother.

Q. Can you recollect any particulars of conversations held with any of the individuals now mentioned, on the subject of war with the English? — *A.* I have frequently heard the Prince of Sarawadi expatiate for half an hour together upon this subject. His language used to be to the following purport.

I render the expressions from the Burman as nearly as I can recollect them. "The English are the inhabitants of a small and remote island. What business have they to come in ships from so great a distance to dethrone kings, and take possession of countries they have no right to? They contrive to conquer and govern the black strangers with caste, (Hindus,) who have puny frames and no courage. They have never yet fought with so strong and brave a people as the Burmans, skilled in the use of the sword and spear. If they once fight with us, and we have an opportunity of manifesting our bravery, it will be an example to the black natives, who are now slaves to the English, and encourage them to throw off their yoke." About a month before my imprisonment, the king's sister, already mentioned, said to me in conversation, that it was obvious the English were afraid to fight; that their conduct on the frontier was mean and cowardly; that they were always disposed to treat, and not to fight; and that upon some occasions, when the Burman and British troops met, the British officers held up their hands to entreat the Burmans not to advance. She insisted that the whole conduct of the British for some time past indicated unequivocal symptoms of fear. She added, "We shall now fight certainly, and will no longer be dissuaded. The new governor general acts foolishly; he is afraid of us, and attempts to coax us, yet continues the usual course of aggression and encroachment."

Q. Did you ever hear the seah wonghee, the king's tutor, express any opinion on the prospect of a war with the English? — *A.* The late seah wonghee was a man of few words and of a cautious disposition. I have often heard him talk of the danger to the Burmans of the neighborhood of the British power, and the necessity of watching their conduct. I once obtained a grant of land for a house through this officer. He took a long time in wording the document, and took especial care to mention to his people, in my presence, calling upon me to understand what he said, that the grant was not in perpetuity, lest it might hereafter be claimed, he said, as the territory of the American government. In this he appeared to me to refer to the history of British aggrandizement in India. It was through his officers, chiefly, that I learned the sentiments of this individual.

Q. Can you recollect the name of any other individual of consequence who expressed in your presence an opinion on the question of a war between the Burman and British governments?—*A.* From the nature of the Burman government, the principal officers of state express themselves with extreme caution on all public questions. The same caution was not so necessary to the king's brothers and sisters, and therefore they expressed themselves more freely. As the war approached, this caution increased; and when the subject, upon one occasion, was introduced before one of the attawuns, this officer did not hesitate to insinuate that the American missionaries were spies of the British government. I have heard the dependants of the chief ministers, and other subordinate officers of government, on innnumerable occasions, express similar sentiments on a war with the British to those which I have ascribed to the Prince of Sarawadi and the Princess of Taungdwen.

Q. Did you hear that any proposition for the conquest of the British territories was ever entertained on the part of the Burman government?—*A.* In the presence of the Princess of Taungdwen, I was once consulted by her officers on the practicability of conquering Bengal. My reply was, that it was as difficult for the Burmans to conquer Bengal as for the English to conquer Ava; which expression was viewed by the Burmans as affording as strong an affirmation of the impracticability of the scheme as words could convey. Their answer was, "You do not believe just now; in a little while you will be convinced." This conversation, to the best of my recollection, took place in March or April, 1824, after the march of Bandula's army, which was the subject of discourse when my opinion was asked.

Q. Can you recollect any other circumstance affording an intimation of the sentiments of the court of Ava on the subject of a war with the British?—*A.* Nothing specific; but I may mention a circumstance which occurred to me one morning, during my second visit to Ava, at the close of the year 1822. I met one of the officers of the young heir apparent, the only son of the king, then a child of about eleven years of age. I asked this person some questions respecting his young master. In the course of the conversation, he used the following expression: "This is the prince who, when he arrives at manhood, is to rule over all your Kula countries." This prediction in favor of the young prince was a matter of general belief among the Burmans, and could refer only to the British territories, being the only Kula countries accessible to the Burmans.

Q. What is the meaning of the term Kula? — *A.* Its original meaning was, men having caste, or Hindus; but now it is extended to all the nations lying west of Ava, who are divided by the Burmans into *black* and *white* Kulas.

Q. Have you understood that any of the Asiatic strangers residing in Ava were instrumental in exciting the Burmans to a war with the British? — *A.* I have uniformly understood that the brahmins, of Cassay, Munnipore, and Upper India, residing in Ava, from hatred of the British rule, were active in instigating the Burmans to war.

Q. Are there many brahmins residing at the court of Ava? — *A.* A great many; and they are particularly favored by the king, and often consulted.

Q. Did you ever hear any person connected with the Burman government complain of any specific act of aggression on the part of the British? — *A.* I have always heard that the principal complaint was, the refusal on the part of the British to deliver up refugees. This had been a subject of complaint during my whole residence in the Burman dominions. At the commencement of the war, I also heard it stated that the British had forcibly seized an island in the Naaf River, belonging to the Burmans. Mr. Lanciego, a Spanish gentleman in the Burman service, who was imprisoned with me, informed me that he had told the king that the dispute concerning the Naaf Island might be settled, and war avoided. The king answered, "We have gone too far, and must proceed." This expression, according to Mr. Lanciego, was pronounced by his majesty in a tone which seemed to indicate that he personally regretted the prospect of war with the English.

Q. Does Mr. Lanciego understand the Burman language, and on what terms was he with the king? — *A.* Mr. Lanciego understands the Burman language perfectly, and was a great favorite of the king. He had high titles, and was collector of the port of Rangoon.

Q. What sensation was produced at Ava by the success of Bandula at Ramoo? — *A.* A strong sensation, as I understood from others; for when the news came I was a prisoner. I saw, from the place of my confinement, the prisoners, their baggage, arms, and ammunition, carried in public procession, and the king himself came out to view the spectacle.

Q. Have you ever heard that the Burman government has felt displeasure at the British power being an obstacle to the extension of its territories to the westward? — *A.* When I was at court for the first time, in 1819, the year of his present majesty's accession to the throne, the late Mr. Gibson, who afterwards went on a mission to Cochin China, was engaged, by the king's orders, in constructing a map of the Burman dominions, together with the adjacent countries of Hindostan, Siam, and Cochin China. Mr. Gibson had exhibited this map to the king, and came to me from the palace, mentioning what had taken place. The king, on seeing the map, used the following expression: "You have assigned the English too much territory." Mr. Gibson said that the map gave a correct representation of the extent of the British dominions. The king answered, with evident feelings of dissatisfaction, "The territory of the strangers is unreasonably large." This was before the conquest of Assam, and it was observed that this country would be a desirable acquisition to the Burmans.

Q. Are you of opinion that the late war might have been avoided on the part of the British by negotiation? — *A.* I am of opinion that war was ultimately inevitable, but might, perhaps, have been delayed for a short time, by the British government yielding to all the demands of the Burmans, especially the restitution of the refugees. The next demand would have been for Chittagong and Dacca.

Q. What reason have you for believing that Chittagong and Dacca would have been demanded? — *A.* The Burmans considered that they had a good claim to them, as having once been dependencies of the kingdom of Arracan. I have heard this claim frequently urged, and, to the best of my recollection, on one occasion by the Prince of Sarawadi. The claim to these parts of the British dominions was so generally maintained by all classes of public officers, that, if I had introduced the subject, I might have heard it insisted upon every day of my life.

Q. Did you ever see any royal proclamations, edicts, or other public documents of the Burman government concerning the late war? — *A.* It is not generally the custom of the Burman government to publish proclamations on such occasions. There was no declaration of war, which is also not customary. The people in general know nothing of war, but by the levy of troops and contributions. When in prison, I heard a royal edict repeated by one of the town secretaries within the prison yard. It was when the British army had reached Sarwa. It stated that, whereas " the rebel strangers " had taken possession of Rangoon, and issued their orders, in defiance of the king's authority in the lower countries, his majesty would take the field in person, with one hundred thousand Burmans and one hundred thousand Shans; and it proceeded to make arrangements for his temporary absence. This was one of five or six edicts of the same nature, respecting his majesty's departure from Ava to conduct the war in person.

Q. What was the reason of his majesty not proceeding in person, in conformity with these edicts? — *A.* I do not believe that he ever seriously intended to march. The proposal to do so was intended to encourage the people, and an artifice to get some of the courtiers to volunteer their services.

Q. Did you ever hear what took place between the king and the Prince of Sarawadi, when the latter was proceeding to take the command of the army to oppose the English? — *A.* It was generally stated and believed, that the prince said to his majesty that, after driving the English out of the country, he trusted he would not be stopped, but allowed to pursue them into Bengal. This was thrown out with the hope of getting a favorable answer from the king, who only smiled, however, without giving any direct reply.

Q. What opinion did the Burmans entertain of the British sepoys previous to the war? — *A.* They had a contemptible opinion of the Hindus, and the Mohammedans of Hindostan also, but did not understand what a sepoy meant. I was frequently asked, by the government officers, after the commencement of the war, and while in prison, who and what the sepoys were — whether they were slaves of the British government, or persons employed on pay, or what? Mr. Lanciego, the Spanish gentleman already alluded to, informed me that, when once consulted by the king respecting the prospect of carrying on a war with the English, he persuaded his majesty against it, and particularly mentioned that the British had two hundred thousand sepoys, well armed and disciplined. Upon that occasion, neither his majesty nor his courtiers seemed to understand what a sepoy meant. His majesty, on hearing what Mr. Lanciego said, retired abruptly; and the courtiers expressed their displeasure at his saying any thing to discourage the king from entering upon a war with the English.

Q. What opinion did the Burmese entertain of the sepoys after the commencement of hostilities? — *A.* They entertained a poor opinion of them, and thought they could easily beat them, after their success at Ramoo, and in an affair which, I understand, took place at Rungpore. It was confidently stated by the Burmans, that, while operations were going forward before Rangoon, the sepoys were amicably disposed towards them, were anxious to spare them, and frequently warned them of the European troops. All this was very generally believed, and I myself entertained no doubt of it at the time. It was also stated that an amicable traffic was carried on by the sepoys and Burmese troops, in which the former, among other articles, occasionally disposed of muskets to the latter.

Q. Where were you when Lieutenant Colonel M'Dowall's detachment was repulsed from Wattigong, and that officer killed? — *A.* I was a prisoner in the Burman camp at Mellun.

Q. What brought you there? — *A.* I was sent from Ava to act as interpreter to the Prince Memiabo.

Q. When were you sent back from thence to Ava? — *A.* Immediately on news being received at Mellun of the British army having advanced from Prome.

Q. While encamped at Mellun, did you see any prisoners of the British army? — *A.* I saw Lieutenant Scott and twenty sepoys, the latter taken at Wattigong.

Q. Do you know what was their conduct when brought before the Burman chiefs? — *A.* Yes. I was present when the sepoys in question were brought, first before the Prince Memiabo, and afterwards before Kaulen Mengi, and interrogated by the latter, through a Hindustani interpreter, with my occasional assistance.

Q. What questions were put to them? — *A.* They chiefly regarded the strength of the British army, and the effects likely to result from the death and defeat of Lieutenant Colonel M'Dowall, who was supposed by the Burmans to be a general of high rank.

Q. How did the sepoys reply, and what was the nature of their demeanor? — *A.* They answered with spirit, and the tendency of all their replies seemed to be for the advantage of their own government. As far as I could judge, they purposely exaggerated the numbers and resources of the British army; and in reference to the death of Lieutenant Colonel M'Dowall in particular, they explained the organization of the British force, stating that the death of a superior officer, even of the commander-in-chief, would be attended with no disorder, as the next senior officer always took his place. The loyalty displayed by them gave offence to Kaulen Mengi, who got out of humor on hearing their replies.

Q. Did the sepoys address you, or did you speak to them? — *A.* They recognized me with emotion, as a European, the moment I presented myself, and seemed to think that I could afford them protection. By direction of Kaulen Mengi, I spoke to them in English; but they did not understand me, and I do not speak any of the languages of Hindustan. In giving the tenor of their answers, I go upon the translations of them rendered to Kaulen Mengi by the Hindustani interpreter.

Q. What impression did the conduct of the sepoys on this occasion make upon you? — *A.* From the unfavorable reports I had heard before, I thought the sepoys lukewarm in the cause of the European government. The conduct observed by them on the present occasion shook that opinion.

Q. Were the sepoys in irons when brought before the Burman chiefs? — *A.* No; they were not in irons, but they had wooden yokes about their necks. They were afterwards put in irons, and sent to Ava.

Q. Did you meet, during your stay in Ava, any of the sepoy prisoners taken on the Bengal frontier? — *A.* Yes; a number of the native officers were confined with me in the same prison; but, from the want of language, no intercourse took place between us. I only heard their sentiments occasionally through Mr. Gouger, an English gentleman who was one of my fellow-prisoners. I think they all died from hard treatment, with the exception of one person, whom I brought down with me to the British camp at Yandabo.

Q. What opinion did the Burmese, previous to the war, entertain of the European troops of the British army? — *A.* They had a better opinion of them than of the Hindus, but considered them luxurious and effeminate, incapable of standing the fatigues of war, and therefore unable to contend with a people hardy like themselves, who could carry on war with little food and no shelter.

Q. What is their present opinion of the European troops? — *A.* They consider them nearly invincible, fierce and blood thirsty, and discovering almost supernatural prowess. I have heard them compare them in action to a particular class of demons, called Balú, that, according to Burman notions, feed on human flesh. They have compared the rapidity of their movements to a whirlwind. The skill of the Europeans in the use of artillery, and especially in that of rockets and shells, astonishes them, and is incomprehensible to them. I should add, that the forbearance and moderation of the European troops after victory, and their obedience to command, and regularity of discipline, is a subject of admiration with them. In comparison with the sepoys, they also observed that they were indifferent to plunder.

Q. Are you aware when this revolution in regard to the character of the European soldiery took place with the Burmans? — A. The first circumstance of the war, which made a deep impression on the Burman court, was the sudden and complete destruction — to use the language of the Burmans themselves — of the thongba wonghee and his party of about one thousand men, in a stockade near Rangoon. I heard from a Burmese who was present in the action, and who, for some political offence, on his return to Ava, became my fellow-prisoner, that this was effected by about three hundred Europeans. The court, being displeased with the procrastination of ki wonghee, had sent thongba wonghee, a brave but hot-headed man, to supersede him. This person was determined to fight. He sent, I think, an Armenian as a spy to Rangoon, who brought back news that the English were preparing to attack his stockade. The messenger was put to death for bringing accounts tending to discourage the troops; but the execution was hardly over, when the British troops presented themselves before the stockade. My informant, and other persons, afterwards gave a most appalling account of the attack of the "Balús," as they called them. The gate of the stockade was choked up by the runaways, and almost every man in it put to death by the bayonet. Thongba wonghee was killed in the fight by one of his own people. This mode of attack was totally contrary to all that the

Burmans knew of war, and struck them with consternation. They stated that, when one of the assailants was killed, another immediately took his place, and that they were not to be discouraged from advancing, even by wounds; so that it was in vain to contend with such an enemy. Their imaginations were so wrought upon, that to these particulars they added many fabulous ones, such as, that the Europeans continued to advance after their hands had been chopped off in scrambling over the stockades; that the arms and legs of the wounded were carefully picked up and replaced by the English surgeons, who were represented to be as skilful as the warriors were bold. The next circumstance which brought about the revolution in question was the defeat of Bandula, in his lines before Rangoon, and his flight to Donabew — an event which struck the Burmans dumb, and for a time made them consider their affairs desperate. They thought the British army would then immediately march upon Ava. The Princesses of Pugan and Shwadong, with the queen mother, when the news arrived in Ava, sent for Mrs. Judson, and communicated to her the particulars of Bandula's defeat. The Princess of Pugan said, on that occasion, " The Bandula's troops have piled up their arms for the use of the foreigners. They have all dispersed, and the enemy has nothing to do but to march to Ava, clapping their hands." Mrs. Judson's advice was asked by the princesses. They wished to know whether they ought to run away or stay; and if they staid, whether there was any chance of safety for them. They entreated her protection and good offices with the English. Upon the failure at Donabew, the Burmans again somewhat recovered their spirits, and Bandula was supported by all the strength the country could afford. The death of Bandula again threw the court into consternation.

Q. What, in your opinion, prevented the Burmans from negotiating during the war? — *A.* All idea of negotiation is repugnant to the pride of the Burmans, and contrary to their custom. They believe the conquering party will always keep what it has got, if it can, and that negotiation is therefore useless. Overtures to treat are always looked upon either as a mark of weakness, or they are considered as an artifice to gain time.

Q. Do you know what was said of the first overture made by Sir A. Campbell to treat from Prome? — *A.* The nine Europeans who were imprisoned were sent for to translate the letter of Sir A. Campbell, which perplexed the court extremely; the idea of treating in the commanding situation in which he then was appearing so utterly unaccountable to them. They endeavored to explain it in various ways. Sometimes they imagined that he was induced to treat from the prevalence of great sickness in the army; at other times, they imagined that the King of England had disapproved of the war; then, that the Seiks had risen against the English, in Upper India; but the most prevalent opinion was, that the King of Cochin China had sent a fleet of fifty ships to assist the Burmans. The king went the length of sending a despatch boat to the mouth of the Rangoon River, to ascertain whether the Cochin Chinese fleet had actually arrived or not.

Q. Do you think the Burmese government now understands the nature of a negotiation with a European government? — *A.* I think they certainly do; but nothing but actual experience could convince them. After the negotiation which led to the peace, they were still incredulous of the good faith of the British, and could not bring themselves to believe that they were sincere until the first retrograde movement of the army. The payment of the money was a desperate experiment on their part, for they thought that the British would take it, and still march on. I was questioned a hundred times over on this subject, by the wonghees and other principal officers of the government, having been sent for at all hours of the day and night, by different parties, for this purpose. I was asked what pledge I would give, and particularly if I was willing to leave my wife and child behind, in order to be put to death, should the English take money and still advance upon the capital.

Q. Do you consider the Burman government very faithless? — *A.* Utterly so. They have no idea either of the moral excellence or the utility of good faith. They would consider it nothing less than folly to keep a treaty if they could gain any thing by breaking it. The fidelity hitherto observed by the British government in fulfilling the stipulations of the late treaty stupefied the Burmans. They knew not what to make of it; but some of them have now begun to admire it. I heard many make use of expressions like the following: "These Kulas, although they drink spirits and slay cattle, and are ambitious and rapacious, have a regard for truth and their word, which is quite extraordinary; whereas in us Burmese there is no truth." The first circumstance in the conduct of the British which struck them with surprise, was the return of Dr. Sanford on his parole; and next, Sir A. Campbell's returning the six lacs of rupees offered, after it was within his power.

Q. Has not the conduct of the British towards Burman prisoners produced a favorable impression? — *A.* This produced a favorable impression on the lower classes, but not on the government, who viewed it as a piece of policy practised by the British to conciliate the people, and seduce them from their allegiance.

Q. While at the court of Ava, did you ever hear of any intrigue going on between the Burmese government and any of the native princes of Hindustan? — *A.* I heard, on three or four occasions, that the late Bandula boasted that he maintained a secret correspondence with several native princes of Hindustan, who, according to him, would rise against the British as soon as the Burmans would set them a good example. Reports of such insurrections were frequently propagated, and received with avidity by the Burman court. There arrived in Ava, I think in 1823, eight or ten Seiks, purporting to be a mission from the rajah of their country. They stated that they had suffered shipwreck in crossing a river, and lost the letter and presents which they had from their master for the King of Ava. I understood that the object of their mission was a treaty, offensive and defensive, to drive the British out of India. For a long time they were honorably received, but during the war they became suspected, and were for a short time imprisoned. They were finally sent back with letters, and a sum of money given to each individual. I heard officers of government state that the alliance would be very desirable, particularly as the king of the Seiks had never been subdued by the English.

Q. Do you know any thing of the object of the late Burman mission to Cochin China? — *A.* I have understood that the object of it was an alliance, offensive and defensive, by which the two powers were to attack the Siamese, from the east and west, conquer the country, and partition it between them.

Q. Do you know of any political connection between the Burmese and Chinese governments? — *A.* An embassy arrived in Ava in 1823, which I have understood to be from the Emperor of China. A white elephant and a princess were demanded in strong language, which occasioned some alarm to the Burman court, under an impression that the Chinese wanted to quarrel with them. The white elephant and the princess, there being none to spare, were refused, and a number of common elephants and other presents were sent.

Q. Have you ever heard that the Burmese claimed the assistance of the Chinese in their war with the English? — *A.* I never heard any mention of such a thing in Ava.

Q. Did you ever hear any of the officers of the Burman government express regret that the Burmese had entered into a war with the English? — *A.* I have, in innumerable instances. During my imprisonment, a great number of public officers, falling under the displeasure of the government, were imprisoned along with me; and, gaining the good opinion of some of them, I conversed intimately with them on the subject of the war. As early as November, 1824, twenty stewards of townships, belonging to various princesses and other ladies of the palace, got into disgrace, and were imprisoned. These stated to me that the king was good natured, and unwilling to disoblige any one; had been teased and over-persuaded into a war with the English, through the intrigues of certain ambitious military leaders, particularly Bandula and Maongkyaio; that, in an evil hour, they induced him to do that which they all now would give the world could be undone. I said to one of the persons in question, " Suppose the English were now to retire, and leave matters as they stood before the war." His answer was, " O, how good that would be!" This feeling became more general as the British army advanced; and latterly, it was universal from the king downwards; for, from the destruction of thongba wonghee and his force, and the retreat of Bandula from the lines before Rangoon, they perceived that they were no match for the British. I may add, that, after these two affairs, their efforts were made with scarcely any hopes of success. Still they went on, because their astrologers continued to predict success, and their wounded pride forbade them to make any concessions.

Q. Are you of opinion, from what you know of the character of the Burman court, that the present peace will be lasting? — *A.* The Burmese have been so severely punished, that I think it will be a long time before any courtier will have the hardihood to propose another war with the British government.

Q. What do you consider the most effectual means for the British government to pursue, in order to maintain peace with the Burmans? — *A.* I think that, since the Burmans are now so thoroughly convinced of the superiority of the British power, that what is chiefly necessary, is to observe towards them a fair and upright course of dealing, and to insist, upon their side, on a strict maintenance of the treaty. By showing them that you religiously observe the treaty, they will, in their turn, take up the same idea, and follow your example.

Q. Do you consider the appointment of a British resident at the court of Ava, in conformity with the treaty, as necessary, or likely to be useful? — *A.* I do not consider the presence of such an officer at the court of Ava absolutely necessary towards the maintenance of peace; but I am of opinion that it will be highly useful in maintaining and extending your commercial relations.

Q. Do you consider that the presence of a consul, or other British agent, at Rangoon, is necessary, or likely to be useful? — *A.* If a resident be appointed at Ava, an inferior agent, depending upon him, will be necessary at Rangoon, as well for the purpose of protecting British commerce as for maintaining a free intercourse between the resident and the British possessions.

Q. Do you consider that an annual mission from the governor general to the court of Ava would be equally useful as a permanent resident? — *A.* No; I do not. A public officer, coming in this manner, would gain no knowledge of the country or people, and therefore would have less influence, and of course be less useful, than an agent residing permanently. The court also will have no knowledge of him — a matter equally necessary. I am of opinion that the residency should, at all events, be permanent, and that, when the chief authority is not present, a subordinate one should be there acting for him.

Q. Are you of opinion that a public agent of the British government residing at Ava is likely, with good management, to obtain an influence beneficial to his own government at the court? — *A.* Yes; I am fully of that opinion. Every thing, however, will depend on the character of the individual. I can conceive that the conduct of many men in that situation might, with the best intentions, be mischievous, rather than beneficial.

Q. What sort of demeanor on the part of the British officers residing at Ava do you consider would tend most to conciliate the Burmans, to maintain peace, and to promote the legitimate interests of the British government? — *A.* I think the demeanor of the British resident and other officers ought to be mild and unassuming. The Burmans have been conquered, and know it. They should not be reminded of it by haughtiness of conduct, or assumption of superiority, on the part of the British officers. Stickling for rank or precedence is generally not necessary at the court of Ava; or, at least, more is to be lost than gained by entering into a contention with the court upon such minute points. Should the Burmese discover that the British envoy is disposed to contend on questions of etiquette, it would arouse their jealousy. They will imagine that he has been set over them as a master, and will be disposed to dispute every point with him. It should be recollected that the present king is himself generally impatient of forms, of an open and playful disposition, easy of access, and disposed to admit familiarity of intercourse. I do not say that this will be the case in the beginning. It is very probable that he will at first consider it necessary to be reserved, until he knows the terms on which he is to stand with the representatives of the British government. The Burman court will certainly, for some time, be suspicious concerning the motives of his appointment.

Q. You have read the depositions of John Baretto and of Jeronimo de Cruz, which I have handed to you? — A. Yes; I have.

Q. What do you think of them? — A. There are some points to which I cannot speak; but in general they appear to me to be very correct.

Q. Are you acquainted with these two individuals? — A. I know John Baretto slightly; the other not at all.

Q. Are you of opinion that there will be war between the Burmese and Siamese? — A. Immediately before leaving Ava, I heard it frequently asserted by the public officers of the government that a war with Siam would, under present circumstances, be highly desirable. They stated that a soldier could not be obtained to fight against the "White Kulas" for one hundred and fifty ticals of flowered silver; whereas, if called upon to fight the Siamese, or Talains, or any such people, they would "go forth dancing."

Q. Have you been frequently admitted into the presence of his majesty the King of Ava? — A. During my second residence in Ava, of five or six months, I saw his majesty almost every day. I sometimes saw him at his public levees, but at all times had free access to the palace, and have frequently conversed with the king on subjects of geography, religion, and history, for ten minutes or a quarter of an hour together. His majesty was incapable of giving his attention to any subject for a longer time.

Q. What is his majesty's personal appearance and character? — *A.* He is a man about forty years of age, of rather a dark complexion, and in person small and slender. His manners are graceful, and in public dignified. In private he is affable, and playful to boyishness. His disposition is obliging and liberal, and he is anxious to see every one around him happy. His mind is indolent, and he is incapable of any continued application. His time is passed in sensual enjoyment, in listening to music, or seeing dancing or theatrical entertainments; but, above all, in the company of his principal queen, to whom he is devoted even to infatuation. His personal activity is remarkable for an eastern prince, and scarcely a day passes that he does not go on the river in boats, or ride on horseback, or an elephant. He is partial to Europeans. No person of this description comes before him without receiving some marks of kindness. The safety of the European and American prisoners is chiefly to be ascribed to this partiality. His majesty is not bigoted to his own religion. From conversations which I had with him on religious subjects, I am inclined to think that he believes in the existence of one God eternal, which is not a part of the Buddhist religion; but, in truth, he is indifferent to all religions. I never saw him perform an act of devotion but once. A handsome image of Gautama stands in a recess in the audience chamber, before which, after the levee, many of the courtiers perform their devotions. His majesty never does, on such occasions; but one day, while I was in the audience chamber, alone, his majesty came walking in in his usual brisk and lively manner. He looked about him, and, appearing to have nothing else to do, knelt before the image, made a hasty prayer and obeisance to it, and jumped up again, proceeding straight to the stables to see his favorite horses fed.

Q. Have you ever been in the presence of her majesty the queen? — *A.* No, never. I was never presented to her majesty; but have seen her three or four times in the palace, passing and repassing. One day I was sitting in the hall of audience, when the king and queen came out together from the inner apartments: his majesty attempted to introduce me, saying "This is the teacher I mentioned to you;" but the queen looked another way, and would pay no attention, pulling the king along with her. She is much more haughty than his majesty; and her character in all other respects differs widely from his, for she is reported to be avaricious, vindictive, intriguing, and bigoted. She was the daughter of a petty officer, a superintendent of jails. She was first the king's concubine, when he was heir apparent. Her influence with his majesty is so unbounded, that the Prince of Sara-wadi and others of the royal family have convinced themselves that she is a sorceress. No one dares hint at the obscurity of her origin. She has convinced the king, in accordance with the doctrine of the transmigration of souls, implicitly believed by all the Burmans, that she was his chief queen in a former state of existence, and that for some peccadillo she was punished by a low birth.

Q. Is her majesty a woman of great personal charms?— *A.* She is about one year older than his majesty. Her face is not handsome, but her person is rather tall and well formed. Her manners are dignified and becoming her station.

Q. Has his majesty any family?— *A.* Yes; one son by his first queen, now about fifteen years of age, and a daughter by her present majesty, about four or five years old, the idol of her parents. When the queen experiences any difficulty in getting the request of a petition granted, the paper is put between the child's hands, and she is thrust in the king's way. This artifice never fails.

Q. Do you know any thing of the queen's brother?— *A.* Yes; I have been presented to him, and visited him in all, perhaps, half a dozen times; but he is of too haughty and reserved a disposition to encourage approach.

Q. What is the character of this person, and in what estimation is he held at court?— *A.* In character he bears a close resemblance to his sister. He is cruel, rapacious, and a great intriguer. He is in the entire confidence of his sister, and through her rules the kingdom. Since the death of the seah wonghee, he has no rival with the king, unless it be his majesty's favorite brother, the Prince of Sarawadi.

Q. You have stated that, shortly after the commencement of hostilities between the British and the Burman governments, you were imprisoned at Ava by the latter. — *A.* Yes.

Q. Were any grounds assigned for your imprisonment? — *A.* Nothing beyond its being stated that it was the will of the king.

Q. Were you ill treated in the act of being arrested? — *A.* Nothing perhaps beyond what is usual in similar cases. I was tightly bound with cords, and thrown down and struck with the knees and elbows in the act of being secured. The cords were so firmly bound round my arms that the skin was cut. By a bribe of ten ticals, the officers somewhat loosened the cords; and when I was brought before the governor of the town, or chief of the police, he reproved them for treating me so harshly.

Q. Were you put in irons? — *A.* Yes, immediately.

Q. What prison were you lodged in? — *A.* That in which all malefactors condemned to death are lodged.

Q. What description of persons were confined with you? — *Q.* Burman thieves and robbers; state prisoners; deserters from the army, of an aggravated description; a few prisoners of war taken from the British; and the different European gentlemen, like myself, arrested in Ava.

Q. How were you treated in prison? — *A.* At first with great severity; but after we had bribed the governor to the extent of about one hundred ticals each, and the jailers and other subordinate officers in proportion, we were treated with more lenity.

Q. What sort of severity was exercised towards you at first? — *A.* We were placed in the inner prison, and put in a sort of stocks, forbid a mat or pillows to sleep on, as well as all intercourse with our friends.

Q. Were you allowed food or clothing by the government while in prison? — *A.* No, never. No prisoners are fed by the government. They must starve unless supplied by their friends. An exception was sometimes made in favor of British prisoners of war. The king ordered each a basket of rice a month — fifty-six pounds; but they never got one half of it.

Q. How long did you continue in the prison at Ava? — *A.* Eleven months — nine months with three pairs of irons on, and two with five.

Q. Where were you imprisoned after being liberated from your incarceration at Ava? — *A.* I was sent, along with the other European prisoners arrested, to a place about ten miles from Ava, and four from Amarapura, called Aongbenlé, and there imprisoned.

Q. What was the cause of your removal to Aongbenlé? — *A.* It was generally stated, and believed, that the American and European prisoners were removed to that place for the purpose of being put to death, as a kind of sacrifice, previous to the pakan-wun taking the field against the English.

Q. Who was this pakan-wun? — *A.* An officer raised to the rank of wonghee, and placed in the command of the army upon the death of Bandula, and the failure of the other chiefs who had acted against the English.

Q. Were you personally acquainted with him? — *A.* I had met him occasionally in the palace, and saw him for a few days in the same prison with myself, during a short confinement, when he had incurred the temporary displeasure of the king.

Q. You state that it was intended to put you and the other prisoners to death; what do you suppose was the reason that this intention was not put in execution? — *A.* The intention of putting us to death was at the instigation of the pakan-wun. This person, after being about a month or six weeks in power, fell into disgrace, was charged with treasonable practices, and executed at an hour's notice. The idea of putting us to death was then dropped.

Q. What character did the pakan-wun bear? — *A.* Of all the chiefs of rank, I think he was the worst man.

Q. Was the intention of putting you to death entertained at any other time than the occasion now alluded to? — *A.* We were assured that the queen's brother had given orders several times to have us secretly executed.

Q. How do you consider that you escaped on these occasions? — *A.* The governor refused to execute the order without the express consent of the king. He hinted it to myself in prison, and told Mrs. Judson and the wife of Mr. Rodgers so, more explicitly.

Q. Were the prisoners' properties confiscated? — *A.* They were seized with a view to confiscation, but not formally confiscated. I afterwards received the value of what was taken from me, at the instigation of the British commissioners.

Q. How did the natives of Hindostan in your employ behave to you during your imprisonment? — *A.* I had two Mohammedan natives of Bengal, who adhered to me faithfully throughout.

Q. Do you know any thing of a Mohammedan native of Bengal, a baker, in the service of Mr. Gouger, one of your fellow-prisoners? — *A.* His conduct was beyond all praise. He adhered to his master at the risk of threats and punishment, and often fed him from his own labor.

Q. Were your Indian servants imprisoned? — *A.* They were confined to the house for a few days, and afterwards liberated, and allowed to attend upon us.

Q. How many native officers of the British army were confined with you? — *A.* Seven or eight.

Q. What has become of those persons? — *A.* They all died in the prison, but one.

Q. What was the cause of their death? — *A.* The want of a regular supply of food. Sometimes they were two or three days without food. When they were supplied, they ate to excess, which brought on bowel complaints, that proved fatal to them.

Q. Do you know what has become of the bulk of the

sepoys of the British army taken prisoners by the Burmans? — *A*. They were sent to a place called Monai, in the country of the Shans, which I suppose to be not less than two hundred miles from Ava. I was informed, before leaving Ava, that, on the demand of the British commissioners, they were ordered back, for the purpose of being delivered up.

Q. What was the reason of their being sent to so great a distance? — *A*. The government, on the advance of the British army, was apprehensive that the prisoners might make a disturbance, and therefore sent them off for security.

Q. Have you read over the depositions which you have made before me, and which I handed over for your perusal? — *A*. Yes.

Q. Are they correctly recorded? — *A*. I have made two or three slight alterations with my pen, and they are now correct.

Q. Are you prepared to swear to them on oath? — *A*. In answer to this question, I beg to explain, that I object, from religious motives, to taking an oath on any occasion. For fifteen years, and since entering upon my present calling, I have not taken an oath. I do not object, however, to making a solemn affirmation of the truth of what I have deposed before you, and beg leave to say, that such affirmation was received from me, in lieu of an oath, by Governor Farquhar, of the Mauritius, in the year 1813.

A. JUDSON, JR.

D.

The following tract has been frequently alluded to in the preceding Memoir. Its circulation has produced great effect on the Buddhist population.

THE GOLDEN BALANCE, TRANSLATED FROM THE BURMAN.

In the time of the prophet Elijah, a thousand years before the manifestation of the Lord Jesus Christ, the Israelites were divided, some worshipping the Eternal, and some worshipping the god Baal. Upon this, Elijah taught the religion of the Eternal, in an assembly of priests and people, and said, "Ye men of Israel, how long halt ye between two opinions? If the Eternal be God, worship him, but if Baal be God, worship him." In like manner the teacher desires to say, Ye Talings and Burmans, how long halt ye between two opinions? If the Eternal be God, worship him; but if Gaudama be God, worship him.

If we desire to know which of two religions is the true one, there is a way of knowing. How shall we know? *The excellent is the true.* The king, for instance, is the most excellent. If we found a person more glorious than he whom we had esteemed the king, we should have to conclude that he whom we had esteemed the king was not the king, but only a tributary prince, or perhaps a rebel; and that the more excellent personage only was the king. So in the case of God. The Supreme, the most excellent of beings, only deserves to be called God. If we should find a being greater or more excellent than he whom we have esteemed God, we must conclude that he whom we first esteemed God is not God, and that the greater, the more excellent being, alone is God. In regard to the law of God, and the ministers of God, the same mode of reasoning holds good.

If, therefore, we desire to know whether the religion of Jesus Christ, or the religion of Gaudama, is the true one, we must first inquire which has the more excellent God.

Do you think that Gaudama is the most excellent, who was possessed of divinity forty-five years? Or is the Eternal the more excellent, who is possessed of divinity without beginning or end, through the endless duration of successive ages?

Do you think that Gaudama is the more excellent, who being in time past, by his own nature, a sinner, and subject to transmigration, has been a quail, a monkey, and all other brute creatures; has suffered hell beyond all calculation; was obliged to perform the greatest austerities to expiate his sins in a small degree; and though at last, for a time, he obtained divinity, could not get free from the consequences of his own sin, but had to endure the sixteen great results of guilt, even while he was deity? Or is the Eternal the more excellent, who, through time present, past, and future, is never subject to illness, old age, or death, but, being possessed of endless life, enjoys, without intermixture of misery, the pure wealth and happiness of Deity?

Do you think that Gaudama is the more excellent, who, being afraid to encounter the results of guilt, and in order to avoid them, forsook the whole creation, and destroying his own body and soul, plunged into the utter perdition of nigban, whence, through all future ages, he will never emerge to life; where he can confer no favor, can save no creature, can enjoy no happiness, and cannot ever come to light, or ever more appear? Or is the Eternal the more excellent, who, being possessed of an eternal nature, exists unchangeable, indestructible, through endless ages?

Do you think that Gaudama is the more excellent, who, though his disciples have promoted him to the supremacy, was of the race of the Hindoos' black Ku-lahs * within the sixteen

---

* The strength of this piece consists in ascribing nothing to Gaudama and his religion, but what the Burmese generally know and acknowledge, though some of the expressions are rather more plain and glaring than they are accustomed to. The position, however, that

countries of India, not the best, but rather a degenerate part of this, the Zam-poo-deep continent, which itself is not the centre and crown of the universe, but situated below the twenty superior and the six inferior heavens, at the edge of the universe, a vile region, full of iniquity, and inhabited by dark sinners? Or is the Eternal the more excellent, who, in virtue of his own nature, is the supreme God, dwelling in the highest heaven, the summit of the universe?

Do you think that Gaudama is the more excellent, who was possessed of no creative power, but, when his disciples inquired about the origin of creatures, was obliged to say that the beginning of transmigratory existence did not appear; who, not to speak of the worlds that are past, appeared as God when this world had been long extant; who, though appearing as a god, had no sovereign authority, but was merely a teacher of religion, with no control over other creatures, with no control over his own life, unable to cope with the king of death, but obliged to follow at his call, and who was the subject of fate from his mother's womb, through his whole existence? Or is he the more excellent, who, being the creator of all worlds, and all beings, is the Lord of life; and who, seated on the summit of heaven, the throne of Deity, rules and reigns throughout universal nature, the Controller of fate, the Monarch of futurity, the eternal God?

Do you think that Gaudama is the more excellent, with whom Kau-ku-than, Gau-nah-gong, Kkah-thah-bah, and many great devotees that have passed, numerous as the sands of the Ganges, can compare, and with whom an innumerable multitude of devotees, that are yet to come, will be able to compare? Or is the one sole Eternal the more excellent, with whom there is none comparable, in time present, past, or future, but who is without a rival, transcendently superior to all beings?

Gaudama was a black Ku-lah, is one exception; and it has been adopted because of its peculiar force, the Burmese all feeling that the black Ku-lahs are inferior to themselves, and because, though the position is rather new and startling, it is seldom objected to, and never disputed.

Do you think that Gaudama is the more excellent, who died saying, "I will take nigban," but gave no proof that he did so; of whose death there were many witnesses, but of whose taking nigban there are none, and who from the day that his breath stopped to the present time has never been able to give any sign or proof that he has actually taken nigban, and is not in confinement for transgressing against the eternal God? Or is Jesus Christ the more excellent, who, though possessed of divine nature, assumed human nature with the name Jesus Christ, in order to save creatures; who, while free from sin himself, laid down his life to expiate the sins of others, rose again from the dead on the third day, and having showed himself for forty days, ascended to heaven, his original abode, in the presence of his disciples, with his holy spiritual body; and who instantly despatched two angels with a celestial communication to his disciples, that, as he had thus visibly ascended, he would again descend, and thereby gave credible proof that he is now actually in the summit of heaven?

Do you think that the substitute of Gaudama is the more excellent, a lifeless, soulless idol, or pagoda? Or is the substitute agent of the Eternal the more excellent, who imparts the celestial conception, the second birth, and dwells in the hearts of his disciples, dispelling doubt, revealing truth, and producing holiness and joy; the third in the three, the Father, the Son, and the Holy Spirit, who unitedly are the one God — the inward Witness, the spiritual Guide, (Comforter,) the divine Spirit?

O ye Talings and Burmans! If ye desire to know which of these two Gods is the more excellent, only open your eyes, and look.

Let us now proceed to compare the two systems of law

The fundamental commands of Gaudama are five, viz.: Kill not. Steal not. Commit not adultery. Lie not. Drink not intoxicating liquor. Do you think that such a defective system is the more excellent, whose commands relate only to outward deeds and words, but not to the thoughts, remove not the root of sin, and comprise not all other commands? Or is the perfect law the more excellent, which says, Love God with all thy heart, and love others as thyself — commands which take cognizance of the thoughts, effectually strike at the root of sin, and comprise all other possible commands?

Which is the more estimable to sinners, a punishing system or a pardoning system? Do you think that the system is the more excellent which says, As the wheel follows the track of the ox, so punishment follows sin, and whoever sins, it is his concern? Or is the joyful news of the gospel the more excellent, which reveals the grace of the Lord Jesus Christ, the Son of God, how he pitied mankind, and took their place, in order to make atonement for their sins, and laid down his life for all who would believe?

Since the most excellent system of religion will impart the most excellent benefits, let us inquire which system imparts the more excellent benefits, the system of Gaudama, or the system of Jesus Christ?

Do you think that the benefits imparted by Gaudama's system, the happiness enjoyed by men, nats, and Brah-mahs, the more excellent, characterized as it is by "mutability, pain, and inanity," and therefore not permanent, not free from sin and guilt, but tending merely to increase the heat of hell fire? Not to speak of ordinary happiness — do you think that the superlative happiness of Tah-wa-ting-thah, the world of nats, deserves to be called excellent, happiness which the nats and the nattesses enjoy four months in the year, while surrounding the Pen-lay-ka-that tree, sprawling about in a state of intoxication? O ye Talings and Burmans! if ye desire to be intoxicated four months in the year, around the Pen-lay-ka-that tree, and afterwards pass through the four states of punishment, be diligent in performing the religious offerings and duties prescribed by the law of Gaudama; or if not so disposed, do you think the other benefit imparted by Gaudama's system is the more excellent, the benefit of nigban, which consists in that frightful, discreditable annihilation which one attains, who, being wearied of worldly enjoyments, and afraid of the fire of hell, desires to kill, not the life of his body merely, but the life of his soul; and not satisfied with temporary death, but eagerly coveting permanent death, performs the duties of Rahandah, and becomes lost in the utter perdition of nigban, where, being lost, he knows not that he is lost, and therefore derives no benefit, and can never make his appearance again through endless ages?

In regard to the benefits imparted by the system of Jesus Christ, his disciples are not only, as mentioned above, freed from the punishment of sin and all the results of guilt, but in the next state they instantly come into the presence of God, in heaven, where perfectly performing the commands of holiness, which require them to love God with all the heart, and to love others as themselves, and placed beyond the possibility of a change as it respects their pure and holy nature, they drink the nectar of immortality, become exempt from illness, old age, death, transmigration, annihilation, and all other evils, and being possessed of immutability, pleasure, and substantiality, enjoy permanent, celestial happiness through the successive ages of endless duration. And is not this happiness the most excellent of all?

As to religion in general — does that religion appear to be true which receives the approbation, and praise, and support of those who are thieves and robbers; those who are intoxicated with worldly wealth and fame; those who, relying on their official authority, are full of pride; those who wallow in the mud of lust; those who seek their own profit only, destitute of truth and virtue; and, in a word, all classes of time-servers? Or does that religion appear to be true which receives the approbation, and praise, and support of those only who comply not with the desires of the flesh, follow not the customs of the world, avoid all sin, and delight themselves in upright, holy conduct?

Does that religion appear to be true which could subsist only under the patronage of worldly government, and being unable to sustain persecution, perished out of all the sixteen countries of India; and subsequently, in foreign countries, can subsist only by means of the authoritative protection of kings? Or does that religion appear to be true which endured the persecution of successive governments for three hundred years after the era of its founder, but incapable of being destroyed, continued to increase by the power of God, and down to the present time proves to be able to sustain itself independent of secular support?

Does that religion appear to be the more excellent which has been gradually declining, is now near extinction, and will ere long become utterly extinct, even as Gaudama himself has attained the extinction of nigban? Or is that religion the more excellent, which from day to day has been increasing, and at the present time, in the near approach of the millennial era, when the disciples are making extraordinary efforts, is beginning to take root in the various countries where it had not been previously established, and will eventually overwhelm and sweep away all other religions, and be established throughout the whole world, and endure forevermore, even as Jesus Christ cannot become extinct, but will endure forever?

Since scriptures that are really excellent will be furnished with credible testimony, let us inquire whether the scriptures of the Be-ta-gat are furnished with credible testimony, or the Scriptures of truth.

Do you think those scriptures the more credible which were written by men who were not the personal disciples of the Lord of the Scriptures, nor even contemporary with him, nor even acquainted with his disciples, nor even acquainted with those who were acquainted with them, but appeared four hundred and fifty-eight years after the Lord of the Scriptures was no more? Or are those scriptures the more credible which were written by the personal disciples of the Lord of the Scriptures, according to what they saw with their own eyes, and heard with their own ears?

Do you think the words of those persons the more credible, who, in the affair of writing their scriptures, obtained worldly fame and worldly profit? Or are the words of the twelve apostles the more credible, who, in the affair of writing their scriptures, endured, one after another, persecution and death?

Do you think that the Be-ta-gat is credible, which contradicts the testimony of eye witnesses who cross the seas? Not to discuss many points, let us touch upon five.

Is the Be-ta-gat credible, which asserts that the Zam-poo-deep (the eastern) continent is ten thousand yoo-ja-nas across, when the ships of England, France, and America have repeatedly encompassed it, and ascertained beyond a doubt that its length is six hundred yoo-ja-nas only, and its breadth three hundred and fifty!

Is it credible that there is in the centre of India a banian tree replete with all the wonders which are stated in the Be-ta-gat, when the English rulers who now control the sixteen countries of India, from Arracan and the Ganges on the east to Persia and the Indus on the west, have never, in searching and rummaging all the towns, and villages, and spots of the whole country, discovered any such banian, or even heard of it?

Do you think the Be-ta-gat credible, which states the eugenia tree, on the northern side of the eastern continent, to be one hundred yoo-ja-nas in height, double the distance between Rangoon and Ava, when Russian and other vessels are continually passing from place to place, on the northern side of the Zam-poo-deep continent, and have never discovered any such wonderful tree, or even heard of it?

Do you think the Be-ta-gat credible, which describes the Myeen-mo Mount and the four great continents, when there are before our eyes two great continents, western, called America, seven hundred yoo-ja-nas long and two hundred and fifty broad, and the eastern, called Zam-poo-deep, six hundred and fifty yoo-ja-nas long and three hundred and fifty broad?

Do you think the Be-ta-gat credible, which describes the seven encircling seas, and the seven encircling mountains, and a great many other strange things, to make people wonder, when ships, on arriving under the North Star, find no Yoo-zan-do Mount, descry no Myeen-mo Mount, nor any thing extraordinary, nothing being there but the little Island of Spitzbergen? * Or are the Scriptures of truth credible, which contain nothing that is contradicted by present testimony?

In comparing the two orders of the priesthood, we will, for fear of being tedious, touch upon three points only.

Do you think those teachers the more excellent who examine not other scriptures; who know not whether their religions are better or worse than their own; who do not even know how many prevailing religions there are in the world; who have neither travelled in foreign countries nor listened to foreign intelligence, but cherishing the idea, "many lents much wisdom," obstinately hold the religion of their ancestors, and though apprised of the superiority of another, reject it perforce? Or are those teachers the more excellent who depend not on the religion of their ancestors, regard not their own character, fear not to be called heretics, but search for wisdom, and examine various religions, rejecting the false and choosing the true?

Do you think those teachers the more excellent, who, full of pride, exalt themselves above other people, applying the superior personal pronoun to themselves, and requiring others to do them homage, and address them by divine appellations? Or are those teachers the more excellent, who, though they know the truth, are penitent and humble?

Do you think those teachers the more excellent, who, while they say with the mouth that they love and pity their fellow-creatures, not only never go to foreign countries to propagate their religion, but never preach even to their own countrymen, but only when they are respectfully invited, and paid, in religious offerings, the wages of preaching; and who, when they do preach, display no strength of mind or power of eloquence, but repeat like a parrot what they have committed to memory?

---

* It is generally understood by the Burmans that the North Star is suspended over the pinnacle of the celestial palace, in the centre of the Myeen-mo Mount.

Or are those teachers the more excellent, who, from motives of love and compassion, forsake their own country, and pass to foreign lands, where, having labored to acquire a new language, they lift up the lamp of truth among a people dwelling in darkness, and though that people, untouched by gratitude, revile, contradict, and persecute them, are yet not discouraged, but go about from place to place, alluring and persuading to salvation those who can be saved; and who, though their hearts are ready to break at the remembrance of their own country, and their country people, yet flinch not, retract not, but spend their whole life unto death in the foreign country, actually laying down their lives, not for their own profit, but for the profit of others?

O ye Talings and Burmans! if, through fear that your dark neighbors will revile you, you dare not open both eyes, do pray open one eye the breadth of a hair, and, from pity to yourselves, take one look.

THE GOLDEN BALANCE IN PEGUAN.

Since these Notes [*] were in course of preparation, a middle-aged man, of sober aspect and respectable appearance, came to the pastor of the church to ask for baptism. He spoke the Burmese imperfectly, and it was soon ascertained that he was a Peguan, from the vicinity of Bangkok, in Siam.

"Why do you wish to be baptized?" inquired the pastor.

"I believe in the Lord Jesus Christ; and I wish to enter his religion, and obey his commands."

"How do you know that this is one of his commands?"

"I have read about it in the Book of Truth."

"How did you first become acquainted with the religion of Jesus Christ?"

"Before I came to this region, a countryman of mine chanced

[*] Notes to the Memoir of Mrs. Sarah B. Judson.

to mention a wonderful little book, which a foreign teacher at Bangkok had given him; and I had the curiosity to procure and read it. I have never worshipped an idol since."

"Indeed! What book was it?"

"The Golden Balance."

The conversation for several moments ceased; for the wheel of time was thrown back too suddenly to admit of any concealment of emotion. The translation of the Golden Balance was one of the earliest of Mrs. Judson's efforts in the Peguan; and the stranger, unconsciously, sat beneath the very roof where she had toiled for his salvation. There had the fingers, now mouldering in a distant grave, given wings to the precious seed, which floated away over vale and mountain, river and woodland, to drop into the soil prepared for it by the Holy Spirit.

After due examination, and the usual preliminaries, the man was admitted to baptism; and the ordinance was administered close beside her former home. The Peguan translator she so often mentions, now a thin, pale, stooping old man, appearing always in russet tunic and sombre-hued waist-cloth, looked on at the scene; and the duty was performed by the hands she would have chosen above all others for administering this sacred rite to one of her spiritual children; but she, who would have been the most joyful of all the spectators, was not there. The bristling pines of the north shake their tasselled branches above the snows of her fathers' home; and the crested hoopoo bird, seeking the golden banana and white flowering cocoa of the south, wings its way across her children's graves; while far away from either scene, upon a rock-bound island, which never felt the pressure of her tread, she is left to her lonely sleep. But by the labor of her hand and pen — by the labor of her lips, engraved on many a throbbing heart — by her prayers — and by the fragrance that clings about her memory, she is living and laboring still.

E.

THE THREEFOLD CORD.

ECCLES. iv. 12.

Written by a Missionary in Burmah.

You hope, my dear brother, that you have repented of sin, and put your trust in the Lord Jesus Christ. You now desire, above all things, to grow in grace, and attain the perfect love and enjoyment of God. But you find yourself perplexed about the way, amidst the various directions of various classes of the Christian world; and you ask for a short manual of advice, plain to the understanding, and convincing to the heart. I present you, therefore, with *the threefold cord*. Lay hold of it with the hand of faith, and be assured that it will draw thy soul to God and to heaven.

The first is the cord of *Secret Prayer*. Without this the others have no strength. Secret prayer is commonly considered a duty which must be performed every morning and evening, in order to keep a conscience void of offence. But do not, my dear brother, entertain an opinion so defective. Consider secret prayer as one of the three great works of thy life. Arrange thy affairs, if possible, so that thou canst leisurely devote two or three hours every day, not merely to devotional exercises, but to the very act of secret prayer and communion with God. Endeavor, seven times a day, to withdraw from business and company, and lift up thy soul to God in private retirement. Begin the day by rising after midnight, and devoting some time, amid the silence and darkness of the night, to this sacred work. Let the hour of opening dawn find thee at the same work; let the hours of nine, twelve, three, six, and nine at night witness the same. Be resolute in this course. Make all practicable sacrifices to maintain it. Consider that thy time is short, and that business and company must not be allowed to rob thee of thy God. At least, remember the morning, noon, and night seasons, and the season after midnight, if not detrimental to thy health.

Dost thou ask how to pray? There is One who is able and willing to teach thee. Whenever thou intendest to pray, draw towards Calvary; kneel at the foot of the mount; lift up thine eyes, tremblingly and in tears, to thine incarnate God and Saviour dying on the cross; confess that thou art the guilty cause; implore his forgiveness; and believe me, my dear brother, that the Holy Spirit will quickly come and teach thee how to pray.

The second is the cord of *Self-denial* — rough, indeed, to the hand of sense, and so abused in the Roman Catholic church, that Protestants have become afraid of it, and thrown it away. But lay hold, my brother, with the hand of faith. It is one of the three; and without it the other two, although they may do some service, will not have firmness and consistency.

It is an acknowledged principle, that every faculty of the body and mind is strengthened and improved by use, weakened and impaired by disuse. It is needless to produce proofs or illustrations; they are to be met with in every day's experience. Self-love, or the desire of self-gratification in the enjoyment of the riches, the honors, and the pleasures of this world, is the ruling principle of fallen man. In the new-born soul this principle, though wounded to death, still lives. And the more it is indulged, the stronger it becomes. But

> "The love of God flows just as much
>   As that of ebbing self subsides;
> Our hearts, their scantiness is such,
>   Cannot sustain two rival tides.
> Both cannot govern in one soul;
>   Then let self-love be dispossessed;
> The love of God deserves the whole,
>   Nor will she dwell with such a guest."

And the way to dispossess self-love is to cease indulging it; to regard and treat self as an enemy, a vicious animal, for instance, whose propensities are to be thwarted, whose indulgences are to be curtailed, as far as can be done, consistently with his utmost serviceableness; or, in the language of Scripture, to deny self, and take up the cross daily; to keep under the body, and bring it into subjection; to mortify the members which are upon the earth; to cease from loving the world and the things of the world.

Alas for those whose days are spent in pampering their bodies, under the idea of preserving their life and health; who toil to lay up treasures upon earth, under the idea of providing for their children; who conform to the fashions of the world, under the idea of avoiding pernicious singularity; who use every means to maintain their character and extend their reputation, under the idea of gaining more influence, and thereby capacity for serving the cause! How can such enter the kingdom of heaven? "Strait is the gate, and narrow is the way, that leadeth unto life; and few there be that find it." Wouldst thou, my brother, belong to the happy few? Wouldst thou subdue that inordinate self-love which has hitherto shut out the love of God from thy heart, and impeded thy progress in the heavenly way? Adopt a course of daily, habitual self-denial. Cease gratifying thy appetite; be content with the plainest diet; reject what most pampers the palate; fast often; keep thy body under. Cease adorning thy person; dress in coarse and poor apparel; discard all finery; cut off the supplies of vanity and pride. Occupy a poor habitation; suffer inconveniences, yea, prefer them ever to slothful ease and carnal indulgence. Allow no amusements; turn away thine eyes from the pleasant sights, and thine ears from the pleasant sounds, of this vain world. Engage in no conversation, read no book, that interrupts thy communion with God; nor indeed any that has not a devotional tendency, unless it be necessary in thy calling. Get rid of the encumbrance of worldly property; sell what thou hast, and give to the poor, especially those who are in spiritual poverty. As to character, that last idol and most deadly tyrant of poor fallen man, follow the advice of that eminent saint, Archbishop

Leighton: "Choose always, to the best of thy skill, what is most to God's honor, and most like unto Christ and his example, and most profitable to thy neighbor, and most against thy own proper will, and least serviceable to thy own praise and exaltation." And again: "Not only be content, but desirous, to be unknown, or, being known, to be contemned and despised of all men, yet without thy faults or deservings, as much as thou canst."* Finally, renounce all terms with this world, which lieth in the arms of the wicked one; renounce all thy worldly projects and pursuits, except what is absolutely necessary for thine own sustenance and that of those dependent on thee; avoid, as much as possible, the contaminating touch of worldly things; and by shutting the avenues of thy soul against the solicitations of the lust of the flesh, the lust of the eyes, and the pride of life, endeavor to weaken that deadly and tremendous influence which the world has gained over thee, and of which thou art scarcely suspicious.† And when thou hast done all thou canst, remember that on account of the hesitation with which thou didst admit the light; the reluctance with which thou didst enter on thy duty; the carnal reasonings which at every step thou hast indulged; the readiness which thou hast sometimes felt to give up the effort; and the unfaithfulness which has marred, the sin which has polluted, thy best performances, — thou deservest nothing but hell.

Art thou ready, on reading these pages, to say in despair

---

* See *Rules and Instructions for a Holy Life*, a piece, which, though not elaborately finished, contains the very marrow of true religion. Study also Law's *Treatise upon Christian Perfection*, and Kempis's *Imitation of Christ*.

† To guard against extremes, take the two following short rules: 1st. Avoid such privations and severities as do really injure thy bodily health. 2d. Avoid affected singularities in dress and deportment, which only cherish pride; and while thou aimest to be poor and mortified in all outward things, still retain the garb and costume of thy country, and respect those national usages which are common to the high and the low, the rich and the poor, unless there be some special reason for a change.

Alas for me! bound by a thousand chains, and loaded with a thousand burdens, how can I ever live a holy life of self-denial? Remember that there is One who is able and willing to help thee. It is commonly, if not always, the case with young converts, that the Holy Spirit draws them towards the path of self-denial. We can all, perhaps, remember the time when we had such a sense of our unworthiness, that we were desirous of denying ourselves of every indulgence; when we had such a sense of the danger of temptation, and the dreadful power of sin, that we were willing to renounce all things, in order to .ive a holy life. But in the Protestant church, we were frightened by the phantoms of Romish austerities, self inflicted mortifications, overmuch righteousness, religious enthusiasm, &c.; we shut our eyes to the dawning light, turned away our ears from the heavenly call, the Spirit ceased to strive, and we have been swept away with the tide.

Return, O mistaken soul, to thy first love. God is still waiting to be gracious. Dost thou not feel a latent impulse, as thou readest these lines? a secret conviction that this is the truth? an incipient desire to comply? Yield thyself to the heavenly influence. Make an immediate beginning. Wait not till thou seest the whole path clearly illumined; expect not meridian brightness, while thy sun is yet struggling with the dark, malignant vapors which rest on thy earthly horizon, the confines of a still darker world. The path of self-denial is, to carnal eyes, a veiled path, a mystery of the divine kingdom. While thou hesitatest at the first sacrifice required, expect no further admonition, no further light. But if thou wilt do what thy hands find to do this hour, if thou wilt, in childlike simplicity and humble obedience, take the first step, thou shalt see the second, which now thou seest not; and as thou advancest, thou shalt find the path of self-denial open most wonderfully and delightfully before thee; thou shalt find it sweet to follow thy dear Lord and Saviour, bearing the cross, and shalt soon be enabled to say,—

> "Sweet is the cross, above all sweets,
> To souls enamoured with thy smiles."

The third is the cord of *Doing good*. This imparts beauty and utility to the rest. It is written of the Lord Jesus, that *he went about doing good*. Art thou his disciple? Imitate his example, and go about doing good. Do GOOD. Let this be thy motto. Do good — all the good in thy power — of every sort — and to every person. Regard every human being as thine own brother; look with eyes of love on every one thou meetest, and hope that he will be thy loving and beloved companion in the bright world above. Rejoice in every opportunity of doing him any good, either of a temporal or spiritual kind. Comfort him in trouble; relieve his wants; instruct his ignorance; enlighten his darkness; warn him of his danger; show him the way of salvation; persuade and constrain him to become thy fellow-traveller in that blessed way. Follow him with all offices of kindness and love, even as thou wouldst be pleased to have another do to thee. Bear with all his infirmities. Be not weary in well doing. Remember that thy Saviour bore long with thee, and is still bearing with thee, beyond all conception, and covering thy pollution with the robe stained with his own blood, that the wrath of God may not strike thee. And when he thus forgives thine immense debt, canst thou not bear with thy fellow-debtor?

Do good to the Lord thy Saviour. Is he far beyond thy reach? True, he reigns on high; but still he lives in all his members. "Inasmuch as ye have done it unto one of the least of these my brethren, ye have done it unto me." As thou hast, therefore, opportunity, do good unto all men, especially unto them who are of the household of faith. As a true follower of Christ, seek not thine own profit, but the profit of many, that they may be saved. Since Christ has suffered, that whosoever believeth on him should not perish, but have eternal life, extend thy good wishes to earth's remotest bounds; and wherever a human being exists, let thy prayers and thine efforts combine to bring down eternal blessings on his beloved soul But let the members of the household of faith, whatever be their language, country, or religious denomination, share in thy warmest love. Regard each one as a part of thine own dear Saviour; and be as happy to wash his feet as if they were the feet of thy Lord himself. Remember that, notwithstanding present imperfections, ye are hastening to be united to one another, and to God, in a manner most ineffable, even as God is in Christ, and Christ in God; that the bosom of infinite love is even now opening to receive you all, and that ye will all bathe together, for endless ages, in "that sea of life and love unknown, without a bottom or a shore."

By practising self-denial, thou weakenest the debasing principle of inordinate self-love; and by doing good, thou cherishest and strengthenest the heavenly principle of holy benevolence. Let these exercises, then, quickened and sanctified by secret prayer, be the regular work of each day of thy life.

Thus I present thee, my brother, with the threefold cord — the three grand means of growing in grace — of gaining the victory over the world, the flesh, and the devil — of drawing the soul from earth to heaven. Means, I say; for I speak not now of faith, the living operative principle within — the hand, with which thou must lay hold of the threefold cord. Wilt thou accept my present? Art thou inclined to lay hold? Cherish the Heaven-born inclination. It is worth more to thee than all the treasures of the earth. Go into thy place of prayer, stretch out the hand of faith, and implore the Holy Spirit, who is even now hovering over thee, to strengthen thee to lay hold for life. Dost thou hesitate? O my brother, do not, I beseech thee. O, do not grieve the Holy Spirit. Disappoint not the fond hopes of thy longing Saviour. Renounce the world, renounce thyself, and flee into his loving arms, which are open to receive and embrace thee. Angels will rejoice over thy second conversion, as they did over thy first. Thou wilt soon find such sweetness as thou hast never yet conceived. Thou wilt begin to live in a new world, to breathe a new atmosphere, and to behold the light of heaven shining around thee; and thou wilt begin to love the Lord thy God in a new manner, when he is "pacified towards thee, for all that thou hast done."

Postscript.

In taking leave of thee, my brother, the thought occurs, that, notwithstanding thy prevailing hope, thou mayst yet have fearful doubts about thy spiritual state, and mayst think that thou hast not yet the hand of faith, with which to lay hold of what I send thee. And I fancy I hear thee cry, What shall I do? Art thou *sensible* of thy maimed state? Then there is some hope. *Do what thou canst:* stretch out what thou hast, however maimed or withered, and try to lay hold. Try to pray in faith, to practise self-denial, and to do good. And be assured, my brother, that thou wilt quickly find the hand of faith where thou thoughtest it was not. There is one near thee, whom yet thou knowest not — He who gave sight to blind Bartimeus, and said to the deaf man, Ephphatha, Be opened; He who heareth the young ravens when they cry, and much more, the cry of man, the dearest of all his creatures; He, who is ever moved with the yearning feelings of a tender parent, when he sees, at a distance, his poor prodigal son returning, famished and forlorn, from the far country.

MIZAR, February 1829.

F.

A BURMAN LITURGY, TRANSLATED INTO ENGLISH.

Homage to the Triune God.

THE Father divine we worship. The Son divine we worship. The Spirit divine we worship. These Three in union, the one sole God, we worship.

The Commands of Righteousness.

1. Love God with all the soul.
2. Love others as thyself.

The Commands of Grace.

1. Repent of thy sins.
2. Believe in the Lord Jesus Christ.

Formulas of Worship.

1. The God without beginning or end, who, free from infirmity, old age, death, transmigration, and annihilation, lives and is permanent during the endless successions of ages, we worship.

2. The self-existent God, who, independent of the influence of good and evil destiny, is possessed of perfections immutable, we worship.

3. The incorporeal, spiritual God, who, beyond the reach of wonder, unites the Father, the Son, and the Holy Spirit, Three in One, we worship.

4. The God, who, dwelling in heaven, by the visible display of his glory is still omnipresent; who knows all things, by omniscience; who can do all things by omnipotence; and who forever enjoys the unmixed, unchangeable, indestructible happiness of Deity, we worship.

5. The God who, free from all darkness and depravity, is perfectly holy and good, all whose deeds are righteous; who feels tenderly compassionate towards all creatures, and desires to make them happy; who, in order to display his perfections and promote the happiness of intelligent beings, has created this system, the heaven and earth, and all things; and who, being the Creator of all, is the sovereign Lord of all, with right to do his own pleasure in all things, we worship.

6. The God who loves righteousness and rewards the righteous; who hates unrighteousness, and punishes the unrighteous; but who, though punishing, pities, and is desirous of bearing with sinners and saving them, so far as may be consistent with the law of righteousness, we worship.

7. The God who pitied the sinful race of man, and sent his only, beloved Son into the world, to save from sin and hell; who also sends the Holy Spirit to enable those to become disciples who were chosen before the world was, and given to the Son, we worship.

8. The God who, with incomparable wisdom, educes good from evil; who is worthy to be worshipped and loved by all intelligent beings; who, as the sun by his rays enlightens the whole world, so, by the light of his countenance diffused abroad, makes the inhabitants of heaven, and all holy beings, joyful and happy, we most reverently worship. Amen.

A Creed, in Twelve Articles; or, A Summary of the Doctrine of the Lord Jesus Christ.

ART. I. There is one only permanent God, possessed of all incomprehensible perfections, eternal, almighty, omniscient, the Creator of all worlds and all things.

ART. II. There are two volumes of the Scriptures of truth, — the Scriptures of the old dispensation, in thirty-nine books, and the Scriptures of the new dispensation, in twenty-seven books, — written under the inspiration of God, by prophets and apostles, the recipients of divine communications.

Art. III. According to the Scriptures, man, at the beginning, was made upright and holy; but listening to the devil, he transgressed the divine commands, and fell from his good estate; in consequence of which, the original pair, with all their posterity, contracted a depraved, sinful nature, and became deserving of hell.

Art. IV. God, originally knowing that mankind would fall and be ruined, did, of his mercy, select some of the race, and give them to his Son, to save from sin and hell.

Art. V. The Son of God, according to his engagement to save the elect, was, in the fulness of time, conceived by the power of God, in the womb of the virgin Mary, in the country of Judea and land of Israel, and thus uniting the divine and human natures, he was born as man; and being the Saviour Messiah, (Jesus Christ,) he perfectly obeyed the law of God, and then laid down his life for man, in the severest agonies of crucifixion, by which he made an atonement for all who are willing to believe.

Art. VI. The Lord Jesus Christ rose from the dead on the third day, and having continued on earth forty days, he ascended to heaven, bodily and visibly, before his disciples; and there he remains in the presence of God the Father.

Art. VII. In order to obtain salvation, we must believe in the Lord Jesus Christ, and become his disciples, receiving a change of nature, through regeneration, by the power of the Spirit.

Art. VIII. Those who become disciples obtain the pardon of their sins through the cross of Christ; and being united to him by faith, his righteousness is imputed to them, and they become entitled to the eternal happiness of heaven.

Art. IX. Disciples, therefore, though they may not in this world be perfectly free from the old nature, do not completely fall away; but through the sustaining grace of the Spirit, they persevere until death in spiritual advancement, and in endeavors to keep the divine commands.

Art. X. At death, the souls of disciples go to the Lord Jesus Christ, and remain happy till the end of this world, at which period he will descend bodily from heaven, all the dead will be raised by his power, and assembled before him to receive his judgment.

ART. XI. At the day of judgment, he will publicly pronounce the pardon and justification of his disciples; and they will then be invested with perpetual life in the presence of God, and enter on the enjoyment of the interminable happiness of heaven.

ART. XII. As to those who are not disciples, since they believe not in the Lord who saves from sin, they will not, on that day, find any refuge, but, according to their deserts, be cast, body and soul, into hell, and come to perpetual destruction.

[After the Creed, or instead of it, an exhortation, or sermon, or portion of Scripture, read and commented on, followed by an extempore prayer, closing, perhaps, with the Lord's Prayer; the benediction in the words of ? Coi xiii. 16.]

Formula for administering Baptism.

Into the religion of the Father, the Son, and the Holy Spirit, I baptize thee.

Formula for administering the Lord's Supper.

1. The Lord Jesus Christ, the night on which he was betrayed, took bread, and having given thanks, broke, and gave it to his disciples, saying, Take, eat; this is my body, which is broken for you; do this in remembrance of me: let us, therefore, in the same manner, eat this bread.

2. He took the cup, also, and having given thanks, he gave it to his disciples, saying, All ye drink of it; this is the blood of the new covenant, my blood, which is poured out to procure for many the remission of sin: let us, therefore, in the same manner, drink this wine.

Formula for appointing an Evangelist, or Missionary.

We, by the imposition of hands, appoint thee an evangelist, in the church of the Lord Jesus Christ. Preach the gospel every where; administer baptism and the Lord's supper; appoint other teachers by the imposition of hands.

Formula for appointing a Pastor, Elder, or Bishop.

We, by the imposition of hands, appoint thee a pastor in the church of the Lord Jesus Christ. Preach the gospel at [such a place] and every where; preside over the church in [such a place;] administer baptism and the Lord's supper; appoint other teachers, by the imposition of hands, in conjunction with two other pastors.

Formula for appointing a Deacon.

We, by the imposition of hands, appoint thee a deacon in the church of the Lord Jesus Christ. Assist the pastor of the church in [such a place;] look after and take care of the members of the church; in concert with the pastor, attend to the management of all the affairs of the church.

Formula for appointing a Licentiate or Itinerant Preacher.

We, by the imposition of hands, appoint thee a preacher in the church of the Lord Jesus Christ. Go about in [such a town, district, &c.,] preaching the gospel.

Provisionary Rules for the Guidance of Native Pastors.

1. In administering baptism, though the power is vested in the pastor, since the baptized person is to be a member of the church, it is well not to baptize but with the consent of the previous church members. If, therefore, one tenth of the members of the church be unwilling to receive the applicant, *it is the opinion of the teachers* that baptism should be deferred.

2. In regard to the Lord's supper, since there is no definite command in Scripture that it shall be received on any particular month or day, but only that it shall be received from time to time; and since various customs have prevailed in Christian countries, as once in seven days, once a month, once in three months, and once in six months, *it is the opinion of the teachers*, that among the Talings and Burmans, who divide the year into three seasons, the hot, the rainy, and the cold, it will be well to receive the Lord's supper at the commencement of each season, or three times a year, viz., on the first Sundays after the full moons of Tah-boung, Wah-zo, and Tanzoung-mong, (answering nearly to March, July, and November.)

3. If any church member shall live in violation of the commands of Christ, and not repent of his conduct, the pastor shall consult with the church, and pronounce such person not sincere, and not worthy to be admitted to partake of the Lord's supper; and when the season of communion arrives, such person shall, accordingly, not be admitted to partake with the church. And if a person thus under censure shall refuse to listen to the pastor, the deacons, and the church, and remain without repenting and confessing for three successive seasons of communion, or one whole year, from the time of his suspension, let him, on the arrival of the fourth season of communion, be deprived of his discipleship, and excluded from the church; let him be anathema — accursed of God; let him be regarded as a heathen and an outcast. But in such proceedings, we are to remember the words of the Lord Jesus Christ to his disciples, "Whatsoever ye shall bind on earth shall be bound in heaven, and whatsoever ye shall loose on earth shall be loosed in heaven," and are, therefore, to proceed with godly fear and caution. Nor on this subject do the teachers give their own opinion merely. See Matt. xviii. 15–18; 2 Thess. iii 6, 14, 15; 1 Cor. v. 11, 13, xvi. 22.

Appendix containing Thirty Precepts, being a Digest of Christian Law.

1. Love God with all the soul. Matt. xxii. 37 ; 1 John iv 16 ; Jude 21 ; 1 John ii. 5.

2. Love others as thyself. Matt. xxii. 39, xix. 19 ; Gal. v. 14 ; James ii. 8 ; Rom. xii. 10, xiii. 9, 10 ; Matt. vii. 12 ; John xiii 34 ; 1 Pet. i. 22.

3. Repent of thy sins. Mark i. 15 ; Acts xvii. 30 ; Luke xxiv. 47 ; Acts ii. 38 ; Luke xiii. 3 ; Acts xx. 21.

4. Believe in the Lord Jesus Christ. Mark i. 15, xvi. 16 ; John vi. 29 ; 1 John iii. 23 ; Acts xvi. 31 ; Rom. i. 17 ; Acts xx. 21.

5. Set not thy heart on worldly good, but keep in view the happiness of heaven. Col. iii. 2 ; Matt. vi. 19–34 ; 1 John ii. 15, 17 ; 1 Tim. vi. 9, 10 ; 1 Cor. vii. 29, 31 ; 2 Cor. iv. 18 ; Heb. xi. 13–16.

6. Avoid idleness, and be diligent in thy calling. Rom. xiii. 13 ; Eph. v. 16 ; John ix. 4 ; Rom. xii. 11 ; 2 Pet. i. 8 ; 1 Thess. iv. 11, 12 ; 2 Thess. iii. 7–12 ; 1 Tim. v. 8.

7. Covet not the property of others. Rom. xiii. 9 ; Col. iii. 5 ; Eph. v. 3 ; 1 Tim. vi. 8 ; Heb. xiii. 5.

8. Do no violence. Luke iii. 18 ; Matt. xxiii. 25 ; 1 Cor. vi. 10.

9. Steal not. Matt. xix. 18 ; Rom. xiii. 9 ; Eph. iv. 28 ; 1 Cor. vi. 10 ; 1 Pet. iv. 15.

10. Defraud not. Mark x. 19 ; Rom. xiii. 7, 8 ; 1 Thess. iv. 6.

11. Lie not. Eph. iv. 25 ; Col. iii. 9 ; 1 Pet. iii. 10 ; Rev. xxi. 8, xxii. 15.

12. Bear not false witness. Matt. xv. 19, xix. 18 ; Rom. xiii. 9.

13. Murder not ; and let the murderer die. Matt. xix. 18 ; Rom. xiii. 9 ; James ii. 11 ; Gal. v. 21 ; 1 Pet. iv. 15 ; Gen. ix. 6 ; Rom. xiii. 4 ; Acts xxv. 11.

14. Be not drunk. Eph. v. 18 ; Rom. xiii. 13 ; 1 Cor. vi 10 ; Gal. v. 21.

15. Commit not adultery. Matt. xix. 18 ; Rom. xiii. 9 ; Heb xlii 4 ; Gal. v. 19 ; Matt. v. 28–32.

16. Besides thine own wife or husband, lust after none. Mark x. 6–8; 1 Cor. vii. 2, 39; 1 Thess. iv. 3–5; 1 Cor. vi. 13–18; Gal. v. 19; Eph. v. 3; Col. iii. 5.

17. Subdue pride, and cultivate a meek and humble spirit. 1 Pet. v. 5, 6, iii. 3, 4; Col. iii. 12; Rom. xii. 16; Matt. xi. 29; Eph. iv. 2; Luke xviii. 9–14.

18. Bear with the faults of others; return not evil for evil; love thine enemies, and do them good. 1 Pet. ii. 20–23, iii. 9; Matt. v. 39; Col. iii. 15; Matt. vi. 14, 15, v. 44; Rom. xii. 14, 17–21.

19. Be charitable to the poor. Gal. ii. 10; 1 Pet. iii. 8; Rom. xii. 13; Luke xi. 41, xii. 33; Matt. vi. 2–4; Acts xx. 35; James ii. 15, 16; 1 John iii. 17.

20. Honor and support thy parents. Matt. xix. 19; Eph. vi. 1–3; Col. iii. 20; Matt. xv. 4–6.

21. Honor ministers of religion, and cheerfully contribute to their support. 1 Thess. v. 12, 13; 1 Tim. v. 17; Heb. xiii. 17; 1 Cor. ix. 11–14; Gal. vi. 6.

22. In regard to rulers, whether disciples or not, honor them; pray for them; obey their orders, not involving sin against God. Rom. xiii. 1–7; 1 Tim. ii. 1, 2; 1 Pet. ii. 13; Acts iv. 19, 31, v. 29.

23. As thou hast opportunity, do good unto all men. Acts x. 38; Luke vi. 30–35; 1 Tim. vi. 18; Heb. xiii. 16; Gal. vi. 10; 1 Cor. x. 33, xi. 1; 1 John iii. 18.

24. In performing worship, avoid idolatry. 1 John v. 21; 1 Cor. x. 14, 20; Gal. v. 20; 1 Pet. iv. 13; Acts xvii. 29.

25. Pray to God always. Matt. vii. 7–11, vi. 5–13; Luke xviii. 1–14; John xvi. 23, 24; Phil. iv. 6; 1 Thess. v. 17; Eph. vi. 18.

26. In all things deny thyself, and seek the will of God. Luke ix. 23; Mark x. 21; 1 Cor. ix. 27; Rom. xiii. 14; Col. iii. 5; John vi. 38; Rom. xv. 1–3.

27. On the first day of the week, assemble with others to worship God and hear the word. Mark xvi. 9; John xx. 19; Rev. i. 10; Acts xx. 7; Heb. x. 25.

28. Profess the religion of the Lord Jesus Christ by re-

ceiving baptism. Mark xvi. 16; Acts ii. 38; Gal. iii. 27; John iii. 5.

29. Afterwards receive the Lord's supper, in remembrance of the divine love. Matt. xxvi. 26-28; 1 Cor. xi. 23-29, v. 7, 8, x. 16, 17.

30. Go into all the world, and preach the gospel to every creature. Matt. xxviii. 19; Mark xvi. 15; Matt. v. 16; Acts viii. 4.

NOTE. — The foregoing "Liturgy," prepared by Dr. Judson, in 1829, was designed to assist young missionaries before they had acquired the language, and as a guide to the native assistants.

G.

LETTER ON ORNAMENTAL AND COSTLY ATTIRE.

To the Female Members of Christian Churches in the United States of America.

Dear Sisters in Christ: Excuse my publicly addressing you. The necessity of the case is my only apology. Whether you will consider it a sufficient apology for the sentiments of this letter, — unfashionable, I confess, and perhaps unpalatable, — I know not. We are sometimes obliged to encounter the hazard of offending those whom, of all others, we desire to please. Let me throw myself at once on your mercy, dear sisters, allied by national consanguinity, professors of the same holy religion, fellow-pilgrims to the same happy world. Pleading these endearing ties, let me beg you to regard me as a brother, and to listen with candor and forbearance to my honest tale.

In raising up a church of Christ in this heathen land, and in laboring to elevate the minds of the female converts to the standard of the gospel, we have always found one chief obstacle in that principle of vanity, that love of dress and display, — I beg you will bear with me, — which has, in every age and in all countries, been a ruling passion of the fair sex, as the love of riches, power, and fame has characterized the other. That obstacle lately became more formidable, through the admission of two or three fashionable females into the church, and the arrival of several missionary sisters, dressed and adorned in that manner which is too prevalent in our beloved native land. On my meeting the church, after a year's absence, I beheld an appalling profusion of ornaments, and saw that the demon of vanity was laying waste the female department. At that time I had not maturely considered the subject, and did not feel sure what ground I ought to take. I apprehended, also, that I should be unsupported, and perhaps opposed, by some of my coadjutors. I confined my efforts, therefore, to private exhortation, and with but little effect. Some of the ladies, out of regard to their pastor's feelings, took off their necklaces and ear ornaments before they entered the chapel, tied them up in a corner of their handkerchiefs, and on returning, as soon as they were out of sight of the mission house, stopped in the middle of the street to array themselves anew.

In the mean time I was called to visit the Karens, a wild people, several days' journey to the north of Maulmain. Little did I expect there to encounter the same enemy, in those " wilds, horrid and dark with o'ershadowing trees." But I found that he had been there before me, and reigned with a peculiar sway, from time immemorial. On one Karen lady I counted between twelve and fifteen necklaces, of all colors, sizes, and materials. Three was the average. Brass belts above the ankles; neat braids of black hair tied below the knees; rings of all sorts on the fingers; bracelets on the wrists and arms; long instruments of some metal, perforating the lower part of the ear, by an immense aperture, and reaching nearly to the shoulders; fancifully-constructed bags enclosing the hair, and suspended from the back part of the head; not to speak of the ornamental parts of their clothing, — constituted the fashions and the ton of the fair Karenesses. The dress of the female converts was not essentially different from that of their countrywomen. I saw that I was brought into a situation that precluded all retreat — that I must fight or die.

For a few nights I spent some sleepless hours, distressed by this and other subjects, which will always press upon the heart of a missionary in a new place. I considered the spirit of the religion of Jesus Christ. I opened to 1 Tim. ii. 9, and read these words of the inspired apostle: " I will, also, that women adorn themselves in modest apparel, with shamefacedness and sobriety; *not with broidered hair, or gold, or pearls, or costly array.*" I asked myself, Can I baptize a

Karen woman in her present attire? No. Can I administer the Lord's supper to one of the baptized in that attire? No. Can I refrain from enforcing the prohibition of the apostle? Not without betraying the trust I have received from him. Again: I considered that the question concerned not the Karens only, but the whole Christian world; that its decision would involve a train of unknown consequences; that a single step would lead me into a long and perilous way. I considered Maulmain and the other stations; I considered the state of the public mind at home. But "*what is that to thee? follow thou me,*" was the continual response, and weighed more than all. I renewedly offered myself to Christ, and prayed for strength to go forward in the path of duty, come life or death, come praise or reproach, supported or deserted, successful or defeated in the ultimate issue.

Soon after coming to this resolution, a Karen woman offered herself for baptism. After the usual examination, I inquired whether she could give up her ornaments for Christ? It was an unexpected blow! I explained the spirit of the gospel. I appealed to her own consciousness of vanity. I read her the apostle's prohibition. She looked again and again at her handsome necklace, — she wore but one, — and then, with an air of modest decision that would adorn, beyond all outward ornaments, any of my sisters whom I have the honor of addressing, she quietly took it off, saying, *I love Christ more than this.* The news began to spread. The Christian women made but little hesitation. A few others opposed, but the work went on.

At length the evil which I most dreaded came upon me. Some of the Karen men had been to Maulmain, and seen what I wished they had not; and one day, when we were discussing the subject of ornaments, one of the Christians came forward, and declared that at Maulmain he had actually seen one of the great female teachers wearing a string of gold beads around her neck.

Lay down this paper, dear sisters, and sympathize a moment with your fallen missionary. Was it not a hard case? However, though cast down, I was not destroyed; I endeavored to maintain the warfare as well as I could, and when I left those parts, the female converts were, generally speaking, arrayed in modest apparel.

On arriving at Maulmain, and partially recovering from a fever which I had contracted in the Karen woods, the first thing I did was to crawl out to the house of the patroness of the gold necklace. To her I related my adventures, and described my grief. With what ease, and truth too, could that sister say, notwithstanding this necklace, "I dress more plainly than most ministers' wives and professors of religion in our native land! This necklace is the only ornament I wear; it was given me when quite a child, by a dear mother, whom I expect never to see again, (another hard case,) and she begged me never to part with it as long as I lived, but to wear it as a memorial of her." O ye Christian mothers, what a lesson you have before you! Can you, dare you give injunctions to your daughters directly contrary to apostolic commands? But to the honor of my sister be it recorded, that, as soon as she understood the merits of the case, and the mischief done by such example, off went the gold necklace, and she gave decisive proof that she loved Christ more than father or mother. Her example, united with the efforts of the rest of us at this station, is beginning to exercise a redeeming influence in the female department of the church.

But notwithstanding these favorable signs, nothing, really nothing, is yet done. And why? This misson and all others must necessarily be sustained by continual supplies of missionaries, male and female, from the mother country. Your sisters and daughters will continually come out, to take the place of those who are removed by death, and to occupy numberless stations still unoccupied. And when they arrive they will be dressed in their usual way, as Christian women at home are dressed. And the female converts will run around them, and gaze upon them, with the most prying curiosity, regarding them as the freshest representatives of the Christian religion from that land where it flourishes in all its purity and glory. And when they see the gold and jewels pendent from their ears, the beads and chains encircling their necks, the finger rings set with diamonds and rubies, the rich variety of ornamental headdress, " the mantles, and the wimples, and the crisping pins," (see Is. iii. 19, 23,) they will cast a reproachful, triumphant glance at their old teachers, and spring with fresh avidity, to repurchase and resume their long-neglected elegances; the cheering news will fly up the Dah-gyne, the Laing-bwai, and the Salwen; the Karenesses will reload their necks, and ears, and arms, and ankles; and when, after another year's absence, I return and take my seat before the Burmese or the Karen church, I shall behold the demon of vanity enthroned in the centre of the assembly more firmly than ever, grinning defiance to the prohibitions of apostles, and the exhortations of us who would fain be their humble followers. And thus you, my dear sisters, sitting quietly by your firesides, or repairing devoutly to your places of worship, do, by your example, spread the poison of vanity through all the rivers, and mountains, and wilds of this far distant land; and while you are sincerely and fervently praying for the upbuilding of the Redeemer's kingdom, are inadvertently building up that of the devil. If, on the other hand, you divest yourselves of all meretricious ornaments, your sisters and daughters, who come hither, will be divested of course; the further supplies of vanity and pride will be cut off, and the churches at home being kept pure, the churches here will be pure also.

Dear sisters: Having finished my tale, and therein exhibited the necessity under which I lay of addressing you, I beg leave to submit a few topics to your candid and prayerful consideration.

1. Let me appeal to conscience, and inquire, What is the real motive for wearing ornamental and costly apparel? Is it not the desire of setting off one's person to the best advantage, and of exciting the admiration of others? Is not such dress calculated to gratify self-love, and cherish sentiments of vanity and pride? And is it not the nature of those sentiments to acquire strength from indulgence? Do such motives and sentiments

comport with the meek, humble, self-denying religion of Jesus Christ? I would here respectfully suggest, that these questions will not be answered so faithfully in the midst of company as when quite alone, kneeling before God.

2. Consider the words of the apostle, quoted above from 1 Tim. ii. 9 — "I will also that women adorn themselves in modest apparel, with shamefacedness and sobriety, *not with broidered hair, or gold, or pearls, or costly array.*" I do not quote a similar command recorded in 1 Pet. iii. 3, because the verbal construction is not quite so definite, though the import of the two passages is the same. But cannot the force of these two passages be evaded? Yes, and nearly every command in Scripture can be evaded, and every doctrinal assertion perverted, plausibly and handsomely too, if we set about it in good earnest. But preserving the posture above alluded to, with the inspired volume spread open at the passage in question, ask your hearts, in simplicity and godly sincerity, whether the meaning is not just as plain as the sun at noonday. Shall we then bow to the authority of an inspired apostle, or shall we not? From that authority shall we appeal to the prevailing usages and fashions of the age? If so, please to recall the missionaries you have sent to the heathen; for the heathen can vindicate all their superstitions on the same ground.

3. In the posture you have assumed, look up and behold the eye of your benignant Saviour ever gazing upon you with the tenderest love — upon you, his daughters, his spouse, wishing above all things that you would yield your hearts entirely to him, and become holy as he is holy, rejoicing when he sees one after another accepting his pressing invitation, and entering the more perfect way.

4. Anticipate the happy moment, "hastening on all the wings of time," when your joyful spirits will be welcomed into the assembly of the spirits of the just made perfect. You appear before the throne of Jehovah; the approving smile of Jesus fixes your everlasting happy destiny; and you are plunging into "the sea of life and love unknown, without a bottom or a shore." Stop a moment; look back on yonder

dark and miserable world that you have left; fix your eye on the meagre, vain, contemptible articles of ornamental dress, which you once hesitated to give up for Christ, the King of glory; and on that glance decide the question instantly and forever.

Surely you can hold out no longer. You cannot rise from your knees in your present attire. Thanks be to God, I see you taking off your necklaces and earrings, tearing away your ribbons, and ruffles, and superfluities of headdress, and I hear you exclaim, What shall we do next? — an important question, deserving serious consideration. The ornaments you are removing, though useless, and worse than useless, in their present state, can be so disposed of as to feed the hungry, clothe the naked, relieve the sick, enlighten the dark minded, disseminate the Holy Scriptures, spread the glorious gospel throughout the world. Little do the inhabitants of a free Christian country know of the want and distress endured by the greater part of the inhabitants of the earth. Still less idea can they form of the awful darkness which rests upon the great mass of mankind in regard to spiritual things. During the years that you have been wearing these useless ornaments, how many poor creatures have been pining in want! How many have languished and groaned on beds of abject wretchedness! How many children have been bred up in the blackest ignorance, hardened in all manner of iniquity! How many immortal souls have gone down to hell, with a lie in their right hand, having never heard of the true God and the only Saviour! Some of these miseries might have been mitigated; some poor wretch have felt his pain relieved; some widow's heart been made to sing for joy; some helpless orphan have been taught in the Sabbath school, and trained up for a happy life here and hereafter. The Holy Bible and valuable tracts might have been far more extensively circulated in heathen lands had you not been afraid of being thought unfashionable, and not "like other folks;" had you not preferred adorning your persons, and cherishing the sweet seductive feelings of vanity and pride.

O Christian sisters, believers in God, in Christ, in an eternal heaven, and an eternal hell, can you hesitate, and ask what you shall do? Bedew those ornaments with the tears of contrition; consecrate them to the cause of charity; hang them on the cross of your dying Lord. Delay not an instant. Hasten with all your might, if not to make reparation for the past, at least to prevent a continuance of the evil in future.

And for your guidance allow me to suggest two fundamental principles — the one based on 1 Tim. ii. 9 — *all ornaments and costly dress to be disused;* the other on the law of general benevolence — *the avails of such articles, and the savings resulting from the plain dress system, to be devoted to purposes of charity.* Some general rules in regard to dress, and some general objects of charity, may be easily ascertained; and free discussion will throw light on many points at first obscure. Be not deterred by the suggestion that in such discussions you are concerned about *small* things. Great things depend on small; and, in that case, things which appear small to shortsighted man are great in the sight of God. Many there are who praise the principle of self-denial in general, and condemn it in all its particular applications as too minute, scrupulous, and severe. The enemy is well aware that, if he can secure the minute units, the sum total will be his own. Think not any thing small which may have a bearing upon the kingdom of Christ and upon the destinies of eternity. How easy to conceive, from many known events, that the single fact of a lady's divesting herself of a necklace for Christ's sake may involve consequences which shall be felt in the remotest parts of the earth, and in all future generations to the end of time — yea, stretch away into a boundless eternity, and be a subject of praise millions of ages after this world and all its ornaments are burned up.

Beware of another suggestion made by weak and erring souls, who will tell you that there is more danger of being proud of plain dress and other modes of self-denial than of fashionable attire and self-indulgence. Be not insnared by this last, most finished, most insidious device of the great enemy. Rather believe that He who enables you to make a sacrifice is able to keep you from being proud of it. Believe that he will kindly permit such occasions of mortification and shame as will preserve you from the evil threatened. *The severest part of self-denial consists in encountering the disapprobation, the envy, the hatred of one's dearest friends.* All who enter the strait and narrow path in good earnest soon find themselves in a climate extremely uncongenial to the growth of pride.

The gay and fashionable will, in many cases, be the last to engage in this holy undertaking. But let none be discouraged on that account. Christ has seldom honored the leaders of worldly fashion by appointing them leaders in his cause. Fix it in your hearts that in this warfare *the Lord Jesus Christ expects every woman to do her duty.* There is probably not one in the humblest walks of life but would, on strict examination, find some article which *might* be dispensed with for purposes of charity, and *ought* to be dispensed with in compliance with the apostolic command. Wait not, therefore, for the fashionable to set an example; wait not for one another; listen not to the news from the next town; but *let every individual go forward*, regardless of reproach, fearless of consequences. The eye of Christ is upon you. Death is hastening to strip you of your ornaments, and to turn your fair forms into corruption and dust. Many of those for whom this letter is designed will be laid in the grave before it can ever reach their eyes. We shall all soon appear before the judgment seat of Christ, to be tried for our conduct, and to receive the things done in the body. When placed before that awful bar, in the presence of that Being whose eyes are as a flame of fire, and whose irrevocable fiat will fix you forever in heaven or in hell, and mete out the measure of your everlasting pleasures and pains, what course will you then wish you had taken? Will you then wish that, in defiance of his authority, you had adorned your mortal bodies with gold, and precious stones, and costly attire, cherishing self-love, vanity, and pride? Or will you wish that you had chosen a life of self-denial, renounced the world, taken up the cross *daily*, and followed him? *And as you will then wish you had done,* DO NOW.

Dear sisters, your affectionate brother in Christ,

A. JUDSON.

MAULMAIN, October, 1831.

H.

SERMON.*

JOHN x. 1-18.—"VERILY, VERILY, I SAY UNTO YOU, HE THAT ENTERETH NOT BY THE DOOR INTO THE SHEEPFOLD, BUT CLIMBETH UP SOME OTHER WAY," &c.

CHRIST is the great Exemplar of his people, and in his ministerial character, the great Exemplar of his ministers. In the portion of Scripture just read, he has represented himself in his ministerial character, as the Shepherd of the flock, the Pastor of the church, not merely of the church then collected, but of the church universal. "Other sheep I have which are not of this fold : them also I must bring, and they shall hear my voice, and there shall be one fold and one Shepherd." The apostle Peter exhorts his brethren in the ministry to act as shepherds of the flock of God, expecting the appearance of the chief Shepherd, who will place on their heads an unfading crown of glory. Let, therefore, all ministers of the church, the subordinate shepherds of the flock, look continually to the chief Shepherd, the Minister of the everlasting covenant, and study the leading traits of character which he has presented for their imitation.

1. Christ is the good Shepherd: he gave his life for the sheep. He saw the wolf coming, the wild beast of hell, to rend and devour his beloved flock, the flock which had been given him by the Father, and on which he had set his heart from all eternity, but which had become involved in the fatal consequences of the fall, and were lying in their blood, without the pale of paradise, exposed to the rage of their fell destroyer. In the hour of impending ruin, he ran to their rescue. And casting a farewell look on the bosom of the Father, where he had reposed in everlasting glory, and withdrawing from the de-

---

* Preached by Dr. Judson on the occasion of the ordination of the Rev. S. M. Osgood, Maulmain, May 10, 1836; supposed to be the only English sermon ever preached by him in Burmah.

lighted, a loving gaze of celestial beings, he descended from the height of heaven, and hid his beauty, his brightness, and his power, in the darkness and imbecility of human nature. He became a poor, laboring man. He walked about, a houseless wanderer on the earth. For though he came unto his own, they received him not. They took advantage of his weakness, his humility, his forbearance, to despise and reject him. And his enemies assailed him with contempt, reproach, abuse; and after many distant attacks, they closed in upon him, and trampled him down, and his heart's blood was mingled with the dust in which he lay. They thought that they had achieved a signal triumph; but the triumph was all his own. He sought the opportunity of laying down his life; and at the last gasp, he cried, "Take, O justice, my life for the life of my people." His prayer was accepted, and his people saved. As Christ spared nothing, shrunk from nothing which would conduce to the salvation of his people, so the faithful minister of Christ will give up all for the good of the people to whom he ministers. When he enters upon the sacred office, and is designated to labor for a particular church, or to itinerate in a certain region, or to devote himself to some portion of the heathen world, he will look around on the people of his charge with such feelings as influenced the Saviour when he looked down from heaven upon this fallen world. When he sees them lying in their ruin, ravaged by their spiritual enemies, death prowling near, and dragging them away to his dreadful charnel house, and the bottomless pit opening to receive and imprison their lost souls in the burning tombs of hell, where the eye of mercy must never, never look, nor angel voice whisper consolation or hope through interminable ages, — when he knows that the cross of Christ is the only refuge from these horrors, the only life-boat which can bear away the struggling, sinking soul from the abyss into which it is rushing, — he will exclaim with the apostle, "I am determined to know nothing among you but Jesus Christ, and him crucified." He will relinquish all his own tastes and inclinations, all literary and scientific pursuits, all ambitious projects, all efforts to acquire celebrity and attain a high standing in society, all that consummation of human folly, the lust of posthumous fame. Still less will the faithful minister aim at amassing the stores of mammon, and enlarging his houses and his lands in the anticipation of a happy old age, supported and propped up, not on the promises of God but on his hoarded treasures and his heaps of bank stock. No, none but the hireling can do this; and he does it because he is a hireling, and careth not for the sheep. The good shepherd is ready to give his very life for the flock; still more to give up all that earth calls good and great; to become all things to all men, that he may, by all means, save some.

2. Another trait in the character of Christ, the good shepherd, he has presented in these words: "I know my sheep, and am known of mine." According to the Hebrew idiom, which prevails in both the Old and New Testaments, *to know* frequently means *to be acquainted with, affectionately acquainted with*, as in such passages as the following: "They that know thy name will put their trust in thee." "O, continue thy loving kindness to them that know thee." "You only have I known of all the families of the earth." "If any man love God, the same is known of God." So when Christ says, "I know my sheep, and am known of mine," he means to say, "An affectionate acquaintance subsists between me and my people." Consider the terms on which Christ held intercourse with his disciples and friends, and learn to imitate his example. In scrutinizing that intercourse, we discover no traces of proud reserve, no assumed state, no pomp, and strut, and supercilious airs, to awe the vulgar, and make religion respectable in the eyes of the world. Nor do we discover any affectation of mystery to impose on the credulous, or crouching and fawning to secure the favor of the great, or low familiarity and arts unworthy of his character to please the crowd. All is open, honest, straightforward, candid, generous, noble, forgiving, affectionate, kind. View him an inmate in the dear family at Bethany. He loved Martha, and her sister, and Lazarus. How affectionate was his intercourse with his dear disciples! and his affection continued unto

the end. Behold John, the best beloved, permitted to recline his head on the bosom of Jesus. Yet John was only a poor fisherman. And how did his disciples and friends reciprocate his love? They followed him every where; they accompanied him when fleeing from his enemies; and when his duty called him back to the post of danger, they were ready to say, "Let us go, that we may die with him." Even when nailed to the cross, though at first, through the impulse of sudden fear, they forsook him and fled, "all his acquaintance, and the women that followed him from Galilee, stood afar off, beholding those things." And though his life was extinct, their love still survived. Though all their hopes were disappointed, they followed him to the tomb, and spared no expense to wrap his mangled body in fine linen, and embalm it in precious ointments and sweet spices; and when they could do no more, they stood weeping before the sepulchre. My brethren in the ministry, and you, my brother, who are about to be inducted into the sacred office, follow the Saviour in these things. Endeavor, as far as possible, to become affectionately acquainted with every individual to whom you are called to minister. Enter into their circumstances, rejoice in their joys, and sympathize with them in their sorrows. Become acquainted with all their wants, especially those of a spiritual nature, which it is your province to endeavor to relieve. And not only know your people, but endeavor to let them know you. Let them become affectionately acquainted with you. Have nothing and be nothing that requires concealment. Live without a disguise, as the Saviour lived, and your people will love you. They will give you their whole hearts. You will acquire an unbounded influence over them; not the influence of learning, or of official rank, but the influence of love. And when, in the providence of God, or by the stroke of death, you are removed from them, you will receive the same testimony to your affectionate faithfulness that crowned the dying moments of the Saviour — the aching hearts and the flowing tears of those to whom you have ministered. Behold Paul kneeling down with the disciples of

Ephesus and praying with them. "And they all wept sore, and fell on his neck and kissed him, sorrowing most of all for the words which he spake, that they should see his face no more."

3. The true shepherd calleth his own sheep by name, and the sheep hear his voice; and when he putteth them forth, he goeth before them, and the sheep follow him, for they know his voice. Christ calls his people by his word; he points out the true and living way; and he has gone before his people in that way, setting them an example which they may safely follow. We come now to consider the main duty of a Christian pastor. First he must call his people. Though enclosed in the Saviour's electing love, they may still be wandering on the dark mountains of sin, and he must go after them; perhaps he must seek them in very remote regions, in the very outskirts of the wilderness of heathenism. And as he cannot at first distinguish them from the rest, who will never listen and be saved, he must lift up his voice to all, without discrimination, and utter, in the hearing of all, that invitation of mercy and love which will penetrate the ears and the hearts of the elect only. And when they listen, he must show them the way — Christ, the way, the truth, and the life; teaching them to observe all things which he has commanded. He must lead them forth to green pastures and beside the still waters. And when he leads them, he must go before them. He must practise the precepts which his lips utter. He must be an example to believers in word, in conversation, in charity, in spirit, in faith, in purity. This constitutes the great difference between the true shepherd and the hireling. The hireling preaches because he is paid for it; but he practises not. And were his stipend withdrawn, how quickly would he withdraw himself from the pulpit which groans under his heartless exhibitions! In that pulpit he does, indeed, assume a ministerial air, and his face is clothed with solemnity befitting the occasion. He will also, perhaps, in order to press into his service some degree of earnestness and obtain the credit of some sincerity, insist on the

externals of the sect to which he happens to belong, the tithe of mint, anise, and cummin; and perhaps, for variety and pathos, he will inveigh with some warmth and acrimony against all deviations from that particular path in which his father and his grandfather have been used to walk. But when he descends from the pulpit, he is like the schoolboy released from his task. Follow him into his retirement and into society. Observe his conduct; listen to his conversation. You see that in the temper and spirit of his mind he is assimilated to the men of the world. Like them, he is ambitious, avaricious, and passionate. Like them he is a stickler for the respect due to his rank. He indulges in the same kind of recreations and amusements. And they all know that he is pursuing the same career with themselves, only in a little different line. He is a hireling minister; he cares not for the sheep; his only care is for the fleece; and dying thus impenitent, unabsolved, he must sink beyond redemption. How different his whole course from that of the true pastor! The latter not only preaches repentance, but daily repents of his own sins; not only preaches faith, but constantly endeavors to cherish in his own soul that holy principle by which alone he can overcome the world. Thus his life attests the sincerity of his word; and the Holy Spirit blesses both his preaching and example to the conversion of sinners and the edification of the church.

4. "As the Father knoweth me, even so know I the Father, and I lay down my life for the sheep. Therefore doth my Father love me, because I lay down my life that I may take it again. This commandment have I received from my Father." Christ, in his mediatorial capacity, as the Saviour of his people, the good Shepherd of the sheep, was influenced, in all his conduct, by a supreme regard to his Father's will. "I came down from heaven, not to do mine own will, but the will of Him that sent me." The love of God was the ruling principle of his whole life. He did nothing for his own aggrandizement in this or a future state. Even his labors and sufferings for the good of his people sprang not so much

from compassion and love to them as from love to the Father, and desire to please him. The true pastor, and, indeed, every true Christian, must be influenced by the same principle. No labors, no self-denial, no deeds of charity, no personal sufferings in the service of religion, are truly estimable, but just so far as they spring from regard to the will of God. All true virtue has its root in the love of God. Every holy affection looks beyond self, beyond every limited circle of creatures, beyond the whole creation, and finds its resting-place in God alone. God must be all in all. What are all created beings in comparison with God — God, who exists from everlasting to everlasting, filling immensity with his presence, and dwelling in his own immortal now; God, who comprises in himself infinitely more worth than can possibly be possessed by all beings through all eternity; God, who enjoys, every moment of his eternal existence, more happiness and glory than can be enjoyed by all beings through all eternity? God loves himself, and ought to love himself, infinitely more than he can love, or ought to love, all creatures which have existed or will exist forever. Who, by searching, can find out God? Every divine attribute is infinite, and the number of the divine attributes is, doubtless, infinite. We obtain some faint idea of a few, — as existence, knowledge, power, benevolence, — from discovering in ourselves and other creatures those attributes existing in a low degree. But there are, doubtless, divine attributes which lie entirely beyond the scope of our present senses or powers of reflection, and of which we can no more form an idea than a person born blind can form an idea of light and color. And there are, doubtless, divine attributes which wait for worlds, and creatures, and combinations of circumstances adapted to their development. The present world has been adapted to the development of mercy, as exhibited in grace to sinners — a gem which had hitherto lain unknown, unsuspected, in the inexhaustible quarry of the divine nature; a new star to be henceforth suspended in the heaven of God's character, transmitting through the dense medium of sin its benign and melting rays to the remotest worlds, through the ever-brightening track of all future eternity. Every new world is, doubtless, designed to display some new attribute of the divine nature — to evolve some new luminary, and furnish a corresponding atmosphere, through which its rays may be modified, and softened, and suited to the apprehension of creatures, or brought into contact with new senses or faculties suddenly roused thereby into susceptibility and activity, and surprising the possessor with the consciousness of new power and new sources of enjoyment which he had never suspected; for the dormant faculties of immortal creatures are probably as numberless and illimitable as the perfections of God, which they are adapted to apprehend and enjoy. What luminaries suspended in the eternity that is past will burst upon our vision when we quit the prison house in which we are now confined; and what new glories we shall see kindling up at each stage of our future happy existence — glories beaming from the divine face, the uncreated sun, the eternal source of all light and glory, forever unveiling to the view of holy beings, yet never, never to be completely unveiled! How infinitely happy must God be in himself, all his infinite attributes ever known and ever enjoyed to full perfection! Herein eminently consists the happiness of God. What is the collective happiness of all creatures in comparison with the happiness of God? How suitable that Christ, in his mediatorial capacity, should have supreme regard to the will of the Father! How indispensable that every minister, every Christian, should refer all his actions to the will of God! On this ground we rest the doctrine of self-denial, renunciation of self-interest, abandonment of self. Still further, even our compassion for souls and our zeal for their salvation must be kept in subordination to the supreme will of God. The love of Christ was so strong as to bring him down from heaven to earth, and to the mansions of the dead; yet so chastened was that love, and so subordinate to the will of God, that, though he foresaw the doom of a certain portion of his hearers, he still would say, "I thank thee, O Father, Lord of heaven and earth, because thou hast hid these things from the wise and prudent, and hast revealed them unto babes. Even so, Father, for so it seemed good in thy sight." And to this sentiment may we be enabled to respond a hearty Amen.

I.

SKETCH OF ELEANOR MACOMBER.

My acquaintance with Eleanor Macomber commenced on her arrival in this country, February, 1836. The first part of her missionary life among the American Indians, at one of the north-western stations, where she acquired the language, and rendered herself extensively useful until obliged to leave on account of her health, her friends in America are doubtless acquainted with. Soon after her arrival here, she was appointed to labor among the Pwo Karens — a people whose language had not been acquired by any foreigner, though a beginning had been made at Tavoy, and in the region of the Zwai-ga-ben hills, where no missionary labor had been performed. After visiting Tavoy, and acquiring the rudiments of the language, she repaired to the wilderness assigned her, about twenty-five miles distant from the habitation of any white person; and there, after parting in tears with the missionary who had conducted her thither, she spread her mat in her loneliness, and sat down in the hut of a petty chief, who gave her reluctant admission — a hard-headed, hard-hearted, notorious drunkard. Though able to say but little, and that in a very imperfect manner, she immediately began to communicate the truths of the gospel to the people around her. It was not long before an elderly person in the neighborhood drank in her instructions; then the wife of the chief, a very sensible, superior woman; and then, to the astonishment of all, the drunkard himself emerged from the fumes of rum, and became a rational being and a devoted Christian. Nearly all their children, a large family, most of them grown up, sooner or later followed their parents into the kingdom. A violent persecution ensued; most of the population forbade her entering their houses; mobs of profligate wretches surrounded her dwelling by night, yelling and throwing stones; several times her house was set on fire; and the house of her principal assistant was burned down. But she breasted the storm in the spirit of the gospel, and finally it died away. The growing church was placed under the pastoral supervision of some of the missionaries. I had the happiness of organizing it in March, 1837; and one and another of the brethren subsequently took the pastoral care. It now consists of thirty members, including two or three promising young men, who, with the first convert, the elderly person above mentioned, — a very steady, substantial Christian, — and the reformed chief, ordained a deacon, have been employed as assistants in spreading the gospel among the neighboring villages.

Besides her labors at Dong-yan, the location first selected, Miss Macomber made occasional tours about the country in search of Karens of the Pwo tribe. Her last tour was up the Houng-ta-ran, above one hundred miles. On her return, she touched at this place; and it soon became evident that somewhere on her tour she had inhaled the pestilential miasma, and symptoms of the jungle fever — so called here, because contracted in a jungle, or wood — began to appear. She at once gave up all hope of recovering; felt that her work was done; and addressed herself to the last trial with the same steadiness of purpose, buoyancy of spirit, and entire trust in God which had marked all her preceding course. "Do you think you shall recover?" "No, no!" "Will you have such or such means used?" "Do all you think proper for your own satisfaction; but it will be of no avail; my time has come." "You are better this morning. Are you willing to get well?" After a pause — "I hope I should be willing, if it be the will of God; but it would be hard to be called back when so near home." "O my Master," — in hardly audible prayer, — "take me *this day* to thyself," — are sentences which may serve to indicate the state of her mind in view of death. The last afternoon she suffered severely. Once she begged those around her bed to join in silent prayer, that her agony might be alleviated. Two or three times, at intervals, she cried out with gasping earnestness, " Why can't I go ? " One by her side whispered, " Sister, the Lord's time is the best," on which she made an evident effort to nod a cordial assent — one of the latest tokens of recognition which we obtained. After a few more struggles with the last enemy, she quietly sank into his arms, and into the arms of the Saviour.

Bitter were the tears and the cries of her converts, who had tended her faithfully by day and night during her sickness, and of others who arrived just in time to witness her interment; and long and lingeringly did they gaze on her face before we closed the coffin lid. She lies by the side of Miss Cummings, a person of similar character, but of much shorter missionary career; and together, I doubt not, their spirits rest in the bosom of Jesus.

We hope that her place at Dong-yan will soon be supplied, and that the seed sown there will continue to spring up and bear fruit, unto the millennium and to the end of the world. Happy sister! Precious was the box of ointment which thou hast poured on thy Saviour's head, and splendid will be the diadem which he will set on thine, inscribed with the praise bestowed on Mary of old, " *She hath wrought a good work upon me.*"

When I consider her unsurpassed missionary spirit, her undiverted, indefatigable efforts, her measure of success, — great when compared with her scanty means and limited time, — and the good judgment which marked all her plans, I am ready to ask, Where shall we find her *equal* among those she has left behind? May my spirit be quickened by contemplating her example, and may my last end be like hers.

A. JUDSON

MAULMAIN, 1840.

J.

SKETCHES OF SERMONS.

No. I.

COL. i. 27: CHRIST IN YOU THE HOPE OF GLORY.

THE birth of Christ and his life in this world are preparatory to his being formed in the souls of believers, and living within them. The one is the external part of Christianity, the other the internal. Kingdom of God cometh not by observation — Is within you — Until Christ be formed within you — Behold, I stand at the door and knock, &c.

I. Christ is in the hearts of his people. 1st. By faith in him. 2d. By love to him. 3d. By his communication of love to us. 4th. By his character stamped on our souls — particularly love to God and to man.

II. Christ within us is the hope of glory. 1st. It is reasonable to believe this, because glorification is only the consistent completion of the incipient indwelling. 2d. Because the divine promises warrant such a conclusion. 3d. Because the indwelling is an earnest of future glory. 4th. Because those whom he loves, he loves "to the end." And then I will profess, I *never* knew you.

Inferences. From the subject we learn, 1st. The indwelling of Christ is the greatest of all blessings. 2d. If destitute of this blessing, woe be to us — no hope — despair. 3d. The first thing, therefore, to which we ought to attend. 4th. If attained in some degree, how careful we ought to be to improve the blessing! It is necessary to peace of mind, usefulness, future eminence.

No. II.

HEB xii. 14: FOLLOW HOLINESS, WITHOUT WHICH NO MAN SHALL SEE THE LORD.

No man hath yet seen the Lord — nor shall, in this state. Shall we in the next? — The greatest good — Comprises all other good. — To see is to enjoy. — Eternal life — eternal happiness.

I. The nature of holiness. 1st. Purity. 2d. Consecration.

II. Holiness essential to being admitted to see God. Why? 1st. God is holy. 2d. Christ. 3d. The Holy Spirit. 4th. The inhabitants of heaven.

III. The certain results of holiness. If we are holy we shall see Him. 1st. The only obstacle removed. 2d. God has promised. 3d. It is the object of the plan of redemption.

IV. The increase of holiness, faith, hope, love.

V. What degree of holiness is attainable in this state. Freedom from actual sin.

[*A sentence is here wholly illegible.*]

K.

TO A LADY, AN INTIMATE FRIEND OF MRS. JUDSON.

MY DEAR MADAM: Since seeing you the other morning, I have felt an uncommon desire to address you on a subject which you have, perhaps, never had a friend faithful enough to present to you without disguise. The fear of offending has frequently prevented me from doing my duty. And there are cases where personal, mental, and moral excellences combine to increase that fear, from the apprehension that a person conscious of possessing such accomplishments may be indignant at the bare suggestion that the one thing needful is yet wanting. I trust, however, that He under whose influence I feel that I am writing will prepare your heart to welcome the truth, however unpalatable. Let me then respectfully ask you, my dear madam, whether you may not be too much influenced by that love of the world which an apostle has declared to be incompatible with the love of God. The Burmans have a story that a certain king, in days of old, received a visit from one of the most beautiful of the goddesses; in consequence of which he lost all relish for his usual enjoyments, and continually repaired to the woods, the scene of the celestial visitation, until his subjects became dissatisfied, and banished him altogether. O, how true it is that when the uncreated beauty of our divine Immanuel is once revealed to the enlightened soul, — when Jesus, in all his glory and condescending loveliness, has really taken possession of the heart, — the glittering bawbles of this world vanish; those subjects which were bright, and beautiful, and magnificent to the natural eye, lose their charms; the face of our celestial Visitant, the sweet accents of his voice speaking to our inmost soul, draw away our affections from all earthly joys, and we come to know the meaning of those mystic words, "He that loveth me shall be loved of my Father, and I will love him, and will manifest myself unto him."

A soul in such a state is ever ready to receive the summons of death, the call of that best beloved Friend, who has prepared the mansion, and is waiting to receive the guest. But alas for that poor soul who looks herself blind in gazing on the idle attractions of this fading, transitory scene, and never gets leisure to open the inner eye of the mind upon the glories that lie beyond! What will that poor soul do when the dark shadows of death begin to gather over all she has loved and honored? She may have been numbered in the church of Christ; to the forms of religion she may have given a vast deal of attention; but she has been a stranger to true penitence and faith; the Saviour's love has never reached her heart — her affections have been supremely set on earthly objects; and when death comes to bear them all away, and present ——

The manuscript remains thus unfinished.|

L.

WAYSIDE PREACHING

By Mrs. E. C. Judson.

IN the preceding volumes the importance of direct preaching to the heathen has been frequently insisted on. The following narrative, from the pen of Mrs. Judson, originally published in the Macedonian, gives an interesting view of the nature and success of this kind of missionary labor.

The sunlight fell aslant upon the fragile framework of a Burmese zayat; but though it was some hours past midday, the burning rays were not yet level enough to look too intrusively beneath the low, projecting eaves. Yet the day was intensely hot, and the wearied occupant of the one bamboo chair in the centre of the building looked haggard and careworn. All day long had he sat in that position, repeating over and over again, as he could find listeners, such simple truths as mothers are accustomed to teach the infant on their knees; and now his head was aching, and his heart was very heavy. He had met some scoffers, some who seemed utterly indifferent, but not one sincere inquirer after truth.

In the middle of the day, when the sun was hottest, and scarcely a European throughout all India was astir, he had received the greatest number of visitors; for the passers-by were glad of a moment's rest and shelter from the sun. The mats were still spread invitingly upon the floor; but though persons of almost every description were continually passing and repassing, they seemed each intent on his own business, and the missionary was without a listener. He thought of his neglected study table at home, of his patient, fragile wife, toiling through the numerous cares of the day alone, of the letters his friends were expecting, and which he had no time to write, of the last periodicals from his dear native land, lying still unread; and every little while, between the other thoughts, came real pinings after a delicious little book of devotion, which he had slid into his pocket in the morning, promising it his first moment of leisure. Then he was, naturally, an active man, of quick, ardent temperament, having such views of the worth of time as earnest American men can scarcely fail to gain; and it went to his heart to lose so many precious moments. If he could only do something to fill up these tedious intervals! But no; this was a work to which he must not give a divided mind. He was renewing a half-tested experiment in wayside preaching, and he would not suffer his attention to be distracted by any thing else. While his face was hidden by his book, and his mind intent on self-improvement, some poor passer-by might lose a last, an only opportunity of hearing the words of life. To be sure his own soul seemed very barren, and needed refreshing; and his body was weary — wearied well nigh to fainting, more with the dull, palsying inanity of the day's fruitless endeavors, than with any thing like labor. Heavily beat down the hot sun, lighting up the amber-like brown of the thatch as with a burning coal, while thickly in its broad rays floated a heavy golden cloud of dust and motes, showing in what a wretched atmosphere the delicate lungs were called to labor. Meantime, a fever-freighted breeze, which had been, all the hot day, sweeping the effluvia from eastern marshes, stirred the glossy leaves of the orange tree across the way, and parched the lip, and kindled a crimson spot upon the wan cheek of the weary missionary.

"God reigns," he repeated, as though some reminder of the sort were necessary, "God Almighty reigns; and I have given myself to him, soul and body, for time and for eternity. His will be done!" Still how long the day seemed! How broad the space that blistering sun had yet to travel, before its waiting, its watching, and its laboring would be ended! Might he not indulge himself just one moment? His hand went to his pocket, and the edge of a little book peeped forth a moment, and then, with a decided push, was thrust back again. No; he would not trifle with his duty. He would be sternly, rigidly faithful; and the blessing would surely come in time. Yet it was with an irrepressible yawn that he took up a little Burmese tract prepared by himself, and saw every word as familiar as his own name, and commenced reading aloud. The sounds caught the ear of a coarsely-clad water bearer, and she lowered the vessel from her head, and seated herself afar off, just within the shadow of the low eaves. Attracted by the foreign accent of the reader, few passed without turning the head a few moments to listen; then catching at some word which seemed to them offensive, they would repeat it mockingly, and hasten on.

Finally the old water bearer, grinning in angry derision till her wrinkled visage became positively hideous, rose, slowly adjusted the earthen vessel on her head, and passed along, muttering as she went, "Jesus Christ! No nigban! Ha, ha, ha!" The heart of the missionary sunk within him, and he was on the point of laying down the book. But the shadow of another passer-by fell upon the path, and he continued a moment longer. It was a tall, dignified-looking man, leading by the hand a boy, the open mirthfulness of whose bright, button-like eyes was in perfect keeping with his dancing little feet. The stranger was of a grave, staid demeanor, with a turban of aristocratic smallness, sandals turning up at the toe, a silken robe of somewhat subdued colors, and a snow-white tunic of gentleman-like length and unusual fineness.

"Papa, papa!" said the boy, with a merry little skip, and twitching at the hand he was holding. "Look, look, papa! *there* is Jesus Christ's man. Amai! how shockingly white!" "Jesus Christ's man" raised his eyes from the book which he could read just as well without eyes, and bestowed one of his brightest smiles upon the little stranger, just as the couple were passing beyond the corner of the zayat, but not too late to catch a bashfully pleased recognition. The father did not speak nor turn his head, but a ray of sunshine went down into the missionary's heart from those happy little eyes; and he somehow felt that his hour's reading had not been thrown away. He had remarked this man before, in other parts of the town, and had striven in various ways to attract his attention, but without success. He was evidently known, and most probably avoided; but the child, with that shy, pleased, half-confiding, roguish sort of smile, seemed sent as an encouraging messenger. The missionary continued his reading with an increase of earnestness and emphasis. A priest wrapped his yellow robes about him, and sat down upon the steps, as though for a moment's rest. Then another stranger came up boldly, and with considerable ostentation seated himself on the mat. He proved to be a philosopher from the school then recently disbanded at Prome; and he soon drew on a brisk, animated controversy.

The missionary did not finish his day's work with the shutting up of the zayat. At night, in his closet, he remembered both philosopher and priest; pleaded long and earnestly for the scoffing old water bearer; and felt a warm tear stealing to his eye, as he presented the case of the tall stranger and the laughing, dancing ray of sunshine at his side.

Day after day went by, as oppressively hot, as dusty, and bringing as many feverish winds as ever; but the hours were less wearisome, because many little buds of hope had been fashioned, which might yet expand into perfect flowers. But every day the tall stranger carried the same imperturbable face past the zayat; and every day the child made some silent advance towards the friendship of the missionary, bending his half-shaven head, and raising his little nut-colored hand to his forehead, by way of salutation, and smiling till his round face dimpled all over like ripples in a sunny pool. One day, as the pair came in sight, the missionary beckoned with his hand, and the child, with a single bound, came to his knee.

"Moung Moung!" exclaimed the father in a tone of surprise blended with anger. But the child was back again in a moment, with a gay-colored Madras handkerchief wound around his head; and with his bright lips parted, his eyes sparkling and dancing with joy, and his face wreathed with smiles, he seemed the most charming thing in nature. "Tai hlah-the!" (very beautiful,) said the child, touching his new turban, and looking into his father's clouded face, with the fearlessness of an indulged favorite.

"Tai hlah-the!" repeated the father involuntarily. He meant the child.

"You have a very fine boy there, sir," said the missionary, in a tone intended to be conciliatory. The stranger turned with a low salaam. For a moment he seemed to hesitate, as though struggling between his native politeness and his desire to avoid an acquaintance with the proselyting foreigner. Then taking the hand of the little boy, who was too proud and happy to notice his father's confusion, he hastened away.

"I do not think that zayat a very good place to go, Moung Moung," said the father, gravely, when they were well out of hearing. The boy answered only by a look of inquiry strangely serious for such a face as his.

"These white foreigners are ——" He did not tell what, but shook his head with mysterious meaning. The boy's eyes grew larger and deeper, but he only continued to look up into his father's face in wondering silence.

"I shall leave you at home to-morrow, to keep you from his wicked sorceries."

"Papa!"

"What, my son?"

"I think it will do no good to leave me at home."

"Why?"

"He has done something to me."

"Who? the kalah-byoo?"

"I do not think he has hurt me, papa; but I cannot — keep — away — no — no."

"What do you mean, Moung Moung?"

"The sorcerer has done something to me — put his beautiful eye on me. I see it now." And the boy's own eyes glowed with a strange, startling brilliancy.

"Mai, Mai! what a boy! *He* is not a sorcerer — only a very provoking man. His eye — whish! it is nothing to my little Moung Moung. I was only sporting. But we will have done with him. You shall go there no more ——"

"If I can help it, papa."

"Help it! hear the foolish child! What strange fancies!"

"Papa!"

"What, my son?"

"You will not be angry?"

"Angry!" The soft smile on that stern, bearded face was a sufficient answer.

"Is it true that she — my mother ——"

"Hush, Moung Moung!"

"Is it true that she *shikoed* to the Lord Jesus Christ?"

"Who dares to tell you so?"

"I must not say, papa; the one who told me said it was as much as life is worth to talk of such things to *your* son. Did she, papa?"

"What did he mean? Who could have told you such a tale?"

"Did she, papa?"

"That is a very pretty *goung-boung* the foreigner gave you."

"Did she?"

"And makes your bright eyes brighter than ever."

"Did my mother *shiko* to the Lord Jesus Christ?"

"There, there! You have talked enough, my boy," said the father, gloomily; and the two continued their walk in silence. As the conversation ceased, a woman, who, with a palm-leaf fan before her face, had followed closely in the shadow of the stranger, — so closely, indeed, that she might have heard every word that had been spoken, — stopped at a little shop by the way, and was soon, seemingly, intent on making purchases.

"Ko Shway-bay!" called out the missionary. A man bearing a large satchel, which he had just nearly filled with books, appeared at the door of an inner apartment of the zayat.

"Ken-payah?"

"Did you observe the tall man, who just passed, leading a little boy?"

"I saw him."

"What do you know about him?"

"He is a writer under government, a very respectable man — haughty —— reserved —— "

"And what else?"

"He hates — Christians, tsayah!"

"Is he very bigoted then?"

"No, tsayah; he is more like a *päramät* than a Buddhist. Grave as he appears, he sometimes treats sacred things very playfully, always carelessly. But does the teacher remember, — it may be now three, four, I do not know how many years ago, — a young woman came for medicine —— "

The missionary smiled. "I should have a wonderful memory, Shway-bay, if I carried all my applicants for medicine in it."

"But this one was not like other women. She had the face of a *nät-thamee*," (goddess or angel,) "and her voice — the teacher *must* remember her voice. It was like the silvery chimes of the pagoda bells at midnight. She was the favorite wife of the sah-ya, and this little boy, her only child, was very ill. She did not dare ask you to the house, or even send a servant for the medicine, for her husband was one of the most violent persecutors —— "

"Ay, I do recollect her, by her distress, and her warm gratitude. And so this is her child! What has become of the mother?"

"Has the teacher forgotten putting a Gospel of Matthew in her hand, and saying that it contained medicine for *her*; for that she was afflicted with a worse disease than the fever of her little son; and then lifting up his hands, and praying very solemnly?"

"I do not recall the circumstance just now. But what came of it?"

"They say," answered the Burman, lowering his voice, and first casting an investigating glance around him — "they say that the medicine cured her."

"Ah!"

"She read the book nights, while watching by her baby;

and then she would kneel down and pray, as the teacher had done. At last the sah-ya got the writing."

" What did he do with it?"

" Only burned it. But she was a tender little creature, and could not bear his look; so, as the baby got out of danger, she took the fever —— "

" And died?" asked the missionary, remarking some hesitation in the manner of his narrator.

" Not of the fever, altogether."

" What then? Surely *he* did not —— "

" No, tsayah; it must have been an angel call. The sah-ya was very fond of her, and did every thing to save her; but she just grew weaker day after day, and her face more beautiful; and there was no holding her back. She got courage as she drew near paradise, and begged the sah-ya to send for you. He is not a hardhearted man; and she was more than life and soul to him; but he would not send. And so she died, talking to the last moment of the Lord Jesus, and calling on every body about her to love him, and worship none but him."

" Is this true, Shway-bay?"

" *I* know nothing about it, tsayah; and it is not very safe to know any thing. The sah-ya has taken an oath to destroy every body having too good a memory. But " — and the man again looked cautiously around him — " does the teacher think that little Burman children are likely to run into the arms of foreigners without being taught?"

" Aha! say you so, Shway-bay?"

" I say nothing, *tsayah*."

" And what of the child?"

" A wonderful boy, tsayah. He seems usually as you have seen him. But he has another look — so strange! He must have caught something from his mother's face, just before she went up to the golden country."

The missionary seemed lost in thought, and the assistant, after waiting a moment to be questioned further, slung his satchel over his shoulder, and proceeded up the street.

The next day, the missionary remarked that the sah-ya went by on the other side of the way, and without the little boy; and the next day, and the next the same. In the mean time the wrinkled old water bearer had become a sincere inquirer. "The one shall be taken, and the other left," sighed the missionary, as he tried to divine the possible fate of his bright-eyed little friend.

The fourth day came. The old water bearer was in an agitated state of joy and doubt — a timid, but true believer. The self-confident philosopher had almost ceased to cavil. Fresh inquirers had appeared, and the missionary's heart was strengthened. "It is dull work," he said to himself, though without any expression of dulness in his face; "but it is the Saviour's own appointed way, and the way the Holy Spirit will bless." Then his thoughts turned to the stern sah-ya and his little boy; and he again murmured, with more of dejection in his manner than when he had spoken of the dulness of the work, "And the other left — the other left!"

The desponding words had scarcely passed his lips, when, with a light laugh, the very child who was in his thoughts, and who somehow clung so tenaciously to his heart, sprang up the steps of the zayat, followed by his grave, dignified father. The boy wore his new Madras turban, arranged with a pretty sort of jantiness, and above its showy folds he carried a red lackered tray, with a cluster of golden plantains on it. Placing the gift at the missionary's feet, he drew back with a pleased smile of boyish shyness; while the man, bowing courteously, took his seat upon the mat.

"Sit down, Moung Moung, sit down!" said the father, in the low tone that American parents use when reminding careless little boys of their hats; for though Burmans and Americans differ somewhat in their peculiar notions of etiquette, the children of both races seem equally averse to becoming learners.

"You are the foreign priest," he remarked civilly, and more by way of introduction than inquiry.

"I am a missionary."

The stranger smiled, for he had purposely avoided the offensive epithet, and was amused and conciliated by the missionary's frank use of it. "And so you make people believe in Jesus Christ?"

"I try to."

The visitor laughed outright; then, as if a little ashamed of his rudeness, he composed his features, and, with his usual courtesy, resumed, "My little son has heard of you, sir; and he is very anxious to learn something about Jesus Christ. It is a pretty story you tell of that man — prettier, I think, than any of our fables; and you need not be afraid to set it forth in its brightest colors, for my Moung Moung will never see through its absurdity, of course."

The missionary threw a quick, scrutinizing glance on the face of his visitor. He saw that the man was ill at ease, that his carelessness was entirely assumed, and that underneath all there was a deep, wearing anxiety, which he fancied was in some way connected with his boy. "Ah, you think so? To what particular story do you allude?"

"Why, that of the strange sort of being you call Jesus Christ — a great *nät*, or prince, or something of the sort — dying for us poor fellows, and so —— Ha, ha! The absurdity of the thing makes me laugh; though there is something in it beautiful, too. Our stupid pongyees would never have thought out any thing one half so fine; and the pretty fancy has quite enchanted little Moung Moung here."

"I perceive you are a *päramät*," said the missionary.

"No; O, no; I am a true and faithful worshipper of Lord Gaudama; but of course neither you nor I subscribe to all the fables of our respective religions. There is quite enough that is honest and reasonable in our Buddhistic system to satisfy me; but my little son" — here the father seemed embarrassed, and laughed again, as though to cover his confusion — "is bent on philosophical investigation — eh, Moung Moung?"

"But are you not afraid that my teachings will do the child harm?"

The visitor looked up with a broad smile of admiration, as though he would have said, "You are a very honest fellow, after all;" then, regarding the child with a look of mingled tenderness and apprehension, he said, softly, "Nothing can harm little Moung Moung, sir."

"But what if I should tell you I do believe every thing I preach as firmly as I believe you sit on the mat before me, and that it is the one desire of my life to make every body else believe it — you and your child among the rest?"

The sah-ya tried to smile, tried to look unconcerned; but his easy nonchalance of manner seemed utterly to forsake him when he most needed it; and finally, abandoning the attempt to renew his former tone of banter, he answered, quietly, "I have heard of a writing you possess, which, by your leave, I will take home, and read to Moung Moung."

The missionary selected a little tract from the parcel on the table beside him, and extended it to his visitor. "Sah-ya," said he, solemnly, "I herewith put into your hands the key to eternal life and happiness. This active, intelligent soul of yours, with its exquisite perception of moral beauty and loveliness," — and he glanced towards the child, — "cannot be destined to inhabit a dog, a monkey, or a worm, in another life. God made it for higher purposes; and I hope and pray that I may yet meet you, all beautiful, and pure, and glorious, in a world beyond the reach of pain or death, and, above all, beyond the reach of sin."

Up to this time the boy had sat upon his mat like a statue of silence, his usually dancing eyes fixed steadfastly upon the speakers, and gradually dilating and acquiring a strange, mystic depth of expression, of which they seemed at first incapable. At these words, however, he sprang forward. "Papa, papa, hear him. Let us both love the Lord Jesus Christ. My mother loved him; and in the golden country of the blessed she waits for us."

"I must go," said the sah-ya, hoarsely, and attempting to rise.

"Let us pray," said the missionary, kneeling down.

The child laid his two hands together, and, placing them

against his forehead, bowed his head to the mat; while the father yielded to the circumstances of the case so far as to reseat himself. Gradually, as the fervent prayer proceeded, his head drooped a little; and it was not long before he placed his elbows on his knees, and covered his face with his hands. As soon as the prayer was ended, he rose, bowed in silence, took his child by the hand, and walked away.

Day after day went by, the sah-ya, as he passed the zayat, always saluting its occupant respectfully, but evincing no disposition to cultivate his acquaintance farther. He was accompanied by the boy less often than formerly; but from casual opportunities the missionary remarked that a strange look of thoughtfulness had crept into the childish face, softening and beautifying, though scarcely saddening, it. And when, occasionally, the little fellow paused for a moment, to ask for a book, or exchange a word of greeting, the gay familiarity of his manner seemed to have given place to a tender, trustful affection, somewhat tinctured with awe.

Meanwhile, that terrible scourge of eastern nations, the cholera, had made its appearance; and it came sweeping through the town with its usual devastating power. Fires were kindled before every house, and kept burning night and day; while immense processions continually thronged the streets, with gongs, drums, and tom-toms, to frighten away the evil spirits, and so arrest the progress of the disease. The zayat was closed for lack of visitors; and the missionary and his assistants busied themselves in attending on the sick and dying.

It was midnight when the over-wearied foreigner was roused from his slumbers by the calls of the faithful Ko Shway-bay.

"Teacher, teacher, you are wanted."

"Where?"

The man lowered his voice almost to a whisper, but putting his hands to each side of his mouth, sent the volume of sound through a crevice in the boards.

"At the sah-ya's."

"Who?"

"I do not know, tsayah; I only heard that the cholera was in the house, and the teacher was wanted, and so I hurried off as fast as possible."

In a few minutes the missionary had joined his assistant, and they proceeded on their way together. As they drew near the house, the Burman paused in the shadow of a bamboo hedge.

"It is not good for either of us that we go in together. I will wait you here, tsayah."

"No, you need rest; and I shall not want you — go!"

The veranda was thronged with relatives and dependants, and from an inner room came a wild, wailing sound, which told that death was already there. No one seemed to observe the entrance of the foreigner; and he followed the sound of woe till he stood by the corpse of a little child. Then he paused in deep emotion.

"He has gone up to the golden country, to bloom forever amid the royal lilies of paradise," murmured a voice close to his ear.

The missionary, a little startled, turned abruptly. A middle-aged woman, holding a palm-leaf fan to her mouth, was the only person near him.

"He worshipped the true God," she continued, suffering the individuality of her voice to glide away in the wail of the mourners, and occasionally slurring a word which she dared not pronounce with distinctness — "he worshipped the true God, and trusted in the Lord our Redeemer — the Lord Jesus Christ; he trusted in him; he called and he was answered; he was weary — weary and in pain; and the Lord who loved him, he took him home, to be a little golden lamb in his bosom forever."

"How long since did he go?"

"About an hour, tsayah." Then joining in the wail again, — "An hour amid the royal lilies, and his mother, his own beautiful mother, she of the starry eyes and silken hand——"

"Was he conscious?"

"Conscious, and full of joy."

"What did he talk of?"

"Only of the Lord Jesus Christ, whose face he seemed to see."

"And his father?"

"His father! — O my master! my noble master! he is going too! Come and see, tsayah!"

"Who sent for me?"

"Your handmaid, sir."

"Not the sah ya?"

The woman shook her head. "The agony was on him — he could not have sent, if he would."

"But how dared *you*?"

There was a look such as might have been worn by the martyrs of old upon the woman's face, as she expressively answered, "*God was here.*"

In the next apartment lay the noble figure of the sah-ya, stretched upon a couch, evidently in the last stage of the fearful disease — his pain all gone.

"It grieves me to meet you thus, my friend," remarked the visitor, by way of testing the dying man's consciousness. The sah-ya made a gesture of impatience. Then his fast-stiffening lips stirred, but they were powerless to convey a sound; there was a feeble movement, as though he would have pointed at something; but his half-raised finger wavered and sunk back again, and a look of dissatisfaction, amounting to anxiety, passed over his countenance. Finally, renewing the effort, he succeeded in laying his two hands together, and with some difficulty lifted them to his forehead, and then quietly and calmly closed his eyes.

"Do you trust in Lord Gaudama at a moment like this?" inquired the missionary, uncertain for whom the act of worship was intended. There was a quick tremor in the shut lids and the poor sah-ya unclosed his eyes with an expression of mingled pain and disappointment, while the death-heavy hands slid from their position back upon the pillow.

"Lord Jesus, receive his spirit!" exclaimed the missionary,

solemnly. A bright, joyous smile flitted across the face of the dying man, parting the lips, and even seeming to shed light upon the glazed eyes; a sigh-like breath fluttered his bosom for a moment, the finger which he had before striven to lift pointed distinctly upward, then fell heavily across his breast, and the disembodied spirit stood in the presence of its Maker.

The thrilling death wail commenced with the departure of the breath; for although several who had been most assiduous in their attentions glided away when it was ascertained that he who would have rewarded their fidelity was gone, there were yet many who were prevented, some by real affection, some by family pride, from so far yielding to their fears as to withhold the honors due to the departed.

"You had better go now," whispered the woman; "you can do no further good, and may receive harm."

"And who are you, that you have braved the danger to yourself, of bringing me here?"

"Pass on, and I will tell you."

They drew near the body of the child, which, by the rush to the other apartment, had been left for a moment alone.

"See!" said the woman, lifting the cloth, reverently. A copy of the Gospel of Matthew lay on his bosom.

"Who placed it there?"

"He did, with his own dear little hand — Amai! amai-ai!" and the woman's voice gave expression to one swell of agony, and then died away in a low wail, like that which proceeded from the adjoining room.

Presently she resumed: "I was his mother's nurse. She got this book of you, sir. We thought my master burned it; but he kept, and may be studied, it. Do you think that he became a true believer?"

"To whom did he *shiko* at that last moment, Mah-aa?"

"To the Lord Jesus Christ — I am sure of that. Do you think the Lord would receive him, sir?"

"Did you ever read about the thief who was crucified with the Saviour?"

"O, yes; I read it to Moung Moung this very day. He

was holding his mother's book when the disease smote him; and he kept it in his hand, and went up with it lying on his bosom. Yes, I remember."

"The Lord Jesus Christ is just as merciful now as he was then."

"And so they are all —— O, *'Ken-payah!* it is almost too much to believe!"

"Where did you first become acquainted with this religion, Mah-aa?"

"My mistress taught me, sir, and made me promise to teach her baby, when he was old enough, and to go to you for more instruction. But I was alone, and afraid. I sometimes got as far as the big banian tree on the corner, and crawled away again, so trembling with terror that I could scarcely stand upon my feet. At last I found out Ko Shway-bay, and he promised to keep my secret; and he gave me books, and explained their meaning, and taught me how to pray, and I have been getting courage ever since. I should not much mind now, if they did find me out and kill me. It would be very pleasant to go up to paradise. I think I should even like to go to-night, if the Lord would please to take me."

It was two or three weeks before the missionary resumed his customary place in the zayat by the wayside. His hearers were scattered widely — in the neighboring jungles, in far-off towns, and in that other place, from whence "no traveller returns."

Where was his last hopeful inquirer?

Dead.

Where the priest?

Dead.

Where the philosopher?

Fled away, none knew whither.

And the poor old water bearer?

Dead — died like a dog in its kennel, and, but that some pitying Christian had succeeded in discovering her at the last moment, without a human witness. But — and the missionary's heart swelled with gratitude to God as he thought of it

— there were other witnesses, nobler, tenderer, dearer to that simple, lone old creature than all the earthly friends that ever thronged a death bed; and these had been her bright, rejoicing convoy to the Saviour's presence.

O, how full of awe, how fearfully laden with the solemn interests of eternity, appeared this wondrous work of his! And how broad and clear seemed his sacred commission, as though at that moment newly traced by the finger of Jehovah!

M.

OBEDIENCE TO CHRIST'S LAST COMMAND A TEST OF PIETY.

DR. JUDSON's last public appearance in this country, before his embarkation in 1846, was on Sunday evening, July 5, at the monthly concert of prayer for missions, in which, on that occasion, the several Baptist churches in Boston united. The following address, committed by him to writing, was read by the Rev. Dr. Sharp : —

It is the most momentous question we can put to our own souls, whether we truly love the Lord Jesus Christ or not; for as that question is answered in the affirmative or the negative, our hope of heaven grows bright or dark. If we take the right way to ascertain, there is no question that can be more easily answered. It is the nature of true love to seek the pleasure and happiness of the person beloved. We no sooner ascertain the object on which his heart is set, than we lend all our efforts to secure that object. What is the object on which the heart of the Saviour is set? For what purpose did he leave the bosom of the Father, the throne of eternal glory, to come down to sojourn, and suffer, and die in this fallen, rebellious world? For what purpose does he now sit on the mediatorial throne, and exert the power with which he is invested? To restore the ruins of paradise — to redeem his chosen people from death and hell — to extend and establish his kingdom throughout the habitable globe. This is evident from his whole course on earth, from his promises to the church, and especially from his parting command, " Go ye into all the world, and preach the gospel to every creature."

The means which he has appointed for the accomplishment of the purpose nearest his heart is the universal preaching of the gospel. Do you, a professor of religion, love the Lord

Jesus Christ in sincerity? Have you set your heart on that object which is dearest to his heart? Are you endeavoring to obey his great parting command? But perhaps you will say, This command is not binding on me. It is impossible for me to obey, and God never commands an impossibility. And saying thus, you disclose the real reason why men do little or nothing for missions — that while they feel under obligation to endeavor to keep the commands which require them to love God supremely, and to love others as themselves, and feel guilty when conscious of neglecting or transgressing those commands, they never make an effort to go into all the world and preach the gospel to every creature — never think of feeling guilty for having neglected and transgressed that command all their lives long!

But let me now submit, that the command can be obeyed by every believer — that it is of universal obligation — and that no profession ought to be regarded as sincere, no love to the Saviour genuine, unless it be attended with a sincere endeavor to obey. But you will reply, How can I, unqualified and encumbered as I am, arise and go forth into the wide world and proclaim the gospel? Please to remember that all great public undertakings are accomplished by a combination of various agencies. In commerce and in war, for instance, some agents are necessarily employed at home, and some abroad; some at the head quarters, and some on distant expeditions; but however differently employed, and in whatever places, they are all interested, and all share the glory and the gain. So, in the missionary enterprise, the work to be accomplished is the universal preaching of the gospel, and the conversion of the whole world to the Christian faith; and in order to this, some must go, and some must send and sustain them that go. "How can they hear without a preacher, and how can they preach except they be sent?" Those who remain at home and labor to send and sustain those that go, are as really employed in the work, and do as really obey the Saviour's command, as those who go in their own persons. See you not, then, that the great command can be obeyed, and is actually binding on every soul? Feel you not that you are under obligation to do your utmost to secure that object at which the Saviour aimed, when he gave that command? It is possible there is some one in this assembly to whom it may be said, You will find, on examination, that you have not done your utmost — that indeed you have never laid this command to heart, or made any very serious effort to obey it; if so, how can you hope that your love to the Saviour is any thing more than an empty profession? How is it possible that you love the Saviour, and yet feel no interest in that object on which his heart is set? What, love the Saviour, who bled and died for this cause, and yet spend your whole existence on earth in toiling for your personal sustenance, and gratification, and vainglory! O, that dread tribunal to which we are hastening! Souls stripped of all disguise there! The final Judge, a consuming fire! "Search me, O God, and know my heart; try me, and know my thoughts; and see if there be any wicked way in me, and lead me in the way everlasting."

THE MISSIONS OF THE AMERICAN BAPTIST MISSIONARY UNION, 1852-3,

Showing present results of the work begun at Rangoon in 1813.

Missions.	Stations.	Out-stations.	Missionaries.	Female Assistants.	Total Missionaries and Assistants.	Native Preachers and Assistants.	Churches.	Baptized.	Present Number.	Boarding Schools.	Pupils.	Day Schools.	Pupils.	Total Schools.	Total Pupils.	Pages printed.
IN ASIA:																
Maulmain Burman,	2	7	9	9	18	8	3	11	181	2	42	8	470	10	512	4,037,400
Maulmain Karen,	2	17	4	7	10	45	40	134	1,750	3	343	17	—	20	343	
Tavoy Karen,	2	17	7	7	14	20	19	74	1,000	—	92	15	250	20	342	
Arracan Burman,	2	2	3	—	—	8	1	1	14	59	—	6	40	2	46	
Sandoway Karen,	1	44	5	4	9	208	45	288	5,000	1	86	2	150	16	230	
Ava,	1	—	2	—	—	—	—	13	27	—	8	2	40	2	40	
Siam,	1	2	3	4	7	—	2	—	33	—	—	—	40	—	40	
Hongkong,	1	4	2	2	4	3	—	—	28	—	—	3	30	4	30	
Ningpo,	1	—	5	3	8	—	1	1	13	1	15	2	50	4	—	
Assam,	3	3	2	3	7	5	3	—	77	—	—	4	25	4	112	
Teloogoo,	1	—	2	—	2	2	—	—	10	—	—	1	25	2	50	
Whole No. in Asia,	18	94	47	43	95	146	117	663	8,180	17	689	65	1,302	72	1,785	9,758,000
IN AFRICA:																
Bassa,	2	2	2	4	6	4	1	1	16	—	—	1	16	2	36	457,400
IN EUROPE:																
French,	14	9†	2	2	4	20	11	100	450	1	7	—	—	1	7	
German,	40	4	3	3	3	27	42	647	4,215	1	7	—	—	1	7	
Greek,	3	—	2	—	2	1	1	—	13	—	—	1	50	1	50	5,285,200
Whole No. in Europe,	57	9	7	5	12	48	54	747	4,678	2	14	1	50	3	64	
INDIAN MISSIONS:																
Ojibwa,	—	1	2	1	3	—	1	—	22	1	5	—	—	1	45	
Ottawa, in Michigan,	2	—	3	2	1	—	1	—	25	2	40	—	40	2	40	
Shawanoe,	1	—	1	2	9	5	1	12	107	2	33	2	—	2	33	
Cherokee,	3	8	2	2	4	9	3	48	1,225	—	—	1	—	1	—	
Whole No. in America,	4	11	9	8	16	8	10	60	1,379	4	138	1	40	5	178	
Totals,	19	88	112	64	66	130	205	182	1,261	14,253	21	861	53	1,208	83	2,063	9,758,000

* Number of pupils in one only reported.   † 50 places for stated preaching.   ‡ 355 places for stated preaching.

www.ingramcontent.com/pod-product-compliance
Lightning Source LLC
Chambersburg PA
CBHW030329240426
43661CB00052B/1576